The Hermeneutical Spirit

The Hermeneutical Spirit

*Theological Interpretation
and Scriptural Imagination for the 21st Century*

Amos Yong
Professor of Theology & Mission
Fuller Theological Seminary

CASCADE *Books* • Eugene, Oregon

THE HERMENEUTICAL SPIRIT
Theological Interpretation and Scriptural Imagination for the 21st Century

Copyright © 2017 Amos Yong. All rights reserved. Except for brief quotations in critical publications or reviews, no part of this book may be reproduced in any manner without prior written permission from the publisher. Write: Permissions, Wipf and Stock Publishers, 199 W. 8th Ave., Suite 3, Eugene, OR 97401.

Cascade Books
An Imprint of Wipf and Stock Publishers
199 W. 8th Ave., Suite 3
Eugene, OR 97401

www.wipfandstock.com

PAPERBACK ISBN: 978-1-5326-0489-8
HARDCOVER ISBN: 978-1-5326-0491-1
EBOOK ISBN: 978-1-5326-0490-4

Cataloguing-in-Publication data:

Names: Yong, Amos. |

Title: The hermeneutical spirit : theological interpretation and scriptural imagination for the 21st century / Amos Yong.

Description: Eugene, OR: Cascade Books, 2017 | Includes bibliographical references and index.

Identifiers: ISBN 978-1-5326-0489-8 (paperback) | ISBN 978-1-5326-0491-1 (hardcover) | ISBN 978-1-5326-0490-4 (ebook)

Subjects: LCSH: Bible—Criticism, interpretation, etc. | Bible—Theology. | Hermeneutics—Religious aspects—Pentecostalism. | Title.

Classification: BS476 .Y62 2017 (print) | BS476 (ebook)

Manufactured in the U.S.A.   NOVEMBER 1, 2017

To Steve Sherman
~ fellow traveler from coast to coast via a post-conservative road
(named otherwise on many other maps) ~

Table of Contents

Preface xi

Acknowledgments xv

Introduction 1
    Theological Interpretation of Scripture: Setting the Stage 1
        Overview and Status Quaestionis: *TIS and the Rule of Faith* 2
        Contemporary Trajectories: Trinitarian Interpretation and the Spirit 4
        Pentecostal Hermeneutics: TIS and the Apostolic Way 8
        Prospects for TIS after Pentecost? An Autobiographical Retrospect 11
    Pentecost, the Spirit, and Scriptural Interpretation:
      Mapping the Argument 14
        Theological Hermeneutics: Pentecostal Perspectives 14
        Theological Anthropology: Luke, the Spirit, and the Human 17
        Pneumatological Soteriology: Pentecost and Salvation 19
        Theological-Scriptural Interpretation: Apostolic Hermeneutics 21

PART I—Theological Hermeneutics: Perspectives after Pentecost

1 The Science, Sighs, and Signs of Interpretation: An Asian American Post-Pentecost-al Hermeneutics in a Multi-, Inter-, and Transcultural World 27
    Multi-, Inter-, and Transcultural Hermeneutics? 28
    Asian American Pentecostal Questions and Trajectories 32

Interpretative Science, Sighs, and Signs: Toward a Pentecostal Hermeneutic 35
- The Science of Interpretation: A Post-Pentecost-al Paradigm 35
- The Sighs of Interpretation: A Modern Pentecostal Assist 38
- The Signs of Interpretation: A Pneumatological Construal 40

2 Understanding and Living the Apostolic Way: Orality and Scriptural Faithfulness in Conversation with African Pentecostalism 43
- Oral Cultures and the Bible: Pentecostal Hermeneutics in African Perspective 45
  - Oral Cultures: Theoretical and African Framings 45
  - Pentecostal Orality and the Scriptural Imagination: An African Phenomenology 50
  - Biblical Orality and African Pentecostal Hermeneutics 53
- Apostolic Faith as Aural Praxis and Confession: Toward a 21st Century Pentecostal Paradigm 57

3 Reflecting and Confessing in the Spirit: Called to Transformational Theologizing 63
- Surprised by the Spirit: When the Living God Shows Up 64
- Pentecostalized by the Spirit: The Trinitarian *Missio Dei* as Normative *Telos* 67
- Reflecting in the Spirit: From Apostolic Theologizing to Christian Confession 71

PART II—Theological Anthropology and the Spirit: The Lukan Imagination I

4 Many Tongues, Many Senses: Pentecost, the Body Politic, and the Redemption of Dis/Ability 79
- Disability Studies and Pentecostal Studies: Roadblocks at the Intersection 80
- What Has (Dr.) Luke to Say? Pentecostal Resources for Rethinking Disability 83
- Many Tongues, Many Senses: The Multiple Modalities of Spirit-Inspired Witness 88
- Pentecostal Contributions to Theology of Disability and Disability Studies? 95

5 Sons and Daughters, Young and Old: Toward a Pentecostal Theology of the Family 99
- Theology of the Family: Current Explorations 100
- The Spirit Poured Out on All Flesh: The Eschatological Family 104

"Children of the Promise": Lukan Intimations for Theology of the Family 109
Transitions: Toward a Pentecostal Theology of the Family 115
6 Children and the Promise of the Spirit: Pneumatology and the Quest for Child Theology 119
Pentecostalism, Pneumatology, and Theology of Children: Whence and Whither? 122
Child Theologies in Lukan and Eschatological Perspective 127
Children and the Coming Kingdom: Aspects of a Third Article Theology 133
Transitions 138

PART III—Pneumatological Soteriology: The Lukan Imagination II

7 The Social Psychology of Sin: A Pentecostal Perspective 141
Sin: Interdisciplinary Formulations 143
Sin in Empirical Perspective 143
Theologies of Sin: Scientifically Informed Understandings 146
Traditional Pentecostal Views of Sin 149
Sin: A Pentecostal Interpretation 151
Sin—In, through, and after Pentecost 152
An Implicit Lukan Theology of Sin 155
Toward a Pentecostal and Scientific Theology of Sin 159
8 Jubilee, Pentecost, and Liberation: The Preferential Option *of* the Poor on the Apostolic Way 162
The Preferential Option for the Poor: Global and Evangelical Developments 163
The Preferential Option of the Poor: Liberationist Routes in Global Pentecostalism 168
Divine Preferences and Options? Apostolic Liberation Today 173
9 Apostolic Evangelism in the Postcolony: Opportunities and Challenges 179
Toward a Pentecostal Theology of Evangelism 180
Toward a Lukan Theology of Evangelism 185
Toward an Apostolic and Pneumatological Theology of Evangelism for the 21st Century 189

PART IV: Theological-Scriptural Interpretation in the Spirit: Apostolic Pathways

10 The Light Shines in the Darkness: Johannine Dualism and the Challenge of Christian Theology of Religions Today 197
    Light and Darkness in John: Aspects of a Classical Christian Theology of Religions 199
    John and the Jews: Reconsidering Implications for Theology of Religions 201
    The Light Shines in the Darkness: John's Prologue and Sectarianism at Qumran 207
    At Dawn and at Dusk: Ambivalence regarding a Johannine Theology of Religions 213
    Pressing the Question: Performing Johannine Theology in the Interreligious Encounter 218

11 Running the (Special) Race: New (Pauline) Perspectives on Disability and Theology of Sport 222
    Contemporary Culture, Sport, and Disability 223
    Running the Race: St. Paul as Disability Theologian of Sport? 228
    Running the Special Race: Pauline Proposals for Theology of Sport 233

12 Reading Scripture and Nature: Pentecostal Hermeneutics and Their Implications for the Contemporary Evangelical Theology and Science Conversation 237
    This is That! Pentecostal Biblical Hermeneutics—A Case Study 239
    That is This! A Pneumatological Hermeneutics of the Creation Narratives? 244
    The Books of Scripture and of Nature: Toward a Hermeneutics of Science 249

Conclusion—Theological Interpretation of Scripture after Pentecost: Trinitarian Hermeneutics for the 21st Century 257
    The *Hermeneutical* Spirit 258
    The Hermeneutical *Spirit* 261
    Trinitarian and Teleological Interpretation of Scripture for the Third Millennium Global Context 263

References 267
Subject Index 309
Scripture Index 318

Preface

I have to confess that it has only been since I arrived at Fuller Seminary in the summer of 2014 that I began to pay attention to the *theological interpretation of Scripture* conversation. Yet my efforts to develop pentecostal theology over the last almost two decades have presumed the viability of a kind of pentecostal hermeneutic that some might see as a species of theological interpretation of the Bible. This book gathers together some of my efforts in this direction over the last few years in order to contribute to but perhaps also further the discussion.

Yet let me be clear that this kind of pentecostal hermeneutic is not one that belongs to any church or even movement of churches but one that proceeds from after the Day of Pentecost as recorded in Acts 2. Christian reading of Scripture, this book urges, follows not only from the Christ event but also from that of the risen Christ's outpouring of the Spirit from the right hand of the Father. Hence to the degree that all churches receives the witness of St. Luke as recorded in his second book, to that same degree the church ecumenical reads Scripture after Pentecost.

Rodney Clapp, my editor, once again not only provided careful editorial feedback but also was enthusiastic about adding this third volume as a follow-up to my *The Dialogical Spirit: Christian Reason and Theological Method for the Third Millennium* and *The Missiological Spirit: Christian Mission Theology for the Third Millennium Global Context*, both published in 2014. This book is, like its predecessors, constituted by twelve essays, almost all previously published and written in response to various invitations for a variety of occasions and audiences. With one exception (chapter 10), they derive from 2009 to the present, with half of them (in parts I and III below) having emerged in the last year, so in this respect they represent a narrower period of time of my thinking than the earlier books. Again, though, I reproduce the previously published pieces as they originally appeared, inserting bracketed footnotes only to register clarifications, new insight/knowledge, or changes of mind, so that readers can follow development in my thinking, however that may be ascertained. The introduction and conclusion are new, the former situating these essays afresh amidst the *theological interpretation of Scripture* scene, which currents I was fairly oblivious to while writing them, and the latter sketching out my own constructive proposal for a pentecostal and pneumatological contribution to the discussion. The reader is thus forewarned: the pieces of the argument collected together here were not initially written to address issues unfolded and developing in the theological interpretation of Scripture area, but the wager of this book is that a pentecostal perspective has something important to contribute here. Whether or not or to what degree this is the case, reviewers will be the judge.

Note that *pentecostal* is uncapitalized except when used as noun or when it occurs within proper names. One way to read the use of *pentecostal* in this book then is to see it functioning adjectivally. I will argue, for instance, that *pentecostal* relates to the Day of Pentecost narrative in the book of Acts that lies also at the heart of the spirituality of the modern pentecostal movement. For me, then, *pentecostal* refers more to the work of the Holy Spirit than it does to a specific denominational and traditioned theological undertaking, although I recognize that my own understanding of such has been nurtured by my growing up within modern Pentecostalism, indeed, as both a pentecostal preacher's kid (PK) and as a pentecostal missionary kid (MK) from my youngest days.

Unless otherwise noted, all Scriptural quotations in this book are from the New Revised Standard Version of the Bible, all rights reserved.

I am grateful to Marty Mittelstadt and Christopher Stephenson, two colleagues in the pentecostal academy, for their critical comments on the manuscript version of this book. Christopher The and Joshua Muthalali, both doctoral students here at Fuller Theological Seminary, also gave me invaluable feedback and perspective on the introductory chapter. The initial footnote of each of the twelve chapters identifies others who have contributed to the texts in their previous iteration. And although the texts of the previously published pieces have been reproduced without revision, I have inserted bracketed footnotes where and when clarifications are now warranted. It goes without saying, however, that all responsibility for errors of fact or interpretation remains my own.

My graduate assistants, Hoon Jung and Nok Kam, helped with preparing publication files, proofreading, and indexing this volume. Scott W. Sunquist, dean of the School of Intercultural Studies where I work, has been supportive in many ways, most importantly in his personal friendship, his care for me and my family, and his ongoing prayer for his faculty in the school. I am grateful also to Jeff Waldrop, director of the David Allen

Hubbard Library here at Fuller, and especially his interlibrary loan staff, for their efficient efforts in enabling research here at the seminary. Jesselynn Clapp and Heather Carraher at Wipf and Stock were efficient and professional in typesetting and copyediting the manuscript and transfiguring it into the book you hold in your hands: thank you both!

As always, my wife, Alma, has been the faithful rock amidst the sea of change characterizing the years over which the pieces of this book have taken shape. The idea for the earliest essay collected here (chapter 10) germinated in our final years in Minneapolis, Minnesota—in conversations with Glen Menzies, a colleague then at North Central University, who challenged me to think about my work in pneumatological theology of religions in light of the biblical dualisms of true versus false religion—before we moved to Chesapeake/Virginia Beach, Virginia in 2005, even as the last chapters and final form of this volume have come together now after another cross-country move to Pasadena, California in the summer of 2014. Alma's love has been steadfast from coast to coast as the essays collected here have been written. This is actually the first self-authored book I have completed since moving to Fuller Theological Seminary, and this task could not have been accomplished without Alma's encouragement, support, and love.

I dedicate this book to Steven B. Sherman, who I first met when he arrived at Regent University in the summer of 2008. Although he had earlier been a bit suspicious of my ideas, I suspected that there were commonalities between his postconservative evangelical approach to theology—given definitive shape in his book, *Revitalizing Theological Epistemology: Holistic Evangelical Approaches to the Knowledge of God* (Wipf and Stock, 2010)—and my own postfoundational pentecostal version. Yet as our friendship grew, these theological compatibilities, as substantial as we soon determined they were, became only a small part of our conversations. We have enjoyed many chats at Starbucks and other places over the years, commiserating over "workplace" issues, celebrating our families, especially our children and more recently grandchildren, praying with each other, and rejoicing in all things good. Our friendship has even lasted through a season of the Yongs as landlords and the Shermans as tenants, until Steve and his wife, Lynne, moved so he could take up a teaching post at Grand Canyon University in Phoenix, Arizona, that now puts them within driving distance to Southern California where both of their families reside. I am looking forward to many more years of conversation with Steve about all things theological, including his own ongoing work in theological method and theological hermeneutics.

* * *

Pasadena, California

Acknowledgments

I thank the editors and publishers for permission to reprint each of the following that were previously published pieces.

Chapter 1: "The Science, Sighs, and Signs of Interpretation: An Asian American Post-Pentecost-al Hermeneutics in a Multi-, Inter-, and Transcultural World," in L. William Oliverio Jr., and Kenneth J. Archer, eds., *Constructive Pneumatological Hermeneutics in Pentecostal Christianity*, CHARIS: Christianity and Renewal–Interdisciplinary Studies series (New York: Palgrave Macmillan, 2016), 177–96.

Chapter 2: "Understanding and Living the Apostolic Way: Orality and Scriptural Faithfulness in Conversation with African Pentecostalism," plenary presentation at international conference, "Pentecostalism and the Catholic Church: Challenges in the Nigerian context," Abuja, Nigeria, 14–17 November 2016.

Chapter 3: "Reflecting and Confessing in the Spirit: Called to Transformational Theologizing," *International Review of Mission* 105:2 (2016) 169–83.

Chapter 4: "Many Tongues, Many Senses: Pentecost, the Body Politic, and the Redemption of Dis/Ability," *Pneuma: The Journal of the Society for Pentecostal Studies* 31:2 (2009) 167–88.

Chapter 5: "Sons and Daughters, Young and Old: Toward a Pentecostal Theology of the Family," *PentecoStudies: An Interdisciplinary Journal for Research on the Pentecostal & Charismatic Movements* 10:2 (2011) 147–73.

Chapter 6: "Children and the Promise of the Spirit: Pneumatology and the Quest for Child Theology," originally presented at the "Child Theologies: Perspectives from World Christianity" consultation, Valparaiso University, August 2011.

Chapter 7: "The Social Psychology of Sin: A Pentecostal Perspective," presented at the Faith & Science Conference, Evangel University, Springfield, Missouri, September 23, 2016.

Chapter 8: Previously unpublished.

Chapter 9: "Apostolic Evangelism in the Postcolony: Opportunities and Challenges," *Mission Studies* 34:2 (2017) 147–67.

Chapter 10: "'The Light Shines in the Darkness': Johannine Dualism and the Challenge of Christian Theology of Religions Today," *Journal of Religion* 89:1 (2009) 31–56.

Chapter 11: "Running the (Special) Race: New (Pauline) Perspectives on Theology of Sport," in Nick J. Watson, ed., special issue of *Journal of Disability and Religion* 18:2 (2014) 209–25.

Chapter 12: "Reading Scripture and Nature: Pentecostal Hermeneutics and Their Implications for the Contemporary Evangelical Theology and Science Conversation," *Perspectives on Science and Christian Faith* 63:1 (2011) 1–13.

Introduction

Greater than the sum of its twelve parts (chapters), the thesis of this book as a whole is that the Trinitarianism prevalent in some of the major segments of the contemporary *theological interpretation of Scripture* (TIS) conversation can be more robustly conceptualized via fresh attentiveness to apostolic spirituality and practice viewed through a pentecostal lens. The concluding chapter at the end of the book revisits this claim in light of the intervening essays. Meanwhile, the following pages set the stage for the prosecution of the thesis in two ways, corresponding to the introduction's two main parts: first by situating its argument within the fields of TIS and pentecostal hermeneutics, in particular exploring the areas where they overlap with my own prior work, and second by laying out step-by-step (chapter-by-chapter) the main cords of the case that is being made.

Theological Interpretation of Scripture: Setting the Stage

What is TIS and how might a pentecostal perspective enter its fluid discursive space? As there are multiple ways to introduce TIS even as there is no one characterization of pentecostal scholarly domains,[1] the following reflects my own take on both and their intersection. Anticipating the overall thrust of this volume—that pentecostal pneumatology can buttress the Trinitarian motif prominent in at least some of the major circles of TIS— our focus will be on these conceptual and thematic sites. We proceed, then, from i) a broad outline of TIS and its developments especially those seeking guidance from the ancient rule of faith, and ii) a brief review of efforts to clarify the theological, and specifically Trinitarian, character of the rule in relationship to contemporary scriptural interpretation, *to* iii) charting developments in pentecostal hermeneutics relevant to the present situation,

---

1. An initial proposal is Fowl, *Theological Interpretation of Scripture*. Overviews of TIS include Treier, *Introducing Theological Interpretation*, and Vanhoozer and Treier, *Theology and the Mirror of Scripture*.

that includes iv) my own efforts to date in understanding TIS in hindsight of the arc of this overview.

Overview and Status Quaestionis: *TIS and the Rule of Faith*

One way to understand the emergence of TIS is in relationship to the ferment in biblical studies in the last quarter of the previous century, in particular the dissatisfaction with the disconnect between biblical scholarship as it had evolved to that time and the churches that embraced these sacred texts as authoritative for the life of faith. Historical methods of investigation that had long focused on the world *behind* the text or sought to explicate or exegete the meaning of the text in its ancient context either minimized discussion of how such texts were relevant beyond the original audiences or suggested that it was beyond the purview of critical scholarship to ask such questions. Yet there was an increasing sense that such modern proclivities not just were out of sync with earlier (patristic, medieval, and Reformation-era) approaches that read Scripture morally, spiritually, and salvifically, but also thereby were incapable of recognizing the fundamentally ecclesial and theological character of these ancient writings.[2] Even within the field of biblical studies, alternative hermeneutical options had begun to appear, most relevant for our purposes being literary and narrative methods that were attentive to the basic plotlines of the scriptural accounts and thereby able to ask fresh questions about divine character and agency attested to across those pages.[3]

The primary concerns raised by biblical scholars, however, were that later theological commitments would be read back into these earlier texts, so the question persisted: what kinds of checks and balances existed to curb eisegesis of texts moved by alien theological presuppositions? One prominent response by TIS proponents in the *postliberal* movement was to emphasize that sacred texts ought to be read in accordance with the ecclesial practices that generated these canonical writings to begin with, and that therefore contemporary readers were best advised to adopt these traditioned postures and their related interpretive habits and goals.[4] Doing so would not just nurture the sensibilities and instincts required for faithful

---

2. As urged by biblical scholar Watson in *Text, Church and World*, and *Text and Truth*.

3. Clearing the way earlier for a fresh appreciation of the narrative aspect of the Bible was Frei, *Eclipse of Biblical Narrative*.

4. Pecknold, *Transforming Postliberal Theology*, is one of the most thoughtful postliberal accounts of TIS.

interpretation but also enable the reparative practices for Christian life and witness attested to in Scripture. Contrary to the concerns that such postliberal privileging of premodern modes of scriptural interpretation would be constraining,[5] the rejoinder was that this also foregrounded an ad hoc hermeneutical sensibility with regard to engaging contemporary issues and realities that made possible a wide variety of deployments.[6] For instance, one vigorous initiative involving a broad range of postliberal practitioners of TIS is the Scriptural Reasoning project that includes Christian, Jewish, and Muslims reading and discussing their sacred texts together, and this is indicative of the potency of TIS in the public sphere, outside of formal ecclesial environments.[7]

Yet the postliberal logic presses the question about theological commitments amidst the diversity of Christian traditions. To get right to the heart of this volume, what kinds of theological warrants are most conducive to and appropriate for TIS and how are the sometimes competing versions of these to be adjudicated? Might there be confessional forms, for instance, a Reformed TIS, or a Baptist TIS, or a pentecostal TIS? More generally speaking, TIS advocates depend on the ecumenical consensus of the early Christian centuries even if they might find themselves located in the Roman Catholic Church or any of the confessional Protestant traditions.[8] What binds them together, then, is the creedal tradition, so that even if some may not fully embrace the first ecumenical councils in their details, there is little objection to TIS being governed in some significant sense by the early

---

5. An articulate apologetic for TIS's premodern approach is Steinmetz, "The Superiority of Pre-critical Exegesis."

6. For more about the ad hoc character of TIS hermeneutics, see Watson, *Text and Truth*, 17, and Fowl, *Engaging Scripture*, ch. 7. As a side note, this ad hoc approach has been prominent especially within the postliberal movement. Discussion of postliberalism's "ad hoc apologetics" can be found in Moulaison, *Lord, Giver of Life*, 56–59. Note that Moulaison's overall project, to infuse postliberal theology of mission in a pluralistic world with a more vigorous pneumatological engine, is one that I am quite sympathetic with, although in my judgment, her work only gets us as far in this regard as her sources—Eastern Christian pneumatologies—are capable of carrying. This book suggests a pentecostal complement to Moulaison's Eastern Christian postliberalism, one that I believe is better primed to take on plurality in its various dimensions.

7. For an introduction to the Scriptural Reasoning conversation, see Ford and Clemson, eds., *Interreligious Reading after Vatican II*. Ford is a prominent TIS participant—see Ford and Stanton, eds., *Reading Texts, Seeking Wisdom*—who has also written about the various sites of interfaith scriptural reading (see Ford, *Christian Reason*, ch. 8).

8. See, e.g., the contributors to Bartholomew and Thomas, eds., *A Manifesto for Theological Interpretation*, who are Roman Catholics as well as Protestants from mainline and evangelical denominations.

Christian *rule of faith*. While including first the Old Roman Symbol and later its expanded version in the Apostles' Creed, the rule of faith has come to refer to the basic scriptural account of God as Father, Son, and Spirit, as creator, redeemer, and sanctifier, encapsulated in the Nicene confession, and such has come to be widely recognized as providing the theological scaffolding for TIS.[9]

Awaiting the pentecostal contribution to TIS promised in this book, a few comments on Wesleyan contributions to the discussion are in order. Two renowned Wesleyan biblical scholars, Robert Wall and Joel Green, have been at the vanguard of TIS almost from its inception,[10] even as they themselves have wrestled with how to formulate a distinctively Wesleyan version of TIS.[11] There is no question that John Wesley's central doctrine of Christian perfection provides an overarching theological and soteriological framework for scriptural interpretation,[12] even while such a vision for TIS has purchase beyond the Wesleyan tradition. At the same time, Green is concerned that the Wesleyan retrieval passes muster with the critical standards of the biblical academy even as Wall has sought to deepen the ecumenical depth of the Wesleyan proposal by anchoring that in the ancient rule of faith.[13] We will return momentarily to see how pentecostal hermeneutical developments compare with and differ from these Wesleyan precedents.

Contemporary Trajectories: Trinitarian Interpretation and the Spirit

Appeals to the church's historic rule of faith put the Trinitarian question at the center of the TIS table. This ought not to be too surprising since another stream into TIS, approaching from the other side of the unease in biblical scholarship noted above, derived from the theological front, in particular developments in the fields of dogmatic and systematic theology. From this direction, the legacy of Karl Barth has been palpable, not unlike across the

---

9. For more on the rule of faith, see, from a Reformed perspective, Billings, *The Word of God for the People of God*, 17–29, and from a Wesleyan perspective, Green, *Practicing Theological Interpretation*, 77–80; see in a moment for more on the Wesleyan aspect of Green's proposal.

10. E.g., Wall, "Canonical Context and Canonical Conversations," and Green and Turner, eds., *Between Two Horizons*.

11. See their contributions, among those of other Wesleyans, in Green and Watson, eds., *Wesley, Wesleyans, and Reading Bible as Scripture*.

12. Koskie, "Can We Speak of a Wesleyan Theological Hermeneutic of Scripture Today?"

13. Green, *Practicing Theological Interpretation*, ch. 4, and Wall, "Reading the Bible from within Our Traditions."

theological arena as a whole. Particularly relevant in this regard has been Barth's theological exegesis, strewn over many pages of his *Church Dogmatics*. As Mary Cunningham has shown, much of Barth's achievements derive from a Trinitarian hermeneutic teased out of a fresh reading of the scriptural narrative, especially but not limited to his understanding of Jesus Christ as the electing God and the elected man distilled from an intertextual reconsideration of the prologue of John's Gospel and Ephesians 1:4's assertion regarding divine election.[14] On the one side, this narrative Trinitarianism, anchored by the work of God accomplished in Jesus Christ, is consistent with if it not also buttresses the Trinitarian structure of the rule of faith guiding the TIS enterprise. On the other side, however, a Barthian form of TIS begs the pneumatological question: what kind of Trinitarianism is at work within a christologically dominant framework that effectively—intentionally or not—subordinates or marginalizes pneumatology?[15] Put alternatively: how Trinitarian is the rule of faith in TIS without a vigorous pneumatology?

It has surely been the case that TIS proponents have insisted on the import of pneumatology in scriptural interpretation. In some respects, this is no new revelation, as the theological tradition has perennially understood the role of the Spirit as both inspirer and illuminator of the Scriptures, and in the present milieu the latter includes explication of the divine word for new situations and different contexts.[16] But there is also recognition of a kind of pneumatic interpretation, perhaps akin to the "spiritual interpretation" or "spiritual exegesis" characteristic of moral-allegorical-ecclesial hermeneutics of the patristic and medieval periods,[17] one perhaps that is

---

14. Cunningham, *What is Theological Exegesis*. Complementing Cunningham's argument, albeit with a robustly pneumatological reading of Barth's exegesis of the Prologue of John, is Smith, *A Theology of the Third Article*, who argues for the Spirit as *inverberate*—meaning, percussively perceptible, especially through the church's kerygmatic proclamation—yet "*not* an additional revelation alongside God incarnate but differentiated continuation of God's revelation in the Word made flesh" (168, emphasis Smith's). I develop another version of a pneumatological ontology of preaching in my essay "Proclamation and the Third Article."

15. Zimmerman, *Recovering Theological Hermeneutics*, is a good example of a robustly incarnational approach to theological interpretation, but the fullness of its Trinitarian potential is yet to be reached because of an anemic pneumatology.

16. On the illumination of the Spirit, see Webster, *Domain of the Word*, ch. 3; Williams, *Receiving the Bible in Faith*, 212–14; and Bartholomew, "Listening to God's Address," 17.

17. See Boersma and Levering, "Introduction: Spiritual Interpretation and Realigned Temporality."

"Spirit-imbued."[18] From the perspective of the rule of faith, such gestures are important steps beyond any (Barthian) christocentrism (at best) or christomonism (at worst) toward a more fully Trinitarian TIS, one that affirms, "the living, speaking reality of the risen Jesus Christ present in the Spirit to the assembly of God's people."[19] There have even been exegetical efforts to explore the contours of such a pneumatological approach to TIS, especially in attending to the practices of the early Christians as recorded in Acts 10–15.[20] Yet what does it mean to conduct a "reading in the Spirit,"[21] or what else does pneumatology contribute to TIS beyond illuminating or applying the scriptural word?

Evangelical theologian Kevin Vanhoozer has made unique headway toward a Trinitarian TIS by delving into, rather than mentioning tangentially, pneumatology. To be accurate, Vanhoozer's pneumatological hermeneutics is part of his larger response to deconstructive theories perceived as dissolving authorship, relativizing textual meaning, and enthroning reader response, and it is within the last domain that his "Spirit of understanding" is developed.[22] Central to Vanhoozer's rehabilitative project is speech-act theory, particularly as such can provide theological account of how divinity is able to utilize the words of others—in the case of Scripture, the *locutions* of its human authors—to accomplish (*illocutionarily*) divine ends in the world at large (the *perlocutionary* effects).[23] Within this framework, then, the activity of the Spirit is largely as perlocutionary force,[24] achieving the divinely intended effects of the scriptural locutions in the lives of believers. Thus the Holy Spirit is tied to Scripture, enables believers to receive and comprehend the scriptural word, convicts them of Scripture's message, sanctifies their attitudes to the biblical witness, and illuminates the letter of the text "by impressing upon [believers] the full force of its communicative action, its illocutions."[25] On the one hand, the Spirit in Vanhoozer plays

---

18. Green, *Seized by the Truth*, 94.

19. Webster, *Word and Church*, 58; for more on Webster's Trinitarian theology of Scripture, see his *Holy Scripture*, ch. 1

20. Fowl, *Engaging Scripture*, ch. 4.

21. Hart, "Tradition, Authority," 201.

22. See Vanhoozer, *Is There a Meaning in This Text?*, 407–31.

23. Bartholomew, Greene, and Möller, *After Pentecost*—to which Vanhoozer contributed the lead chapter—is mostly about speech-act theory as applied to philosophy of language and biblical interpretation, and hardly at all about pneumatology.

24. Ibid., 428–29.

25. Ibid., 413, 421, 427; see also Vanhoozer, *First Theology*, 233.

the familiar role of illuminating the biblical word,[26] and in that sense, this could be viewed as typical subordination of pneumatology to Christology. Yet within a certain Trinitarian frame of reference, the indispensability of the perlocutionary dimension of scriptural communication can also be understood as highlighting the essential work of the Spirit, particularly as unfolded within, and constitutive of, the life of the church as the believing community.[27] Further, Vanhoozer also recognizes that while Christ is the one who sends the Spirit, Christ is also who he is only by the power of the Spirit, so that there is a mutuality between Word and Spirit, albeit with different functions as the latter is primarily the "executor" of—advocate for and witness to—the former.[28]

Last but not least, and perhaps most important for the purposes of this book, Vanhoozer is forthright about what he calls a "Pentecostal plenitude" that, while presuming texts have a single, literal sense and therefore determinate meaning, also welcomes manifold applications and explications.[29] This is the way forward as "a responsible pluralist,"[30] one that enables navigation between rigid absolutism and unrestrained pluralism, and that recognizes the plurality of readers in diverse contexts and various methods of reading. To be sure, the distinction between single determinate textual meaning and multiple significances is too neat and does not adequately account for the fact that even the determination of original textual meaning involves interpretive assessment of significance,[31] but my point is that Vanhoozer

---

26. The scriptural rationale is that, "When the Spirit of truth comes, he will guide you into all the truth; for he will not speak on his own, but will speak whatever he hears, and he will declare to you the things that are to come" (John 16:13); see Vanhoozer, *Is There a Meaning in This Text?*, 415.

27. So Vanhoozer, *The Drama of Doctrine*, chs. 6–7, talks about the church as "performance of the Spirit" and about the "Spirited" church discernible within the ecclesial "history of canonical effects," whether of prayer, ritual, or covenantal life.

28. Ibid., 193–94, 197.

29. Unpacked in Vanhoozer, *Is There a Meaning in This Text?*, 415–16.

30. Ibid., 415.

31. The contours of this debate can be seen in Adam et al., *Reading Scripture with the Church*, especially Fowl's argument therein about the underdeterminacy of scriptural meaning versus Vanhoozer's account. Green as biblical scholar sides with Fowl—e.g., Green, "Scripture and Theology," 34, and "Learning Theological Interpretation from Luke," 57—although not deploying his categories. Spinks, *The Bible and the Crisis of Meaning*, brilliantly captures how Fowl and Vanhoozer are right in what they are wary about (absolutism for the former and relativism for the latter) but are too beholden to modern dyadic constructs to see a constructive way forward, which requires a triadic semiotic. My response, complementary to Spinks and also drawing at least in part from C. S. Peirce as he does, is pneumatological and Trinitarian, initially

has done more than anyone to think about "interpretation after Pentecost,"[32] and this as a Reformed and evangelical theologian.

Pentecostal Hermeneutics: TIS and the Apostolic Way

Whence and whither pentecostal hermeneutics amidst this discussion? Related entries in the *Dictionary of Theological Interpretation of Scripture* are uninformingly descriptive as well as cautionary about the need for a *via media* between the anthropocentrism of the liberal tradition and the "pneumatic excess" of global charismaticism.[33] Yet although pentecostal scholars and theologians have been largely disengaged with the TIS conversation,[34] Joel Green has observed that they have led the way to thinking in more tradition-specific ways—*confessionally* is not quite the right word given pentecostal wariness about creedalism—about hermeneutics, perhaps in part because of "persons nurtured in the Pentecostal tradition coming to the table of biblical studies rather late, when the rules of the game of critical scholarship had been somewhat loosened, allowing for critical reflection on the Enlightenment project."[35] In the following, with neither time nor space to cover the full gamut of pentecostal hermeneutics,[36] I focus on what I have called the "Cleveland School" alongside another stream of pentecostal hermeneutics in pneumatological key, both of which are relevant to TIS concerns.

If pentecostal hermeneutics received its initial impetus in the early 1990s via the openings afforded by postmodern sensibilities to hitherto

---

argued in *Spirit-Word-Community* and developed in many books since, this one being a further deepening of the point.

32. See Vanhoozer, *First Theology*, 196–98.

33. See Tennison, "Charismatic Biblical Interpretation," and, for the quotation, Badcock, "Holy Spirit, Doctrine of the," 305.

34. With two exceptions, perhaps: Green, *Sanctifying Interpretation*, about which I will have occasion to refer to in the conclusion, and Thomas and Macchia, *Revelation*, which is a contribution to The Two Horizons New Testament Commentary series written by a biblical scholar and systematic theologian, both from the pentecostal tradition (although the commentary itself, as a final product, does not read as "pentecostal" in most senses of that word).

35. Green, *Practicing Theological Interpretation*, 11.

36. Chapters 1 and 2 below cover some of this ground; overviews include Martin ed., *Pentecostal Hermeneutics*, and (more historically oriented) Oliverio Jr., *Theological Hermeneutics in the Classical Pentecostal Tradition*, although see more recently, Keener, *Spirit Hermeneutics*, for a major, constructive formulation.

marginalized voices or particularized perspectives,[37] Rickie D. Moore and John Christopher Thomas, faculty in Old and New Testament respectively at the then Church of God Theological Seminary (now Pentecostal Theological Seminary)—the flagship institution of graduate theological education for the Pentecostal Holiness Church of God (Cleveland, Tennessee)—were busy establishing the *Journal of Pentecostal Theology* and its Journal of Pentecostal Theology Supplement series.[38] Moore in particular also began writing about how his pentecostal spirituality and charismatic encounters with the Spirit provided perspective on the First Testament inhibited by the historical-critical methods he had imbibed in his graduate education,[39] and the duo began publishing arguments regarding a distinctive pentecostal approach to scriptural interpretation in their journal and book series.[40] For them as pentecostal scholars, the emergence of literary and narrative criticism in the biblical academy allowed for focus on the scriptural text in ways important for their ecclesial contexts but also the postmodern milieu did not require bracketing their charismatic experiences and perspectives in the interpretive task.[41]

Most important within this venue was the twenty-eighth volume of the Supplement series, Kenneth Archer's *A Pentecostal Hermeneutic for the Twenty-First Century* (2004). Consistent with the preferences of the Cleveland School, *pentecostal* in this volume is delineated according to the beliefs and practices of the Azusa Street generation, and from this vantage point,

37. Inaugurated, arguably in the fall 1993 issue of *Pneuma: The Journal of the Society for Pentecostal Studies*; see Dempster, "Paradigm Shifts and Hermeneutics," and, in hindsight, Noel, *Pentecostal and Postmodern Hermeneutics*.

38. I have overviewed this "Cleveland School" in my article, "Pentecostal Theology," section 2. Note though that far from being a monolithic whole, biblical scholars at Lee University and at the Pentecostal Theological Seminary, both in Cleveland, Tennessee, do not all operate in unison. In that respect, what I am calling the "Cleveland School" masks a diversity of approaches by those working in these two institutions. However, for heuristic purposes, and more importantly to contrast the approach I will be describing in what follows with other options across the pentecostal academy, this designation suffices, at least for the time being and for the present discussion.

39. Most important in initiating this line of inquiry was Moore, "Canon and Charisma in the Book of Deuteronomy" (1992) and "Deuteronomy and the Fire of God: A Critical Charismatic Interpretation" (1995), later reprinted in Moore, *The Spirit of the Old Testament*, part II.

40. Leading the way was McQueen, *Joel and the Spirit*, ch. 5. Important in the next decade was Waddell, *The Spirit in the Book of Revelation*, ch. 3; Martin, *The Unheard Voice of God*, ch. 3; and Archer, *'I Was in the Spirit on the Lord's Day'*, ch. 2. See also Thomas, *The Spirit of the New Testament*.

41. For more on the literary and narrative "turn" in pentecostal biblical scholarship, see Mittelstadt, *Reading Luke-Acts in the Pentecostal Tradition*, 82–91.

Archer urges a distinctively pentecostal hermeneutic that features an attentiveness to the voice of the Spirit in the pentecostal community's engagement with Scripture. The emerging pentecostal story then acts as a kind of hermeneutical filter that guides ongoing pentecostal biblical interpretation, which in turn reshapes the pentecostal narrative and its core convictions, etc. To his credit, Archer has identified in a coherent if not compelling fashion at least one way of understanding the hermeneutical circle within the pentecostal tradition, even as the putative success of his endeavor invites the question about whether every Christian hermeneutic ought to be qualified according to the sub-tradition within which it has been nurtured. This may not be a bad thing if in fact ecclesial traditions—e.g., pentecostal, Wesleyan, Baptistic, Reformed, Lutheran, Catholic, Orthodox, and so on—have their distinctive charisms for the church ecumenical and the fruits of such are to be discerned at least in part in and through their hermeneutical or methodological offerings.

A spectrum of options has thus opened up before us, ranging from an intra-pentecostal proposal designed to shore up pentecostal self-understanding on the one side to a more general stance intended to be both more ecumenical to the wider church and more defensible vis-à-vis the purported objectivity of the scholarly guild on the other side.[42] Leaning toward the latter trajectory are two more recent collections that consider the viability of any pentecostal hermeneutic as resting on its capacity to address not just those within pentecostal interpretive communities, ecclesial or academic. Both urge adjustments from *pentecostal* to *pneumatic* nomenclature, albeit via distinct routes. *Spirit and Scripture: Exploring a Pneumatic Hermeneutic*, edited by Kevin Spawn and Archie Wright (2012), insists on widening the pentecostal tent to include charismatic and related renewal movements not just on the contemporary horizon but also going back historically, even into ancient Israel. Their quest is to identify a mode of interpreting "in the Spirit," so to speak, one that might characterize not just those situated in self-identified pentecostal churches and movements but as representative of how the people of God have perennially encountered the divine in history. By contrast, a wide ranging set of essays, *Constructive Pneumatological Hermeneutics in Pentecostal Christianity*, edited by William Oliverio Jr., and Kenneth

---

42. The former more augustly pentecostal perspective is attempted by Wyckoff, *Pneuma and Logos* (although perhaps its success limits its extra-pentecostal relevance), while the latter more rigorously acceptable scholarly orientation is represented by the work of exegete Gordon Fee, for instance. As already noted, Keener's *Spirit Hermeneutics* may carve out the needed *via media* for the next decade and beyond, albeit its achievements still need to be filled out from majority world, feminist, and postcolonial perspectives.

Archer (2016), manifests a collaborative effort to consider the potency of a pentecostal hermeneutic that is pneumatologically empowered toward multiple tasks: generating a general hermeneutical horizon capable of engaging the human condition with transcendence; nurturing an ecumenical sensibility that welcomes cross-confessional interpretation; attending to the sociocultural pluralism that marks not just the global renewal movement but world Christianity as well; and facilitating the multidisciplinary dimensions of human knowing across the broad scope of the human and natural sciences. Clearly, pentecostal hermeneutics as catalyzed in these ventures is not only substantively pneumatological but seeks, precisely through such a pneumatic itinerary, to attend to the many voices of a post-Pentecost world.

Prospects for TIS after Pentecost? An Autobiographical Retrospect

It is against the preceding discursive matrix—in TIS and in pentecostal scholarship both as convergent and divergent platforms—that my own work has unfolded. In order to appreciate the arguments of the chapters in this book, I will briefly overview how TIS has evolved in my work. As may be argued, its cumulative effect might well be denoted as PIS: pneumatological interpretation of Scripture.[43]

My second book, *Sprit-Word-Community: Theological Hermeneutics in Trinitarian Perspective* (2002), attempted to argue both that there is a sense in which any general hermeneutical dialectic is pneumatological and that any Christian Trinitarian hermeneutic required a robust pneumatological component. These twin convictions have undergirded my work since, and it is from within this frame of reference that my pentecostal type of TIS took a pneumatological form thereafter. More precisely, concerned as I was that any pentecostal hermeneutic be not just for modern pentecostal communities or those self-identified with such, I was led to explore what it might mean to read the Day of Pentecost narrative hermeneutically. Even if Acts 2 was surely at the heart of modern pentecostal spirituality yet as canonical Scripture, it also belongs to all Christians. Such a way forward invited a distinctively Lukan hermeneutical imagination, one that gave hermeneutical priority to the book of Acts generally. My initial foray in this direction was in *The Spirit Poured Out on All Flesh: Pentecostalism and the Possibility of Global Theology* (2005), which utilized Lukan themes to talk about pentecostal and global soteriology, ecclesiology, the doctrine of God, theology

---

43. Those interested in connecting the dots between how I describe my developing thinking in TIS here and the arc of my broader *oeuvre* can see Yong, "Between the Local and the Global" and "The Spirit, Vocation, and the Life of the Mind."

of religions, and theology of creation. A few years later, I deployed a similar approach for public theology: *In the Days of Caesar: Pentecostalism and Political Theology* (2010) takes its cues from the fact that the story of Jesus and the early messianists unfolds "In those days [when] a decree went out from Emperor Augustus that all the world should be registered" (Luke 2:1), and then derives from the apostolic movement's Spirit-empowered efforts to navigate the Roman imperial world a pneumatological vision of "many tongues, many political practices" for the contemporary arena.

If *Spirit Poured Out* and *Days of Caesar* were both distinctively Lukan in its scriptural frames, their central Day of Pentecost hermeneutical orientation was preserved in my other TIS efforts. *Hospitality and the Other: Pentecost, Christian Practices, and the Other* (2008) furthered earlier work I had done in pneumatological theology of religions via the motif of interfaith hospitality, but now this was not only grounded in a Lukan understanding of hospitality but also, from that scriptural locus, embraced the hospitality of ancient Israel, especially as revealed in its wisdom literature.[44] Then my *The Bible, Disability, and the Church: A New Vision of the People of God* (2011), also extending earlier thinking in theology of disability,[45] is motivated centrally via a pentecostal vision of "many tongues, many forms of ability" to revisit the broad scope of the biblical narrative—First Testament accounts of Jacob, Mephibosheth, and Job, Levitical passages on impairments, and the psalms of lament, among other materials, and New Testament materials starting with Luke and Acts but also including but not limited to the Fourth Gospel (the story of the man born blind in John 9) and the Pauline letters—in order to redeem disability tropes for an inclusive and welcoming ecclesiology in the present time. Last but not least in terms of reflecting how my pentecostal starting point has opened up to a pneumatic hermeneutic is *Spirit of Love: A Trinitarian Theology of Grace* (2012), which basic thrust, consistent with that initiated in *Spirit-Word-Community* and continued elsewhere, suggests in part via a close reading of Lukan, Pauline, and Johannine pneumatological texts, that starting with the Spirit leads to a more authentically Trinitarian (rather than actually binitarian) theological vision.[46]

In the last half decade I have also become increasingly more engaged with TIS. My *Who is the Holy Spirit: A Walk with the Apostles* (2012) was forged alongside the *Days of Caesar* volume but crafted out of a close

---

44. See Yong, *Hospitality and the Other*, 100–17.

45. Yong, *Theology and Down Syndrome*.

46. The latter two textual sites are to be read from a post-Day of Pentecost perspective established by the Third Evangelist; see Yong, *Spirit of Love*, chs. 6–8.

reading through the entirety of the book of Acts—with forays almost every other chapter into the Third Gospel to pick up thematic linkages between the apostolic experience and their remembrance of the Jesus story[47]—and devoted to explicating what might be called a political theology (or pneumato-theology) for the late modern world. Then, in a one-volume systematic (pneumatological) theology,[48] *Renewing Christian Theology: Systematics for a Global Christianity* (2014), I insisted that starting with the Spirit of Pentecost meant beginning eschatologically and thereby reversed the traditional sequence of the loci so as to end with the doctrine of Scripture;[49] yet with each of the eleven dogmatic chapters, the third section was devoted to reading one book of the New Testament relevant to that doctrinal locus. Even now, I have begun work, expected to persist over the next few years, on a commentary on the book of Revelation, contracted for Westminster John Knox's Belief series, which contributions are written by systematic theologians (of which mine may be the last volume to be published, God willing, and perhaps appropriately so due to the circumstances amidst which the invitation and assignment arrived).

As should be evident, I did not start out in TIS but have found my way into the discussion through work as a pentecostal theologian seeking to understand more clearly what it meant to do theology, and read Scripture as part of this process, in light of the Pentecost event. This is not quite the same as imitating the early apostles as interpreters of their Scripture, but there is a sense in which I am after an apostolic hermeneutic: engaging with Scripture as being of the apostles (who were writers of what we call the New Testament and readers of the First Testament) and as divine word in light of encounter with the risen Christ through the power of the Spirit. I submit that such an apostolic and pentecostal approach to TIS is both more deeply scriptural, and more deeply Trinitarian, precisely because the work of the Spirit then (in scriptural writings), since (in the Christian tradition), and

---

47. Hence this is to read Luke in light of Acts, although the pneumato-logic behind this approach is that the narrative of the Third Gospel is not just post-Easter but post-Pentecost: nothing in the New Testament, in other words, precedes the Pentecost event, and therefore, all should be read in its light.

48. The seeds of which were planted during my graduate studies when I read Clark Pinnock's *Flame of Love: A Theology of the Holy Spirit*, which is less a pneumatology than a reconsideration of the various dogmatic loci from a pneumatological perspective, hence a pneumatological theology, strictly speaking.

49. As Wesleyan TIS scholar Robert Wall puts it: "every episode of Acts is understood against this [Acts 2:17] eschatological horizon"; see Robinson and Wall, *Called to Be Church*, 24.

now (in our contemporary situation) is foregrounded, rather than subservient, marginalized, or ignored altogether.⁵⁰

Pentecost, the Spirit, and Scriptural Interpretation: Mapping the Argument

Unlike the two predecessor volumes of previously published essays—*The Dialogical Spirit* and *The Missiological Spirit* (both 2014)—to which the book you hold in your hands is intended to be a sequel, the chapters in this volume are organized not chronologically but topically. But even if readers of this volume will be less able to trace development in my thinking as in those works, this is because, as already indicated, my turn to TIS has gathered momentum only more recently. The rest of this introductory chapter explains the four parts to come, summarizes each chapter within each part, and explicates its role in relationship to the TIS thesis of this volume, viz., that the Trinitarianism dominant in contemporary TIS can be more robustly conceptualized via fresh attention to the apostolic and scriptural narrative viewed through a pentecostal lens.

Theological Hermeneutics: Pentecostal Perspectives

The three essays in part I of this book originated within a few months of each other in the spring of 2016, each in response to distinct invitations. Together, they summarize my views about pentecostal hermeneutics at the time of writing. In brief, pentecostal hermeneutics is Christian hermeneutics that is defined explicitly by the horizon of the Pentecost event: all Christian interpretation of Scripture in this regard is pentecostal, undergirded by the presence and activity of the Spirit poured out on all flesh.

"The Science, Sighs, and Signs of Interpretation: An Asian American Post-Pentecost-al Hermeneutics in a Multi-, Inter-, and Transcultural

---

50. In this respect, *apostolic* in this work is certainly rooted in Reformation and post-Reformation restorationist movements, included for our purposes but not limited to apostolic type emphases in pentecostal and charismatic Christianity, while insisting that such retrieval of the apostolic writings (by which I mean the New Testament specifically, which can only be comprehended in light of the Acts narrative, and through which then the significance of the First Testament is discovered) is informed by the ongoing life of the Spirit discerned in the church and the world. *Apostolic* in this book hence includes classic and ecumenical notions of apostolicity as being based on or authorized by the apostles, albeit, again, as generated for us via charismatic and pneumatic spirituality. The rest of this volume clarifies and expands on this understanding.

World," suggests that the way forward for pentecostal hermeneutics in a pluralistic world is to develop not so much a confessional approach founded on any genealogical connection with the Azusa Street Revival at the turn of the twentieth century, but to adopt the Day of Pentecost apostolic experience as exemplary for biblical and theological interpretation. Such a *post-Pentecost-al*—the dual hyphenation of this neologism highlighting connections first and foremost to the Day of Pentecost rather than to the modern Pentecostal movement—proposal is delineated by looking at the challenges for hermeneutics in contemporary glocal context that need to navigate multi- and inter-cultural projects in search of a more transcendent, overarching, or trans-cultural vantage point; by unfolding the opportunities inherent in this hybrid space for Asian American Pentecostals in particular;[51] and by sketching the contours of a hermeneutical paradigm that is observant of its interpretive rules (science), its subterranean impulses (sighs), and its historical practices and teleological performances (signs). The goal is to invite further hermeneutical reflection not only from pentecostal Christianity but all who believe there is something else to be considered when understanding human interpretation in relationship to divine presence and activity opened up in the Day of Pentecost narrative.

TIS scholars are also beginning to recognize the need to account for interpretive habits, sensibilities, and practices of the modern pentecostal movement. Daniel Treier, for instance, addresses the opportunities and challenges for postcolonial hermeneutics from the site of global pentecostal Christianity, observing that particularly in the majority world, the focus on the Old Testament, notions of immediacy vis-à-vis encounter with the divine, and cultural diversity invite if not require a "critical contextualization" or "critical syncretism" between gospel and culture in the present era.[52] My own efforts have been less focused on postcoloniality although I agree global Pentecostalism provides a generative site for approaching the important issues.[53]

"Understanding and Living the Apostolic Way: Oral Culturality and Hermeneutics after Pentecost" shifts from the Asian to the African horizon (through an invitation to present at a conference on African Pentecostalism), and makes the bold claim in conversation with African pentecostal perspectives that there is a pentecostal way of reading and interpreting

---

51. Herein expanding on Yong, *Future of Evangelical Theology*, and, on the notion of theological hybridity, also Yong, "From Every Tribe, Language, People, and Nation."

52. Treier, *Introducing Theological Interpretation of Scripture*, 182; Treier relies mostly on Jenkins, *The Next Christendom* and *The New Faces of Christianity*, for his analysis.

53. See Yong, "Conclusion: The Missiology of Jamestown."

Scripture that has normative implications for all Bible believers and practitioners in the third millennium. We start with a longer more descriptive discussion of African pentecostal hermeneutics as understood within oral-cultural matrices, and then briefly outline a pentecostal proposal for biblical hermeneutics that is argued as viable for the twenty-first century global context. The key is to unfold the pentecostal model according to its biblical frame, following specifically clues within the Day of Pentecost narrative that sheds light on apostolic ways of understanding and living sacred scripture.

The lens of orality central to this chapter is an extension of prior work in this arena applied to a pentecostal and pneumatological theology of preaching.[54] Yet such efforts are connected with their application in TIS projects. The late Donald Juel drew on orality perspectives to observe how the public or verbalized reading of scripture enables hearing even the "silences" communicated by the text, which in turn can inform our understanding of what is being "said."[55] If TIS intends to *hear* the voice and address of God,[56] then its proponents need to overcome the literary bias of the modern West and listen again to the oral-cultural imagination that remains vibrant across the majority world.

The final chapter of part I, "Reflecting and Confessing in the Spirit: Called to Transformational Theologizing," shifts from scriptural to theological hermeneutics. It asks the question about whether pentecostal and charismatic renewal has anything to contribute to global mission *theology* and *theologizing* in the present time, and suggests that the Spirit-filled and empowered life invites a pneumatological imagination, hermeneutic, and theological method that carves out a via media between a fundamentalistic scripturalism that neglects the ongoing work of the Spirit on the one side and a subjectivistic experientialism that is untethered to the biblical and theological tradition on the other. Such an approach is not just laid out propositionally (or "scientifically" in the old tradition of hermeneutics understood as the science of interpretation) but forged via a close reading of the Day of Pentecost narrative as recorded in the book of Acts.

Together, the chapters in the first part of this volume triangulate around a vision of how the Pentecost event precipitates its own hermeneutical vista. As Pentecost belongs to the church ecumenical, my own perspective shaped by modern pentecostal ecclesiality and spirituality is surely not the only way to formulate such a hermeneutical vision. More importantly, here I suggest that such a pentecost-al approach is not just another hermeneutical option

---

54. Yong, "Proclamation and the Third Article."
55. Juel, *Shaping the Scriptural Imagination*, ch. 2.
56. See, e.g., Seal, "Sensitivity to Aural Elements of the Text."

but may indeed be intrinsic, in this or other related versions, to any Trinitarian TIS. The rest of the chapters in this volume seeks to add fuel to the fire of this claim.

Theological Anthropology: Luke, the Spirit, and the Human

The theological-anthropological thread through part II of this volume is a happy coincidence, or fortuitous Spirit-led (pneumatological) providence, as the case may be. Written over a span of approximately four years (from 2008 to 2011—with chapter 4 first and the other two toward the latter part of this time), in retrospect, the movement in each case was from the Day of Pentecost narrative toward a more expansive Lukan exploration. Together, we can view these chapters as various incursions into theological anthropology from a Lukan frame of reference.[57]

What do disability studies and pentecostal studies have in common? "Many Tongues, Many Senses: Pentecost, the Body Politic, and the Redemption of Dis/Ability" responds to this questions in four steps (sections): 1) identification of some of the reasons behind the lack of interaction, so far, between disability and pentecostal studies; 2) exploration of how disability perspectives might bring to the fore previously unrecognized resources for rethinking pentecostal understandings of disability; 3) explication, with the help of a disability hermeneutic, of the pentecostal theology of "many tongues" bearing witness to the gospel with the resulting motif of "many senses" capable of receiving and giving witness to the wondrous works of God; and 4) reassessment of the possibility of pentecostal contributions to theology of disability and disability studies in light of the "many senses" motif. Dialogue at the intersection of disability studies and pentecostal studies will be challenging but also helpful for both sides, even as such joint efforts might also bear witness, in a creative and distinctive way, to the marvelous works of God in and through the diversity of embodied human experiences.

Chapter 4 took shape as part of the outworking of my theology of disability, specifically progression from systematic considerations to the arena

---

57. That Luke is as much theologian as historian is by now taken for granted (e.g., Bovon, *Luke the Theologian*; Kee, *Good News to the Ends of the Earth*). Yet if the first forays into this question in modern scholarship focused on Luke in his two volumes as "reinterpreting early Christian history to come to terms with the 'delay of the parousia'—the collapse of the expectation that Jesus would return soon" (Walton, "Acts," 75), my reading throughout presumes the Lukan posture of the "last days" inaugurated on the Day of Pentecost (Acts 2:17) that invites contemporary Christian faith and practice in every generation to be lived in anticipation of the coming reign of God.

of biblical theology.[58] It helped me fill out the underdeveloped pneumatology of the former volume via what might be loosely conceived as a biblical theology of disability that flowered in the latter book. The means was via delving more deeply into Luke's pentecostal and pneumatic theology and mining these Lukan resources—from Acts and the Gospel—in dialogue with disability perspectives for theological anthropology. My cue was to follow the multisensory manifestations of the Spirit in the Pentecost event to developing a (Lukan) theology of many senses (and many sensory abilities).

The fifth and sixth chapters of this book were written around the same time (circa early 2011), initially for presentation at two different conferences, one devoted to theology of the family and the other to theology of children. As I was invited to share a pentecostal perspective on the topic in both cases, I asked (myself initially) what such would be and was led, as with the disability topic, to the Day of Pentecost, and from there, to broader considerations across the two Lukan volumes.

"Sons and Daughters, Young and Old: Toward a Pentecostal Theology of the Family," urges that a Lukan and pentecostal approach will understand the family as an eschatological sign of the coming reign of God, and from this stage explores implications for a theology of parenting, for filial and sibling relationships, and for thinking about the intergenerational family, all in eschatological perspective. "Children and the Promise of the Spirit: Pneumatology and the Quest for Child Theology" deepens the nascent theology of the family by taking up the theology of children. Again, a pentecostal (Acts 2) and pneumatological emphasis discloses elements of what has now come to be known as a Third Article theology, in this case, of children, again situated in eschatological framework, with distinctive implications for Christian beliefs and practices drawn especially from material in the Third Gospel.[59]

As will be clear, although the aspects of theological anthropology covered in part II are ineluctably ad hoc—related to the conferences themes toward which I was invited to present a pentecostal perspective—this is not inconsistent with how at least the postliberal strand of TIS interacts with the historic dogmatic loci (as discussed above). Yet the pneumatological lens that at least for me is inspired by a pentecostal imagination also brings to bear resolutely theological commitments, including but irreducible to the

58. See the development from Yong, *Theology and Down Syndrome*, to Yong, *The Bible, Disability, and the Church*, which unfolded over approximately half a decade.

59. My eschatological hermeneutics is distinctively pneumatological and pentecostal, which secures the theological credentials, in my estimation, of eschatological approaches derived on other grounds, as in Webster, "Reading Scripture Eschatologically (1)," and Rowland, "Reading Scripture Eschatologically (2)."

eschatological, soteriological, and Trinitarian shape of the Pentecost account. From this vantage point, those interested in the almost decade-long development of my own theological anthropology can observe the movement from its initial formulation in theology of disability (in 2007) to the more recent systematic discussion (2014) within an eschatological framework.[60] But more importantly, beyond the theoretical gains to be made in thinking theologically about the nature of being human, a pentecostal and pneumatological reading of Luke-Acts urges Spirit-inspired practices, whether as temporarily able-bodied or impaired creatures,[61] or whether as spouses, parents, or children, in order to witness appropriately to the coming reign of God.

Pneumatological Soteriology: Pentecost and Salvation

The soteriological cord woven through part II comes more fully into view in chapters 7–9. Written also over a few months in 2016, like the first three chapters of the book, they were produced in response to different invitations, projects, and initial audiences. Yet as before, foregrounding my pentecostal perspective gave me opportunity to press further into Luke's understanding of the saving work of God through the coming of the Son and the gift of the Spirit.

Although the most recently completed essay in the book (in July 2016), chapter 7 on "The Social Psychology of Sin: A Pentecostal Perspective" launches this part as hamartiology supplies the theo-logic for soteriology. As said initially by Reinhold Niebuhr, sin is the "only empirically verifiable doctrine of the Christian faith."[62] If pentecostal sensibilities regarding the doctrine of sin may have been shaped as much by early twentieth century Victorian mores as by scriptural considerations, this chapter conducts an exploratory dialogue between literature at the nexus of the social and psychological sciences and theologies of sin on the one side and pentecostal theological readings of the Day of Pentecost narrative on the other side. The

---

60. See Yong, *Theology and Down Syndrome*, ch. 6.3, and Yong and Anderson, *Renewing Christian Theology*, chs. 8–10 (theological anthropology in this latter text does not have its own locus but is dispersed across the doctrines of healing/embodiment, soteriology, and theology of creation).

61. Engaging disability perspectives alerts us to the fact that what able bodied people considered normal is nevertheless contingent, even in the natural scheme of things; see further the discussion in ch. 4 below.

62. Niebuhr, *Man's Nature and His Communities*, 24.

goal is a preliminary pentecostal contribution to both contemporary efforts to formulate a multidimensional and interdisciplinary theology of sin.

The seed for this chapter was planted when I was invited to give one of the plenary addresses for the biennial "Faith and Science" conferences hosted by Evangel University, a leading Assemblies of God liberal arts institution of higher education. Delivering the keynote was Baylor University biomedical neuroscientist Matthew Stanford, who was going to speak on his book *The Biology of Sin* (2010). Having also done extensive work at the theology and science interface,[63] I thus begun to think about what a pentecostal and even pneumatological theology of sin might look like in dialogue with the sciences. But because Luke did not in his two volumes clearly address hamartiological matters, I approached my task from another angle: what was it that was wrong with the world that the Day of Pentecost outpouring of the Spirit was projected to repair or resolve? Might this provide a route to Luke's implicit theology of sin?

"Jubilee, Pentecost, and Liberation: The Preferential Option *of* the Poor on the Apostolic Way" was initially drafted for an edited volume exploring the relationship between evangelical theology and liberation theology. Inspired both by recent trends in liberation theology that show remarkable diversification compared with the perceived Marxist underpinnings of the first generation's efforts and alerted by the widely repeated anecdote that while liberation theologians opted for the poor, the poor were opting for Pentecostalism, chapter 8 considers how pentecostal spirituality that has served the poor across the majority world has *both* gained further theological traction and specification *and* expanded evangelical thinking on this topic via sustained engagement with the "many tongues" of liberation theology in the present global context as refracted through the apostolic witness, particularly of the third gospel and its sequel volume. Starting with contemporary liberationist impulses in global and evangelical theological discourses, the argument moves from there to developments of pentecostal liberationist thought, and concludes with scriptural reflections, focused particularly on Luke-Acts.

If the Exodus narrative has been central to liberation theology since its emergence, the Third Gospel has arguably been its principal New Testament locus, one that even pentecostal scholars have been drawn to.[64] Intriguingly, however, although conceived separately, there is a correlative thread

---

63. See Yong, *The Spirit of Creation*, among other edited ventures on pentecostal theology and the sciences.

64. Compare, for example, the Roman Catholic Michael Prior's *Jesus the Liberator* and the pentecostal Darío López Rodriguez's *The Liberating Mission of Jesus*.

between the holistic soteriology promoted by liberationist perspectives and the multidimensional hamartiology elicited from an interdisciplinary reading of the Lukan texts. The pentecostal work of the Spirit intends to bring liberative good news to human beings at the many levels of their sin-impacted existence.

The final chapter of part III, "Apostolic Evangelism in the Postcolony: Opportunities and Challenges," explores how such good news is communicated. Delivered as the plenary address to the 2016 annual meeting of the Academy for Evangelism in Theological Education, it asks what evangelism, the proclamation of the Christian gospel, looks or sounds like in a postcolonial era, a time in which there is a reluctance to assert a metanarrative that marginalizes the many voices of the pluralistic public sphere. Part of the response is: perhaps like how it may have originally gone forth in the first century via the apostolic followers of Jesus the Messiah. This answer is queried through a rereading of Luke-Acts, connecting the central themes of the Spirit's empowerment for apostolic witness and evangelistic praxis across the first century Pax Romana, and then asking about the significance and application for contemporary evangelism across the global postcolonial landscape. In the end, the point is, as all pentecostally inspired reading gestures toward, performing Christian witness—evangelism in this case—which is the desired perlocutionary effect of the Lukan locutions (to resort to the discourse of speech-act theory prevalent among at least some TIS advocates).[65]

Part III thus sketches the full sweep of what might be understood as a Lukan soteriology, one that begins with the Third Evangelist's implicit theology of sin, progresses through his doctrine of salvation as disclosed in the ministry of Jesus and the mission of the Spirit, and culminates in the apostolic practice of evangelism through which such good news is made known to the world. The ad hoc character of our inquiry through these chapters also consists in what occasioned their writing: a science-and-faith conference on the one side and an evangelism colloquium on the other, for instance, resulting in diverse contextual elicitations that contribute toward this soteriological exercise. Yet the consistent Lukan vision, grounded by the pentecostal message of the Spirit's redemptive work through Christ, brings together a perhaps not-so-surprisingly coherent pentecostal and Christian soteriology for the present era.

---

65. I have drawn on speech-act theory myself sparingly, albeit dating back to *Spirit-Word-Community*, 254–56.

Theological-Scriptural Interpretation: Apostolic Hermeneutics

The last triad of chapters veers away from Luke and Acts but they provide alternative windows into my readings of Scripture over the last ten years that I believe is relevant for the dialogue between pentecostal hermeneutics and TIS. If the *apostolic* label pertains to the full scope of the New Testament writings, then the dominant focus on Luke-Acts in this book is merely a starting point for considering apostolic interpretation of Scripture after Pentecost. Fundamentally, all of the apostolic writings were produced in light not only of Easter (the resurrected and ascended Christ) but also of Pentecost (the Spirit's gift to the world). From this Trinitarian perspective, we read the New Testament to find out not only what the apostles believed but also how they so believed, and we read the Old Testament to see how they read their sacred Scriptures from their pentecostal location.

The tenth chapter, "'The Light Shines in the Darkness': Johannine Dualism and the Challenge of Christian Theology of Religions Today," is the first essay I wrote that is now collected in this volume. Situated amid my earlier efforts in pneumatological theology of religions,[66] the burden of this essay to move theology of religions to engage more deeply with some of the historically exclusivistic positions deemed rooted in biblical depictions of the people of God as being in the light and others as being in the darkness. Even in the face of the pervasiveness of this theme in the Gospel of John, this chapter seeks to make the case for a less exclusivistic approach to Christian theology of religions—especially through considerations of the Johannine account as an apologetic against confrontational and hostile Jews set against the background of Qumranic sectarianism—in order to open up to the possibilities of a more dialogical and hospitable set of postures and practices vis-à-vis those in other faiths.

Some readers of this book interested primarily in the theology of religions arguments might compare my reading of the Fourth Gospel with that of others who have also observed how important it is to wrestle with the Johannine message in a pluralistic world.[67] For TIS purposes, however, chapter 10 contrasts with the dominant thrust of my pentecostal hermeneutic manifest in the rest of this book both in providing a reading of an entire single New Testament book, and in looking at the world behind the text and asking about its exegetical, applicational, and theological implications.

---

66. Ch. 10 was written after Yong, *Discerning the Spirit(s)* and *Beyond the Impasse*, but before my third book in theology of religions: *Hospitality and the Other*.

67. See Köstenberger, "Sensitivity to Outsiders in John's Gospel," and the chapter, "Peculiar Politics: John's Gospel, Dualism, and Contemporary Pluralism," in Volf, *Captive to the Word of God*, ch. 4, for such readings.

Although there is no appeal to the Pentecost event in this essay, I suggest in hindsight that it assumes the theological conviction that the New Testament writings, John's Gospel included, are all post-Pentecost in derivation, and hence, acknowledges one way in which to receive the Johannine witness, in its diversity also, as part of the many tongues of the Spirit.[68]

The penultimate chapter of this book, "Running the (Special) Race: New (Pauline) Perspectives on Theology of Sport," addresses the hypothetical question: what if St. Paul was to address the commissioners of the Olympics, Paralympics, and Special Olympics, simultaneously? I submit, drawing in particular from the specific reference to athletic ideals and imagery in 1 Corinthian 9, that as (arguably) the first theologian of disability, Paul would urge them indeed to revision what it means to train for, compete in, and pursue goals that are imperishable rather than perishable. This means, then, that the model for sport, even for disability sport, becomes something like the Special Olympics, particularly inasmuch as its "wisdom" belies the conventional wisdom of the sporting world in its emphases on ability, competition, self-achievement, and self-exaltation. This essay suggests that rereading 1 Corinthians 9 from the perspective of disability in general and intellectual disability in particular highlights aspects of Paul's argument that counters any uncritical appropriation of his ideas in support of the contemporary Christian embrace of sport. It applies a disability lens to the Pauline materials even while extracting from the latter disability-related insights for a contemporary theology of sport.

It might seem that this book's pentecostal approach to scriptural interpretation has been displaced here by a disability hermeneutic. Not so, I counter, particularly when it is realized how my turn to St. Paul in this essay extends both my pentecostal and pneumatological reading of Paul begun elsewhere as well as deepens my disability reading of Paul informed by charismatic theological perspectives.[69] Its inclusion here also means that there is at least one example of a close reading of a short scriptural passage (in 1 Corinthians 9) in this volume, even as the exegetical moves made can be seen as exemplifying how TIS might take up and engage with topics of contemporary relevance, no matter how ad hoc such might appear to be.

The final chapter, "Reading Scripture and Nature: Pentecostal Hermeneutics and Their Implications for the Contemporary Evangelical Theology

---

68. This is my pentecostal version of what biblical theologians like Francis Watson, "Are There Still Four Gospels?," argue from the fact of the multiple gospels in the New Testament.

69. The former, pentecostal reading of Paul, is found in my *Spirit of Love*, ch. 8, while the latter, charismatic reading of Paul for theology of disability, is in my *The Bible, Disability, and the Church*, ch. 4.

and Science Conversation," was originally an attempt to suggest how pentecostal hermeneutics might be relevant to conservative Protestant or evangelical interactions with the theology and science dialogue. In particular, it focuses on the creation narrative in the book of Genesis, seeking to resist the concordism prevalent in some conservative Christian circles that insists on harmonizing Scripture with science and inevitably ends up either misreading the former or rejecting the latter. Instead, I suggest that pentecostal Bible-reading practices and hermeneutical sensibilities not only allows for a reading of nature that is complementary with a reading of Scripture but also has the potential to shape a theology and hermeneutic of nature and creation that can sustain the scientific enterprise even while registering pentecostal perspectives, especially in the dialogue between theology and science.

As with chapter 7 in this book, this essay is part and parcel of my ongoing endeavors within the theology and science arena. It here tests the viability of the pentecostal "this is that" hermeneutic in reading the early chapters of Genesis.[70] More relevantly for TIS purposes, it suggests a pneumatological hermeneutic, even a pneumatological theology of creation, through which to both appreciate the creation narratives and interact with, rather than dismiss, mainstream science.[71] Last but not least, chapter 12 provides us with a glimpse of a pentecostal TIS reading of the Old Testament.

* * *

We now turn to readings of the Bible, particularly Luke and Acts, from a pentecostal perspective that is rooted first and foremost in the Day of Pentecost event. The following is intended both to argue for how such a hermeneutical posture is intrinsically Trinitarian in its overarching orientation, and to demonstrate such a pneumatic-Trinitarian TIS at work. We will ask in the conclusion if and to what degree the arguments in these chapters are compelling.

---

70. First articulated in Yong, "The 'Baptist Vision' of James William McClendon Jr."

71. I have considered Gen 1–3 in other places also: e.g., *Spirit of Creation*, ch. 4, and *The Cosmic Breath*, ch. 3.

PART I

Theological Hermeneutics: Perspectives after Pentecost

CHAPTER 1

The Science, Sighs, and Signs of Interpretation

An Asian American Post-Pentecost-al Hermeneutics in a Multi-, Inter-, and Transcultural World[1]

I have been writing about hermeneutics in global and cross-cultural perspective as a Pentecostal theologian for a while.[2] Along the way, my hermeneutical considerations have been enriched—or complicated, depending on one's perspective—by work on theology's dialogue with the natural sciences, by inhabiting more fully my location as a 1.5 generation (born in Malaysia but raised and educated in the USA since my middle school years) Asian American naturalized immigrant, and by research about the role of affectivity in the theological task.[3] The following thus represents my current thinking about Pentecostal hermeneutics in global context.

---

1. The idea for this paper was instigated by Megan Musy and Dan Morrison of the Society for Pentecostal Studies when, as chairs of the Diversity Committee, they asked me to be a panelist on "Non-Western and Western Hermeneutical Traditions" at the annual meeting at Life Pacific College, San Dimas, California, in March 2016. I am grateful for the opportunity provided by Bill Oliverio and Ken Archer to develop that outline into the essay for their book. Thanks to Ryan Seow, my graduate assistant, for reading an earlier draft, and to Christopher The and other members of the "Informal Pneumatology Seminar" group at Fuller Seminary's Center for Missiological Research who met to discuss this chapter on November 1, 2016. All remaining errors of fact or interpretative misconstruals are my own responsibility.

2. Going back to my second book, *Spirit-Word-Community*.

3. E.g., Yong, "Reading Scripture and Nature" (ch. 12 below); Yong, *The Future of*

In brief, my argument is that the way forward for Pentecostal hermeneutics in a pluralistic world, understood variously as the following will unpack, is to develop not so much a confessional approach founded on any genealogical connection with the Azusa Street Revival at the turn of the twentieth century,[4] but to adopt the Day of Pentecost apostolic experience as exemplary for biblical and theological interpretation. I will delineate such a *post-Pentecost-al*—the dual hyphenation highlighting connections first and foremost to the Day of Pentecost rather than to the modern Pentecostal movement—proposal in three steps, working backward across the triads in the title of this essay. First, we will look at the challenges for hermeneutics in contemporary glocal context that need to navigate multi- and intercultural projects in search of a more transcendent, overarching, or transcultural vantage point; second, we will unfold the opportunities inherent in this glocal (all situatedness being irreducibly local, but yet now also global in various respects in our interconnected world) space for Asian American Pentecostalism in particular; finally, in the longest part of this essay we will sketch the contours of a hermeneutical paradigm that is observant of its interpretive rules (science), its subterranean impulses (sighs), and its historical practices and teleological performances (signs). The following is intended to invite further hermeneutical reflection not only from Pentecostals but all who believe there is something else to be considered when thinking about human interpretation in relationship to divine presence and activity opened up in the Day of Pentecost narrative.

Multi-, Inter-, and Transcultural Hermeneutics?

Our contemporary context is rife with proposals in intercultural hermeneutics.[5] Such projects come in many forms, but the underlying theme is how to generate a coherent interpretive stance amidst a global situation constituted by many oftentimes conflicting vistas or standpoints. In order to elaborate

---

Evangelical Theology; and Coulter and Yong, eds., *The Spirit, the Affections, and the Christian Tradition*, especially my concluding reflections: "The Affective Spirit."

4. In this respect, I would differ from the proposals of the so-called "Cleveland School" of Pentecostal studies—about which I have written briefly: "Salvation, Society, and the Spirit"—that seeks inspiration from the first generation of modern Pentecostal spirituality; I am appreciative of their proposals as charting important trajectories for contemporary Pentecostal scholarship, but see my suggestion as providing a broader—albeit surely more generalized and abstract—account that would include theirs with other modern Pentecostal hermeneutical options.

5. A more general philosophical discussion is Xie, *The Agon of Interpretations*.

on the issues, let us focus for a few moments on the triad of multi-, inter-, and transculturality.

Although *multiculturalism* has become politically charged vis-à-vis the politics of identity and representation, at the descriptive level such a notion highlights nothing more than that there are *many* cultural, linguistic, ethnic, and other groups within human history and experience. While this has been the case for millennia, our present information and global age simply means that we are confronted by the multiplicity of human difference more starkly than ever before. Even the notion of *culture* masks more than it communicates since often we think of cultures homogeneously and we overlook (consciously or unconsciously, usually the latter) the heterogeneity and developmental character of cultural formation.[6]

Yet to stay within the *cultural-linguistic* orbit for a moment in order to have a handle by which to discuss the issues,[7] the point is that in our contemporary postmodern, postcolonial, post-Western, and even post-Christian time, it is accepted that there are many viable hermeneutical starting points for Christian biblical and theological interpretation.[8] Cultural-linguistic horizons and ways of life provide perspective on the biblical and theological tradition that are understood to be representative of at least some aspects of the diversity of world Christianity and are (generally) assumed to enrich the ongoing task of Christian traditioning.[9] What needs to be emphasized here is that the plurality of cultural-linguistic springboards for hermeneutics ought not to be conflated prematurely. Rather, the process of each quest for biblical understanding and theological reflection ought to be respected. In other words, multiculturality, at least in this view, emphasizes the distinctiveness of each cultural-linguistic project, and the need for such to be attended to, each one on its own terms.

From a biblical and Lukan perspective, such hermeneutical multiculturality can be seen as embraced within the Day of Pentecost narrative. Acts 2 notes that at the sound of winds (of the divine spirit), "the crowd gathered and was bewildered, because each one heard them speaking *in the native language of each*. Amazed and astonished, they asked, 'Are not all these who are speaking Galileans? And how is it that *we hear, each of us, in our own*

---

6. For a brilliant discussion of cultures as constituted by internal differentiation, even occlusion and marginalization, see Medina, *Mestizaje*.

7. Here in part to connect to how the cultural-linguistic domain has emerged in contemporary theological discourse, largely in the wake of Lindbeck, *The Nature of Doctrine*.

8. See here my *The Dialogical Spirit*.

9. *Traditioning* here refers to the ongoing work of forging Christian faith for the next generation; see Irvin, *Christian Histories, Christian Traditioning*.

native language?"' (Acts 2:6–8, italics added). Following this Lukan account, the particularity of each cultural-linguistic witness is not to be subsumed too quickly under other discourses.[10] This does not mean every cultural testimony is to be accepted uncritically, but that each needs to be weighed and understood according to its own norms and terms, at least initially. Translated into our contemporary global scene, such a multicultural stance insists on the plurality of hermeneutical and theological approaches in local contexts that need to be valued and engaged.[11]

Yet even if we embraced multiculturality, no cultural-linguistic frame is static and, as already indicated, each is impacted by cross-cultural fertilization. Hence without undermining the importance of cultural-linguistic particularity and diversity, there is also no hard and fast line between multi- and interculturality, the latter denoting the perennial and ongoing meeting and overlapping of cultural-linguistic encounters. Over prolonged periods of time, new syntheses emerge, reflecting an intercultural mixture that often later becomes incomprehensible to those of the originally distinct cultures. In considering intercultural contact and transformation, we need to take into account not just synchronic but also diachronic factors: the ongoing tasks of traditioning involve intercultural work not only with living cultural-linguistic options but also with those mediated by texts and traditions from the bygone past. We are just as apt to develop intercultural proposals from cross-cultural conversations with contemporaries as with the ancients (e.g., Plato, Aristotle, Confucius, Buddha, Shankara).

It might well be the case that the meeting of many cultures and languages in Jerusalem on the Day of Pentecost generated just such an intercultural project that we call Christian faith. We see snapshots of such an interculturalism in the nascent Hellenistic, Hebraic, and Judean group of messianists that struggled to survive in the ensuing weeks, months, and perhaps years. As the Acts narrative depicts, such interculturality was not without its challenges, even if there were clearly many other factors that impinged on the dispersal of that early apostolic community.[12] What needs to be recognized in the present context is what we will further develop in the next section: that there is a sense in which all local hermeneutical and

---

10. See more on this in ch. 4 of my *The Spirit Poured Out on All Flesh*.

11. Thus the import of translation projects; see, e.g., Sanneh, *Translating the Message*.

12. I discuss some of these developments in my *Who is the Holy Spirit?*, esp. parts II & III.

theological work is also intercultural in various respects, especially in light of migration and globalization realities.[13]

Theologically, however, registration of the specificities of the witness of particular cultural-linguistic perspectives (the project of a multicultural approach as I have defined it here) and exploration of cross-cultural achievements (the result of intercultural efforts here understood, and to be elucidated further in the next section), beg for synthesis having transcultural applicability. Whatever any particular cultural perspective might insist upon, whether on its own terms or in cross-fertilization with other cultural dynamics, theological claims ultimately aspire to universality: what is true theologically is true for more than that cultural group, even if its initial articulation derives from a particular vantage point or even from intercultural exchange. This is because "God so loved the world" (John 3:16), even if such an insight first emerged, in all probability, within around the turn of the second century CE in a community in Asia Minor. In other words, multicultural and intercultural *theological* formulations are sustained as they are deemed to be viable across as many cultures as they might encounter while not losing their distinctive contributions.[14] As such they are deemed to be of transcultural import, having cross-cultural relevance, even if forged within particular cultural-linguistic environments (and thus distinctively so according to our multicultural construct) or from out of specific intercultural developments (and thus exhibiting synthesizing aspects).

One caveat, however, before proceeding. Any presumed transcultural theological claim always emerges historically and thus is particularly constituted by some cultural-linguistic ferment or combination thereof. Hence, transcultural theological truths are articulable only through the process of their contestation, certainly preliminarily if not also in the longer run. Such disputation may result in the demise of such claims, or else their (gradual) reception across space and time will be indicative of their transculturality, however provisional such might be. The point is that theological claims are posited contextually in faith, and their ultimate truthfulness will have to run the gamut of multi- and intercultural adjudication. Going forward I will focus on Asian America as my intercultural site, but in order to invite also the multiple other cultural articulations that are essential for a truly transcultural achievement to emerge.

13. For my thoughts on migration in conversation with the Acts narrative, see Yong, "The Im/Migrant Spirit," and "Informality, Illegality, and Improvisation."

14. In contrast here to *deculturation*, wherein specific cultural contributions are so transformed through cross-cultural syncretism that they have lost their particularity. I get the notion of deculturation from Rodríguez, *Racism and God-Talk*, who draws in turn from the work of Afro-Cuban scholar Fernando Ortiz.

Asian American Pentecostal Questions and Trajectories

I now explore the relevance of Asian American Pentecostal perspectives on hermeneutics in light of the preceding discussion.[15] My goal here is to clarify the historicity of hermeneutical dynamics striving toward transcultural relevance. We shall see how multi- and interculturality facilitates and prompts, however challenging the obstacles, transcultural theological thinking.

We begin with the obvious, that the Asian American Pentecostal site is triadically constituted and in that sense, triadically contested, but at three different levels. First, each of the terms of *Asian American Pentecostal* is irreducibly plural. *Asia* can be understood historically (perennially disputed surely), politically, geographically, culturally, or religiously, among other dimensions, but the result is the same: dynamic and shifting perspectives that can be broken down into practically innumerable categories of analysis.[16] Similarly, *American* is no less pluralistically comprehensible. Even at the explicitly theological level (as opposed to any other register such as the political or geographical, just to name two important categories of analysis), one encounters not only ethnic perspectives but also a range of theological traditions claiming to represent the American experience.[17] This does not mean that the notions of *Asia* or *America* cease to be meaningful, but that any assertions regarding Asianness or Americanness inevitably function at high levels of abstraction and can only be deployed as placeholders for certain functions and then only provisionally engaged in ways that invite further specification. In short, whatever Asian or American might mean are generalizations that serve certain (theological) purposes, and these speak not only for segments of both groups but only in certain (not exhaustive) respects.

At a second level, dyadic combinations multiply the difficulties exponentially, much more than as if issues were merely the sum of the two considered disparately. For instance, *Asian American* invites qualification not only in terms of both sides of this binary, but also with regard to the

---

15. The following expands on previously published work, particularly in thinking about hermeneutic; see my essays: "The Future of Evangelical Theology"; "Whither Asian American Evangelical Theology?"; "Asian American Evangelical Theology"; and "Asian American Historicity."

16. For starters, see England et al., eds., *Asian Christian Theologies*.

17. There are thus, e.g., Native, African American, and Latino/a theologies, not to mention arguments for Jonathan Edwards as America's theologian (Robert Jenson, Gerald McDermott, and Mark Noll, among others), for the philosophical pragmatists as inspiring to an inculturated North American theology (Donald Gelpi), or for Douglas John Hall's Canadian project as representative of a more inclusive North American hemisphere.

conditions of their togetherness. First generation immigrants are different than 1.5-generation sojourners and these are in turn distinct from second-generation experiences, and migrants and students have different vantage points, as do those who are here on shorter- to longer-term work permits or visas or who are Asian American biracially, etc. The point is that *Asian American* can mean so many different things not only in what each category represents on its own but then vis-à-vis their various possible combinations.

Here it is now appropriate to consider what difference *Pentecostal* makes when factored into the equation. Initially, Pentecostal as an adjective can refer to a specific set of ecclesial traditions that trace their roots back to the Azusa Street revival in the early twentieth century, and in many contemporary contexts, such includes churches and denominations derived from these movements and often (though far from always) including that specific word in their title.[18] Yet there is a sense in which the notion Pentecostal has expanded to include charismatic movements in the mainline Protestant, Catholic, and Orthodox traditions and even other groups indigenous to Christianity in the majority world that exhibit Pentecostal-type spirituality but oftentimes go by other labels.[19] The point is that apart from geographical markers, *Pentecostal* is already problematic as a blending of ecclesial movements across spectra in multiple directions.

Following from this, the notions of *American Pentecostal* and *Asian Pentecostal* (to move on to the other possible dyadic registers of our triadic Asian American Pentecostal formulation) invite cautious procession for additional reasons related to historiographical debates.[20] *American* in the former case now includes not only the pluralisms inherent in the United

---

18. Even this sidesteps the heated debate in Pentecostal studies about whether the origins of this modern movement are America-centric (according to the Azusa Street thesis) or global (originating in multiple locations around the world in the first decade of the twentieth century without explicit links connecting these various sites). I tend to favor the latter hypothesis, particularly in light of its theological and hermeneutical implications (to be extrapolated in the next section below), although I also grant the preeminent role of Azusa Street as a central node in the emerging Pentecostal network after 1906. From this latter angle, Anderson's *Spreading Fires* is as fair a proposal as any other.

19. See Yong, "Global Renewal Christianity and World Christianity," and "Poured Out on All Flesh."

20. Compare, for instance, Synan and Yong, eds., *Global Renewal Christianity*, vol. I, with Synan and Yong, *Global Renewal Christianity*, vol. IV, eds., in order to track the differences between these two spheres of the global Pentecostal movement. Beyond these edited volumes, see also Alexander, *Black Fire*, and Anderson and Tang, *Asian and Pentecostal*, for alternative comparative perspectives on the differences between America and Asia.

States (and Canada too), but also the intricacies related to the influence of the North American versions of the movement across the global South. American Pentecostal perspectives hence cannot be assumed to be located only in the North American context, but may be prevalent across the majority world as well, albeit perhaps with varying features. Similarly, the *Asian Pentecostal* construct involves not only the varieties of Asianness but also American influences, more marked in some cases because of missionary efforts to be sure, but not absent because of globalization trends in any case. The point is thus that *American Pentecostal* and *Asian Pentecostal* perspectives are already inclusive of the "other" (in all its complexity, we should be reminded), and we have not even begun to consider how there are additional flows, for instance from Africa or from Latin America, each no less diverse than America and Asia, that also ought to be considered.

But our task is to explore, at least in a preliminary manner, the contours of a triadic hermeneutic as qualified by Asian American Pentecostal perspectives. And while it would be important at some point in this inquiry to consider this matter at the intersection where the hybridic realities of *Asian American* and *Asian Pentecostal* and *American Pentecostal* meet, to do so would remain at the historical and even phenomenological plane of multi- and interculturality. I would suggest that in order to make some progress toward a transcultural hermeneutic, a shift to theology is in order. In that case, *Pentecostal* cannot be defined only historically or phenomenologically but has to be negotiated theologically. Here, I focus not on the Oneness-Trinitarian theological divide (in order not to hopelessly complicate our task),[21] but propose we turn back to the basis for understanding the *multicultural* stance briefly articulated above: that from the perspective of Christian faith seeking understanding, the Day of Pentecost narrative (in Acts 2) provides scriptural warrant for defining Pentecostal hermeneutics and even theological method. Hence, while historical Pentecostalism is manifest only in its various cultural guises—as American or Asian, or Asian American, in our cases that are under consideration—arbitrating its contestations inexorably leads to explicitly theological matters. To be sure, appeals to scriptural texts rarely resolve the quarrels, but this means that their interpretations have to be justified, which leads us back to the hermeneutical question.

---

21. Although compare the Pentecostal hermeneutic deployed in preeminent Oneness scholar Bernard's recent *The Glory of God in the Face of Jesus Christ*, that reflects a maturing set of interpretive sensibilities.

Interpretative Science, Sighs, and Signs: Toward a Pentecostal Hermeneutic

My proposal is that an Asian American Pentecostal hermeneutic will be resolutely theological in the Day of Pentecost sense of the Spirit being poured out on all flesh, even as such a possibly transcultural pneumatological imagination will include, but not obliterate the specificities of Asian and American—considered separately and together—experience and perspectives, broadly considered. The goal, however, will be to demonstrate, at least in part, the distinctiveness of Asian American contributions to this broader conversation not in order to argue that they are indispensable to theological hermeneutics but to exemplify how multi- and intercultural approaches are unavoidable and can be fruitfully developed.[22] This final section will outline the parameters for this thesis via exposition of the triad of terms in the essay's main title. We will discuss, in order, how rules, affections/motivations, and behaviors/purposes are hermeneutically significant within this Pentecostal and, more precisely, post-Pentecost-al proposal.

The Science of Interpretation: A Post-Pentecost-al Paradigm

I denote what is being proposed as a "post-Pentecost-al" model because I do not want to conflate prematurely the apostolic hermeneutic with that of modern Pentecostalism. Surely my own formulation of such an apostolic approach to interpretation has been forged out of my own Asian American Pentecostal experience, but insofar as our goal is a transcultural hermeneutical ideal, any modern Pentecostal set of sensibilities, even if colored by Asian American lenses, that are to be viable will need to be warranted biblically. Within this framework, however, post-Pentecost-al means not only *with* the apostles, but also *after* the apostles, in particular, after and with the reception of the apostles and their witness in the Christian testament.

Toward this end, then, our Asian American articulation of a post-Pentecost-al hermeneutic can be understood as normed by at least three sets of "rules" or guidelines. First, we have to read Scripture as the apostles themselves read Scripture. The Acts 2 narrative indicates that the Pentecost experience was understood scripturally, according to the prophecy of Joel.[23] Here I am looking less for interpretive rules as developed in the modern so-called *science* of hermeneutics than to observe how apostolic

---

22. The following presumes both my *Spirit-Word-Community* and *Future of Evangelical Theology*.

23. For exegesis and elaboration, see McQueen, *Joel and the Spirit*.

meaning-making grasped their experience of the Spirit's outpouring via appeal to their scriptural tradition. Herein was what might be called a "this-is-that" approach that comprehended their present experience (the Day of Pentecost manifestation of the Spirit) according to their canonical heritage (in this case, the Joel prophecy immediately but then later in Acts 2, also via retrieval of Davidic, wisdom, and psalmic texts). In short, such a post-Pentecost-al hermeneutics follows the apostolic example, less in terms of attempting to specify *how* they received their authoritative writings than *that* they sought to understand present experience in light of the established tradition. In this specific case, theirs was the experience of the divine spirit, and therefore they returned to the promise of such spirit in the prophetic literature.[24]

At a second level, a post-Pentecost-al hermeneutical paradigm interprets Scripture following the established "rules" of post-apostolic traditions, as received generally within the broad consensus of the church ecumenical. Here of course "post-Pentecost" simply is extended to include the full scope of the Christian tradition after the apostolic generations. I include within this scheme, surely, the modern hermeneutical traditions as developed academically and in this respect "scientifically," whether those advocating historical and grammatical criticism or other literary, canonical, and related approaches developed since the early modern period.[25] Yet besides these established hermeneutical "sciences," we ought not forget patristic and medieval traditions foregrounding multiple levels of discerning the divine word via spiritual, moral, allegorical, and related interpretive methods. In many respects, these earlier paradigms are more amenable to the pneumatic dimension of scriptural reception that not only seeks to understand texts in their original context but also how they might be applied in any contemporary horizon. If some proponents of modern historical critical methods are wary about how such so-called subjective perspectives might undermine the quest for the putatively objective meaning of texts in their original contexts, other more late- and postmodern hermeneuticians sug-

24. Such an apostolic hermeneutic, I might suggest, is confirmed at the Jerusalem Council when they said, after consideration of the prophet Amos (Acts 15:16–18), that "it has seemed good to the Holy Spirit and to us" (15:28a), thus again reiterating that present experience had to be correlated with or rendered intelligible according to the accepted canonical sources by a process of pneumatic discernment. For further explication of this apostolically defined pneumatic hermeneutic, see Thomas, "Women, Pentecostals, and the Bible."

25. In the modern Pentecostal tradition, the "Cleveland School" of hermeneutics prioritizes literary approaches through which the living word of the Spirit might be deciphered for contemporary life and practice; e.g., Thomas, *The Spirit of the New Testament*, and Moore, *The Spirit of the Old Testament*.

THE SCIENCE, SIGHS, AND SIGNS OF INTERPRETATION   37

gest that reader-response hermeneutics is unavoidable and thus simply need to be acknowledged and disciplined.[26] At this second level, however, what is important is to highlight how there are a variety of hermeneutical approaches developed throughout Christian history that enable what might be understood as "living into the spirit of biblical texts" in subsequent ages and contexts.

It is perhaps from this reader-response perspective that we ought to specify a third level of guidelines for a post-Pentecost-al hermeneutic: that related especially to the Asian American site where I am located. As already indicated, if the original Pentecost account valued the particularity of each language, then the specificity of the Asian American witness, no matter how generalized its designation, ought not to be minimized. While Asian American hermeneutics is open to multiple trajectories of exploration, more generally speaking for the moment, I suggest simply that there are bridges for connecting contemporary Pentecostal testimony in its many modes with Asian (and Asian American, by extension) storied approaches to the hermeneutical and theological task.[27] Asian (and Asian American) story theology in this case connects to the narratives embedded in the Asian cultural, religious, and philosophical imagination and brings them to bear on the scriptural traditions as mediated by the contemporary experience of the Holy Spirit.[28] The point here is not to elide the differences between such disparate "spaces" of ecclesial and cultural inhabitation but to seek common categorical ground, with transcultural potency, from which to engage the "this-is-that" instincts of post-Pentecost-al interpretation.

My claim here is that a post-Pentecost-al hermeneutical paradigm ought to embrace three levels of interpretive guidelines: that following the apostolic reception of Scripture, that related to the methods of receiving Scripture as the living word of God manifest across the Christian tradition, and that emergent from out of multiple intercultural spaces and that draws upon the resources in such domains for the task of glocal biblical reading and living.[29] Yet to stay only at this realm of rules—"scientifically"

---

26. Pentecostal scholars who have advocated for reader response models include Archer, "The Spirit and Theological Interpretation," and Noel, *Pentecostal and Postmodern Hermeneutics*.

27. Compare for instance Cartledge, *Testimony in the Spirit*, and Song, *Tell Us Our Names*.

28. Preliminarily, see, e.g., Yun, *The Holy Spirit and Ch'i (Qi)*, which accomplishment highlights one of the reasons for my ongoing work in interreligious encounter and dialogue, theologies of religions, and comparative theology, e.g., Yong, *Hospitality and the Other*.

29. Daniel Topf, one of my students, remarked that there is a "subtle shift" (his

generated, it might be claimed, in parts of this conversation—is to remain at a conjectural and speculative level. But what if intellectual decisions are rooted more deeply in the affective dimension than we might care to admit?

The Sighs of Interpretation: A Modern Pentecostal Assist

I therefore want to expand on our post-Pentecost-al hermeneutical model by shifting from the intellective to affective sphere.[30] The Day of Pentecost narrative suggests that comprehension of the Spirit's presence and activity is not just an intellectual task but is a perceptual one as well, one mediated through the full range of human senses. To be sure, there is the speaking in "other languages" (Acts 2:4) and the hearing, "each of us, in our own native language" (2:8). But even before this level of cognition, there is "a sound like the rush of a violent wind ... [and] .... Divided tongues, as of fire, [that] appeared among them" (2:2a, 3a). These highlight the manifestation of divine *pneuma* as first heard and seen, long before such is cerebrally explicated, and even more so, *felt*: "a tongue *rested on each of them*" (2:3b, emphasis added). The point is that the work of the Spirit is embodied, and the divine is not only read textually, but also encountered affectively and experienced perceptually.

If the Petrine explanation of this event via the Joel text situated this divine arrival "in the last days" (Acts 2:17a), then this provides a bridge to consider how the many tongues of the Spirit in Luke's Acts parallel with or connect to the eschatological "sighs" and "groans" of the Spirit in Paul's Romans. In the latter, Paul writes about believers "who have the first fruits of the Spirit, groan inwardly while we wait for adoption, the redemption of our bodies," and also about how "the Spirit helps us in our weakness; for we do not know how to pray as we ought, but that very Spirit intercedes with sighs too deep for words" (Rom 8:23, 26).[31] Here we are considering the role of affectivity at least at two levels: that of what the texts point to in hu-

---

description) in this third guideline from the specificity of Asian American (earlier) to more generic "intercultural spaces"; I agree, responding that the Asian American hybrid of my own location is hereby mapped onto the Jerusalem—"other" hybridity embedded in the Acts 2 narrative—with "other" replaceable here with any of the localities or people groups (Phrygia, Crete, Rome, etc.) mentioned in Acts 2:9–11—as a means of inviting, even insisting upon, all persons to both recognize their dynamic hybridity, or least as the hybridic character of their identities, and to appreciate the theological (and pneumatological) warrants for embracing these aspects of who they are.

30. Fuller discussion of the following can be found in my *Spirit of Love*, part II.

31. For further discussion, see Bertone, "The Experience of Glossolalia and the Spirit's Empathy."

man experience, and that of how human perception and feeling can provide perspective on the text.

The point is that the post-Pentecost-al "this is that" approach not only invites but even insists that understanding the Bible is facilitated by engagement with its pathos: the emotions, feelings, sentiments, and passions embedded in the scriptural message.[32] If *homo sapiens* are not only thinking but feeling animals, and even more so, are thinking creatures precisely because they are sensing and perceiving—loving, desiring, hoping—creatures, then there is no right thinking (orthodoxy) about biblical or theological interpretation without also right feeling (orthopathos).[33] And from this perspective, global Pentecostal sensibilities are much more conducive, it seems, to developing this orthopathic dimension in transcultural ways particularly since majority world cultures are much more oral and embodied, and thereby also more affectively attuned in their overall orientation, than literary cultures.[34]

So if a post-Pentecost-al hermeneutics is also embodied, then such interpretive sensibilities are nurtured not only in the classroom but also in the sanctuary, not only through study but also through singing and worship, not only cognitively but also affectively. Thus Pentecostal liturgy and worship become incubators that precipitate life in the Spirit, and this in turn nurtures hermeneutical instincts and dispositions.[35] How we read Scripture and discern what the Spirit might have said formerly through these sacred texts is informed by how we have been touched by the Spirit in the present, so that "this helps interpret that." This is not only about discerning the nature of the signs and groans explicit in the Bible but also about feeling the passions embedded in the scriptural narrative from beginning to end.

From an East Asian cultural perspective that oftentimes minimizes the expression of emotion, we might wonder how affectivity might be hermeneutically relevant. However, the point about affectivity, and about the sighs and groans in general, is less about felt emotions than about embodied knowing. In this respect, then, Asian American epistemologies could foreground the ritual character of human sociality and epistemology since awareness of and attentiveness in this ritualized environment is nurtured

---

32. See the essays on affectivity vis-à-vis Pentecostal hermeneutics in Martin, ed., *Pentecostal Hermeneutics*.

33. See here the work of Smith, both his *Thinking in Tongues*, and *Imagining the Kingdom*

34. Compare here Land, *Pentecostal Spirituality*; Hollenweger, *Pentecostalism*; and Solivan, *Spirit, Pathos and Liberation*. I develop the idea of affectivity in relationship to oral cultures in my essay, "Proclamation and the Third Article."

35. I develop this point in my "Improvisation, Indigenization, and Inspiration."

by habitual and bodily practice.³⁶ A post-Pentecost-al hermeneutic and theological method would, in this Asian American context, ask about how Scripture is to be received and how the Spirit is to be discerned within the fivefold relationality that structure human interaction with the world. There would also be need for asking how the Spirit might then spawn novelty within the routinized ritual and liturgical practices of the church toward a catholic, ecumenical, and transcultural witness.

My argument is that a post-Pentecost-al hermeneutics concentrates not only on the rules of interpretation as defined and normed by ecclesial, confessional, academic, and other traditions, but also is prompted by reasons shaped by the heart and its hopes and loves, no less than its fears and worries. Orthodox hermeneutics is governed less by scientifically delineated rules than affectively generated passions. But that does not mean that orthodoxy gives way to orthopathy, since we have yet to consider orthopraxy.

The Signs of Interpretation: A Pneumatological Construal

In the end, right thinking and right feeling are intertwined with right behaving and acting. The point about hermeneutics is reading or interpreting, and although much of the hermeneutical question is focused on texts, a post-Pentecost-al approach wonders about life in the Spirit in relationship to such texts. As such, hermeneutics involves reading and interpreting life, and particularly the events of human acting, behaving, and living. These life events are themselves signs for interpretation and discernment.³⁷

The Day of Pentecost event itself was part of a larger story of the Spirit's activity, particularly in connection with the Spirit's empowering the witness of the disciples "in Jerusalem, in all Judea and Samaria, and to the ends of the earth" (Acts 1:8b). Put in other words, interpreting the signs of the Spirit's events, whether or not facilitated through human activity or agency, always involves the wider narrative that anticipates the mission of God and the heralding in and through many tongues and languages of the divine reign, "the coming of the Lord's great and glorious day" (2:20b). What needs to be emphasized is that the significance of signs relates to what they are pointing to, and with respect to the works of the Spirit—in and through human agents or otherwise—this has to do with their purposes and goals. Understanding the "this is that" of the present human drama in relationship

---

36. As argued by my teacher Neville, *Ritual and Deference*; cf. Neville, *Boston Confucianism*.

37. I work here with the semiotics of Charles Sanders Peirce; see Yong, "The Demise of Foundationalism and the Retention of Truth."

to the biblical narrative involves this practice-related, performative, and teleological dimension.[38]

The works of the Spirit, put alternatively, inspire and are manifest through human agents and their purposes, practices, and performances. Post-Pentecost-al interpretation thus reads the scriptural witness to the Spirit's activity ("that") in and through contemporary expressions ("this"), especially but not only within the church (the people of God, the body of Christ, and the fellowship of the Spirit), as intimated in light of the already-but-not-yet reign of God. To some degree, we can discern the normative shape of that reign in the person and work of Jesus, but in other respects, "now we see in a mirror, dimly" (1 Cor 13:12a). This means that we read, interpret, and discern in and through the Spirit betwixt and between: after Pentecost, but in and through the multi- and intercultural witness that expects, transculturally, the divine reign.[39]

From an Asian American perspective, then, such pragmatic and teleological interpretation includes the proclamation of the gospel (good news) story betwixt and between the processes of globalization. Migration, transnationalism, and the fluctuations of the global market impinge upon life in the Spirit in the present era. How can the gospel narrative provide norms for and yet also inspire faithful Asian American and transcultural Spirit-filled living amidst the current pressures? How might the forging of Asian American Pentecostal faithfulness be redeemed toward a transcultural instantiation that is in turn a sign of the coming reign of God? How might Asian American innovation anticipate transcultural and eschatological purposes and performative praxis within global ebbs and flows? In short, how might we read the "that" of Spirit's apostolic mission as a transcultural ideal for the "this" of the contemporary multi- and intercultural mission of God?

A post-Pentecost-al hermeneutic emphasizes the signs of the Spirit's presence and activity, especially as expressed in how the people of the Spirit attempt to bear witness to the person and message of Jesus that announces the coming divine reign. These signs of the Spirit are unfolded in the scriptural narrative, particularly in and through the apostolic testimony, as a template for the ongoing Spirit-led and empowered life. Yet insofar as the "science" of hermeneutics is less rigidly describable in propositional mandates for interpreting Scripture and is fundamentally informed by the sighs of human hopes and yearnings especially for what is yet to come, then the

---

38. See Yong, "The Hermeneutical Trialectic."

39. This is the eschatological horizon within which all interpretation proceeds; for more on such eschatological framing, see Yong and Anderson, *Renewing Christian Theology*, ch. 2.

signs of the Spirit's work are both discerned in the biblical account and also in every generation's ongoing efforts to bear faithful witness toward the Day of the Lord.

Hence, orthodoxy (right thinking), orthopathy (right feeling), and orthopraxy (right living) are intertwined so that a post-Pentecost-al hermeneutics is a threefold chord of life in the Spirit practiced multiculturally, performed interculturally, and aspired to transculturally betwixt and between the "that" of the apostolic testimony and the "this" of witness that the Apocalypse describes variously as deriving from every tribe and language and people and nation.

CHAPTER 2

Understanding and Living the Apostolic Way

Orality and Scriptural Faithfulness in Conversation with African Pentecostalism[1]

How do Pentecostals read and interpret the Bible? How should Pentecostals do so? The former can be empirically determined,[2] and what may be discovered may not be defensible, desired, or warranted from a normative Christian point of view. This begs the questions of how Christians in general read and interpret the Bible, and how they should do so. And again, we can conduct empirical investigations to answer the former question,[3] and what we find may also not be recommended as worthy of emulation. The overarching issue, of course, concerns whether there are norms of biblical interpretation that are relevant for all Christians and, within that frame, also for Pentecostals. The related question then is whether there are distinctive

---

1. I am grateful to Dr. Marco Moerschbacher of the German Bishops' Conference, Research Group on International Church Affairs, in collaboration with the Catholic Bishops' Conference of Nigeria, for the invitation to participate in and present a previous draft of this paper at their international Conference, "Pentecostalism and the Catholic Church: Challenges in the Nigerian Context," held in Abuja, Nigeria, 14–17, November 2016. Nimi Wariboko gave me immensely helpful feedback on an earlier draft of this chapter and saved me from many embarrassing mistakes. Last but not least, Anna Droll led other students in my "Informal Pneumatology Seminar" group at Fuller Seminary's Center for Missiological Research in a discussion of this chapter on December 6, 2016 that led to some final, minor, revisions. I am alone responsible for the version here.

2. For instance, Jenkins, *The New Faces of Christianity*.

3. See for instance the anthropological study of Bielo, *Words upon the Word*.

pentecostal ways of interpreting Scripture that might be justifiable, and then whether such would also be feasible for non-pentecostal Christians. This initial round of considerations seems preposterous in a postmodern, postcolonial, and even post-Christendom world: aren't there many ways of reading and understanding the Bible, much less the majority world and the so-called global South, each contextually relevant? Isn't there not one biblical hermeneutics but many?

This essay makes the bold claim that there is a pentecostal way of reading and interpreting Scripture that has normative implications for all Bible believers and practitioners in the third millennium, and does so in conversation with African pentecostal perspectives. The two parts of this essay move from the descriptive (what is) to the prescriptive (what can be and even ought to be). We start with a longer discussion of African pentecostal hermeneutics as understood within oral-cultural matrices, and then briefly outline a pentecostal proposal for biblical hermeneutics that will be argued as viable for the twenty-first-century global context. The key, it will be seen, is to unfold the pentecostal model according to its biblical frame, following specifically clues within the Day of Pentecost narrative (Acts 2) that sheds light on apostolic ways of understanding and living sacred Scripture.

A number of interrelated caveats ought to be noted before proceeding. The normative argument here is theological, specifically, pneumatological, based on Luke's Pentecost account. Yet here we approach this text with help from African Pentecostalism understood from oral cultural perspectives. None of what follows, however, ought to be understood in any essentialist way. Pentecostalism is certainly not monolithic, nor is African culture. More important for our purposes, orality is not to be understood merely as contrasting with literacy or textuality—as if contemporary global and even Western cultures, technological and otherwise, could be said to be either oral or not, or either textual or not—nor is Africa or Pentecostalism to be reducible to their oral dynamics as if African culture or pentecostal spirituality were devoid of literacy or textuality. Rather than presuming with prior generations of scholarship that African orality is associated with cultural inferiority, the argument here seeks to draw from African perspectives for the purposes of both comprehending the oral dimensions of human experience and exploring the formulation of a global biblical hermeneutic from such vantage points.

Oral Cultures and the Bible: Pentecostal Hermeneutics in African Perspective

This first section seeks to understand how pentecostal Christians read and engage the Bible, and we will attempt to do so by way of looking at the African context. I will be relying here on the scholarship of others who are familiar with the African region in ways that I am not,[4] although I believe the generalizations that follow will be plausible as a point of entry into the hermeneutical issues at stake in large part because of the oral cultural framework of analysis that is being deployed.[5] Hence we begin by delineating what oral culturality entails and then elucidate what might be called a phenomenology of African pentecostal interactions with the Bible from such an orality perspective before sketching the contours of a pentecostal hermeneutic for the third millennium.

Oral Cultures: Theoretical and African Framings

Over the last generation and more, Walter Ong, an American Jesuit scholar, has opened up the nature of human orality as an interdisciplinary discussion.[6] In brief, the appearance of the printing press precipitated an increasingly intensifying chirographic and typographic world, bringing with it a shift from reliance on intersubjective modes of personal relations to dependence on literary forms of communication. Thus traditionalist or premodern sociality was facilitated primarily by voice, sound, and hearing, and even if these have not been displaced into the modern and late modern periods, in Western contexts with high literacy rates the authority of the spoken word is subordinated to that of the printed text that is visualized and read. Hence also the import of literacy: only the elite who have had access to education and are able to read can participate in and contribute to the important discourses that shape public life. Yet our immersion in the literacy of modernity has occluded the potency of the oral cultural imaginary that persists and may now be resurging in our postmodern context. A brief analysis of the epistemological and ontological underpinnings of these

---

4. I have worked with others on African Pentecostalism—e.g., Synan, Yong, and Asamoah-Gyadu, eds., *Global Renewal Christianity*, vol. III; cf. Alexander and Yong, eds., *Afro-Pentecostalism*.

5. My initial foray into the literature on oral cultures was in an essay on pentecostal preaching: "Proclamation and the Third Article"; our focus here shifts from proclamation to reading and interpretation.

6. See Ong, *The Presence of the Word*, and *Orality and Literacy*, for starters; much of the next three paragraphs derives from my reading of Ong's work.

distinct modalities of human intercourse highlights the important issues for our consideration.

Epistemologically, the differences amount, for starters, to that separating primarily communal and predominantly individualistic ways of knowing. Oral interactions engage two or more persons over time, whereas texts are now read privately and even silently.[7] In the former, meaning emerges from out of the embodied, affective, facial, and other dynamics that constitute social relations, but in the latter, meaning is mentally constructed and hence more abstract, theoretical, and even speculative. Thus, oral cultural forms of literature are narrative-oriented—e.g., poetry, epic, drama—whereas modernist discourse is (generally) analytical, linear, and propositional. The communicative power of orality accentuates rhetorical performance whereas that of textuality enables both logical argumentation and descriptive depth. It needs to be emphasized that these divergences are not hard and fast, as if oral cultures are absent in modernity or that there are no overlaps in orientations. Yet these broad brushstrokes clarify where the emphases are placed and make explicit how modern literacy has shaped current preoccupations. We can therefore be better attuned to how more social and dynamic ways of knowing contrast with epistemological concerns that are focused on engaging subjective minds with objective writings about the world.[8]

The disparate ontological presuppositions can also now be clarified. Whereas the distance between the subject and the object is presumed in visual perception, such is absent in the aural dimension since sound surrounds and is felt within the hearer. Hence if textuality not only prioritizes but also distinguishes authors and their intentions, not to mention the objects of their textual references, then orality foregrounds the dynamic sociality between speakers and hearers, between communicative agents and their vocalizations. It is not as if orality is more audience- or reader-oriented, as might be emphasized in (postmodern) hermeneutical constructs, even if this is not entirely incorrect. More accurate would be to say that textual referentiality enables focus on the particular and the determinate

---

7. Recall that in the patristic and medieval periods, texts were read aloud, with Augustine even commenting about St. Ambrose reading silently: "But when he was reading, his eye glided over the pages, and his heart searched out the sense, but his voice and tongue were at rest"; see Augustine's *Confessions*, book 6 (Pusey trans.), available at http://www.sacred-texts.com/chr/augconf/aug06.htm (last accessed May 13, 2016).

8. Preliminarily this is why modern biblical criticism asks different types of questions about the nature of Scripture than the ancients; an initial foray into the biblical world informed by oral cultural perspectives is Kelber, *The Oral and the Written Gospel*.

while oral interrelationality presumes a more open-ended and even cosmic situatedness within which communicative speech acts are sounded. Textual representations thus proceed as if reality is stable enough, sufficiently mechanistic, even, to be reducible to words, while oral communication is funded, arguably, by an organic and even animistic cosmos.[9] Ironically, even if texts are linked to authorial intentions, they can convey meanings apart from authorial presence; voices, however, are carried only sonically by speech and thus invite a more fluid (Heraclitean) view of the world. If textuality thereby locates meaning in words, orality engages communicative subjects in the fullness of their perceptual interiority; voices, after all, derive from agents, and are carried by sound waves, thus inserting human communicators into the overall cosmic soundscape. Texts are static, carried by the materials upon which they are printed or electronically presented, whereas voices are vital, breathed out by human spirits, and thereby resonate sonically within a sound-filled and in that sense spirit-filled world.

The preceding moves far too quickly over somewhat contested terrain and does not even begin to explicate properly the relationships between traditionalist orality, modern textuality, and postmodern digitality,[10] but enough has been said to alert us to why contemporary hermeneutics ought not neglect oral cultural modalities of interpreting texts. And although orality is by no means only a non-Western phenomenon, any consideration of the encounter with and use of Scripture in global Christian context foregrounds this dimension of human experience.[11] So whereas the foregoing discussion of oral culturality has been conducted primarily vis-à-vis the Western academy, it would be irresponsible to neglect majority world and

---

9. Ong (*The Presence of the Word*, 227–28) suggests that "earlier man, under the influence of oral-aural or preliterate communications media, the world tended to be vaguely animistic.... Economies of thought built around the study of nature are thus vaguely animistic, for *natura* means at root birth"; by contrast, the scientific and Newtonian revolution, especially with its "accompanying exaltation of the sense of sight at the expense of hearing, spelled the end of the feeling for a vitalized universe.... The old more or less auditory syntheses had presented the universe as being, which was here and now acting, filled with events. For the new, more visual synthesis, the universe was simply there, a mass of things, quite uneventful."

10. On the electronic turn and its implications for the orality-textuality field, see Purves, *The Web of Text and the Web of God*.

11. I say this with full awareness that Pentecostalism in the Western world is fast minimizing its earlier oral sensitivities and instincts—see, e.g., Ellington, "'Can I Get a Witness,'" 55–59—but the emergence of a global pentecostal conversation alongside other theological discussions and explorations bodes well for now thinking more specifically about these matters; cf. Medina, "Orality and Context in a Hermeneutical Key."

subaltern voices on the topic. More specifically, scholars have also begun to insist that the contribution to global philosophical and other scholarly conversations in the humanities from the African region of the world cannot be appreciated without attentiveness to the orality of human life.[12]

For instance, African thinkers have been calling attention to the import of *oral literatures* for comprehending not just the African worldview but also the African mode of thinking and form of life.[13] Thus the literary genres of narrative, stories, fables, folktales, lyric, song, chants, poetry, proverbs, riddles, sayings, tongue twisters, dramas, etc., are carriers of African values and commitments. What is therefore needed is a kind of hermeneutics of ordinary language use that can engage African wisdom with wider discursive traditions (philosophical and otherwise). As, if not more, important, oral literatures clarify how African cultures identify their problems and resource their cultural traditions for resolutions to their situations. In short, such oral literary forms operate both analytically and teleologically: to query and to repair existing conditions.

Although African theologians have begun to engage with the dogmatic traditions of the church catholic and hence have developed hermeneutical strategies capable of probing the conceptuality of these ecumenical, predominantly Western, frameworks,[14] we are still a long way from thinking with and through oral literatures for not just the African but also the world Christian theological task, especially to the degree that global Christianity is largely now a majority world phenomenon. Toward that end, then, oral literatures have relevance not just for local theological reflection but also for the church ecumenical. Nevertheless, oral literatures themselves are not generic but particular, and any theology of orality will need to be regionally focused in order to build, from there, toward a more catholic paradigm.

And such indigenous African theological initiatives featuring the centrality of oral literatures are, fortunately, underway.[15] In these arenas, African oral literatures are not only sources for theological reflection but also central both to authentic inculturation and effective mission and evangelism across the continent. But access is needed therefore both to the literatures that emerge from out of oral discourse, and to the latter in their original forms: sermons, prayers, testimonies, liturgies, and other generators of the African literary corpus within the churches. What needs to be emphasized

---

12. E.g., Bell, *Understanding African Philosophy*, ch. 6, and Irele, *The African Imagination*, ch. 2.

13. Okpewho, *African Oral Literature*, and Anoka, *African Philosophy*.

14. See Kombo, *The Doctrine of God in African Christian Thought*.

15. E.g., Healey and Sybertz, *Towards an African Narrative Theology*.

is that theological and other content cannot just be extrapolated from these oral literatures but that the forms of the latter are intrinsic to any message that might be deciphered. Put aurally: *how* something is uttered and heard is not to be subordinated to *what* is said.

Now African culture certainly cannot be reduced to orality.[16] Yet there is no excuse for neglecting the oral dimension of human interaction and every reason to gain facility in this area for the contemporary hermeneutical task. Attentiveness to the oral modality highlights that the Bible is understood not just as a source of information but is a medium for experiencing the saving work of God. The words of Scripture are therapeutic for the healing of persons in communities, are potent for protection against malevolent forces, and are productive of success (as opposed to setbacks) in life.[17] If western hermeneutical interpretations focus on divining the meaning of texts in their original contexts, oral cultural approaches can help to address contemporary opportunities and especially challenges, and are thus more likely to trouble the status quo, whether that be physical, relational, economic, or other needs, and more likely be transformational in instinct.[18] The point is that if textuality invites hermeneutical guidelines designed to assist in historical interpretation and understanding, orality derives such meaning from use: how the sacred text is sounded, chanted (to invite the Spirit's presence), sung (to express devotion to God), prayed (to make known human needs), recited (to reorient the soul), retold (to be reminded of the divine story), memorized (to edify and nurture the soul's character), ritualized (to express obedience to divine injunctions), claimed (as coming to pass), pronounced (to ward off evil forces), declared (for its promises and blessings), or otherwise deployed toward various ends.[19]

---

16. Hence Wariboko, "Senses and Legal expression in Kalabari Culture," helps us appreciate a multisensory African epistemology, but this is in itself further reason to overcome the predominant textual or literary orientation of the modern Western imagination that in effect operates in denial of its *de facto* oral modalities.

17. See Adamo, *Reading and Interpreting the Bible in African Indigenous Churches*.

18. See, for instance, how the biblical Proverbs is received to counter the felt poverty on the African continent: Kimilike, *Poverty in the Book of Proverbs*.

19. Thus from such a perspective, there is an "interpenetration" between the spoken and written word that persists even into the present time; for discussion of these oral modalities of Christian scriptural engagement, see Graham, *Beyond the Written Word*, 62–55 and 123–25 (more historical assessment of orality in the Desert fathers and mothers, and in Luther is in chs. 10–11 of this book, and the reference to "interpenetration" is on 157).

Pentecostal Orality and the Scriptural Imagination: An African Phenomenology

Clearly what is needed is not what the Western hermeneutical tradition calls interpretive rules for exegeting texts since such presumes a sharp distinction between former meaning residing in authors and contemporary application in the hands of readers. It is not that oral cultures collapse the distinctions between speakers and hearers but that the exegesis-eisegesis binary is less applicable to the dynamic gateway within which orality reverberates. Hence what is more urgent is a kind of hermeneutics of sound and speech, one that can discern how oral communicative forms empower salvific meaning and redemptive faith and action in a broken world.[20] Toward this end, we explore in what follows two case studies of African pentecostal-charismatic biblicism in order to see how its message is received, enacted, and performed.

I begin with the Masowe Apostolics of Zimbabwe not because they are ideally representative of pentecostal-charismatic Christianity in the African context but because their oral biblicism puts the issues we are considering into stark relief. Also known as the Friday Masowe (because they congregate on Fridays) and formally as the Gospel of God Church, this group was founded by Johane Masowe (ca. 1914–1973) in the 1930s as part of a wider reaction by African Christians not just to the political upheavals of colonial rule but also to the religious elements that were deemed to support the European agenda.[21] As such, the Friday Apostolics rejected all indicators of colonial religion including sacraments, institutional hierarchies, and even church buildings (they meet in open-air environments). Part and parcel of such an *immaterial* faith is that, by their own conviction, they are "the Christians who don't read the Bible."[22] It is not that they do not know the biblical contents, but that as an object the printed Bible potentially inhibits, rather than mediates, the presence and activity of the divine.

In what sense then can the Friday Apostolics be considered to be part of the Christian tradition that depends on scriptural authority? In the sense that they receive the word of God not through printed biblical texts but through prophecy, (noninstrumental) singing, and other oral activities. If literate cultures rely on the printed medium for reception of tradition, oral cultures depend on mnemonic devices to enable recitation and memory.

---

20. Webb, *The Divine Voice*, initiates such a project in the Western context although it has been largely marginalized as a homiletical theology rather than as having hermeneutical and even dogmatic import.

21. The most comprehensive study of the Friday Apostolics is by Engelke, *A Problem of Presence*, upon whose research I depend.

22. Engelke, *A Problem of Presence*, 4.

The group's prophets thus become human megaphones that, by the power of the Holy Spirit, render the word of God for the people, while the singing of the people, again regarded as Spirit-inspired, sound out the divine word through standard or routinely sung verses (oftentimes saturated with Scripture), local favorites (in which scriptural allusions have contemporary application), and special improvisations (through which personal testimonies echo scriptural themes). As people of the ear, the material Bible for them is ineffectual as the word of God; instead, the Spirit of God uses human voices as "the proper material channel through which God becomes present. It is live and direct in a way that a written text or musical instrument is not."[23]

Another indigenous or independent group from Southern Africa is the Spirit Apostolic Church (a pseudonym) researched by anthropologist Thomas Kirsch.[24] If the physical Bible is sounded out but not otherwise *used* by the Friday Apostolics, the Scriptures in all their physicality are pervasive among the Spirit Apostolics even as they are also performed orally in various ways. Here the reaction to the colonial powers is not at the material level but the power of the printed word is understood to sustain and perpetuate alternative—read: local—forms of African agency. Hence, it is not just that the Bible enables spiritual authority but its local tactility and articulation legitimizes homegrown—read: African—hierarchies and bureaucracies. If classic Weberian theory of the charismatic opposed spirituality and the institution, for the Spirit Apostolics bureaucracy is spiritualized and respiritualized continuously via biblical enunciation, and spirituality is generative of bureaucracy when undergirded by the verbal appeal to written Scripture. In that sense, the institutionalizing trends of the Spirit Apostolics is inconceivable apart from the public reading of and open appeal to the scriptural text.

Central here is the aural interaction between the utterance of speakers and the reception of hearers as mediated through the congregational reading and exposition of scriptural texts.[25] Spirit Apostolic speakers and preachers unleash the biblical content orally with the belief that the Holy Spirit thereby endows these scriptural words with life-giving powers. The congregation in effect completes these proclamations or declarations not

---

23. Engelke, *A Problem of Presence*, 206. In these respects, the Friday Apostolics can be understood as embracing the scriptural admonition, "for the letter kills, but the Spirit gives life" (2 Cor 3:6), and as embodying the biblical conviction, "the word of God is living and active" (Heb 4:12).

24. Kirsch, *Spirits and Letters*.

25. Ibid., 145, writes: "'Aurality is distinguished from 'orality'—i.e., from a tradition based on the oral performance of bards or minstrels—by its *dependence on a written text as the source of the public reading* . . . ."; here quoting Coleman, *Public Reading and the Reading Public*, 28 (italics Kirsch's).

only in the call-and-response rhythms of the homiletic context but in discerning the relevance of the word of God as applied to their existential situations and lives. Exemplary in this regard is how, when addressing specific communal anxieties about witchcraft, the prophet utilizes biblical allusions, tropes, and even concrete texts—for instance: Revelation 19:20 and 1 Samuel 17:35, thus linking biblically a witch (at Endor) with a geographic reference (the lake of fire)—leaves open-ended the contemporary references, and assumes that the audience would be able to discern how to apply what is said for their purposes. In this instance, the congregation was led by these scriptural cues to identify the perpetrator so that, "For the elders of African-initiated Pentecostal-charismatic churches . . . , referring to and quoting biblical verses allowed the shifting of responsibility for the identification of witches from themselves to the authority of the Bible and to the listeners, who were burdened with the hermeneutic task of making sense out of seemingly disparate verses."[26]

The point is that on its own the text of Scripture does nothing. Yet from the mouths of prophets, or through the vocal cords of those filled with the Spirit, the biblical letter becomes the life-giving word of God. The Spiritual Apostolics are thereby people of the book, but the book is understood as not just opened and read but expressed and said.[27] Hence God's word may impart knowledge for Christian to believe, but more importantly invites participation, performance, experience, and interaction. In that case, beyond hermeneutical guidelines for interpreting the biblical text, the people of God need discernment principles for deciphering such scriptural practices. In the end, then, the Spirit not just inspired the words of Scripture in their original authorial context but inspires ongoing enactments of Scripture among believers in various reception contexts in every age.[28]

Our presentation of these two cases presumes not that Africa is essentially an oral society in the present time but is designed to focus analysis on the orality ignored in hermeneutical discussions at large, much less pentecostal hermeneutics. Further, if the Friday Masowe operate according to a kind of oral fundamentalism that rejects textuality altogether, the Spiritual Apostolics presume a togetherness of orality and textuality that ought to further undermine any naïve distinction between the two. And although neither group is easily understood within the *pentecostal* category,

---

26. Kirsch, *Spirits and Letters*, 99.

27. See also Horsfeld and Asamoah-Gyadu, "What Is It about the Book?"

28. "Against this background, the Holy Spirit was presumed never to reside permanently at any particular material location, whether in the Bible or in any other object of Christian practice"; Kirsch, *Spirits and Letters*, 141.

their charismaticism is not easily dismissed in any effort to develop African pentecostal thinking.

The important point at this juncture is that oral cultural transmission in the African context presumes textual impotence apart from their inspiration and exhalation. But verbalization through (human) breath catalyzes interpersonal causality, in effect activating other breath- or spirit-beings.[29] However we might want to envision the interrelationality between human and extra-human or spiritual domains, oral culturality presumes an intersubjective ontology and morality in the sense that the fluctuations of the spoken word do not merely fade into oblivion but spark cosmic forces and reactions.[30] The preceding phenomenology of African pentecostal-charismatic scriptural practice, then, has ontological implications for how the "word of God" works to bring about divine answers in the creational sphere.

Biblical Orality and African Pentecostal Hermeneutics

While there is, to my knowledge, no book-length discussions of African pentecostal hermeneutics,[31] for the last generation, Walter Hollenweger, doyen of pentecostal studies, has been arguing that the core of pentecostal-charismatic Christianity is informed by what he calls an "oral root" that he traces to the African continent via the slave spirituality of William Seymour at the Azusa Street revival.[32] Canvassing the journal literature in this area confirms that the emerging field of African pentecostal hermeneutics is consistent with the preceding phenomenological overview, indicating how the pentecostal orality sketched above is translated into hermeneutical theory in the nascent African pentecostal scholarly discourse. We see that pentecostal scriptural locutions extend in at least three interrelated pathways: the personal, the spiritual, and the political.

At its foundational level, African pentecostal hermeneutics can be considered as a form of reader-response hermeneutics, particularly in the sense that its emphasis lies not on the world of or behind the text, but on

---

29. For more on such personal causative potency stimulated by speech in the African context, see Ellis and ter Haar, *Worlds of Power*.

30. See also in this regard Bongmba, *African Witchcraft and Otherness*, 130–32.

31. The closest thing here is the work of Assemblies of God missionary scholar, Tarr, *Double Image*, although the hermeneutical discussion in this book is constrained, even as the pentecostal perspective is more under the surface than explicit; see, however, Tarr's argument for the importance of attending to oral worlds given our literacy bias in ch. 6 of his book.

32. See Hollenweger, *Pentecostalism*, part I.

that in front of the text, on the world of the contemporary readers and hearers of the biblical word. Thus, African pentecostal hermeneutics is a "reader-centred, faith-oriented approach . . . that aims at concretising the Word of God" for their context.[33] The Bible's promises of blessing are declared in order to realize and actualize wealth and prosperity; the Scripture's imprecatory prayers are intoned to pronounce judgment on perceived enemies; the healing stories of sacred writ are designed to nurture faith in a healing God for those who are sick, etc.[34] The Word of God, in other words, orients hearers toward and enables encounter with the divine, and this in turn empowers human responses to life's dilemmas, and this happens in their voicing and intonation.[35]

Yet this "performative" and "declarative" feature of the scriptural world and reality means that is efficacy depends not just on the part of biblical speakers but on the responses of their audiences.[36] The biblical narratives are true both because they accurately recount what happened so long ago and because they provide present opportunities to receive, experience, and actualize the power of God for today's challenges. This means that the proclamation of the word of God demands choices, decisions, and allegiances from those within earshot. If there are concerns that western scholarship relativizes the Bible to its original context, then in this case there might be qualms that African Pentecostals relate the scriptural message too directly to and for their contemporary contexts.[37] No one can say African Pentecostals believe the Bible to be too far removed from their life affairs and situations.

Yet, the applicability of the Bible to the material, existential, and real lives of believers depends precisely on the indigenous conviction that the historical and spiritual planes are intertwined. The biblical message about the spirit world is hence not about an other or non-terrestrial realm but about real world human interactions. Precisely because what happens on

---

33. Omenyo and Arthur, "The Bible Says!," 67; note that our authors are actually critical that pentecostal hermeneutics—what they call in their article "neo-prophetic hermeneutics"—is over-literalized or over-spiritualized, and that leads to excess in various respects (an issue we return to later in this essay).

34. See Asamoah-Gyadu, *Sighs and Signs of the Spirit*, ch. 4, on pentecostal prosperity hermeneutics.

35. Cf. Gallegos, "African Pentecostal Hermeneutics."

36. Asamoah-Gyadu, *Contemporary Pentecostal Christianity*, 163.

37. Compare Olwa, "Pentecostalism in Tanzania and Uganda," 180–84, with Masenya, "Foreign on Own Home Front?," 384–89, both of whom highlight variously, for good or ill, how such approaches expecting of immediate encounter with the divine are far from critical approaches to the Bible in the theological academy that keep divinity at arm's length.

earth is interrelated with what happens in the spiritual fields of reality, the power of Scripture is needed to address, control, and transform these interwoven domains. Precisely because of intuitions regarding the "mystical causality" of biblical worldview as perceived through African lenses, the scriptural word is sounded out to counter cosmic principalities and powers and their presumed destructive aims for human lives.[38]

On the one hand, pentecostal believers around the world, including those in the Western and Euro-American orbits, are convinced that such African biblicism more accurately comprehends the scriptural worldview and message than secularized discourses and this explains, from such a perspective, the expansion and even explosion of pentecostal Christianity in the majority world. On the other hand, others are concerned that such approaches not only remythologize indigenous traditions in a time when scientific forms of rationality are needed for economic and political development,[39] but even exacerbates precisely the fears and apprehensions that beset the masses when they perceive threatening spiritual forces in their midst. The point, however, is that in oral cultures, the vitality of the spoken and sounded word relates to the prominence of the sonic dimension of human being–in-the-world, and such foregrounds the pneumaticism that sustain both, even interlaces, the dynamics of breath and vocalization on the one side and the metaphysical reification of spiritual beings and entities on the other side.[40]

From this, then, we can see that not only are the personal and the spiritual intermingled, but these together are also not divorced from the social and public ground. There is here a communal aspect to pentecostal Bible reading and hermeneutics that recognizes how a scripted word of God can nevertheless address the present realities of believing communities in places and times far removed from the original utterances.[41] Such a communal approach to and engagement with Scripture could precipitate liberative transformation not only at personal but also at ecclesial and even social levels, at

38. Asamoah-Gyadu, "Pulling Down Strongholds," 316.

39. Asumang, "Powers of Darkness," 13, is worried about what he identifies as the "hyper-mythologization" which systematizes too neatly along African traditional animistic lines what St. Paul's principalities and powers leave more vague and general; see also Zalanga and Yong, "What Empire? Which Multitude?," and Ngong, *The Holy Spirit and Salvation in African Christian Theology*.

40. Thus some African scholars believe that a kind of "conflationist" hermeneutic blends too easily both testaments and the indigenous African worldview; see Acheampong, "I Will Pass over You," 211–12, electronic version available at http://d-nb.info/1076359868/34.

41. See Jonker, "Towards a 'Communal' approach for Reading the Bible in Africa."

least that is the promise of African pentecostal communal hermeneutics.[42] This is an urgent question across the continent, particularly when it is understood in light of failed African states and the need for the rule of law in the political sphere, and for effective solutions for the economic and social development of the region. Palpable Pentecostal resurgence in the African public square raises hopes that these churches might contribute to political stability and the economic betterment of the continent.

Yet the verdict thus far is ambiguous at best and negative at worst in that pentecostal Bible reading and application remains more personalized and individualized than catalytic of wider sociopolitical or economic impact.[43] Even if there were biblical themes and ideas related to the coming reign of God that could be drawn upon to prophetically critique and correct the socioeconomic status quo, pentecostal reception of Scripture by and large avoids issues the churches suppose to be too "political."[44] Communal pentecostal hermeneutics thus remains by and large focused on the scriptural relevance for ecclesial life at most, with the well-being of individual believers here prioritized. And even here, pentecostal biblical consideration generally marginalizes social or systemic issues even when they impinge on the day-to-day struggles of more than half of the members of their churches: women and children. Along this vein, they allow instead what is thought to be the clear canonical teaching about the role of women to remain uninterrogated, even when there are texts from the center of the pentecostal canon-within-the-canon—the book of Acts and the Day of Pentecost narrative for instance—that just as clearly teach otherwise.[45]

The preceding highlights the potency of African pentecostal approaches to the Bible while also prompting concerns (first and foremost among African scholars, pentecostal and otherwise, themselves). If emphases on

42. Nadar, "'The Bible Says!'" 145, thus notes that pentecostal communities read the Bible "for transformation" in these various spheres.

43. For instance, Chitando, Gunda, and Kügler, eds., *Prophets, Profits and the Bible in Zimbabwe*, reveal how the Bible is drawn upon to develop prosperity teachings but is not, at least not yet, viewed as related to economic growth and development on a wider scale; on a more hopeful note, albeit not ignorant of the fact that much needs to be done to bridge pentecostal spirituality and socioeconomic transformation, see the chapter by The Center for Development and Enterprise, South Africa, "Under the Radar: Pentecostalism in South Africa and Its Potential Social and Economic Role."

44. See the insight and bold stance of pentecostal biblical scholar, Masenya, "The Bible and Prophecy in African-South African Pentecostal Churches."

45. Gabaitse, "Pentecostal Hermeneutics and the Marginalisation of Women," argues that in this sense, pentecostal hermeneutics is presumptively fundamentalistic, reading proof texts in isolation rather than according to pentecostal perspectives or priorities.

textuality include hermeneutical pros and cons, it ought not be surprising that oral-cultural instincts and sensitivities bring their own sets of strengths and weaknesses. Put positively, the Bible remains a potent resource for guiding human social interactions, at least with regard to protecting believers and enabling their success, if not in terms of empowering sociopolitical witness and mission. In these ways, the hermeneutics of orality is concerned first and foremost with the sonic field wherein the biblical message is pronounced: put charitably, the powers are neutralized or exorcized, lives are touched and transformed, and the word of God attains and accomplishes good things for hearers who receive such in faith. On the other hand, overemphases are prominent and the need for discernment is urgent.

Apostolic Faith as Aural Praxis and Confession: Toward a 21st-Century Pentecostal Paradigm

In this concluding section, I want to briefly delineate the contours of a pentecostal hermeneutic in light of the above analysis. My goal here, however, is not to assume I speak for African Pentecostals—much less all Pentecostals—but to be attentive to and build constructively upon the preceding perspectives in crafting a hermeneutical orientation that potentially has global purchase. Hence I want to return to the Day of Pentecost narrative at the heart of pentecostal spirituality in order to think through such a hermeneutical posture that is related to, albeit capable of navigating what might be reckoned as excessive of, oral cultural sensibilities. Our goal is to do no more than denote the contours of a hermeneutical framework that, grounded in the scriptural witness, has the capacity to address the challenges and opportunities confronted by contemporary global Christianity. I urge that there are three interrelated facets of such a pentecostal and Christian hermeneutic and that these can be explicated in terms of orthopathy (right feeling), orthopraxy (right actions), and orthodoxy (right belief).[46]

Orthopathy, related to right affections, passions, and emotions, concerns the heart, which in religious language connotes what is central to human embodiment.[47] Orality attends to how the human voice sounds out the desires, hopes, fears, aspirations, etc., deep in the human spirit, even if oftentimes such can be no more than "sighs too deep for words" (Rom

46. Here I supplement from the perspective of oral culturality what I have developed elsewhere, specifically with Jonathan Anderson in *Renewing Christian Theology*, ch. 1 and passim.

47. For elaboration of the otherwise obscure notion of *orthopathos*, see Yong, *Spirit of Love*, part II.

8:26b). This is the language of human interiority, communicated audibly but also through the touch, the smile, the groan, etc. If there is no minimizing the unique personal characteristics of the biblical authors as contributing to their texts, there is also no marginalizing of these aspects from readers and users of these Scriptures in succeeding generations.[48] It is also the language of the spirit, and the portal through which the human and the divine resound.

On the Day of Pentecost, the outpouring of the Spirit was upon "all flesh" (Acts 2:17a), indeed on human bodies. There is audiality: "suddenly from heaven there *came a sound* like the rush of a violent wind"; visuality and viscerality: "Divided tongues, as of fire, *appeared* among them, and a tongue *rested on* each of them"; and aurality: "All of them were filled with the Holy Spirit and *began to speak* in other languages, *as the Spirit gave them ability*" (Acts 2:2-4, emphases added). The point is that the pentecostal message was not only heard, although it surely was, but also perceived and experienced in and through human bodies. The divine word is received not merely cognitively but affectively.[49] Thus this embodied aspect of encountering the divine, of primary import in oral cultural perspective, ought not to be minimized. Instead, it is prioritized in considerations of encountering, sensing, and perceiving the divine manifestation, all of which are a prelude to interpreting and understanding its significance.[50]

Orthopraxy, related to right actions, behaviors, and agency, is much more prevalent in theological discourse, especially in the wake of liberation theology and its impulses that have been forcefully felt in the last generation. Yet if liberation theologians emphasize moving from theology to praxis, pentecostal the concerns for right activity are the prior side of the aural field: before theology is applied practically, words are heard via their performance or enactment. Thus, praxis calls attention to how language

---

48. Hence the focus on the readers' and communities' responses is not only appropriate but imperative, as has been done by postmodern pentecostal scholars such as Noel, *Pentecostal and Postmodern Hermeneutics*.

49. Pentecostal scholars are thus slowly but surely developing the notion of affectivity as part and parcel of a biblical hermeneutics for the contemporary world. A preliminary formulation is Baker, "Pentecostal Bible Reading." Leading the way among pentecostal biblical scholars otherwise is Martin: "Psalm 63 and Pentecostal Spirituality"; "'Oh Give Thanks to the Lord for He Is Good'"; and "Rhetorical Criticism and the Affective Dimension of the Biblical Text."

50. Other pentecostal scholars—e.g., Spawn and Wright, eds., *Spirit and Scripture*—have been emphasizing that the inspiration of the Spirit not only preceeds *behind* the text with its authors but also follows *beyond* the text with readers; my point is that the Spirit's role *beyond* the text is not limited to enabling interpretation but in the prior reception and use of sacred Scripture.

not just inspires practical implementation but can be effective in achieving intended changes in the world. If oral communications in this vein are in general speech acts that bring about, potentially or actually, new states of affairs, orthopraxic utterances—that which are *right* according to certain theological standards—as such accomplish divinely intended objectives. This is the language of human exteriority that enables human agents to realize divine aims in the power of the Spirit. In effect, the prophetic performance precedes prophetic speech or the latter receives its authorization precisely through the former.

The Pentecost narrative here not just tells of a historic event inaugurating the church (as in conventional accounts) but invites participation in the ongoing mission of the Spirit of the living God. If Acts 1 promises the power of the Spirit to bear witness to the ends of the earth (1:8), then Acts 2 indicates that the outpoured Spirit occurred initially among those gathered from these geographic ends in Jerusalem, and the rest of the Acts narrative unfolds how these sojourners returned back to the far corners of the known world to carry out the messianic message. Pentecostal reading thus presumes the lavish gift of the Spirit is intended for "everyone who calls on the name of the Lord [to] be saved" (2:21), and that its ongoing relevance is "for you, for your children, and for all who are far away, everyone whom the Lord our God calls to him" (2:39), precisely in order to enable involvement in the divine mission. Hence the Acts narrative continues after the final 28th chapter so that each successive generation write out a new 29th chapter of the ongoing story of the mission of God.[51] In this way, pentecostal praxis assumes that the biblical message (the *that* of the scriptural witness) maps onto or undergirds the experiences of all believers in the post-apostolic era (the *this* of contemporary life and mission).[52]

Orthodoxy, right beliefs and confessions, is located third not because it is least important—note that in this account, orthopathy, orthopraxy, and orthodoxy are interlinked strands of a threefold cord[53]—but because historically, the church's teachings follow from its encounter with the triune

---

51. One version of this Acts 29 account is by pentecostal feminist theologian Holmes, "Acts 29 and Authority."

52. For more on this pentecostal version of the "this-is-that" hermeneutic, see my essays, "The 'Baptist Vision' of James William McClendon Jr.," and "Reading Scripture and Nature" (ch. 12 of this book).

53. I and other pentecostal scholars have developed a range of hermeneutical correlations for these three domains, all framed pneumatologically: e.g., Yong, *Spirit-Word-Community*; Archer, *A Pentecostal Hermeneutic for the Twenty-First Century*; and Stronstad, *Spirit, Scripture and Theology*.

God and concomitant practices.⁵⁴ Yet in oral cultural perspective, right beliefs are not limited to propositions but are carried in a full range of sayings and genres: proverbs, laments, songs, narratives, and the like. This is the language of intersubjective interrelationality, forged from out of the interpersonal interactions that constitute human being-in-the-world, expressed not only volubly but with the full scope of communicative gestures and actions available to embodied agents. In the ancient church, the Latin motto *lex orandi lex credenda*—loosely: the law of praying is the law of believing—captures the basic thrust that speech acts are directed not only to other creatures on the horizontal plain but also addressed to the deity that is vertically transcendent,⁵⁵ and as such, the orality of orthodoxy is multi- and transdimensional.

The Day of Pentecost was not devoid of orthodox explication. The manifestation of the Spirit resulted in bewilderment, amazement, astonishment, and perplexity (Acts 2:6, 7, 12): "What does this mean?" (2:12), the crowd wondered? Peter's response appeals to the Old Testament prophet Joel, explicating Joel's vision of the divine response to the plague of locusts as being eschatologically fulfilled with the Spirit's outpouring (2:16–21). From there, Peter—via St. Luke, the author of this account—connects the life, death, and resurrection of Jesus to the story of David, his persecution at the hands of Saul and other enemies, and the resulting laments, song, and narrative (2:22–36). Here the apostolic believers located the significance of their own experiences in the collected scriptures of ancient Israel. That which had been handed down from childhood orally from generation to generation (2 Tim 1:5, 3:15) was now "useful for teaching, for reproof, for correction, and for training in righteousness" (2 Tim 3:16). The apostolic community would continue to rely on these orally transmitted accounts as guided by the Spirit, in their discernment when disputes arose in the following years and decades (e.g., Acts 15:12–29).⁵⁶ The pentecostal people of the Spirit in all subsequent generations have these apostolic exemplars as models of not just *what* to believe and confess but *how* to discern, formulate, and forge such belief and confession.⁵⁷

---

54. See here the derivation of the fourth-century creeds in Yong, *Hospitality and the Other*, ch. 2.

55. See Stephenson, "The Rule of Spirituality and the Rule of Doctrine."

56. Thus during the first Jerusalem council (Acts 15), the apostles drew from the Old Testament prophet Amos (15:15–17), and reasoned therefrom toward a resolution as "it has seemed good to the Holy Spirit and to us" (15:28).

57. See the application of this apostolic Acts 15 model for normative purposes by Thomas, "Women, Pentecostals and the Bible"; a more descriptive but no less informative account of pentecostal Bible reading in communal and ecclesial contexts is by

My claim in this essay is that orality perspectives help us to appreciate both what the Bible says in its textuality and how such is said. Pentecostal hermeneutics, then, resounded through the African continent, concerns not just the orthodoxy of biblical interpretation but also the orthopathy of how the Bible is received and the orthopraxy of how it is used in relationship to the ultimate mission and purposes of God. I have attempted therefore to reflect on the phenomenology of oral cultural engagement with sacred writ in dialogue with the Day of Pentecost narrative in order both to illuminate the orality inherent in the biblical text and to elucidate how the performance of Scripture also participates in that oral traditioning. Along the way, I have also suggested how developments in pentecostal biblical and theological hermeneutics in the last generation have made explicit commitments otherwise embedded in the orality and spirituality of the global renewal movement.

Yet beyond clarifying pentecostal practices to scriptural interpretation, the wider goal attempted in the preceding pages is to make plausible the suggestion that an orality orientation—articulated in the preceding in conversation with pentecostal perspectives—might also be helpful for thinking about biblical hermeneutics in global/catholic, intercultural, and transcultural contexts.[58] Traditionally formulated biblical hermeneutics thus responds to the transmission side of the sacred text, illuminating the world *behind* the text in critical ways. The hermeneutical accents focused upon in this essay, however, explore the reception side of the biblical message, explicating the world *beyond* or *in front of* the text in ways essential for comprehending its ongoing power to address human lives and affairs. If traditionalists are concerned about the subjectivity of oral approaches to the Bible, they need to be reminded that historical critical analysis is not entirely objective even as the myth of scientific positivism and objectivism has also been exposed. More importantly, as the preceding hints at, the criterion for correcting excessive interpretations and applications of Scripture will always be contested ecclesiologically (vis-à-vis the historic and ongoing unfolding Christian tradition), theologically and christologically (as the Spirit is not free-floating but is always the Spirit of God and the Spirit of Jesus), and missionally and practically (e.g., assessed according to the fruits of the Spirit, for instance),[59] even as these more general norms will also always be

---

Grey, *Three's a Crowd*.

58. As such, I consider this chapter as complementing the argument for a pneumatological hermeneutics and methodology recently made in Yong, *The Dialogical Spirit*.

59. As unpacked in the concluding chapter of my *The Missiological Spirit*.

contextually and culturally adjudicated.[60] The point is not to dispense with historical, grammatical, linguistic, and other staples of traditional biblical criticism, but to realize that the power and significance of Scripture for any age is only half-grasped when that is accomplished. Orality dynamics help us to appreciate that the concentrated effort on the other half of the equation brings orthopathic and orthopraxis perspectives to bear on the task of being transformed by the Spirit of the triune God so as to more faithfully move into and live within the apostolic witness.

---

60. For instance, see Wendland, "Study Bible Notes for the Gospel of Luke in Chichewa," 144.

CHAPTER 3

Reflecting and Confessing in the Spirit

Called to Transformational Theologizing[1]

Some might argue that pentecostal and charismatic Christianity presumes a fundamentalistic biblicism that has so far resulted in an underdeveloped hermeneutics and theological method, that is literalistic about what they presume to be the scriptural worldview so as to collapse the world of the text and the world in front of the text in a sometimes naïve sense. Others might counter-argue that pentecostal and charismatic Christians rely too much on what they perceive to be the Spirit's leading, or at least legitimize what is no more than their own assumptions with pneumatic inspiration, and in that sense, justify their biblical interpretations even if these seem to go far beyond what the text might allow or what the Christian tradition might sanction. As a pentecostal theologian I recognize that both of these perspectives identify worrying tendencies of charismatic spirituality, but precisely for that reason, I have devoted significant effort over the last two decades to articulating a hermeneutical posture and theological method that is not viewed as provincially pentecostal-charismatic but might also be representatively Christian and even normative for Christian faith.[2]

---

1. I am grateful to Rev. Dr. Jooseup Keum, Director of Commission on World Mission and Evangelism, for inviting my contribution to this issue of the *International Review of Mission* that he edits. Thanks also to Joshua Muthalali, a Keralite pentecostal PhD student here at Fuller Seminary who is working on a postcolonial pentecostal hermeneutics (which final results I am eager to see) and on whose doctoral committee I serve, for proofreading carefully and providing extensive comments on an earlier version of this essay. Responsibility for the final draft remains my own.

2. Starting with Yong, *Spirit-Word-Community*, and continuing most recently Yong, *The Dialogical Spirit*. If some of my readers tire of what seems like an excessive

The following outlines what might be called a pneumatological hermeneutic and methodology that takes seriously the Day of Pentecost narrative as described in the book of Acts as a starting point for biblical and theological reflection. Such a "pentecostal" approach is no doubt informed by my life experience as participant and member in the modern pentecostal-charismatic movement, yet as articulated herein, I invite consideration of how it presents a more robustly Trinitarian perspective that all Christians would or should desire to embrace.[3] In brief, I suggest that hermeneutical imagination and theological method after Pentecost ought to proceed in the Spirit following the apostolic community. I unpack this thesis in three steps in dialogue with the apostolic narrative, especially in the book of Acts: regarding the experience of the Spirit, in relationship to the *missio Dei*, and with reference to apostolic theologizing. As I trust will become clear, Christian theologizing consists not only in the recitation, retrieval, and repetition of biblical and apostolic teachings but in taking seriously encounter with the Spirit and then following earnestly the Spirit's guidance as normed by apostolic belief and practice.

Surprised by the Spirit: When the Living God Shows Up

I begin with the Day of Pentecost narrative given my conviction, informed by a modern Pentecostal perspective, that a fully Trinitarian theological vision is centered on the person and work of Jesus Christ as Lord and Son of God but that access to this personal reality comes only through the Holy Spirit (e.g., 1 Cor 12:3)[4] whose outpouring and gift to the people of God is recounted in Acts chapter 2. In that case, then, I suggest that Christian knowing and reason is not just post-Easter (after the risen Christ) but also always post-Pentecost, meaning via the Spirit's surely unexpected raising of Jesus from the dead (Rom 1:4) and through the then obscurely anticipated, via the prophetic Scriptures, the pentecostal outpouring of the Spirit of the living God upon all flesh (Acts 2:17, drawing from Joel).[5] In that respect,

---

self-referencing in what follows, I apologize in advance; those looking for further explication as well as for insights into my prior research and other conversation partners will not need to guess about where to search next.

3. My Trinitarian theology is not exclusive of those who come from Oneness Pentecostal traditions; see how I navigate the issues in my *The Spirit Poured Out on All Flesh*, ch. 5, and *Renewing Christian Theology*, ch. 11.

4. I have learned about this pneumatological prioritization from, more than anyone else, articles and essays by Dabney, including the lead chapter, "Starting with the Spirit."

5. Chapter 1 above urges such to be a *post-pentecost-al* hermeneutics in the sense

one might argue that the book of Acts provides the interpretive frame or point of entry into the biblical narrative as a whole.[6] While such a pentecostal thesis can be variously understood, for our purposes, I suggest that it is no less than, or at least, christological, pneumatological, and eschatological.

First, the pentecostal hermeneutic and theological method is resolutely christological not only in that the Spirit poured out on the Day of Pentecost comes from the risen Christ at the right hand of the Father (Acts 2:32–33), but also that the Spirit bears and enables heretofore inexplicable witness to the Jesus as Messiah. Thus the outpouring of the Spirit at Pentecost inspires Peter's message (2:14–40)—as recorded by Luke—that culminates in proclamation about Jesus of Nazareth (2:22–36), in particular so "the entire house of Israel [can] know with certainty that God has made him both Lord and Messiah, this Jesus whom you crucified" (2:36). Yet Jesus' messiahship is constituted in his anointing with the Spirit. Later in Acts, Peter tells Cornelius and his household about how "God anointed Jesus of Nazareth with the Holy Spirit and with power; how he went about doing good and healing all who were oppressed by the devil, for God was with him" (10:38), and this is consistent with Jesus' own self-understanding as preserved in Luke's (first volume) gospel account wherein his public ministry is inaugurated at Nazareth as the Spirit's messianic work: "The Spirit of the Lord is upon me, because he has anointed me to bring good news to the poor. He has sent me to proclaim release to the captives and recovery of sight to the blind, to let the oppressed go free, to proclaim the year of the Lord's favour" (Luke 4:18–19; cf. Isa 61:1–2a).[7] Thus even the instruction of the risen Christ proceeds "through the Holy Spirit" (Acts 1:2). The point is twofold: that a pentecostal hermeneutic and theological method both lifts up Jesus who is Christ and messiah precisely through the anointing of the divine Spirit and enables apostolic witness to Jesus' messiahship through that same Spirit.

More expansively, the apostolic experience as a whole is christological because it is pneumatological: the experience of the resurrected Christ is recounted as good news *after* Pentecost. The former appearance was startling and terrifying (see Luke 24:37) and needed the descent of the Holy Spirit (24:49) for appropriate perspective and comprehensible witness (Acts 1:8). Yet such reorientation also was not achieved except through further

---

that it is a modern pentecostal construct but derived from the Day of Pentecost narrative; in this chapter, such a *post-pentecost-al* approach is understood synonymously as a *pentecostal hermeneutics* so as not to overly complicate things.

6. For more on Acts as the pentecostal canon-within-the-canon and its ramifications for Christian hermeneutics, see my *In the Days of Caesar*, ch. 3.

7. My book, *Who is the Holy Spirit?*, thus reads Luke's Christology (in the Third Gospel) through his pneumatology (in Acts).

disorientation. The promised Spirit given on the Day of Pentecost thus reordered the apostolic imagination and thinking through its cognitive dissonance, catalyzing in those who had followed Jesus for three years bewilderment, amazement, astonishment, and perplexity (Acts 2:6, 7, 12).[8] In large part the confusion assuredly was "because each one [among the large crowd gathered from around the Mediterranean] heard them speaking in the native language of each" (2:7), and yet through that cacophony, "in our own languages we hear them speaking about God's deeds of power" (2:11). Without minimizing this communicative miracle of speech or hearing (either is warranted from Luke's text), I want to focus also on the fact that this experience of the Spirit cannot be reduced to either the oral or sonic register. Rather, this was a fully embodied, intersubjective, and interpersonal confrontation with the transcendent. Note that the wind is not merely heard sonically but felt, "like the rush of a violent wind, and it filled the entire house where they were sitting" (2:2), and further, that the descent of the Spirit was not just felt as precipitative of speech, but also perceived palpably and tangibly, "as of fire," again not just appearing as if visually to (and therefore over and against) them but touching upon and resting on each of them (2:3).[9] The point, central to the thesis of this essay, is that meeting the living God by the Spirit transfigures human cognition precisely because it is wholly transformative of human knowing and perceiving in its multiple dimensions of tactility, affectivity, and emotions.[10] We think and live differently *after* the Spirit because we have been changed.

Historically, however, the Pentecost narrative has been treated as a one-off event, usually understood as founding the church as the people of God. Without denying this inaugural aspect of the people of God as the fellowship of the Spirit (hence also introducing a more Trinitarian articulated ecclesiology),[11] my claim is that there is a normative character to the pentecostal outpouring witnessed to in Luke's account as the promise of the Spirit "is for you, for your children, and for all who are far away, everyone whom the Lord our God calls to him" (2:39). This is why pentecostal hermeneutics has long stressed, consistent with other restorationist and baptistic approaches, a "this-is-that" connectivity between the contemporary hori-

---

8. I get this characterization from Welker, *God as Spirit*, ch. 5.

9. See ch. 2 above; cf. Synan, Yong, and Asamoah-Gyadu, eds., *Global Renewal Christianity*, vol. III.

10. For more on a pneumatology of affective transformation, see my *Spirit of Love*, part II; cf. also Coulter and Yong, eds., *The Spirit, the Affections, and the Christian Tradition*.

11. I develop further an ecclesiology of pneumatic fellowship in Yong, "Renewed and Always Renewing."

zon of Spirit-filled involvement with the living God (this) and the apostolic account of the same (that).[12] Yet the issue is not just epistemological, as if the Christian knowing of generations subsequent to the apostolic age is presumptively the same as that of their ancestors; rather, the claim is more ontological, actually theological and Trinitarian: that this promise persists because we remain in the eschatological age between the *then* of the initial coming of Christ (incarnation) and his Spirit (Pentecost) poured out from the right hand of the Father (Acts 2:33) and the *that* of Jesus' future return (the Parousia and the end of this age). Hence it is in this eschatological time of the "last days" (2:17) that pentecostal hermeneutics unfolds. Mention of the "last days" is an interpolation, even interpretation, of Joel 2:28, which simply says, "Then afterwards . . ." (after the plague of locusts).[13] This apostolic hermeneutic, one shaped by being face-to-face with the living God, invites consideration of how "all who are far away," including but not limited to geographic and temporal distance—both dimensions, it should be noted, are included in the "ends of the earth" (1:8) which maps the entire Acts narrative[14]—are also to read Scripture in light of the experience of the Spirit.

The preceding christological-pneumatological-eschatological trajectories are interwoven and, for our purposes, foreground the triadic character of a Christian hermeneutic after Pentecost. The centrality of Christ is pneumatologically understood, even as the pneumatic and eschatological nature of Christian understanding in this time between the times is not marginalized. Hence Christian interpretation in the footsteps of the apostles engages Scripture dynamically as they did, in and through perceiving the risen Christ by the power of the Spirit, and the latter always leads back to a fresh reading of the scriptural testimony.

Pentecostalized by the Spirit: The Trinitarian *Missio Dei* as Normative *Telos*

We will return in the final section to address the questions of hermeneutics more explicitly, but in the meanwhile we have to ask pointedly: toward what ends is such pentecostal rereading and reflecting directed? This is the important question since anxiety about pentecostal subjectivity in hermeneutics

---

12. More on pentecostal "this-is-that" hermeneutics can be found in my essays: "The 'Baptist Vision' of James William McClendon Jr.," and "Reading Scripture and Nature" (ch. 12 of this volume).

13. For further discussion of Joel 2 in relationship to Acts 2 and vice-versa, see McQueen, *Joel and the Spirit*.

14. See further Yong, *Renewing Christian Theology*, chs. 2, 3.

are, rightly, driven by the disquiet that we can always justify our own preferences and desires by appeal to Scripture. On the other hand, to historicize the scriptural message in a positivistic sense is to open up a chasm between the *that* of the biblical world and the *this* of any contemporary generation which seemingly cannot be crossed, at least in hermeneutical traditions that prioritize the historical-critical method. I will argue here that interpretation presumes guiding goals and that the telos of pentecostal hermeneutics is normed by the mission and coming reign of the Trinitarian God.[15]

How does Luke, the author of Acts and also of the prequel, the Gospel that bears his name, characterize this Trinitarian mission? Certainly Jesus himself was motivated to "proclaim the year of the Lord's favour" (Luke 4:19), which in effect was understood according to the Jubilee model in the Pentateuch.[16] Yet the more prevalent description of the central core of Jesus' message is as the "good news of the kingdom of God" (4:43; cf. 8:1, 9:11). Jesus urged his disciples to declare this same gospel of the reign of God (9:2, 60, 10:9) and also to pray for its soon arrival (11:2; cf. 12:32), even as he understood his exorcisms as indicative of the divine reign breaking through (11:20). Yet his teachings suggested multiple perspectives: that "the kingdom of God is [already] among you" (17:21) on the one hand and that it is delayed (19:11; cf. 22:16) and on the other, along with the admonition "that the kingdom of God is near" (21:31), and is in that sense coming.

In Acts, it is not that the disciples never proclaim the reign of God—there are a few indications that this constituted their account of the gospel (Acts 8:12, 14:22, 19:8, 20:25, 28:23, 31)[17]—but when asked by the disciples about its imminent arrival (1:6), Jesus promised the gift of the Spirit instead (1:7-8).[18] That his response is central to the book of Acts, not only its message but also in how it structures the book's arc, suggests that the Pentecost account frames the unfolding of early Christianity not as a descriptive history but as a normative telos, one that involves the expansion of the faith from Jerusalem to the ends of the earth as being at the heart of the mission

---

15. In earlier work—e.g., *Spirit-Word-Community*, ch. 7, and *Hospitality and the Other*, ch. 2—I wrote of hermeneutical and methodological teleology in terms of pragmatic performance; here I complement these more philosophical and formal accounts from a scriptural perspective.

16. See Sloan, *The Favorable Year of the Lord*, and Ringe, *Jesus, Liberation, and the Biblical Jubilee*.

17. See further discussion of apostolic preaching in ch. 12 below.

18. Costantino, *The Relationship of Jesus and the Kingdom of God*, argues that although explicit references to the reign of God are much less common in the second Lukan volume, this is because the kingdom is defined by Jesus as Son of God and messianic Lord and the fact that this is the focal point of the apostolic kerygma in Acts.

of the triune God as carried out through the pentecostal outpouring of the Spirit.

I suggest that pentecostal hermeneutics follows pentecostal praxis, which is oriented teleologically toward realization of the reign of God to the ends of the earth. Against any colonial, imperial, or triumphalistic rendition of such a hermeneutical and missionary posture,[19] I counter that apostolic border crossing from Jerusalem through Samaria to Rome (the ends of the earth from a Jewish perspective that is Jerusalem-centric) is marked by mutuality and dialogical humility. Hence the many tongues on the Day of Pentecost represent not only *others* receiving the witness of the apostles but "God's deeds of power" (2:11) resounding in the languages of those from around the Mediterranean world. In fact, even before the apostolic delegation had stepped foot beyond the Judean countryside, Hellenistic Jews "from every nation under heaven" had already been gathered in Jerusalem (2:5) so that, in fact, one might argue apostolic proclamation from the beginning went forth on the terms and conditions defined by "the ends of the earth." Not surprisingly, perhaps, it would be Hellenist believers who later took the gospel to Samaria when the apostolic leaders hunkered down under persecution (see Acts 8:1–4).

That apostolic mission praxis continued to be marked by mutuality and reciprocity is seen in the remainder of the Acts narrative. Peter's visit to Cornelius featured mutual conversion: the latter came to repentance, baptism, and reception of the Spirit according to the apostolic preaching (cp. 2:38 and 10:44–48) while the former arrived at a new awareness (of the purity of Gentiles; see 10:34–35) and a transformed community (consisting of Jews and Gentiles).[20] Later, both when dealing with the heathen at Lystra and Derbe and when interacting with the philosophers of the Areopagus, Paul resorts to natural theological arguments (14:15–17) and to citing and referencing pagan poets (17:28). In both of these cases, I proffer Paul is being consistent in following the Pentecost principle that invites, if not insists, that witnesses to the Messiah "become all things to all people, so that [they] might by any means save some" (1 Cor 9:22). Last but not least, observe Pauline mission among the Maltese barbarians (from Greek: *barbaroi* in Acts 28:2) in the final chapter of Acts. After their shipwreck on the island, it is the natives who "showed us unusual kindness" (28:2) and who "entertained us hospitably for three days" (28:7b), and there is actually no verbal proclamation of the gospel recorded in the account. Christian mis-

---

19. All of which are certainly an ever-present dangers in pentecostal circles, as superbly diagnosed by Courey, *What Has Wittenberg to Do with Azusa?*

20. On this mutual conversion, see Nguyen, *Peter and Cornelius*.

sion to and in Malta thus unfolded out of apostolic praying as guests of the hospitality of others and the Spirit's healing intervention instead (28:8–10), rather than from any authoritative pronunciations.[21]

The end of the Acts narrative has Paul in chains awaiting a hearing before Caesar, yet given full freedom even under guard to share his faith. So Luke ends his story of the gospel's arrival to the ends of the earth rather unpredictably and abruptly, telling of Paul "proclaiming the kingdom of God and teaching about the Lord Jesus Christ with all boldness and without hindrance" (28:31). If the reader asks what happened next, the text invites the ongoing performative proclamation in the spirit of mutuality and reciprocity instead. Pentecostals have said that the inconclusive and open-ended character at this juncture urges new permutations of Spirit-inspired and empowered witness to and from the ends of the earth, as if to fill in a twenty-ninth chapter of the book of Acts.[22] Thus the pentecostal this-is-that approach would connect the missional efforts of every succeeding generation to the apostolic efforts, all as being Spirit-driven toward the coming divine reign.

So far I have suggested that Christian hermeneutics and theological method are furnished pneumatologically: through responsiveness to the initiative of the Spirit poured out on all flesh, and as oriented toward the mission of the Spirit to establish the reign of the triune God. These reflections thus provide a Trinitarian alpha (source) and omega (goal), as it were, for Christian theological reflection, which presumes that what happens in between, after Pentecost but before Parousia, involves boundary crossing to and from the ends of the earth in and through the Spirit. In these respects, the present and ongoing pentecostalization or charismatization of world Christianity observed by various scholars is suggestive also of a similar pentecostalization (also charismatization) of Christian hermeneutics and theological method.[23] Scriptural reading and theological reflection are precipitated by encounter in and with the Spirit and oriented toward the Spirit's

21. For more on the apostolic mission to Malta and other account of missional mutuality in reciprocity in Acts, see my *The Missiological Spirit*, ch. 6.

22. One version of this Acts 29 perspective is by pentecostal feminist theologian Holmes, "Acts 29 and Authority." In more conventional exegetical terms, Kee, *Good News to the Ends of the Earth*, 106–7, puts it this way: "Rome is not the end of the story, even though it is the literary conclusion of Acts. . . . [T]he open nature of the new community excludes no one on the basis of present condition, but is open across all humanly-established boundaries. The world is open. God is in control, and has provided the message and the means to communicate it."

23. On the pentecostalization and charismatization of world Christianity, see, e.g., Jenkins, *The Next Christendom*; Omenyo, *Pentecost Outside Pentecostalism*; and Thorsen, *Charismatic Practice and Catholic Parish Life*.

mission to bear witness to the gospel of the Messiah to and at the ends of the earth. However, such undergirding still leaves obscure how biblical interpretation might proceed, or how theological methodology might operate. The next and final section of this essay probes into the Acts narrative more deeply to see if there is apostolic exemplarity in this regard.

Reflecting in the Spirit: From Apostolic Theologizing to Christian Confession

Methodologically, this essay has proceeded on the assumption that any contemporary pentecostal contribution to hermeneutics and theological method originates not from the parochial experiences of modern pentecostal believers (no matter how many there are) but are established normatively from the scriptural witness. In brief, Christian biblical interpretation follows the apostolic example in receiving and reappropriating their Scriptures in light of their experiences and with regard to their communicative goals in their first-century contexts.[24] Yet at the same time, their, and our, biblical arguments are never only textually funded but, as I have portrayed, derived from contact with the Spirit of the living God. So also then, with regard to the question at hand about the *how* of scriptural engagement, we shall see that biblical hermeneutics and theological reflection after Pentecost can only be pneumatically charged. We will consider three accounts of this thesis of scriptural retrieval via pneumatic or pneumatological interpretation and reflection: that manifest with St. Stephen, depicted at the first Jerusalem council, and portrayed in the ministry of St. Paul.[25]

I am drawn to Stephen the martyr for this task for a number of reasons, not the least of which is that he provides the first instance of someone not part of the Twelve whose sermon is recorded.[26] He is a Hellenist, said to have been "a man full of faith and the Holy Spirit" (Acts 6:5; cf. 6:3, 10), who is also said to be "full of grace and power, [who] did great wonders and signs among the people" (6:8). As the "word of God continued to spread; the number of the disciples increased greatly in Jerusalem, and a great many of the priests became obedient to the faith" (6:7), other Jews from the

---

24. Flemming, *Contextualization in the New Testament*, is the most extensive argument of this thesis.

25. Consider the following a (minor) assist to the efforts of Spawn and Wright, eds., *Spirit and Scripture*.

26. The following expands on an earlier discussion of Stephen (in Yong, *Renewing Christian Theology*, ch. 7.1) where I focus on his contributions to apostolic ecclesiology.

synagogue of the Freedman (6:9) were no doubt then stirred to charge him with "saying things against this holy place and the law" (6:13).

I have argued elsewhere that, "filled with the Holy Spirit" (7:55a), Stephen's apologetic for a Messianic faith that was foundationally based upon but not reducible to narrow Jewish concerns itself was informed, at least in part, by his Hellenist experience and perspective beyond the borders of Judea.[27] Thus Stephen's own sojourns from around the Mediterranean world (we are not informed about where specifically he hailed) enabled his appreciation of Abraham's journey from Mesopotamia, through Haran and the land of the Chaldeans, not to mention the dynamic history of the Abrahamic brood leading up to and then settling through Egypt (7:2-19). His Greco-Roman education may also have allowed him to accept that "Moses was instructed in all the wisdom of the Egyptians and was powerful in his words and deeds" (7:22). Later on Moses settles in Midian for forty years (7:29-30), thus effectively becoming a Midianite. Read from the perspective of the Pentecost narrative of witness going to the ends of the earth, Stephen presents a remarkably cosmopolitan understanding of ancient Israel, one continuous with his own experience of the messianic way and community itself constituted by those from around the known world.

If the Freedman then desired to limit authentic Jewish practice to that of the Temple and according to a stricter interpretation of the law, Stephen counters that "the Most High does not dwell in houses made by human hands" (7:48), and appeals on this point to a postexilic messianic prophecy regarding the living God having the entire earth as his Temple (7:49-50; cf. Isa 66:1-2).[28] Hence while these observant Jews could not grasp how messianic faith might reconfigure divine presence beyond Temple precincts, apostolic leaders after Pentecost realized that the people of the Spirit were drawn from many cultures, languages, and regions of the world. In short, the pentecostal gift that reconstituted the people of the Temple as the fellowship of the Spirit led Stephen to a reconsideration of ancient Israel as similarly constituted by encounters with others and incorporation of their contributions. For our purposes, Stephen becomes an exemplar of the pneumatological imagination post-Pentecost.

The lesson from the Jerusalem Council for our purposes is no less important for a pentecostal and pneumatological hermeneutics.[29] The major

27. See Yong, *Who is the Holy Spirit?*, ch. 16.

28. On Isaiah 61 as a post-exilic writing, see my *The Spirit and the Missio Dei: Trinitarian Mission in Canonical Perspective* (work in progress), ch. 4.3.

29. Another pentecostal reading of the apostolic council in Acts 15 as pneumatological, hermeneutical, and methodological model is provided by Thomas, "Women, Pentecostals and the Bible."

question concerned how the young messianic community with a majority Jewish cast ought respond to the "reported . . . conversion of the Gentiles" (Acts 15:3). Despite Peter's own newfound realization (see above), there was "no small dissension and debate" that it was nevertheless "necessary for them [the Gentiles] to be circumcised and ordered to keep the law of Moses" (15:2, 5b). How then would this nascent apostolic community adjudge the issues?

Experientially, scripturally, and pneumatologically, it seems. The apostles and leading elders first heard, again, Peter's testimony (15:6–11), in particular about how God had given to the Gentiles "the Holy Spirit, just as he did to us" (15:8b). Then Barnabas and Saul also "told of all the signs and wonders that God had done through them among the Gentiles" (15:12), in effect reiterating that apart from these developments, there would be no issue to dispute or contest. Then, James recalls a prophetic word to the effect that there would come a messianic time when "all other peoples may seek the Lord—even all the Gentiles," and that this promise had come from "the Lord, who has been making these things known from long ago" (15:17–18; cf. Amos 9:11–12). In their letter to the fledgling Gentile congregations, then, the apostolic leaders provide theological guidance and practical resolution believed as pneumatically merited. Their recommendations ensued, they underscored authoritatively, as "it has seemed good to the Holy Spirit and to us" (Acts 15:28a).

It did not matter that the prophetic text appealed to could be said to have been, at best, partially fulfilled and in that sense only somewhat applicable to the contested situation. But even if "the remnant of Edom" (Amos 9:12) had not yet been restored, at least not in any literal sense—and this is not referenced in the Acts version—from the apostolic perspective after Pentecost, this prophetic passage provided scriptural warrant for receiving the Gentiles onto the messianic Way and into the Spirit-impelled community.[30] Within the wider scheme of the apostolic experience, it should also be noted that the experiential, scriptural, and pneumatic judgment rendered at this first council was consistent with the mission of the Spirit to establish the divine reign to the ends of the earth.

The final set of apostolic considerations for a pneumatic hermeneutic and theological method I will briefly discuss are St. Paul's retelling of his own conversion experience when speaking to the crowd at Jerusalem

---

30. For further discussion of Amos 9 in relationship to Acts 15, see Meek, *The Gentile Mission in Old Testament Citations in Acts*, ch. 4; Meek's wider argument is that Luke's use of the first testament for a variety of purposes relates to contested aspects of the apostolic understanding of the gospel witness, including to buttress the rationale for the Gentile mission.

(22:4-16 within 22:2-21) and to King Agrippa (26:12-18 within 26:2-23).[31] The significance of these Pauline testimonies is that they unfold and can be compared and contrast with the narrated account earlier in Acts (9:1-19). There is neither time nor space here to go into the scholarly discussion of these three passages.[32] My interest is in reading these subsequent recollections in light of the Spirit's empowering apostolic witness to the ends of the earth. From this perspective, Luke's more descriptive initial narration provides the basic plotline later variously accentuated by Paul.

For instance, in his apology before the Jews in the Jerusalem Temple area, Paul emphasizes his Jewish credentials (22:3-5), and acknowledges the assistance of Ananias, "a devout man according to the law and well spoken of by all the Jews living there" (22:12). The former Jewish backdrop is not altogether absent in his explanation before Agrippa but it is subordinated comparatively to highlighting the more theoretical and philosophical questions like that concerning the plausibility of the idea of the resurrection from the dead (26:6-8) and focused on Paul's commissioning as apostle to the Gentiles (26:15-18). If in the former speech there is a preoccupation with the blinding light from heaven (thrice mentioned: 22:6, 9, 11; cf. 9:3), then in the latter emphasis is placed instead on the apostle's empowerment to turn Jews and Gentiles from darkness to light (26:18, 23).[33] Hence the parallel accounts spotlight diverse aspects of the conversion related to the audience and purpose of the testimony. These can thus be understood as contextualization cases that foreground the Spirit's enabling witness in different arenas.

What is to be emphasized in this discussion is that a post-Pentecost hermeneutic and theological method involves revisiting the received tradition afresh vis-à-vis every new visitation with the triune God. Such "thinking in the Spirit" is holistically experiential and communally adjudicated, albeit in and through wrestling with the inherited scriptural and authoritative traditions in light of new circumstances.[34] In a post-New Testament

---

31. The standard study of these parallel passages is Lohfink, *The Conversion of St. Paul*; Lohfink's predominantly form critical approach comes to conclusions that are not unamenable to my own pentecostal consideration.

32. Hedrick, "Paul's Conversion/Call," suggest these are three genres, for instance; we need not adjudicate the scholarly issues for purposes of this article.

33. Our discussion here proceeds as if the Pauline apologies are strictly historical over and against Luke's own telling when in reality, even the Pauline testimonies are unfolded by the Acts author; hence it is important to keep in mind, as Lohfink, *The Conversion of St. Paul*, 89-91, reminds us, that Luke's own purposes are to undergird the Gentile mission of which he presents Paul as the foremost exponent.

34. More philosophically articulated is Smith, *Thinking in Tongues*.

context then, the pentecostal way of the Spirit invites not just a recitation of the apostolic writings but revitalized testimonies to and innovative confessions about the work of the Spirit in every subsequent place and time.

* * *

I wish to make three final points. First, there is no denying that the most vigorous vanguard of the world Christian movement is being carried by pentecostal and charismatic type churches, communities, and movements. These include not just the so-called classical pentecostal denominations with historic links to the Azusa Street revival in the early twentieth century but also charismatic renewal movements from out of mainline Protestant as well as Roman Catholic and Orthodox traditions in the last fifty years plus, along with indigenous spiritual churches especially in Africa but also prevalent across the majority world.[35] Adherents of these communities might presume special divine favor as sparking such expansion and growth, but a more somber assessment should ask what this means and what it demands from participants or those so associated. Here the earliest modern pentecostal convictions ought to be reiterated: that even among those "come outers," the point was not mere sectarianism but to consider how best their own newfound brush with the Spirit of God might be conduits to the revitalization of their churches.

As a pentecostal theologian at the front end of the twenty-first century, I present with some trepidation the preceding as part of the fruits of pentecostal and charismatic spirituality, now submitted back to the church catholic as a pneumatic hermeneutic and theological method that might perhaps be what is needed for such a global time as this.[36] If before the charisms of the pentecostal-charismatic movement were its accents on the spiritual gifts or evangelistic zeal or missional energy, the question must be posed: what are the hermeneutical and methodological correlates, both that can be made explicit from such pentecostal-charismatic practices and sensibilities on the one hand and that can be discerned as having stimulated the scriptural imagination toward such contemporary performances of the biblical narratives on the other hand? In other words, what kind of hermeneutical

---

35. I provide a cartography of these developments in this essay: "Global Renewal Christianity and World Christianity."

36. The emphasis on the hermeneutical contribution in this essay complements that proposed on the theological method front in my "Pentecostal and Charismatic Theology."

and methodological presuppositions precede and follow from pentecostal-charismatic praxis, mission, and spirituality?

This essay proposes a pentecostal hermeneutic and theological method, not one that is merely insular to the modern pentecostal movement but one that seeks to live substantively into and out of the apostolic way initiated by the Day of Pentecost outpouring of the Spirit on all flesh. Such a pentecostal and pneumatological imagination belongs to all followers of Jesus, the messianically anointed (by the Spirit), who live in every place and time subsequent to the era of the first disciples. Yet those who have come later, including us in our own generation and our children, are not bereft of the apostolic witness, not only because we have their written convictions in the New Testament but because we have available to us the same Spirit that was given to them by the risen Christ. Hence we also have met the triune God and are enabled to walk in his Spirit to receive and reappropriate the scriptural and theological traditions in light of our unique experiences, circumstances, and challenges. Thereby we also are called, as they were, to the kind of transformational theologizing that connected their unique experience of and encounter with the living God with the record bequeathed by their ancestors on the one hand, but that also sought, through Spirit-led theological reflection, to both regulate and vulnerably hasten future transformations on this apostolic way. The church ecumenical—the fellowship of the Holy Spirit—in the second decade of this third millennium is obligated to do at least this much in order to witness to the world now and leave a legacy for those coming after.

PART II

Theological Anthropology and the Spirit: The Lukan Imagination I

CHAPTER 4

Many Tongues, Many Senses

*Pentecost, the Body Politic,
and the Redemption of Dis/Ability*[1]

What do disability studies and pentecostal studies have in common? Are intersections between these two scholarly fields of inquiry possible or profitable? Can each discipline learn from and yet critically inform the other?

The following pages seek to respond to these questions in four steps, correlating with the four sections of this essay: 1) identification of some of the reasons behind the lack of interaction, so far, between disability and pentecostal studies; 2) exploration of how disability perspectives might bring to the fore previously unrecognized resources for rethinking pentecostal understandings of disability; 3) explication, with the help of a disability hermeneutic, of the pentecostal theology of "many tongues" bearing witness to the gospel with the resulting motif of "many senses" capable of receiving and giving witness to the wondrous works of God; and 4) re-assessment of the possibility of pentecostal contributions to theology of disability and

---

1. Thanks to the following for their comments on a previous version of this paper: Rosemarie Scotti Hughes, Jack Levison, Stephen Fettke, Martin Mittelstadt, Timothy Lim, and Frank Macchia. Needless to say, all errors of fact and misinterpretations remain my own fault.

This essay is also dedicated to the memory of Nancy Eiesland (see also note 5 above), who passed away on March 10, 2009 after a lifelong struggle with a congenital bone defect. I wrote this essay before her passing and she graciously commented on a previous draft during what turned out to be some of the last months of her life. Her scholarship pushed the boundaries of the discussion in theology and disability, and if this essay does, even minimally, something similar for the pentecostal studies and disability studies interface, it is only because I have attempted to follow in professor Eiesland's footsteps (better: wheel-paths) as she has attempted to follow after Christ.

disability studies in light of the "many senses" motif. I will argue that the intersection of disability studies and pentecostal studies will be challenging but also helpful for both sides, even as our joint efforts might also bear witness, in a creative and distinctive way, to the marvelous works of God in and through the diversity of embodied human experiences.

Disability Studies and Pentecostal Studies: Roadblocks at the Intersection

The field of disability studies has exploded into prominence over the past generation, and especially during the last two decades.[2] Landmark events informing this new discipline include the emergence of the disability rights movement in the early 1970s, in the wake of the civil rights movement and the Vietnam War, and then the passing of the Americans with Disabilities Act in 1990.[3] Albeit focused on the human experience of disability, scholars approach the topic from a variety of (inter- and multi-) disciplinary perspectives, including the medical, technological, social, and political sciences, economics, law, literature, history, philosophy, and even religious and theological studies, just to name a few.[4]

Why then has disability studies not interacted or interfaced with pentecostal studies? One can think of a few reasons, including the relative youth of both scholarly enterprises.[5] Yet, there are also at least two other specific reasons why disability studies scholars have ignored pentecostal studies. First, disability studies has been, by and large, motivated by a sociopolitical agenda directed toward the achievement of disability rights and the inclusion of people with disabilities into the mainstream of society. Insofar as pentecostal studies is understood (rightly or wrongly) as being apolitical in its representing the overall orientation of the pentecostal movement, it would be seen as being out of alignment with rather than supportive of the

---

2. The standard introductions to the discipline are Davis, ed., *The Disability Studies Reader*, and Snyder, Brueggemann, and Garland-Thomson, eds., *Disability Studies*.

3. See Fleischer and Zames, *The Disability Rights Movement*, and Colker, *The Disability Pendulum*.

4. Disability studies have now been represented for awhile in discussions in both the American Academy of Religion (through the Religion and Disability Studies group) and the Society of Biblical Literature (through the Disability Studies and Healthcare in the Bible and the Near East program unit). See, respectively, Betcher, "Rehabilitating Religious Discourse," and Schipper, *Disability Studies and the Hebrew Bible*.

5. Pentecostal studies itself had its genesis also in the early 1970s; see my brief "history" in "Pentecostalism and the Theological Academy."

goals of disability scholarship. Second, the experience of disability scholars like Nancy Eiesland suggests that the pentecostal movement's emphasis on healing is counterproductive and even offensive to those scholars of disability who themselves have disabilities but understand these not as problems to be resolved (or healed or cured) but as part and parcel of their identity as human beings.[6] In this case, the assumption would be that pentecostal studies is interested more in legitimating the ideology of healing prevalent in the movement than in interrogating how such ideologies legitimate the oppressive status quo that marginalizes rather than values the experiences of people with disabilities. When combined, it is easier to see why disability studies scholars have either neglected or distanced themselves from, rather than sought to engage, pentecostal studies.

On the pentecostal side, we should note that the movement's emphasis on healing is a central conviction with deep theological rather than ideological roots.[7] At the heart of pentecostal theology, for example, is the Fourfold Gospel of Jesus as savior, *healer*, baptizer (with the Holy Spirit), and coming king. This is predicated on the pentecostal biblical hermeneutic that identifies the apostolic experience, especially that recounted by St. Luke in the book of Acts, as normative for the ongoing life of the church. Hence, the healings experienced by the early Christians—e.g., that of the lame man at the Gate Beautiful, Aeneas, the crippled man at Lystra, Publius on the isle of Malta (Acts 28), and many others (e.g., Acts 5:16, 8:7, 28:9)—are thought to reflect God's primary intentions for believers. Further, believers empowered by the Holy Spirit to bear witness to the gospel are supposed to emulate Jesus himself, who through the power of the same Spirit "went about doing good and healing all who were oppressed by the devil" (Acts 10:38; cf. Luke 4:18). Along with the many healings recorded in the Gospel of Luke, Jesus is said to have responded when asked if he was the messiah to come: "Go and tell John what you have seen and heard: the blind receive their sight, the lame walk, the lepers are cleansed, the deaf hear, the dead are raised, the poor have good news brought to them" (7:22). In sum, if the ministry of Jesus and the apostles are marked by the healing power of the Holy Spirit,

---

6. Eiesland herself grew up in the Assemblies of God with a congenital form of degenerative bone disease; for her account of her experiences in the church, see her by now classic book, *The Disabled God*, 116–18, and also "Avoiding Hospital Chaplains and other Venial Sins." For further discussion of this disability self-understanding, see my *Theology and Down Syndrome*, 242–44.

7. Two recent studies of pentecostal healing are Hardesty, *Faith Cure*, and Alexander, *Pentecostal Healing*.

then so will the ministries of the followers of Jesus who are filled with the Spirit.[8]

More to the point, the healings accomplished by the power of God are thought to be signs heralding and inaugurating the coming kingdom.[9] It is typically assumed, in conjunction with the eschatological vision of the Apocalypse about there being no more tears in the new heavens and new earth (Rev 21:4), that sicknesses, diseases, and disabilities will be eliminated before or, finally, with the resurrection of the body in the life to come. The presence of these bodily infirmities and afflictions are a mark of the present fallen order. Their persistence, and the lack of healing, either is thought to signal the ongoing effects of sin (and, concomitantly, the lack of repentance or of faith) or, alternatively, to represent God's testing of our trust in him. For the able-bodied, the unfortunate sufferings of people with disabilities serve only as occasions for acts of charity toward them.

Given this background, I suggest it is important for both disability studies and pentecostal studies to engage in a mutual discussion. Pentecostal scholars are increasingly realizing not only that contemporary etiology of disability requires a rethinking of the connection between sin and disability,[10] but that Jesus himself had already called this into question (cf. John 9:2–3). Further, that Jesus' resurrected body retained the marks of impairment in his hands and sides should give pentecostals pause about too simplistically dismissing the "presence" of disabilities in the new heavens and new earth; might it be that God's wiping away every tear from our eyes signals not so much the elimination of disabilities but their redemption and the removal of the social and even ecclesial stigmatization that comes with them?[11] Last but not least, healing is itself now seen to have not only bio-

---

8. Hence we can better understand the disability studies critique that Jesus' healings functions "as erasure rather than acceptance of disability"; that "the restoration of bodies to normative health through acts of faith healing ultimately devalues our commitments to the demands of embodiment overall"; and that, in this view, redemption becomes "a form of social cleansing"; see Mitchell and Snyder, "Jesus Throws Everything Off Balance," 178 and 179.

9. See Irvin, *Healing*.

10. Taking mental incapacities, for example, the biblical traditions identify its causes in terms that include God himself, sin (of one's ancestors, if not oneself) and its effects, or the devil and his demons. By contrast, contemporary etiologies of mental disabilities include environmental, genetic/chromosomal, and pre-natal explanations, among others; see, e.g., Harris, *Intellectual Disability*, ch. 5. The theological issues are much more complex, of course, but my point is that we cannot proceed as if contemporary diagnoses do not exist.

11. For elaboration of this point, see my "Disability, the Human Condition, and the Spirit of the Eschatological Long Run."

logical but also social dimensions; this means that disabilities are, at least in some cases, as much if not more social constructions as they are physical conditions.[12] All this to say that pentecostal scholars should now rethink popular pentecostal theologies of suffering and healing in light of the work of disability studies which challenges a one-dimensional medical, biological, and individualistic model of the human experience of disability.[13]

On the other hand, I invite disability studies scholars to reconsider what pentecostal studies might have to offer toward what Eiesland calls a "liberatory theology of disability."[14] At the same time, I recognize as a pentecostal theologian that unless and until pentecostal scholars themselves begin to explicitly engage issues pertinent to disability,[15] their work will remain inconsequential to disability scholarship. Yet I wonder if there are resources within what I call the "pneumatological imagination" of pentecostal spirituality that not only contribute to disability studies but also help rethink altogether the binary contrasts of able/disabled. This essay is motivated in part by my anticipation of a positive response to this question.

What Has (Dr.) Luke to Say? Pentecostal Resources for Rethinking Disability

As a first step toward a constructive pentecostal theology of disability, I turn to the pentecostal canon within the canon, St. Luke's Acts of the Apostles.

---

12. See Barnes, "*Cabbage Syndrome*," Hughes and Paterson, "The Social Model of Disability and the Disappearing Body," and Goggin and Newell, *Digital Disability*.

13. Both are already happening—e.g., Mittelstadt, *The Spirit and Suffering in Luke-Acts*, has begun to re-work pentecostal theology of suffering, and my own *Theology and Down Syndrome*, esp. ch. 8, has sought to re-conceptualize theology of healing. The present essay is an extension of my theology of disability work in an explicitly pentecostal idiom.

14. E.g., Lovett, "Liberation: A Dual-Edged Sword," Volf, "Materiality of Salvation," Sepúlveda, "Pentecostalism and Theology of Liberation," and Melander, "'New' Pentecostalism Challenges 'Old' Liberation Theology."

15. Some members of the Society for Pentecostal Studies are beginning to do this—for example, three papers presented at the thirty-seventh annual meeting of the Society at Duke Divinity School in Durham, North Carolina, in March 2008: Brothers and Biddy, "Theology of Disability Within the Church," Fettke, the published version being "The Spirit of God Hovered Over the Waters," and Rouse, also published as "Scripture and the Disabled"—although these remain "in house" discussions within pentecostal circles rather than intentional efforts to interact with disability scholarship. For a further call for such pentecostal engagement with disability, in response to my book, see Mittelstadt and Hittenberger, "Power and Powerlessness in Pentecostal Theology."

In making this move, I am relying neither on external testimonies regarding Luke as a physician (Col 4:14) nor on the assumption that he was therefore more sympathetic to people with disabilities. In fact, the former has been contested,[16] and, as we have already seen, there is plenty in Luke's text regarding the ambiguous status of the blind and the lame, etc., that would perpetuate discriminatory stereotypes regarding people with disabilities.[17] Equally problematic is the issue that our contemporary category of disability is anachronistic when applied to the biblical material.[18] At the same time, I think the tradition of Luke the physician can provide resources for a renewed theology of disability when his text is approached and carefully reread using a disability hermeneutic.

Helpful in this regard is the recent work of Mikeal Parsons on physiognomy (the study of bodily or outer characteristics) in the Lukan writings.[19] While in the ancient Greek world, physical bodily forms were thought to represent inward moral tendencies and characteristics through anatomical, ethnographic, and zoological correlations, Parsons argues in his groundbreaking study that Luke deploys widely accepted physiognomic characterizations only to subvert their usual moral associations. Of his four cases studies—of the bent over woman, Zaccheus, the lame man at the Gate Beautiful, and the Ethiopian eunuch—the last is particularly illuminating as all three of the ancient Greek stereotypes are undermined: neither his Ethiopian background (the ethnographic aspect), nor physical deformity as a eunuch (the anatomical), nor association with the weakness represented by sheep in the Isaianic passage being read (the zoological) hindered the eunuch's baptism and inclusion in the kingdom of God.

Following Parsons's lead, I want to reflect further on Luke's accounts of Zaccheus and, especially, the eunuch to see how they might provide new insights for a pentecostal theology of disability.[20] For those who are doubtful

---

16. E.g., Cadbury, *The Style and Literary Method of Luke*, 39–51. Yet defending the traditional view is Ramsey, *Luke the Physician*, 58–60. The recent study of a physician and clinical haernatologist, Dawson, *Healing, Weakness and Power*, 152–55, is rather conclusive, in my view, against the traditional understanding. See also a summary of the discussion that concludes that while Luke may not have been a doctor in the ancient sense of the word, he was knowledgeable to some extent about ancient medicine—in Weissenreider, *Images of Illness in the Gospel of Luke*, 330–35.

17. On this point, see also Roth's study about how Lukan references to the blind and the lame, among others, depict their weaknesses and vulnerability; Roth, *The Blind, the Lame, and the Poor*. We will return to this issue later.

18. As I argue in *Theology and Down Syndrome*, esp. ch. 3.

19. Parsons, *Body and Character in Luke and Acts*.

20. The following discussion of the eunuch is an abridgment of my *Who is the*

that eunuchs are to be included with the disabled, note that in the biblical traditions, castrated males were categorized among those with physical, sensorial, and functional disabilities—the blind, lame, mutilated, hunchbacked, dwarfed, etc. (Lev 21:17–23)—and, more problematically for first-century Jews, the law explicitly excluded eunuchs and those with crushed testicles from participating in the liturgical cult and worship of ancient Israel (also Deut 23:1).[21] Yet Luke's inclusive vision of the redemption of Israel and the kingdom of God is revealed even in this case of people long marginalized because of their bodily mutilation. Just as Jesus had accepted the socially despised and short-statured (physically disabled) Zacchaeus, so also does Luke here record the early church's acceptance of the physically impaired eunuch. Yes, in many other cases, Jesus and the apostles healed the sick and "disabled" by the power of the Spirit. However, in these two cases, Jesus pronounced the arrival of salvation to Zacchaeus's household (Luke 19:9) and Philip baptized the eunuch (Acts 8:38) without any reversal of their physical conditions.

Further, the acceptance of the eunuch began to fulfill the promise of YHWH to include eunuchs just as they were in the eschatological redemption of Israel (Isa 56:3–5).[22] Jesus' own teachings foreshadowed the eschatological inclusion of people like the eunuch. In two parables, of the wedding feast and the eschatological banquet (Luke 14:7–24), Jesus intentionally taught about humility rather than self-promotion, overturned the rules of "you-invite-me-and-I-invite-you" reciprocity, and warned his hearers that the kingdom would include those at the bottom rather than at the top of the social, political, and religious hierarchy. At the same time, his hearers (and Luke's audience) would have been shocked at the presence of people with clearly recognized disabilities—the crippled, the lame, and the blind—at the *eschatological* table of the king (14:21; cf. 14:13). These were the outcasts who had no status, and were incapable of reciprocating the "generosity" of the host. For that very reason, social conventions would have dictated that they politely decline the invitation to begin with, so that Jesus insisted they needed to be compelled to attend the banquet and, by implication, that they be carried in if necessary (14:23). So while Jesus' healing of people with disabilities would have confirmed some prophetic pronouncements that the blind, lame, and otherwise impaired would be cured on the coming Day of

---

Holy Spirit?, ch. 19.

21. For a disability rereading of these Levitical prohibitions, see Melcher, "Visualizing the Perfect Cult."

22. Saul Olyan thinks this Isaianic passage is perhaps the only text in the Hebrew Bible which contests the stigmatization of those with bodily "defects" (*mumim*); see Olyan, *Disability in the Hebrew Bible*, 11–12 and 84–85.

YHWH, in this case Jesus' inclusion of such people *just as they are* in the Great Banquet picks up on other prophetic themes (e.g., Jer 31:8–9, Mic 4:6–7, Zeph 3:19) about the coming kingdom involving the flourishing of all people not because we are physically cured but because YHWH has acted to remove the barriers that segregate temporarily able-bodied people from those with disabilities and alleviate the social stigma attached to disabilities.[23] In this view, the restoration and redemption of Israel would include people like the eunuch and Zacchaeus, not "fixed" so that they can conform to our social standards of beauty and desirability, but precisely as a testimony to the power of God to save all of us "normal" folk from our own discriminatory attitudes, inhospitable actions, and exclusionary social and political forms of life. Here, then, we find another ironic Lukan reversal:[24] wherein the redemption of disability consists not necessarily in the healing of disabilities but the removal of those barriers—social, structural, economic, political, and religious/theological—which hinder those with temporarily able bodies from welcoming and being hospitable to people with disabilities!

I suggest that these inclusions—of the physiognominally suspect and stigmatized figures like Zacchaeus and the Ethiopian eunuch—should actually be taken for granted within the theological imagination centered on the Spirit's eschatological outpouring on all flesh on the Day of Pentecost (Acts 2:17).[25] Let me elaborate on this proposal along three lines.[26] First, pentecostal theology has perennially understood the miracle of Pentecost to consist, at least in part, of the miracle of inspired speech. But this miracle is only a means to an end, which is the manifestation of "God's deeds of power" (Acts 2:11). Read this way, the means can be seen as subordinate to the end,

---

23. For discussion of these inclusive-of-disability prophetic texts, see Melcher, "I Will Lead the Blind by the Road They Do Not Know."

24. Luke's theology of ironic reversals is announced in Mary's Magnificat—"He has brought down the powerful from their thrones, and lifted up the lowly; he has filled the hungry with good things, and sent the rich away empty" (Luke 1:52–53)—as well as pronounced by Jesus: "some are last who will be first, and some are first who will be last" (13:30). For further discussion, see York, *The Last Shall Be First*.

25. Here I extend also the thesis I argued in *The Spirit Poured Out on All Flesh*.

26. I realize that my interpretation of Acts 2 in the following paragraphs is more inferential than some may be comfortable with. I am simply proposing a possible rather than necessary reading, as informed by a disability hermeneutic. While in the end readers will probably agree or not for different reasons, my claim is that Luke can be read from a contemporary perspective as being more friendly to rather than hostile against disability. Hence this particular disability interpretation of Acts 2 needs to be understood against my rereading of Luke-Acts as a whole, a rereading of which this essay can be considered a down payment anticipating future work.

and God could just as well choose other means to accomplish these ends. Following out this line of thinking, if God not only is capable of inspiring speech but has also created the bodily members through which speech is produced, I suggest the incapacity to speak is of no hindrance to what God can do. From a disability perspective, then, the God who creates the mute or enables the speech of the stutterer (Exod. 4:10-12) is the one who empowers all communication about God's wondrous and powerful works.

But second, there is also a minority reading of the Pentecost narrative which views its miracle to be one of inspired hearing. Luke records the crowd's response that "each one *heard* them speaking in the native language of each" (Acts 2:6) and that "in our own languages we *hear* them speaking about God's deeds of power" (2:11).[27] So, the Spirit empowers not *xenolalia*, the speaking of unlearned languages, but *akolalia*, the understanding of unlearned languages.[28] But again, his miracle of hearing can be understood as being subordinate to the intended ends that manifest God's deeds of power. So in this case, if God not only is capable of enabling hearing but has also created the bodily members through which hearing is accomplished, I suggest the incapacity to hear is in and of itself no hindrance to what God can do to reveal his glorious works. Hence, a disability perspective would simply then insist that God who creates the deaf or enables communication through signs—e.g., as seen in Zechariah (Luke 1:22, 62-63)—is also the one whose speech-acts are capable of being manifest and received through the diversity of phenomenological and embodied discourses.

This leads, third, to my proposal that God's communicative speech-acts engage human beings through the multiplicity of our sensory capacities. On the Day of Pentecost, Peter himself recognized that the outpouring and gift of the Holy Spirit was both seen and heard (Acts 2:33). Pentecostals have generally focused on what has been most explicit in the Acts 2 narrative: the "sound like the rush of a violent wind" and the "divided tongues, as of fire" which alighted on each one (2:2-3). I suggest, however, that such *explicitly thematized* sounds and images, along with the sensory capacities that mediate them (hearing and seeing), are not exclusive of the other sensory modalities that constitute our being-in-the-world. What if the miracle of Pentecost is not only that of either speaking, hearing, or seeing, but also that of touching, feeling, and perceiving? What if inspired speech is not the only means to bear witness to the wondrous works of God but is one of a plurality

---

27. I have added the italics in both verses; thanks to Steven Fettke for reminding me to emphasize this point.

28. For some of the distinctions between *xenolalia* and *akolalia*, see Spittler, "Glossolalia," 670.

of sensory capacities through which God is present and active in our midst? What if the Pentecostal gift of the Spirit redeems all people—Zacchaeus and the Ethiopian eunuch included—neither by transforming "them" into able-bodied standards of normalcy nor by "fixing" their incapacities or impairments so that they can interact with us on our terms, but by transforming and fixing all of us so that we can together be the new people of God?

I would see this set of proposals as an extension of the view that the list of ethnic and national provenance in Acts 2:7–11 is a representative rather than exhaustive one.[29] My point is that Luke's inclusive vision of the kingdom intersects not only with the coordinates of language, ethnicity, gender, class, and culture, but also with that of disability. If I can demonstrate this point, then regardless of whether or not Luke's credentials as a physician withstand critical scrutiny, in effect he can be understood to have fulfilled the medical doctor's Hippocratic oath—except that rather than (merely) reporting about the healing of the sick and disabled, his narrative would be a performative speech-act, an illocutionary invitation to each of us to inhabit the new world of the Spirit in which the stigmatization and marginalization of people with disabilities and sensory impairments will be no more.

Many Tongues, Many Senses:
The Multiple Modalities of Spirit-Inspired Witness

Let us now see if the case can be made for the following pneumatology of "many tongues and many senses" capable of giving testimony to and receiving the witness of the wondrous works of God. There are two basic steps to the following argument: a general overview of the epistemology operative in Luke's narrative that shows how there are multiple modes of human knowing and interaction, and a more focused discussion of Luke's holistic soteriology, especially in its kinesiological dimensions as manifest in the touch that is inspired by the Spirit. Throughout, I presume the Spirit's charismatic anointing of the entire life and ministry of Jesus in the Third Gospel and the extension of that anointing in the outpouring of the Spirit on all flesh in Acts, so that the entirety of the Lukan narrative can be understood to be about the "acts of the Holy Spirit." My goal is to sketch a holistic pentecostal theology of embodiment that in turn opens up conceptual space for a pneumatological theology of disability beyond emphasizing only the healing of disabled bodies and minds.

To begin, I want to explore further the significance of both seeing and hearing as central to Luke's theology of bearing and receiving the witness

---

29. I argue this point in my *The Spirit Poured Out on All Flesh*, ch. 4.3.3.

of the Spirit. This couplet occurs throughout Luke's account. The shepherds praised God "for all they had heard and seen" (Luke 2:20); the disciples have seen and heard what prophets and kings have not (10:24), and later they cannot but testify to what they had seen and heard (Acts 4:20); the Samaritan crowds heard and saw the signs that Philip did (8:6); and Paul himself was called to bear witness to the world of all he had seen and heard (22:15). Whereas this combination of seeing and hearing is a fairly standard characterization of the two dominant epistemic senses—as is evident from the preceding, neither is privileged over the other; there is no standard form whereby one always precedes and the other follows—I suggest that from a disability perspective their pairing together is significant as it points to not one but two basic modalities of human knowing.

This observation already advances the discussion of pentecostal and pneumatological epistemology.[30] Within a pentecostal schema in which inspired speech is perhaps the central manifestation of the Spirit's empowerment for witness, the principal form of communication is speaking and the primary mode of knowing is hearing. Yet our discussion shows that seeing is also important, and not only when paired with hearing. Thus there are also occasions within the Lukan narrative that the salvation of God is specifically noted as seen rather than heard (Luke 2:30, 3:6; Acts 3:17). Even at the heart of the Pentecost narrative itself, not only will sons and daughters prophecy, but "your young men shall see visions, / and your old men shall dream dreams" (Acts 2:17b). Here, seeing occurs under the power and inspiration of the Spirit even when our eyes are closed, even when we are asleep! My point is that besides speaking and hearing there is seeing, and that the Spirit's revelatory and saving work is accomplished not only through the oral medium of testimony but is also received through the visual media of seeing, envisioning, and dreaming.

The narrative of the blind man in Luke 18:35–43 is a case in point of the multisensory modalities and the multi-dimensional activities in and through which he witnessed (to) the presence and activity of God. 1) While *sitting* on the roadside, he is nevertheless not entirely passive; rather, he is *begging*. 2) He *hears* the crowd going by, and *asks* about what is going on. 3) His persistence results in his *being brought* or *led to* Jesus (by others). 4) He *persists in shouting*, "Jesus, Son of David, have mercy on me!" and when asked by Jesus what he wanted, *replies*, "Lord, let me see again." 5) Upon

---

30. Proposals for a pentecostal epistemology are still in the initial stages; for a starter discussion, see Cartledge, *Practical Theology*, ch. 3. In my own work, I have sketched the contours of what I call a "pneumatological epistemology" as informed by pentecostal spirituality; see Yong, *Spirit-Word-Community*, part II.

receiving his sight, he *follows* Jesus and *glorifies* God.[31] Note that the blind man bears witness to the wondrous works of God not only in the reception of his sight at the command of the Spirit-anointed Son of God, but also in his exhibition of faith—as manifest in his alertness, aggressiveness, and response. Note also that his healing is mediated by those around who took the time to witness to and interact with him (leading him to Jesus), and then rejoiced with him.[32]

My claim is an extension of David Daniels' 2007 Society of Pentecostal Studies presidential address that emphasizes the reception end of sound and hearing rather than what pentecostals traditionally focus on (speech and words).[33] Insofar as pentecostalism is constituted as much if not more so by its music, worship, sound, "primal cries," and joyful noises, pentecostal orality requires pentecostal audio for its completion. Hence hearing is central to pentecostal spirituality and piety, perhaps as much as if not more than is speech to pentecostal witness. Daniels also mentions in passing the sense of touch (in the gift of instrumentalization), sight (seeing visions), speaking (singing), and writing (poetry), and concludes, "Within the Pentecostal sensorium, the orality-literacy binary of the Enlightenment was recast in ways that challenged the coupling of reason and literacy and the hierarchy of the senses that privilege sight."[34]

Building on Daniels's proposals, a disability perspective would observe that rather than "normalizing" *both* seeing and hearing in ways that marginalize people who are blind and/or deaf,[35] the Lukan text suggests instead

---

31. Blind theologian John Hull suggests that the main point of this pericope is just as much to demonstrate the conversion of the blind man toward discipleship in the way of Jesus as it is to highlight Jesus' healing power; see also Hull, *In the Beginning There was Darkness*, 44–45.

32. On the other hand, the social discrimination enacted against the man is also clear from the exclusionary attempts to silence him, prohibit him from addressing the Son of David, and by doing so, reject his claim to belong as a member of good standing to the inner circle of Davidic progeny. My thanks to Frank Macchia for this insight.

33. Daniels, "'Gotta Moan Sometime.'"

34. Ibid., 29.

35. Thus the disability studies agenda would reject "normalization" theory in as much as it presumes what the disability community calls "ableism"—the oppression of people with disabilities via sociobiologically and economically exclusive structures and practices that privilege the temporarily able-bodied; rather, what is "normal" is precisely the recognition, acceptance, appreciation, and "unleashing [of] multiple forms of corporeal flourishing" (see Betcher, "Monstrosities, Miracles, and Mission," 82; cf. Betcher, *Spirit and the Politics of Disablement*, ch. 3). For further discussion of normalization theory in disability studies, see Flynn and Lemay, eds., *A Quarter-Century of Normalization and Social Role Valorization*, and Carlson, "Rethinking

that only one of these sensory capacities are needed for encountering and then bearing witness to the work of the Spirit. If so, then neither blind nor deaf people are excluded from being recipients or vehicles of the Spirit's gracious and charismatic work. By extension, the deaf-mute would also be capable of receiving the gift of the Spirit and bearing the fruits of the Spirit.[36]

Yet in the remainder of this section I want to expand our discussion to include the somatic sensory capacities which will, in turn, have implications for dealing with a much wider range of disabilities than blindness and deafness. I begin by noting, for example, the epistemic function of the body's affective and perceptual sensibilities.[37] On the road to Emmaus the two disciples saw and heard Jesus, but did not recognize him until the breaking of bread. Yet at that moment, they both realized, "Were not our hearts burning within us while he was talking to us on the road, while he was opening the scriptures to us?" (Luke 24:32). Then later, the resurrected Christ invites the disciples to "Look at my hands and my feet; see that it is I myself. Touch me and see; for a ghost does not have flesh and bones as you see that I have" (24:39). While in the latter case, the touch plays an evidentiary role that confirms what is seen, in the former case it is plausible to view the entire somatic system as affectively engaged in a process of discernment.[38]

When we turn from epistemic to ministerial and missiological modalities, however, the touch can be seen to play a much more expansive role in the Lukan narrative. Jesus' welcoming of children, for instance, led to the people bringing their infants to him "that he might touch them" (18:15). Jesus' palpable acceptance of children and people on their own terms no

---

Normalcy, Normalization, and Cognitive Disability."

36. Recent research on deaf theology bearing out this point are Hitching, *The Church and Deaf People*, and Lewis, *Deaf Liberation Theology*.

37. Moore, *Mark and Luke in Poststructuralist Perspective*, esp. chs. 4–8, provides an intriguing analysis of the ears, mouth, eyes, nose, and body in the Lukan text. At one point, for example, he writes, "To smell is to draw in air, wind, *pneuma*, Spirit. The Gaspels are in-spired, then inhaled. Their sense is their essence or fragrance. To devour a book is to digest its meaning, but to sniff out its es-sense is a more intimate act" (152), and then cross-references 2 Cor 2:14–16, Phil 4:18, Eph 5:2, and Gen 8:20–22, among other passages. My own inspiration derives more from a disability studies hermeneutic than it does from Moore's poststructuralist approach (about which many questions can be raised), although I think our goals converge in seeking to interrogate the assumptions regarding any normative epistemology in the biblical narrative in general and in Luke-Acts in particular.

38. As argued, e.g., by Howard, *Affirming the Touch of God*. Pentecostal theologians like Steve Land and Samuel Solivan have also called attention to the centrality of the affections in the knowing that is graced by the Spirit; see Land, *Pentecostal Spirituality*, esp. ch. 3, and Solivan, *The Spirit, Pathos and Liberation*, esp. chs. 4–5.

doubt invited such a public response. One concrete expression of the fully affective and embodied ministry of Jesus involved a "reverse" situation in which Jesus was the recipient of the sinner woman's washing his feet with her tears, drying them with her hair, and kissing them in gratitude (7:36–50).[39] As Simon's reaction seemed focused more on *who* was touching Jesus rather than on the fact he was being touched, we may detect in the background a widespread recognition and appreciation of the affective and somatic dimensions of Jesus' ministry.[40]

Yet there was probably more to the desire for Jesus to touch their babies in these gestures of the people. There was also the expectation of receiving the life-transforming and -transcending power of God associated with Jesus' touch.[41] Adults thus sought to touch Jesus whenever they realized that healing power exuded from his body (6:19), with the case of the woman with the issue of blood being the most notable (8:44). Otherwise there is one account—that involving the severed ear of the high priest's slave (22:51)—of Jesus' intentional healing accomplished via his mere touch, as well as a number of other occasions, as with a leper (5:13), the crippled woman (13:12–13), and the son of the widow of Nain (7:14), when his touch combined with his spoken word to bring about healing or a bodily resuscitation.[42] If we recall that Jesus' accomplishments were empowered by the Holy Spirit, then we can recognize the revealing and saving work of the Spirit at work through the embodied and somatic-sensory ministry of Jesus. Unsurprisingly, then, the Spirit's empowering of the disciples also produced miraculous healings and even exorcisms, in some cases mediated through Peter's shadow (Acts 5:15–16) and handkerchiefs and aprons that had come into contact with Paul's skin (19:12).

---

39. The woman's kissing and tears may be ambiguous—e.g., communicating joy, sorrow, or mourning—but these somatic and kinesthetic cues leave no doubt that she is wholly taken up in her interactions with Jesus; see Malina, *Social-Science Commentary on the Synoptic Gospels*, 378.

40. Which raises the intriguing question about whether or not Jesus' affective-somatic ministry is but the completion of the affective-somatic ministry of Simeon (Luke 2:25–35), on whom the Spirit "rested," who was guided by the Spirit, and who took Jesus "in his arms" in order to dedicate the life and ministry of this infant to God. My thanks to John H. (Jack) Levison for helping me see this connection.

41. See Epperly, *God's Touch*.

42. Amidst the background of the Hellenistic world, the uniqueness of Jesus' ministry of touch is explored by Lalleman, "Healing by a Mere Touch as a Christian Concept." Kliner, "Assessing Healing Stories in the Gospels," 35, further notes that Jesus' touches frequently violated Hebrew purity codes, which may also explain why the "unclean" felt he was approachable to begin with.

From a pentecostal perspective, I would suggest that these somatic-sensory cues in the Lukan narrative have been internalized within the spirituality and piety of the movement, and therefore manifest themselves most obviously in the palpability, tactility, and embodied expressivity of pentecostal worship.[43] Glossolalic utterances, the dance, the shout, the laying on of hands, prostrations, tarrying at the altar, being slain in the Spirit, etc.—each of these are affective-somatic signs of the Spirit's presence and activity in pentecostal contexts. Note also that pentecostal healing insists that God touches human bodies, restores human psyches, reconciles the psychosomatic dimensions of human life, and reconciles human beings. In short, God reveals himself to us through the multiple sensory modalities of the human constitution, even as God redeems and saves us as fully embodied creatures.[44]

I suggest further that such a multisensory pentecostal and pneumatological epistemology and holistic spirituality open up to and invite critical theological reflection on issues central to disability studies.[45] Let me elaborate briefly on these along two lines. First, following in the footsteps of Jesus means that our Spirit-inspired engagement with the world is neither limited solely to that of speech (and hearing), even if such may be the usual way that the Spirit enables our witness to others, nor even to that of our deeds (which are seen), even if these are also essential to bearing adequate witness to the world. Rather, the power of touch should not be underestimated as a vehicle of the Spirit, and this is *felt* rather than heard or seen. From a disability perspective, then, Luke's narrative implicitly challenges modes of ministry, ecclesial structures and practices, and communal forms of life that privilege seeing and hearing at the expense of touching and feeling. In other words, people with multiple sensory impairments should not be excluded simply because they do go not about being in the world like most of the rest of us.[46] Instead, the church should dare to be different and creatively reconsider

---

43. For more on the kinesthetic dimensions of Pentecostal worship, see Albrecht, *Rites in the Spirit*, 147–48. For further discussion of the centrality of embodiment in pentecostal spirituality and practice, see also Baer, "Redeemed Bodies," and Coleman, "Textuality and Embodiment among Charismatic Christians."

44. The preceding fleshes out what is indicated in the title of Owens, "On Praising God with Our Senses."

45. Consider the following a pentecostal expansion and elaboration of Avalos, "Introducing Sensory Criticism in Biblical Studies."

46. The work of Brent Webb-Mitchell has been exemplary in pointing the way forward toward an ecclesiological vision that is inclusive of people with disabilities— e.g., *Unexpected Guests at God's Banquet*, and *Dancing with Disabilities*.

how the Spirit might empower interactions that are inclusive of people who are blind, deaf, blind and deaf, and sense-impaired in other respects.[47]

Second, Luke's multisensory epistemology and holistic spirituality suggests that embodied and affective reason is just as important as cognitive reason,[48] and therefore that the church should also be a haven specifically for people with intellectual disabilities.[49] Of course, there is a broad spectrum of intellectual disabilities, ranging from mild to profound retardation (to use the classification adopted by the World Health Organization),[50] and for many people with intellectual disabilities, visual and auditory interactions suffice when supplemented with other communicative strategies. The more severe or profound the retardation, however, the less capacity there is for cognitive understanding. At this level, however, pentecostals should be among the first to affirm the power of the Spirit-inspired touch to affect lives, to bring people together who may otherwise never relate to one another, and to mediate the presence and activity of God. Yes, the profoundly disabled will never be able to experience *koinonia*, the liturgy, or the call of God in the same way as others. However, this does not mean that they are excluded from the fellowship and communion of the Spirit. It just means that the church needs to be sensitive to the workings of embodied and affective reason, and to nurture the capacities of each of its members—"strong" and "weak" according to their own particular needs—to utilize these modes

---

47. Here I am thinking of that icon of disability, Helen Keller, who was blind, deaf, and mute, but yet was nurtured toward a full life, as well as an engaged spirituality. While disability studies has produced a growing amount of literature on Keller—e.g. Nielsen, "Helen Keller and the Politics of Civic Fitness"—to my knowledge, no scholarly study of Keller's faith has yet been done. For a selection of her religious writings, with some commentary, see Belck, ed., *The Faith of Helen Keller*.

48. The centrality of the body and the affections to human reason is increasingly being recognized by many philosophers—e.g., Damasio, *Descartes' Error*; Wainwright, *Reason and the Heart*; and Lakoff and Johnson, *Philosophy in the Flesh*. While I agree with the general claim that cognitive reason is informed by and assumes embodiment and the affections, I would go further to insist, in the light of our understanding of profound disability, that embodied and affective reason is operative even when no evidence for cognitive reason exists (cf. Yong, *Theology and Down Syndrome*, esp. 207-15).

49. An electronic search of the digitized archives at the Flower Pentecostal Heritage Center of the Assemblies of God reveals only two hits for the word "retarded" as compared with 167 for the word "deaf" and 123 for the word "blind"; see the search engine at http://ifphc.org/ (thanks to Regent University librarian Robert Sivigny for pointing me to this database).

50. See World Health Organization and Joint Commission on International Aspects of Mental Retardation, *Mental Retardation*.

of interaction more intentionally and effectively.[51] Here I am referring not only to the accessibility of our congregational events, whether understood in terms of physical and topological (i.e., are there ramps or elevators), sensory (i.e., are there interpreters), or rhetorical and discursive (i.e., are we sensitive to using disability rhetoric in our publications and other oral discourses) terms. Rather, each of these aspects of accessibility contributes to the presentation of our churches and faith communities as being hospitable to, welcoming for, and seeking to be inclusive of people with disabilities.[52] Hence, the goal cannot be just to minister to such people as objects of care, concern, or charity—although such ministry is precisely what is needed in many cases—but full inclusion of them and reception of their contributions resulting in the enrichment of our own lives.[53] In many respects, this requires our own conversion so that our eyes can truly see, our ears can really hear, and our other senses can be fully activated to receive and be transformed by what such people have to offer.[54]

Pentecostal Contributions to Theology of Disability and Disability Studies?

In the preceding, I have explained why there has not been much interaction previously between pentecostal studies and disabilities, identified some resources from within the pentecostal theological tradition and pentecostal spirituality and piety for rethinking disability, and elaborated on a multi-sensory epistemology and holistic spirituality (utilizing a hermeneutic informed by disability studies) in the service of a pneumatological and pentecostal theology of disability. In this concluding section, I would like to highlight what a pentecostal theology of disability can contribute both to the wider theological discussion and to the discipline of disability studies.

First, a pneumatological and pentecostal theology of disability, informed by the preceding reflections, points the way forward toward a

51. Leading the way in this regard is the vision and ministry of L'Arche; see Vanier, *An Ark for the Poor*, and Young, ed., *Encounter with Mystery*.

52. I provide a sketch of the practices involved in such an ecclesiology of hospitality in my *Theology and Down Syndrome*, ch. 7.

53. Thus the argument of Hans Reinders that we might even receive the gift of friendship from people with profound disabilities! See Reinders *Receiving the Gift of Friendship*.

54. That Luke is interested not only in the conversion of Jews and Gentiles to Christ but also in the conversion of Christ-followers is evident in the Cornelius episode where Peter's conversion is as if not more important than Cornelius's in their mutual encounter. For discussion, see Newbigin, *The Open Secret*, esp. 59–62.

renewed vision of the church as a charismatic fellowship of the Spirit, one that is inclusive of people with disabilities.[55] Such a pneumatological ecclesiology will appreciate all members of the body equally, because each one "speaks" in his or her own voice (whether or not he or she has the charismatic gift of tongues!) and fulfills his or her own role, as empowered by the Spirit. Thus there will be no segregation in the fellowship of the Spirit since the mentality of "us" versus "them" or "able bodied" and "disabled" will have been overcome. At the same time, there is also no totalitarian homogeneity that ignores the distinctiveness and particularity represented by each member, both in terms of what he or she has to contribute as well as what he or she may need.[56] On the Day of Pentecost, the many voices were recognized, each in its own language. Similarly, a pneumatological and pentecostal ecclesiology that is hospitable toward all people, including those with disabilities, will be sensitive to the particular needs of each one, as well as receptive to the gifts that each brings. In this way, as the Apostle Paul indicated, "the members of the body that seem to be weaker are indispensable. . . . God has so arranged the body, giving the greater honour to the inferior member, that there may be no dissension within the body, but the members may have the same care for one another. If one member suffers, all suffer together with it; if one member is honoured, all rejoice together with it" (1 Cor 12:22, 24–26, NRSV).[57]

With regard to the pentecostal contribution to disability studies, it should be clear from the preceding that such will come obliquely rather than directly. Pentecostalism is a religious movement, rather than a social services agency or political organization. It is true that pentecostal churches and members of pentecostal churches are socially engaged and that the stereotypes regarding an apolitical pentecostalism are increasingly recognized

---

55. Here I am extending the notion, developed by my colleague Veli-Matti Kärkkäinen, of the church as a charismatic fellowship of the Spirit; see Kärkkäinen, *Toward a Pneumatological Theology*, part II; cf. my *Spirit Poured Out on All Flesh*, ch. 3, and *Theology and Down Syndrome*, ch. 7.

56. This emphasis on difference and yet on overcoming marginalization and oppression is at the center of disability studies; see, e.g., Gadacz, *Re-thinking Dis-ability*; Mitchell and Snyder, eds., *The Body and Physical Difference*; Rogers and Swadener, eds., *Semiotics and Dis/ability*; and Michalko, *The Difference that Disability Makes*.

57. Note, however, that Paul's use of the language of "inferior members" (literally, "weak" or "lacking members," from the Greek ὑστερουμένῳ) is not one that should be understood as devaluing the lives of people with disabilities; in fact, it is precisely the Apostle's point that those which our social conventions would view as inferior are in fact those upon whom God has bestowed the greater honor. For a disability reading of this Pauline metaphor, see Moede, "God's Power and Human Ability."

as wrongheaded.[58] At the same time, pentecostal social and political engagement are more by-products of living out the gospel and being the church empowered by the Holy Spirit than they are first and foremost sociopolitical agendas. Similarly, pentecostal scholarship is, in general, designed to serve pentecostal theological reflection, and in that respect, it seeks not to do the work of disability studies. Yet, insofar as pentecostalism implies and then makes explicit a theological vision, it becomes, like all authentically theological discourses, a meta-discourse that has implications for other disciplines given the Christian convictions regarding the lordship of Christ and the universal work of the Spirit. Hence, in each of these respects, disability service providers, advocates, and scholars looking for pentecostal studies to support the disability agenda on its own terms will continue to be disappointed.

That said, perhaps pentecostal studies can contribute to the cause of disability studies precisely by doing the kind of theological work such as that which has been attempted here so that pentecostal churches and practices can be reordered to embody more concretely the hospitality of God for all people, including those with disabilities.[59] As a subset of religious and theological studies, then, pentecostal studies can contribute to those conversations, perhaps enriching them with insights not so readily available outside the tradition of pentecostal spirituality and piety so that such more general religious and theological discourses can then in turn have an impact on disabilities studies. In addition, perhaps pentecostal scholars may also discover creative ways to retrieve and revitalize the virtues of the biblical and classical Christian traditions so that novel methodological approaches that include, involve, and empower people with disabilities in our congregations, communities, and lives will become regular features of not only pentecostal praxis but also of the wider church. Pentecostal studies can thus inform and transform pentecostal praxis so as to provide further data for the work of disability studies—data that might either further illuminate or even challenge the methods, assumptions, and theories of disability studies.

Is this too much to ask or hope for from the intersection of pentecostal studies and disability studies? As a pentecostal theologian, I think that the many tongues of the Spirit potentially include the many discourses of the modern academic disciplines.[60] Might not the Spirit who empowers many

---

58. See Miller and Yamamori, *Global Pentecostalism*, and Yong, *In the Days of Caesar*.

59. I develop a pneumatological theology of hospitality in my *Hospitality and the Other*, ch. 4; see also Reynolds, *Vulnerable Communion*.

60. See my "Academic Glossolalia?"

tongues also speak through the many languages of the academy, including that of disability studies? Further, might not the Spirit who declares the wondrous works of God in and through the many senses also enable a diversity of gifts from and for people with disabilities so that each member of the fellowship of the Spirit will be edified? If this is indeed possible—and pentecostals should be the first to recognize that "What is impossible for mortals is possible for God" (Luke 18:27)—then so is it possible for God to redeem disability in ways that, in the process, redeems us all, even the world itself.

CHAPTER 5

Sons and Daughters, Young and Old

Toward a Pentecostal Theology of the Family[1]

The emergence of pentecostal theology within the wider academy is a relatively recent phenomenon. This means, in part, that pentecostal theologians are still at the very early stages of thinking theologically about the various academic loci, and that there are therefore many topics about which they have given scant, if any, consideration. Theology of the family is one of those topics. The fact is that Pentecostals, at least in North America, register as being rather conservative in terms of family practices, sexual mores, anti-abortion, anti-homosexuality, and even opposition to birth control.[2] So in some circles, the issue about a pentecostal theology of the family is a closed one: why not just reiterate traditional evangelical or even fundamentalist

---

1. I am grateful to Jan-Ake Alvarsson for the invitation to present this plenary lecture to the European Research Network on Global Pentecostalism, sixth annual conference in Uppsala, Sweden, May 21, 2011. Thanks also to my then graduate assistant, Timothy Lim, and to an anonymous reader for *PentecoStudies* for their comments on an earlier draft of the paper. They are not to be held responsible, however, for any infelicities that remain.

2. See Greeley and Hout, *The Truth about Conservative Christians*, ch. 11. I note here that my claims regarding "Pentecostalism" are informed more by my own North American perspective and location than anything else, so readers should keep this in mind. However, given the influence of North American Pentecostalism in the global South, and even given that the partriarchalism of the North American versions find parallel expressions across the various cultures within which Pentecostals in the global South find themselves, many of my generalizations remain applicable in the world pentecostal context. To be sure, exceptions abound, but only a full study, rather than an exploratory article, can tease out the diversity of family issues and perspectives with the global renewal movement.

views on the matter? For others, however, it is precisely this uncritical traditionalism that needs to be interrogated. Yet while there have been a growing number of studies of various aspects of family life in Pentecostalism, none of these have been sustained constructive theological efforts.

This essay intends to initiate theological reflection on the family among Pentecostals. In brief, it asks if there is an explicitly pentecostal set of perspectives on theology of the family and if so, what these might be. The three parts that follow thus are primarily prolegomenal in nature: initially in order to identify possible trajectories of approach, then with regard to pentecostal hermeneutical and scriptural intuitions, and finally to chart lines of inquiry for theological thinking about the family. My goal in what follows will be to invite pentecostal engagement with this topic by teasing out how the central motif of pentecostal spirituality, the outpouring of the Spirit on the Day of Pentecost, might contribute toward the articulation, at least in outline, of a theology of the family that resonates with scholars of the global renewal movement. An emerging thesis, one with possible implications for discussions about theology of the family for Christians in general (beyond the circle of Pentecostalism), is that the family might also be considered as an eschatological sign of the reign of God, in which case, the family in all of its historical configurations remains ambiguous and fragmentary, awaiting the final redemption wrought by Christ in the power of the Spirit.[3]

Theology of the Family: Current Explorations

A wide-ranging discussion of theology of the family can be found across the spectrum, informed by a multitude of disciplinary approaches. To be sure, for Christians as people of the book, biblically oriented explorations are surely in the mix.[4] Not surprising, given the many challenges confronted by families since the dawn of the modern age and particularly now in an increasingly globalizing world, theologians have reflected on the family

---

3. My remarks remain first and foremost at the prolegomenal level because I am not a specialist on the family; yes, I am a husband and father, but this gives me experiential perspective, rather than scholarly understanding. With regard to the latter there is a growing amount of literature that I have not been able to engage, so my comments remain horribly uninformed by the ongoing debates in theology of the family. Still, I hope that my considerations from a distinctively pentecostal vantage point will not only precipitate conversation among pentecostals but perhaps bring in a fresh voice that can potentially advance the discussion a step forward.

4. A more evangelically informed approach is Hess and Carroll R., eds., *Family in the Bible*, while a more history-of-religion set of discussions can be found in van Henten and Brenner, eds., *Families and Family Relations*.

with practical questions and concerns as well, which explains in part why theological and social ethicists have entered into the discussion alongside practical and applied theologians.[5] Last but not least, there have been also more "confessional" proposals authored by scholars and theologians situated within and drawing from specific Christian traditions for thinking about the family.[6] The emergence of such more explicitly confessional approaches invites pentecostal scholars and theologians also to reflect on what, if anything, they have to contribute to thinking about theology of the family.

Within Pentecostalism in general and pentecostal scholarship as a whole, there has been neither sustained studies of the family nor, as already indicated, explicitly theological reflection on the topic. This is not to say that there has been a complete absence of research on the family in Pentecostalism. However, much of this has been conducted by anthropologists and others working in the social sciences and humanities, and even some of what is available are tangential rather than focused explorations. For example, fitting the latter description is the work of Pacific Lutheran University anthropologist Elizabeth Brusco.[7] Yet her project is actually focused on gender issues in Colombian evangelicalism (or Pentecostalism, a practically synonymous term in the Latin American context), rather than on the family, more broadly considered. We surely learn much about the dynamics of pentecostal conversion and their implications for Latin American families in Brusco's study—i.e., about how women are empowered, how men are transformed so as to take responsibility for their families, and how pentecostal families are set on trajectories of upward social, economic, and ecclesial mobility, among other developments—but in the end, these anthropological insights in the nature of pentecostal families are in effect incidental to other concerns that animate the research.[8]

There are other smaller-scale research projects that have shed light on pentecostal family structures, configurations, and practices. An early

---

5. The former includes Post, *More Lasting Unions*. The latter feature two field establishing volumes in 2007: Browning, *Equality and the Family*, and Thatcher, *Theology and Families*.

6. Reformed proposals include those by Stackhouse, *Covenant and Commitments*, and Deddo, *Karl Barth's Theology of Relations*, while Roman Catholic offerings include Rubio, *A Christian Theology of Marriage and Family*; McCarthy, *Sex and Love in the Home*; and Ouellet, *Divine Likeness*. It is not surprising that the latter have been more energetic about this topic given the official Catholic position about the procreational purposes of human sexuality.

7. Brusco, *The Reformation of Machismo*.

8. In another study, Brusco, "The Peace that Passes All Understanding," focuses on the issue of violence within the Colombian evangelical and pentecostal family.

study of the Catholic charismatic movement in the late 1970s by Mary Jo Neitz, a sociologist, focused on the pro-family ideology prevalent within the renewal and compared and contrasted this view among the masses with the more pro-life ideology of the Catholic hierarchy.[9] Neitz has not, to my knowledge, retained her attention on the family in pentecostal or charismatic movements, although she has continued to work around the topic over the years, especially in her studies of gender, women's roles, and motherhood.[10] More recently, Maria das Dores Campos Machado, a sociologist at the Universidade Federal do Rio de Janeiro, compared responses within pentecostal and Catholic charismatic communities in Brazil to perennial familial structures challenges—i.e., unfaithfulness, single motherhood, or homosexuality—with the former tending to spiritualize (even demonize) the issues much more so than the latter.[11] Both cases, of course, are prime examples of sociological analyses of families in Pentecostalism, and they should be taken into consideration in any interdisciplinary treatment of the topic.

More social scientific analyses, however, have also uncovered that many pentecostal churches are modeled after what they consider the New Testament to say about first-century households as congregating centers for the earliest followers of Jesus. In these "home church" scenarios, the lines between families and churches are blurred: husbands are likened to priests of the home, and the family is structured like a church. For instance, the pentecostal Russian Church of Christians of the Evangelical Faith has as part of its 2002 statement of faith an article titled "The Home Church," which reads:

> We believe that the blessing and well-being of the church to a great extent depends on the holy institution of the home church, which consists of the members of the family. The duty of the home church includes the parents' holy and exemplary life before God, their children and the surrounding world. Parents must raise their children in the word of truth, together they must pray, sing spiritual songs, and read the Holy Scriptures. Together with their children they must attend the Divine service.[12]

9. Neitz, "Family, State, and God."

10. This area of women and Pentecostalism has also been the focus of other studies, the most prominent being Lawless, *God's Peculiar People*, Toulis, *Believing Identity*, Alexander, *The Women of Azusa Street*, and Soothill, *Gender, Social Change and Spiritual Power*.

11. Machado, "Family, Sexuality, and Family Planning."

12. This article is quoted in Löfstedt, "Gender Roles among Russian and Belarusian Pentecostals," and derives from an earlier version of the church's statement of faith.

These developments should not be surprising if we keep in mind that pentecostal churches are growing in developing regions of the world experiencing high social mobility, and in these contexts, migrating families have left "home" and thus find new "family" support networks, particularly among others of pentecostal faith.[13] Yet the emergence of these forms of pentecostal families/churches beg for more explicit theological reflection and elucidation.

One of the first and perhaps still only theological assessments remains a short essay written by then Associate Professor of Christian Education and Theology at the Seminario Sudamericano in Ecuador, Virginia Trevino Nolivos.[14] Nolivos here undertakes, in a very preliminary way, the task of developing a pentecostal theology of the family. Deeply informed by the work of what is now the Centre for Pentecostal Theology affiliated with the Pentecostal Theological Seminary in Cleveland, Tennessee (affiliated with the pentecostal Church of God denomination), Nolivos approaches her topic utilizing the framework of the pentecostal "five-fold gospel" of Jesus as savior, sanctifier, Spirit-baptizer, healer, and coming king.[15] What emerges are initial reflections about how these commitments and sensibilities can help shape pentecostal understandings of the family. The emphasis here is on the redemptive or ideal aspects of the family as envisioned in the saving, sanctifying, healing, and eschatological work of Christ in the power of the Holy Spirit. Thus does Nolivos present her ideas as a transformational proposal or paradigm.

The following discussion builds on Nolivos's suggestions, particularly in light of her eschatological vision. As someone committed to interdisciplinary research, I would surely want to draw from and even highlight the empirical and social scientific research that has been done on the family in pentecostal movements, churches, and communities. Yet as a systematician, I would also insist that any theological proposal will need at some point to interpret the data across the spectrum of the sciences in theological

---

I am grateful to Prof. Löfstedt for sharing an electronic version of his paper with me.

13. At least two other papers presented at the GloPent Conference also discussed pentecostal churches which structured themselves according to the New Testament model of the family—viz., Karagiannis, "More than a Metaphor," and Frei, "The Pentecostal Church as a Family."

14. See Nolivos, "A Pentecostal Paradigm for the Latin American Family." Nolivos, "Pentecostalism's Theological Reconstruction of the Identity of the Latin American Family," is more social-scientifically and historically oriented than theological, although many of the same insights as from her earlier articles reappear.

15. This theological framework revolving around the "fivefold gospel" also structures my reflections on public theology: *In the Days of Caesar*.

terms. In other words, there ought to be a specifically theological framework of interpretation that enables us to make sense of the disparate data presented through historical and social-scientific research. My own work has presumed what I have called a pneumatological starting point, related to the experiences of the Spirit embedded within pentecostal spirituality.[16] My claim is that such a pneumatological approach to pentecostal theology dovetails nicely with Nolivos's intuitions regarding the eschatological nature of the family and the need for a transformational paradigm of understanding that can help us work toward a normative and redemptive theology of the family.

For my theological starting point, however, I turn to the New Testament book of Acts. As members of a restorationist movement, many pentecostals read this Lukan account of the lives of the earliest followers of Jesus as providing a template for Christian life as a whole. In the past, the Acts narrative has been understood not merely as providing a history of the incidental truths of the apostolic ministry but as having normative import for the Spirit-filled life and for both theological self-understanding and doctrinal self-definition. Why then should pentecostal theologians not return to this same account for resources to deal with issues across the theological spectrum? This is not to confine pentecostal theology to Acts or even to the two volumes of Luke-Acts; but it is to say that the pentecostal canon within the canon has served and can continue to function as a springboard for constructive theological reflection among pentecostal scholars, even if the topic were theology of the family.

The Spirit Poured Out on All Flesh: The Eschatological Family

Pentecostalism derives its name from the Day of Pentecost narrative about the outpouring of the Spirit in Acts 2. In response to the crowd's amazement and perplexity about what they were seeing and hearing (Acts 2:12–13), Peter responded, quoting also from the book of Joel:

> In the last days it will be, God declares,
> that I will pour out my Spirit upon all flesh,
>   and your sons and your daughters shall prophesy,
> and your young men shall see visions,
>   and your old men shall dream dreams.
> Even upon my slaves, both men and women,

---

16. See my book *Spirit-Word-Community*, wherein the details of this methodology is articulated, and then my *The Spirit Poured Out on All Flesh*, wherein the methodology is exemplified.

> in those days I will pour out my Spirit;
> and they shall prophesy . . .
> Then everyone who calls on the name of the Lord shall
> be saved (2:17–18, 21).

I would like to invite reflection on this kerygmatic retrieval of the Hebrew Bible as a springboard to developing what we might call a Lukan, and then by extension pentecostal, theology of the family. Three themes stand out for explicit comment and consideration.

First, note the eschatological self-understanding foregrounded in this appeal to the prophet Joel (2:17). There are multiple levels of possible analysis here, including the original *Sitz im Leben* of Joel's prophecy, the reception and canonical history of Joel, Peter's own retrieval of Joel's text (assuming the historicity, at some level, of the Acts 2 narrative), and Luke's use of this Petrine sermon, among other hermeneutical approaches.[17] My point is that Luke, following Peter (as his source), situates the Day of Pentecost outpouring of the Spirit within an eschatological framework. Yet these "last days" refer not first and foremost to the end of time, but to the days of God's promised redemption, restoration, and renewal of Israel.[18] So Luke is not thinking about, nor should pentecostals focus on, the end of history. Instead, the appearance of the Spirit marks the expansion of God's redemptive age, initially inaugurated in the life, ministry, death, and resurrection of Christ, but now made available by Christ to all through his giving of the same Spirit who empowered his messianic mission.[19] In short, pentecostals have always been right to emphasize the eschatological character of the Spirit's outpouring;[20] yet in developing what might be called their eschatological imagination, they have misjudged the signs of their own times insofar as they have framed the "last days" according to dispensationalist categories rather than attending to Luke's own vision of what these last days mean and how they are to unfold.[21]

---

17. A number of these various levels have already been identified and explored by McQueen, *Joel and the Spirit*.

18. See, for example, Turner, *Power from on High*; compare my *In the Days of Caesar*, ch. 3, 2.2.

19. Here I build on my proposal for understanding pentecostal eschatology on its own or on Lukan terms, rather than according to the categories of futuristic dispensationalism, presented in my *In the Days of Caesar*, ch. 8, esp. 331–32.

20. For example, Land, *Pentecostal Spirituality*, and Faupel, *The Everlasting Gospel*.

21. Here I follow the path blazed by Sheppard, "Pentecostalism and the Hermeneutics of Dispensationalism," which has now been developed in multiple directions in Althouse and Waddell, eds., *Perspectives in Pentecostal Eschatologies*.

So what does this eschatological orientation have to do with thinking about theology of the family? I suggest—and this is my second set of comments—that the prophecy of Joel retrieved by Luke through Peter can help us begin to develop some basic intuitions about these matters. Consider, for example, what might be deemed the egalitarian character of the Spirit of prophecy: both sons and daughters, male and female servants, are empowered by the Spirit. While the Lukan witness to the role of women as equivalent with that of men is certainly incommensurate with contemporary notions of egalitarianism, it is also undeniable that women play a much more prominent role in the Third Gospel, not to mention the Acts narrative as well, than elsewhere in the New Testament writings, and that these images anticipate if not resource contemporary egalitarian visions.[22] Further, while there is no slighting of elders, who continue to dream dreams, there is also no recognition that age, and the sageliness that comes with that, is a privileged medium for revelatory insights of the Spirit. Instead youth, or young men, are not inhibited from seeing visions, even in tandem with the elders of the community. Last but not least is the suggestiveness in this passage for the extended family. As is well-known, ancient Israelite, Second Temple, and early Christian households—note that the New Testament uses the term *oikos* (household) instead of the Latin *familia* (family)—included servants (as in the case of Philemon). Yet the Christian message of Christ and his followers as servants of the living God introduced a new dynamic that began to unravel traditional master-slave relations.[23] In the eschatological perspective of Luke, servants are no less worthy as vessels of the Spirit or as conduits for the Spirit's prophetic witness.

Now we need to tread carefully here. It would be both anachronistic and exegetically irresponsible to say that Luke's retrieval of Joel constitutes his own theology of the family. In fact, as we shall see more clearly in the next section, Jesus himself called younger disciples, some who might have been young heads of households, into an itinerant ministry that was probably not conducive to the kinds of family structures desired at least by some

---

22. This is not to say that pentecostal scholars have automatically gravitated toward a feminist hermeneutical perspective. In fact, while there is more to work with in the Lukan texts toward a feminist reading, feminist scholarship has also illuminated that patriarchal assumptions still reign in Luke's two volumes and so a hermeneutics of suspicion nevertheless should be engaged. Still, we await a feminist pentecostal reading of Luke-Acts, and this would also be especially important with regard to thinking about a Lukan theology of the family such as the one that is being outlined here. For preliminary considerations of women in Luke-Acts, see my *Who Is the Holy Spirit*, chs. 29–30.

23. See Klein, "A Liberated Lifestyle."

in the contemporary world, even as he also expected that itinerant discipleship relied to some degree on an older generation of established heads of households (older fathers) to provide hospitality without reciprocity or other forms of social compensation.[24] In other words, Luke's portrait of Jesus' life and ministry itself operated according to an eschatological model that would have challenged also the social status quo in the first-century Mediterranean world. Hence we ought to understand the Day of Pentecost narrative not just eschatologically but also ecclesiologically. The upshot of God's redemptive visitation of Israel in these last days is to renew and restore the exiled, oppressed, and dispossessed people of God. What emerges on the other side of the Spirit's outpouring upon all flesh is the reconstituted people of YHWH, the church. But the key here is that God's renewal of Israel and establishment of the body of Christ and the fellowship of the Spirit is envisioned in familial—not to mention familiar—terms: the church is constituted as a new set of social relationships in which males and females play similar roles, in which the elders and the youth of the community are joined together in leadership and common cause, and in which the free and the slave—core and extended members of the household or the community, in short—are all recipients of the Spirit's gift and empowerment.[25]

This leads to my third set of observations: that this pneumatological, eschatological, and ecclesiological vision of the people of God is also finally soteriological: "Then everyone who calls on the name of the Lord shall be saved" (Acts 2:21).[26] When does this happen? ". . . before the coming of the Lord's great and glorious day" (2:20b), which is the day of the reign of God itself. This eschatological redemption and renewal of Israel is part of God's grand soteriological design, except that the earliest followers of the Messiah never anticipated that this restoration would involve the gathering and grafting (to use one of St. Paul's metaphors) of the Gentiles as well, through the outpouring of the Holy Spirit. Thus all the peoples of the earth would finally partake of the promises made to Abraham (3:25). Thus also

---

24. See Destro and Pesce, "Fathers and Householders in the Jesus Movement."

25. Here the lines between ecclesiological and familial discourse begin to blur, particularly as ecumenical conversation proceeds to take up the doctrine of the church utilizing models derived from family life; on this development in Roman Catholic ecclesiology, see, for example, Shorter et al., *Theology of the Church as Family of God*, and Ryan, ed., *The Model of "Church-as-Family."*

26. Waters, *The Family in Christian Social and Political Thought*, ch. 7, also suggests that the church witnesses to the eschatological nature of the family even as the family witnesses to the providential sustenance of the church; yet Waters' eschatological framework is driven more by the doctrine of the resurrection and Christology compared to my more pneumatological emphases.

does Luke record, at the conclusion of Peter's Day of Pentecost sermon, that the forgiveness of sins and gift of the Holy Spirit is available to all: "For the promise is for you, for your children, and for all who are far away, everyone whom the Lord our God calls to him" (2:39).

Here again we have a familial reference. Not only is there is no reason to exclude biological children from this promise, but the biological aspect appears explicit, alongside others, even "all who are far away" (geographically, chronologically, and otherwise). Thus, the eschatological work of the Spirit and its attendant salvific benefits are meant for biological families within the reconstituted people or household of God, even as families are invited to nurture their children to live into this promise associated with God's redemptive plan.[27] Later on in the apostolic narrative, Luke confirms the ongoing unfolding of this promise in the lives of the household of the Philippian jailer who cared for Paul, Silas, and other prisoners: "At the same hour of the night he took them and washed their wounds; then he and his entire family [including non-blood related household members if there were any] were baptized without delay" (16:33).[28]

Thinking about a Lukan theology of the family in light of the Day of Pentecost outpouring of the Spirit, then, invites consideration of the household—first of God, and then of human families—in eschatological perspective. Here I wish to push pentecostal intuitions about the church as household or family, which we introduced in the first section (above), in a more explicitly theological, viz., soteriological and eschatological, direction. Such households are precisely what the Spirit of God is forming and constituting in these last days, both in order to renew and revitalize the fallen world and to save through the forgiveness of sins and the gift of the Spirit. The prophecy of Joel thus provides a template for the eschatological and Spirit-filled household. Pentecostals have now begun to give some consideration to the nature of the church (ecclesiology) as a community of the Spirit;[29] might it also be possible to extrapolate from this discussion the beginnings of a pentecostal theology of the family?

---

27. See Davis, "Perpetuating Pentecost through the Family." This volume is one of the few "manuals" for pentecostal family raising that includes—certainly in some chapters more than others—some theological reflection.

28. Some charismatic Christians from mainline Protestant, Catholic, or Orthodox churches might see in this reference justification for infant baptism; my proposals in this paper do not turn on any dogmatic stance regarding this matter. Pentecostally, in any case, baptismal efficacy is pneumatological rather than liturgical, as I argue in my *The Spirit Poured Out on All Flesh*, 156–60.

29. For example, Kärkkäinen, *Toward a Pneumatological Theology*, and Kärkkäinen, *An Introduction to Ecclesiology*, 72–74.

"Children of the Promise": Lukan Intimations for Theology of the Family

For preliminary considerations of this task, I consider moving backward from the early apostolic experience to the portrayal of the Christ in which steps they hoped to follow. Luke's Gospel actually includes a number of references to household members that have deeply informed pentecostal beliefs and practices. Engaging with the Third Evangelist on these matters will enable us to accomplish at least three related purposes. First, it will help us to further navigate the hermeneutical circle by rereading the Day of Pentecost account in light of the life of Christ, which preceded in historical and even chronological terms in the order of Luke's writings; in this way, we can see how the early Christian experience as the household of faith may or may not have implemented or even extended Jesus' teachings about the family.[30] Second, as shall be seen, there are a number of "hard sayings" of Jesus regarding the family that have been internalized in pentecostal piety; engaging with Luke on this matter will provide an opportunity for Pentecostal scholars to interrogate critically not only their own beliefs and practices but also their hermeneutical sensibilities. Finally, of course, as the Bible does not provide any systematic presentation of theology of the family, any attempts to sketch the contours of a pentecostal view on such matters will need to proceed ad hoc; my own approach is thus to mine especially the teachings of Jesus in order to outline a framework for thinking theologically about the family in light of the eschatological and pentecostal outpouring of the Spirit on all flesh.

Inklings about the family in the life of Christ leap off Peter's invocation (as recorded in Acts) to the crowd about the promise being for their children and others. This refers, of course, to the assurance of the forgiveness of sins and of the gift of the Spirit. More precisely, this is the guarantee of God the Father, originally and vaguely made to the ancestors (in particular to Abraham) of Israel (Luke 1:55 and 72), explicitly connected to the Spirit by Jesus at the conclusion of his teaching the disciples to pray (11:13), and then referenced again just before his ascension (24:49). Luke reiterates this aspect of Jesus' final instructions at the beginning of his second volume: "While staying with them, he ordered them not to leave Jerusalem, but to wait there for the promise of the Father" (Acts 1:4). This promise of the Spirit has been a perennial theme in early pentecostal history. Originally a

---

30. See also the introduction to my *Who Is the Holy Spirit*, where I explain more about this strategy of reading Luke's account of Jesus from the standpoint of the apostolic and early Christian experience.

legacy of the American Holiness movement,[31] which was a central part of the ferment for the emergence of Pentecostalism at the turn of the twentieth century, the promise of the Father was believed to have found further fulfillment in the last days as part of the latter rain outpouring of the Spirit at the Topeka, Kansas and Azusa Street revivals.[32] Pentecostal historiography and theology, then, has been long informed by the notion of a promising Father.

What does this have to do with a pentecostal theology of the family? My suggestion is that the depiction of the Father's promise assumes both the patriarchal and hierarchical worldview of the ancient Near East. The father represents the primordial source of life (or of all things, in the case of the divine Father) and serves as the family authority figure.[33] The Father's willingness to make promises and then to bring them about presumes his responsibility to oversee the well-being of the family and to provide for its members. Similarly, of course, pentecostal pastors become father figures as well who provide leadership, oversight, and at least spiritual provision for members of their congregation, the household of God. Prayers are thus addressed to the heavenly Father, even as it is also the Father's prerogative to give good gifts to his children (Luke 11:13; 12:32). To be sure, Jesus' own relationship with the Father contrasted with standard expectations for filial relationships of his time,[34] but the problem is that pentecostal readings of the Fatherhood of God is less christologically informed than achieved through unexamined patriarchal assumptions.

In short, pentecostal reception of the promising Father within the various male-dominated societies that shape the global renewal movement have led to a sacralizing of a patriarchal theology of fatherhood. Traditional family values, among other conservative views of the family, are preserved within this scheme of things, even if much of the details of such understandings are developed from out of patriarchal cultural values and practices more than they are from the Bible.[35] Problems then unfold in light of

---

31. Especially in the work of Phoebe Palmer, a Holiness preacher, whose *The Promise of the Father* was a best-seller that influenced Holiness and, later, pentecostal traditions in North America.

32. See Dayton, *Theological Roots of Pentecostalism*, 87–89; cf. Everts and Baird, "Phoebe Palmer and Her Pentecostal Protégées."

33. This is clearly articulated by Jeffrey, "Naming the Father"; I would agree that the Father's authority is clear in the Gospel accounts (not just in Luke) although I wonder sometimes how this authority is to be understood—which is part of the goal of this essay to ponder.

34. See, for example, Mowery, "God the Father in Luke-Acts," and Thompson, *The Promise of the Father*.

35. In North America, pentecostal "family values" are thus more or less Victorian;

the specific challenges such father figures confront in attempting to live up to certain expectations in a post-agrarian, post-industrial, and (for Latin American cultures) machismo world.[36]

I would urge pentecostals (and other Christians) to reconsider the nature of the Father within the eschatological perspective of the pentecostal outpouring of the Spirit (Acts 2). Two alternative trajectories are opened up within such an eschatological reconfiguration. The first suggests that the paternal authority of the Father is either not yet fully revealed or that it has not yet been fully and properly established. Signs of such an eschatological paternalism are registered in the prophecy from Joel and inaugurated in the Pentecost outpouring of the Spirit. This allowance for a more egalitarian conception of father-mother-family relations is then also seen as anticipated in the life of Christ's extended family or household, wherein the authority of Zechariah to name his newborn son after himself is checked by Elizabeth's insistence that he be called John (Luke 1:59-60). Recall that Elizabeth herself anticipates the eschatological outpouring of the Spirit, in her case being filled with the Spirit in meeting with Mary, the *Theotokos* (1:39-41).[37] Such an eschatological theology of fatherhood, then, would be neither hierarchical nor authoritarian vis-à-vis mothers (women); instead it would emphasize the coequality of male and female—and by extension of husbands and wives and of fathers and mothers—in the eschatological household of God.[38]

A second trajectory opened up by re-situating the Lukan doctrine of fatherhood within the eschatological framework of the Day of Pentecost is that the Fatherhood of God is recast in a Trinitarian framework, not that of a Nicene or post-Nicene construct, but that of the salvation or redemption

for details, see Ittmann, *Work, Gender, and Family in Victorian England*, 223-36.

36. O'Neill, *City of God*, ch. 4, describes the issues confronting pentecostal fathers in the Latin American context.

37. Note that Mary's relationship with Elizabeth provides a window into the latter's role as the aunt of Jesus. While there is not much in the Gospel accounts to flesh out Jesus' relationship with his aunts, uncles, and extended family, given the nature of first-century wider Mediterranean and more specifically Palestinian family life—e.g., extended families travelled together to Israel's festivals (Luke 2:44)—there is no doubt that Jesus would have had significant interactions with broader family members. From a theology of the family perspective, I recommend consulting something like Ellingson and Sotirin, *Aunting*, for insights into thinking about the roles of extended families in general and about aunts in particular.

38. Pentecostal women are already making such transitions, rejecting more secular versions of feminism on the one hand but yet seeking equality in the home and in the church through adherence to the biblical injunctions regarding mutual submission and spousal partnership; see Billingsley, *It's a New Day*, esp. ch. 2-3.

history of Luke's narrative. What I mean is that the Fatherhood of God now not only involves, but is in a sense completed by, the economies of the Son and Spirit: "Being therefore exalted at the right hand of God, and having received from the Father the promise of the Holy Spirit, he has poured out this that you both see and hear" (Acts 2:33). According to such a salvation-historical interpretation, then, the Fatherhood of God is not absolute; instead, as Jesus responded to the man who wanted to bury his father before heeding the call to discipleship, "Let the dead bury their own dead; but as for you, go and proclaim the kingdom of God" (Luke 9:60). The point here is not to dishonor the deceased father, but to relativize the father's role within the eschatological horizon of the redemptive work of the Son and the Spirit.[39] This in turn helps us to understand the role of the father in particular and of the family as a whole in eschatological and soteriological perspective.

Having introduced such a relativizing of the father, however, we must now confront a whole host of Lukan texts that are troublesome because they have been used to legitimate traditional theologies of the family and of family values as these have been formed from out of the modern Enlightenment period. I am referring to the various sayings of Jesus that seem to minimize the importance of the family in contrast to personal commitment to the coming reign of God.[40] Representative are the following:

- ". . . they will be divided: father against son and son against father, mother against daughter and daughter against mother, mother-in-law against her daughter-in-law and daughter-in-law against mother-in-law" (Luke 12:53).

- "Whoever comes to me and does not hate father and mother, wife and children, brothers and sisters, yes, and even life itself, cannot be my disciple" (14:26).[41]

---

39. Or as Joel Green puts it, "the presence of dual references to the kingdom of God announces the reorganization of former allegiances, with the result that one may be called upon, in this case, to engage in behavior deemed deviant by normal conventions"; see Green, *The Gospel of Luke*, 408.

40. On the surface, the following might suggest Jesus thought less than positively about his family: "Then his mother and his brothers came to him, but they could not reach him because of the crowd. And he was told, 'Your mother and your brothers are standing outside, wanting to see you.' But he said to them, 'My mother and my brothers are those who hear the word of God and do it'" (8:19-21); yet the Lucan version, in contrast to the Markan parallel (3:20-21) could be said to lift up Jesus' mother and brothers "as model disciples"; see Fitzmyer, *The Gospel according to Luke (I-IX)*, 723. Thanks to Marty Mittelstadt for this reference.

41. To "hate" means not to abhor, detest, or loathe, but to love less in comparison to something else, in this case, to the call of discipleship, so notes Bruce, *The Hard*

- "And he said to them, 'Truly I tell you, there is no one who has left house or wife or brothers or parents or children, for the sake of the kingdom of God'" (18:29).

- "You will be betrayed even by parents and brothers, by relatives and friends; and they will put some of you to death" (21:16).[42]

From within the eschatological horizon of the last days outpouring of the Spirit, these texts bear witness consistently to Jesus' commitment to doing the work of establishing the reign of God to restore, renew, and redeem Israel.[43] From this perspective, there can be no partial allegiances since the oppression of Israel has persisted for far too long and any stragglers will simply perpetuate the wilderness wandering of the people of God. Any fuller discussion of these issues should then also explore the similarities and differences between Luke and the other Gospels in which similar sayings appear in order to tease out a more specifically Lukan theology of the family. Yet from the perspective of needing to craft a contemporary theology of the family, these are hard sayings that exacerbate the tensions and stresses confronted by families in a globalizing and post-traditionalist world. This is particularly the case when pentecostals, like other conservative or fundamentalist Christians, read the scriptural witness fairly literally. The result is often the justification of practices that subordinate care of the family—either those of parents for their children or those of grown up children for their elderly parents—to the larger and, ostensibly, more worthwhile purposes related to the work of the kingdom.[44]

Sayings of Jesus, 120. Yet this mode of alleviating the sting of this "hard saying"—not to mention the others cited, or not, here—should not numb the force of the challenges involved in responding to the call of the reign of God.

42. In an illuminating article, Lambrecht, "The Relatives of Jesus in Mark," suggests that one way to understand the ambiguous nature of Jesus' relationship with his relatives in the Gospel of Mark is against the assumption that the relatives represent the unbelieving readers among Mark's audience. This is open, however, to objections from a number of angles, including the speculative nature both with regard to Mark's intentions and of his audience. I prefer the explanation given by Watson, which I mention in a moment.

43. Clearly articulated in Borgman, *The Way According to Luke*, ch. 12, titled "Relinquish Family and Religion."

44. As Karl Barth rightly puts it—in his discussion of the relationship between parents and children—these sayings of Jesus "are anything but an invitation to engage in all kinds of perverse spiritual adventures"! This advice came too late, of course, for the earliest modern pentecostal missionaries, although it is doubtful that they would have read him then anyway! See Barth, *Church Dogmatics*, vol. III/4, 265.

More extreme forms of neglect are, thankfully, much less prevalent today than in the first few generations of the pentecostal revival when many—according to a broad spectrum of anecdotal evidence—left (some say neglected and others say abandoned) their families in order to pursue what they felt was the call of God to the mission field or to evangelistic work, since the time was short and the days were evil.[45] Yet while this may not occur much if at all in today's climate, nevertheless pentecostals have not thought through the biblical and theological issues related to texts like these such that they have been left in a profoundly ambiguous situation: feeling as if the call of God requires a radical forsaking of the family on the one hand, but yet somehow sensing on the other hand that there is something not quite right with the radical nature of such a divine vocation.

One way to understand the nature of these family-negating sayings is to compare the social milieu of the first century messianic movement with its eschatological orientation. For an eschatological people who understood themselves as the restored and renewed people of God, previous allegiances had been displaced. This new ecclesial context thus served "as a new court of public opinion, displacing the natural family in importance. This new court of public opinion would function as the primary context in which Christians secured honor."[46] The Gospels can thereby be understood as providing for an alternative means of Christians securing honor, a means not measured according to former natural family ties but to new criteria related to "doing the will of God, becoming a servant, becoming 'last,' becoming like a child, taking up the cross—in other words, acting in ways entirely opposed to the reckoning of honor in the wider culture."[47] If this is true, then, the eschatological orientation does not undermine the nature of the family per se, but reconfigures family ties within a soteriological and ecclesial framework.[48]

This leads us, then, to the one passage where Jesus blesses the children brought to him:

45. See for example Wacker, "Living with Signs and Wonders," 429–32, and McGee, *Miracles, Missions, and American Pentecostalism*, 148–49. Blumhofer, "The Role of Women in the Assemblies of God," 13, also notes: "In the movement's earliest phases, William Seymour (pastor of the Azusa Street Mission in Los Angeles) reminded husbands and wives of their responsibilities to one another and to their children. Contemporary conditions seemed to Seymour to render such advice necessary: situations in which one spouse neglected family obligations to follow a 'leading,' leaving a family in economic hardship, were all too common." Thanks to Darrin Rodgers for some of these references.

46. Watson, *Honor among Christians*, 148.

47. Ibid., 149. See also Neyrey, "Honor and Shame," 95–96.

48. This focus on Jesus' attitude toward children is also the strategy deployed by Thatcher, "Beginning Again with Jesus."

> People were bringing even infants to him that he might touch them; and when the disciples saw it, they sternly ordered them not to do it. But Jesus called for them and said, "Let the little children come to me, and do not stop them; for it is to such as these that the kingdom of God belongs. Truly I tell you, whoever does not receive the kingdom of God as a little child will never enter it" (Luke 18:15–17).[49]

This pericope is followed by one in which Jesus interacts with a rich ruler who wants to know how to inherit eternal life; in response, Jesus reaffirms the commandments, including the one about honoring one's parents (18:18–20). Here we see Jesus' actions and teachings as an adult mirror what was enacted in his childhood, when he was cared for by his parents and sought to honor them while going about the work of the kingdom. What Jesus does in this case with children—i.e., receive them, bless them, and locate them at the center of the reign of God—provides a performative speech act through which to interpret his other teachings with references to the family. Whatever else an eschatological and salvation-history perspective entails— and there is much more with regard to the preceding material that we have not discussed, and which will need to considered in any fuller articulation of a Lukan theology of the family—it does not involve the neglect of the most vulnerable in society who are nevertheless harbingers of the very reign of God toward which all of creation is called.

Transitions: Toward a Pentecostal Theology of the Family

The preceding reflections have attempted to proceed from the eschatological imagination at the heart of pentecostal spirituality toward what might be considered as an eschatological notion of the family. One of the consequences of such an eschatological approach is that the family as we know it is still in the process of being fully redeemed and hence remains in significant aspects unformed, even as we can grant that it is also in other respects malformed. Hence human experiences of family life remain fragmented, unstable, and ambiguous, whether instantiated in so-called traditional nuclear forms or in its many variants (single-parent, extended, adopted, legal guardianships, foster families, etc.).[50] In fact, such an eschatological perspective sits in some tension with traditionalist models of the family,

---

49. In the next chapter, I develop also what might be called a pentecostal and pneumatological theology of the child drawing from Lukan resources in particular.

50. For a succinct discussion of the fluid nature of the family across human history, see Browning, *Equality and the Family*, ch. 9.

particularly those informed by conservative evangelical "family values" perspectives that at least some pentecostals have adopted and embraced.

At the same time, this does not mean that anything goes. The life, death, and resurrection of Christ in the power of the Spirit—a deeply Lukan set of motifs that we have not elaborated on here—provide us with general theological norms by which to assess the viability of families in historical life before the eschaton. In this in-between time, we recognize the dynamic nature of families in and amidst various times, places, contexts, and constraints—and this is where empirical studies of the pluralistic and diverse character of families across the global pentecostal landscape are essential— while simultaneously recognizing that the Spirit seeks to renew, restore, and redeem the human family fully and wholly within and as the eschatological household of God.

Still, in the meanwhile, pentecostal theological reflection cannot remain only at this level of eschatological abstraction. In order to reconsider fully the many issues involved, pentecostal theologians will need to reflect more broadly on the scriptural data, building on the pentecostal theology of Luke-Acts sketched in the preceding pages. But there is space left only to make suggestions about what issues need to be taken up more fully in light of the remainder of the New Testament witness in order to develop a pentecostal theology of the family:

- What does it mean to read St. Paul's injunctions to husbands and wives to love one another as Christ has loved and served the church (Eph 5:22–23) in light of the eschatological outpouring of the Spirit to empower all flesh equally, sons and daughters, male and female?[51]

- How might we similarly understand St. Paul's command to fathers— "do not provoke your children to anger, but bring them up in the discipline and instruction of the Lord" (Eph 6:4)—and his (or that of the Pauline "school" of thought's) exemplary citation of mothers like Lois and Eunice (2 Tim 1:5) in the eschatological perspective of the Spirit's empowering equally the younger and the elder in the household of God?[52]

---

51. As Keener, *Paul, Women and Wives*, ch. 5, decisively argued, the Ephesians 5 passage requires "mutual submission" when we read 5:22–23 in light of 5:21; thanks to Marty Mittelstadt for this reminder.

52. Church mothers in African American pentecostal denominations and traditions may embody this eschatological motherhood in palpable ways which in turn mediate the experience of motherhood in the home as well as relationships with fathers; see, for e.g., Butler, *Women in the Church of God in Christ*, ch. 1, Trulear, "Ida B. Robinson," and Hardy, "Church Mothers and Pentecostals in the Modern Age."

- What about St. Paul's admonishment, "Children, obey your parents in the Lord, for this is right. 'Honour your father and mother'—this is the first commandment with a promise: 'so that it may be well with you and you may live long on the earth'" (Eph 6:1–3)? How might we understand this as an eschatological expression of family life within the coming reign and household of God?

- How else might the early Christian experience of filial love—of brothers and sisters of (the body of) Christ through (the fellowship and power of) the eschatological Spirit under the fatherhood of God—provide a template for filial relationships between biological family members in anticipation of the coming reign of God?[53]

- How might we reconsider intergenerational and extended family relations in light of the formation of the household of God as an eschatological community of equality and mutual sharing (Acts 2:42–47, 4:32–37, and 6:1–7)?

- Last but not least, does the eschatological baptism of the Ethiopian eunuch—of whom it was said that he resonated with the Isaianic Scripture which told of the suffering servant's descendent-less future (cf. Acts 8:32–33 and Isa 53:7–8)—have anything to say about how to understand the issue of homosexuality in general or its implications for theology of the family in particular?[54]

I am certainly not insisting that the preceding set of trajectories is the only or even the best way forward for pentecostal theological reflection on the family.[55] I am merely suggesting that insofar as pentecostals have perennially begun their theological reflections from a consideration of the apostolic experience, there is no good reason why we should not also turn there, at some point if not at the beginning, for thinking about the family.

---

53. The analogy here would be to move from the doctrine of the church (ecclesiology) to theology of the family (of filial love); I provide some orientation along these lines in my *Spirit of Love*.

54. For further discussion of the Ethiopian eunuch, although not one that presses the issues of theology of family or theology of sexuality, see my *Who Is the Holy Spirit*, ch. 19. An illuminating ethnography of lesbian, gay, bisexual & transgender communities (LGBT) with many congregations that also identify with the charismatic movement is Wilcox, *Coming Out in Christianity*.

55. Another route worth exploring toward an eschatological theology of the family is the Corinthian letters, through which we have clear indications of the issues that confronted what we know to have been one of the most charismatic "households" of the early Christian communities; I thank Mark Cartledge for pointing out this connection.

If we do so, I propose that a more dynamic and eschatological perspective on the family opens up, one that provides us with fresh angles on neglected or contested aspect of contemporary family life and realities. These provide, at least at this rudimentary stage, not so much clear-cut templates for the formation of contemporary families, but they invite people of the Spirit to attempt to live in and after the Spirit and to discern perspicuously the ways of Christ in the power of the Spirit in order to live more faithfully in light of the eschatological and redemptive work of God, which we now only dimly foresee. Perhaps along the way, pentecostal perspectives might help not just forge greater understanding for pentecostal communities and churches but also advance broader discussions that will remain urgent in the foreseeable future of this globalizing world.

CHAPTER 6

Children and the Promise of the Spirit

Pneumatology and the Quest for Child Theology[1]

The following seeks to make a contribution to pneumatological theology from a pentecostal perspective as informed by developments in theology of children.[2] As a pentecostal theologian, I am sensitive to the global expansion of pentecostal, charismatic, and related movements and to the diversity of its expressions.[3] Global Pentecostalism is a very diverse phenomenon, one irreducible to any one definition. Central to the name of the movement, however, is the Day of Pentecost narrative (Acts 2), which includes an explanation of what was happening in terms of the outpouring of the Holy Spirit upon all peoples. Pentecostal theology has traditionally focused on developing the doctrine of the baptism in the Holy Spirit or on a theology of the spiritual gifts (*charismata*), both of which are central to the vibrancy of pentecostal spirituality. More recently, however, pentecostal theologians have been thinking creatively and constructively from out of the pentecostal experience and reconsidering traditional, classical, and ecumenical theological themes and even doctrines.[4] These reflections have been important

---

1. I am grateful to Marcia Bunge for the invitation to present this paper at the "Child Theologies: Perspectives from World Christianity" consultation that met at Valparaiso University in August 2011, and to attendees there for their feedback. Thanks also to Frederick Longino (Leeds University) and my then graduate assistant, Timothy Lim (now PhD), for their helpful comments on an earlier draft of this essay.

2. For further discussion of the diversity of Pentecostalisms and the problem of nomenclature, see my *The Spirit Poured Out on All Flesh*, 18–22.

3. See, e.g., Hollenweger, *Pentecostalism*; Jenkins, *The Next Christendom*; and Anderson, *An Introduction to Pentecostalism*.

4. E.g., Macchia, *Baptized in the Spirit* and *Justified in the Spirit*.

not only for pentecostal churches and self-understanding but also for the catholic and ecumenical church, in large part because some of the most vigorous growth of Christianity in the global South has been of the pentecostal and charismatic type.

My own work in pentecostal theology, then, has been intentionally global in orientation and thoroughly pneumatological both materially with regard to the doctrine of Spirit (pneumatology) and methodologically in terms of doing theology from the standpoint of the experience of the Spirit.[5] Historically, pneumatology has been one of the classical theological loci and even then, the Spirit has been traditionally the neglected topic of theology, even to the point of being known as the "shy" or "hidden" member of the Trinity.[6] In the last half of the twentieth century, there has been a renaissance of Trinitarian theology and, along with that, a resurgence of pneumatology as well. The latter has brought with it developments not just on the doctrine of the Spirit but also a pneumatological revision of the traditional theological or doctrinal loci.[7] What is being explored is not only an understanding of the person and work of the Spirit but also a consideration of how starting with the Spirit might lead to a rethinking of other theological or even dogmatic themes as well.[8] It is also increasingly clear that the doctrine of the Spirit is concerned not with ethereal, spiritual, or otherworldly dimensions of Christian faith, but is eminently connected with the embodied, social, and environmental nature of human life in this world.[9]

These developments in pneumatology hold forth promise for thinking about theology of children and vice-versa. In the past, what had been important was to identify how the Holy Spirit might touch or form children; the task was preeminently that of applied theology. Our present undertaking, however, focuses on child theology, a path of inquiry committed to the systematic reconsideration of the beliefs and practices of the church especially in light of theologies of children and involving the commitment to seeing children as being essential to rather than at the periphery of the theological enterprise.[10] This chapter is thereby a reflection on theology in

---

5. Starting with my PhD dissertation, published as *Discerning the Spirit(s)*, and developed since in many other books, some of which are cited below.

6. E.g., Hordern and Bruner, *The Holy Spirit*.

7. E.g., Pinnock, *Flame of Love*.

8. As suggested by Dabney, "Otherwise Engaged in the Spirit."

9. E.g., Rogers Jr., *After the Spirit*.

10. Note that "child theology" understood in this manner is still in its very preliminary phases, building on but extending contemporary theologies of children. See, e.g., Berryman, *Children and the Theologians*, esp. ch. 7, for an overview of the current ferment, although the entire volume is a beautiful history of theology of children. An

general and pneumatology in particular informed by the child or children as a category of analysis. It is motivated not only by the realization that children have their own theological voice, but also by our increased solidarity with children, our sensitivity to children's perspectives and concerns, and our awareness that the child or children is more at the center than at the margins of the biblical narrative. Thus, the question here is twofold: how can a pneumatological theology illuminate a theology of children and how can such an interface in turn contribute to the task of child theology?

The three sections of this essay provide some methodological orientation to pentecostal and pneumatological theologies of children, resource the exploration through a retrieval of references to and narratives about children in Luke-Acts read through this hermeneutical lens, and sketch some practical and theological implications of this programmatic exercise of doing theology in the light of children. My thesis is that the particular insights generated by the constellation of themes and approaches I am suggesting invites what might be called a pneumato-eschatological theology that understands children as embodying the principles and values of the coming reign of God.[11] This exploration is thus motivated by my pentecostal perspective, although it is equally informed by developments in pneumatology and the child theology enterprise.

Our overarching goal is to contribute to pentecostal and pneumatological theologies, but specifically in dialogue with theologies of children. If successful, this chapter will feature two main theoretical achievements: on the one hand, pentecostal and pneumatological approaches might provide further insights into child theology, and on the other hand, attention to the experiences, perspectives, and realities of children will enrich and transform pentecostal and pneumatological theologies. At a practical level, our success should also translate into a more inclusive ecclesial environment *for* children (the church as a fellowship of the Spirit), an empowered ministry *with* children (the people of God as inspired by the Spirit to bear witness), and a world that is more hospitable *to* children (the cosmos as the dwelling place of the Spirit).

---

article length introduction to the whole child theological enterprise is Bunge, "Theologies of Childhood and Child Theologies."

11. There are obviously non-pentecostal pneumatological theologies, and these applied to the task of child theology would undoubtedly highlight different emphases. In this essay, I use "reign of God" instead of "kingdom" language primarily because I wish to avoid the patriarchal and kyriarchical connotations of the latter.

Pentecostalism, Pneumatology, and Theology of Children: Whence and Whither?

Pentecostal scholars and theologians have only rather recently arrived at the academic roundtable.[12] As such, pentecostal contributions to theological conversations across the board are still at a preliminary stage. Take any theological topic, and there is in all probably a dearth, if not absence, of pentecostal reflection. This is no different in the developing discussions in child theology, particularly since this theme and undertaking itself is of even more recent provenance.

Yet, of course, Pentecostals have had children, raised them, and these youngsters become adults in turn. So it is not as if Pentecostals lack perspective on children—we have all been one at some point or other in our lives, some of us acting as such longer than others, probably! In the extant literature, of course, children have been an explicit part of the pentecostal experience from the beginning. At the Azusa Street revival, for example, there were testimonies of miraculous healings involving children.[13] In addition, typical of many evangelical and conservative Protestant movements of the first part of the twentieth century, pentecostal evangelism and missionary ventures have always been concerned about the plight and welfare of children, often establishing orphanages for their care and in order to raise and form them within a distinctively pentecostal ethos.[14] Children have always thus participated in pentecostal revivals, church services, and other religious activities—i.e., there were "child evangelists" from the very beginning of the Azusa Street mission[15]—and they have always been expected to manifest in their personal lives the unique elements of pentecostal spirituality. Not surprisingly, then, it has been an ongoing pastoral question about how to nurture children so that they may be open to and actively embrace these pentecostal expressions, including the all-important experience of receiving the baptism of the Holy Spirit subsequent to Christian initiation.[16]

---

12. The inaugural volumes were Dayton, *Theological Roots of Pentecostalism*, and Land, *Pentecostal Spirituality*. See also my "Pentecostalism and the Theological Academy."

13. Welchel, Morris, and McCowan, *Azusa Street*.

14. White, "Insights into Child Theology through the Life and Work of Pandita Ramabai."

15. Wacker, "Living with Signs and Wonders," 427; see also Robinson and Ruff, *Out of the Mouth of Babes*.

16. Rostrup, "Teaching Children about the Baptism in the Holy Spirit," Myers, "Encouraging Youth to Receive the Baptism in the Holy Spirit," and Dresselhaus, "Can Children Receive the Baptism?"

In many respects, however, pentecostal beliefs about and practices relating to children, especially in the North American context, have been characteristic of those to whom they were closely connected, their conservative Protestant and fundamentalist cousins. Parents were strict, and children were disciplined; these were in accordance with Scriptures such as, "He that spareth his rod hateth his son: but he that loveth him chasteneth him betimes" (Prov 13:24, KJV), which were believed to be consistent with the overall portrait of the fatherhood of God as one who "disciplines those whom he loves, and chastises every child whom he accepts" (Heb 12:6, KJV; cf. Prov 3:12). To be sure, some pentecostal parents used these Scriptures as justification for what in other contexts would be child abuse, and in doing so, they provoked their children to wrath and failed to "bring them up in the nurture and admonition of the Lord" (Eph 6:4, KJV). In general, however, Pentecostals took their child-rearing seriously because they sought to raise them up in the ways of the Lord. Their methods were inevitably also informed by the strictest mores of their time, in hopes that their children would adhere to the Christian way for the rest of their lives.[17]

Times are, of course, changing, and in our contemporary context this has involved the complex dynamics of globalization as well. Migration has meant that the customs and conventions for child-rearing have shifted, even within pentecostal communities, so that non-negotiables of a previous generation are now being adjudicated in various contexts.[18] This means, at least in part, that we can no longer take for granted the existence of any type of homogeneous view regarding children among Pentecostals. There are probably many different understandings of children among lay Pentecostals, and just as many forms of child-rearing practices across the global renewal movement.

But our task is not merely phenomenological or historical but theological. In other words, regardless of what pentecostals might believe or what their practices are with regard to children, how might their perspectives contribute to a pentecostal theology of children or to the child theology initiative? This raises, of course, methodological questions about the nature of pentecostal theology. At a fundamental level, I have argued that Pentecostals' spirituality opens up intuitively to a pneumatological orientation.[19] There are three interrelated reasons for this correlation. First, Pentecostal-

17. For fundamentalist theologies of the family, see Rice, *The Home*, and Hendricks, *A Theology for Children*. See also Barnes, *In the Wilderness*, and Huffey, *The Hallelujah Side*, for autobiographical and highly engaging accounts of "growing up pentecostal" and all of the challenges that entailed in then adjusting to a larger world.

18. E.g., Hunt and Lightly, "Work in Progress."

19. See my *Spirit-Word-Community*.

ism derives its name from the Day of Pentecost narrative in Acts 2. The outpouring of the Holy Spirit, signified by the speaking of many tongues and languages, has been intrinsic to the modern pentecostal movement from its beginning. From this, second, follows the fact that not just glossolalia but the entire range of charisms or spiritual gifts are embraced by pentecostal believers as characteristic of the Spirit-filled life. Being filled with the Spirit is, for most Pentecostals, to be fully and authentically Christian. Last but not least, then, Pentecostals are bound together not by any creed (in fact, many, like other restorationists, are anti-creedal) or by institutional bonds; rather, as a protean and global movement, what unites pentecostal Christians is its spirituality, in particular its openness to the ongoing manifestation of and interaction with the Holy Spirit.

The preceding overview is suggestive not only for pentecostal theological methodology but also for its hermeneutical orientation. By this I am referring not only to how pentecostals read the Bible but also to what portions of Scripture they are most immediately attracted to. With regard to the latter, as already noted, Pentecostals focus first and foremost on the book of Acts, desiring as primitivists to experience the fullness of God as did the apostolic leaders and early followers of the messianic Way. It is the Acts narrative that has thus functioned intuitively as the pentecostal canon within the canon, in contrast to the Reformation focus on St. Paul in general and the Epistle to the Romans in particular.[20] This has given impulse to a unique pentecostal approach to Scripture, one that might be characterized as a form of reader-response hermeneutic, although I prefer to call it a soteriological and even eschatological mode of reading the Bible.[21] What I mean is that Pentecostals spend much less time worrying about historical-critical matters—as biblical literalists, by and large, they take what the Bible says at face value in terms of its descriptions of what happened—and are much more concerned that they enter into and experience for themselves the realities of the "Word of God." Taken together, then, it becomes clear why the book of Acts catches and holds the attention of Pentecostals more than the New Testament epistles. Narrative genres invite reader self-identification with the described events in ways that the more propositionally-framed discourses of early Christian letters do not.

The result is that Pentecostals read the Bible in general as they do the early Christian account of the Acts: pneumatologically (or pneumatically—"in

---

20. On this pentecostal emphasis, see the work of Stronstad, *The Charismatic Theology of St. Luke*; *Spirit, Scripture and Theology*; and *The Prophethood of All Believers*.

21. See my "Reading Scripture and Nature" (ch. 12 in this book,) esp. 4–6.

the Spirit") and soteriologically.[22] What they are seeking here, or what had led them to the text of Scripture to begin with, is a living encounter with the Holy Spirit. This means that they both read "in the Spirit" and in anticipation and expectation of deeper and more intense experiences of the Spirit. These pneumatic occasions are soteriological—in classical terms involving regeneration, justification, sanctification, etc.—through and through. What the Scripture witnesses to in terms of the work of the Spirit among the apostles and prophets is also expected, even prevalent, today.

What does all of this mean for the prosecution of the child theology project? I propose we meditate momentarily on the primordial pentecostal narrative, the Day of Pentecost outpouring of the Holy Spirit. There are two key passages within Acts 2 that may be suggestive for thinking pneumatologically about a theology of children: the beginning and end of Peter's apologia to the crowd for what was happening. The former is recorded by Luke as involving reference to the prophet Joel, wherein Peter says:

> this is what was spoken through the prophet Joel:
> [17] "In the last days it will be, God declares,
> that I will pour out my Spirit upon all flesh,
>   and your sons and your daughters shall prophesy,
> and your young men shall see visions,
>   and your old men shall dream dreams.
> [18] Even upon my slaves, both men and women,
>   in those days I will pour out my Spirit;
>   and they shall prophesy.
> [19] And I will show portents in the heaven above
>   and signs on the earth below,
>   blood, and fire, and smoky mist.
> [20] The sun shall be turned to darkness
>   and the moon to blood,
>   before the coming of the Lord's great and glorious day.
> [21] Then everyone who calls on the name of the Lord shall be saved." (Acts 2:16–21)

Two elements are here noteworthy for preliminary consideration. First, the visitation of the Spirit involves both sons and daughters, young men and young women, as manifest in their activity of prophesying, dreaming divinely appointed dreams, and seeing God-given visions (visions and dreams are to be taken in v. 17 as part of the parallelism between young and old men and thus as making the mutual point that "God will be accessible

---

22. E.g., Kärkkäinen, *Toward a Pneumatological Theology*, chs. 1–2; Noel, *Pentecostal and Postmodern Hermeneutics*, ch. 7; and Archer, *The Gospel Revisited*.

to and direct his people").[23] This is, of course, the basis for pentecostal expectations that children will be involved in any pentecostal revival and that they will be participants in and recipients of the gracious visitation of God whenever the Spirit is present in any extraordinary manner. This will surely be significant for the task of formulating child theology.

Second and more importantly is the eschatological horizon of the apostolic understanding. Peter and Luke—remember that from a pentecostal perspective focused on the soteriological dimension of the biblical text, there is less of a need to have to sort out historical-critical issues about whether or not Peter really said this or if it is merely Luke who puts this in Peter's mouth—understand the gift and outpouring of the Spirit upon all flesh as an eschatological event, one that inaugurated "the last days" (Acts 2:17). According to this exposition of the prophet Joel, these last days are the days of God's visitation, manifest through a variety of media (tongues, prophecies, visions, and dreams, etc.), and they accomplish, or at least begin to bring about, God's salvation. These salvific works of God (2:21) portend, if not precipitate, "the Lord's great and glorious day" (2:20). Modern Pentecostals often read this through the lens of dispensational eschatology, although there are other ways to understand the eschatological significance of this text.[24] What is undeniable, however, is that modern Pentecostals have embraced this eschatological message and have been thereby inspired to respond to the Great Commission and to take up urgently the evangelistic mandate of the church.[25] For them, to experience the Spirit of Pentecost is not merely to manifest charismata like glossolalia, but to be consigned into the "last days" apostolic mission to the world. The Spirit of Pentecost is the eschatological Spirit, and the Spirit of the last days is the Spirit of Pentecost.[26]

So from the preceding, what else then can or should be said about the work of child theology? Now we fast forward to the end of Peter's Day of Pentecost sermon. Here, he holds an altar call, one in response to a crowd eager to make a commitment: "Now when they heard this, they were cut to the heart and said to Peter and to the other apostles, 'Brothers, what should we do?' Peter said to them, 'Repent, and be baptized every one of you in the name of Jesus Christ so that your sins may be forgiven; and you will receive

23. Bock, *Acts*, 114.
24. E.g., McQueen, *Joel and the Spirit*.
25. See Goff Jr., *Fields White unto Harvest*, and Faupel, *The Everlasting Gospel*.
26. There are revisionary accounts of this relationship underfoot, but the basic message remains intact—e.g., Althouse, *Spirit of the Last Days*, and Yong, *In the Days of Caesar*, ch. 8.

the gift of the Holy Spirit. For the promise is for you, for your children, and for all who are far away, everyone whom the Lord our God calls to him.'" (Acts 2:37–39) Again, we find the pneumatological and soteriological self-understanding of the apostolic church: salvation at least culminates in, if it does not also consist centrally of, the gift of the Holy Spirit. What is further noteworthy for our purposes, however, is the reference to children. In this case, the apostolic response was that the promised gift of the Spirit was going to be liberally available. The crowd, who had already been indicted for the murder and crucifixion of Jesus (2:36), was promised full salvation in Christ by the power of the Spirit. Not only that, salvation was also accessible to their children, near and far, geographically close by and distant. From an eschatological perspective, those "far away" mean not those removed from Jerusalem, but descendants separated by generations in time.[27] To be sure, "children" in this context means more literally descendants than it does those youngsters who remain under the oversight of their parents. However, my point is that the metaphorical reference to "children" in the broader context of Peter's (and Luke's) explanation of the Pentecost event does not exclude those who are not adults; rather, the thrust of the pentecostal message here involves "all flesh" getting caught up in the soteriological and eschatological work of the Spirit of God.

Child Theologies in Lukan and Eschatological Perspective

Our pentecostal intuitions have highlighted at least the metaphorical role of children in the apostolic experience of the Spirit of Pentecost. I suggest, however, that this can also be understood in an explicitly theological key. More to the point, the children of whom Peter (and Luke) speak are eschatological agents and subjects who have not only encountered the Spirit but also participated in the salvation-historical events of the last days. But what might this mean theologically and practically in our time?

In order to pursue this line of theological reflection, I propose to continue reading Acts, and the Gospel of Luke in particular, through this pneumato-eschatological lens. Such a hermeneutical approach, I suggest, is not only deeply pentecostal in its overall orientation but is also one viable mode of pursuing pneumatological theology. What I mean can be briefly explicated at three levels: with regard to pentecostal theology, with regard to the theology of St. Luke, and with regard to pneumatological theology. (1) Pentecostally speaking, as has already been indicated, the Acts narrative has

---

27. For this reading of the "last days," I am indebted to Luther theologian Westhelle, "Liberation Theology," 320–23.

functioned principally as the point of entry into the scriptural canon. What I am proposing here involves, then, reading about the life of Christ (in the Third Gospel) from the standpoint of the Spirit's outpouring on all flesh.[28] The same Spirit who was given without measure to the apostolic community also empowered the life and ministry of Jesus (Luke 4:18–19; Acts 10:38). (2) With regard to Luke, the life of Christ is not a detached historical account but a theological understanding deeply informed by the apostolic experience as that unfolded through the expansion of the early church around the Mediterranean world.[29] More particularly, in light of Luke's own major themes, Jesus is not merely configured as a risen savior but is understood as one anticipating and then enacting the outpouring of the Spirit (Acts 2:32–33 says explicitly that the Spirit is given by Jesus); in other words, this is not merely a post-Easter perspective, but a post-Pentecost one as well. (3) Finally, my claim is that St. Luke the theologian is the most charismatically oriented of the Gospel writers. The gift of the Spirit most prominently highlighted in the Day of Pentecost narrative is not just an incidental event in the life of the early church, but is central to the Luke's understanding of the life and ministry of Jesus and of church as a charismatic and missionary fellowship of the Spirit.[30] In other words, those seeking to formulate or develop a pneumatological theology cannot do much better than entering into a sustained dialogue with the two volumes of Luke's writing.

Moving in this direction results, I suggest, in what might be called a pneumato-eschatological theology of children. Such a theological perspective emerges particularly when we observe what Luke has to say about children in light of the previously identified pneumatological and eschatological framework. We unpack this claim in light of brief glances at select passages in the book of Acts before moving "backward" to a more sustained consideration of children in the Third Gospel.

In the book of Acts, sons and daughters are rarely mentioned after chapter 2.[31] There are references to Moses's sons (7:29), the sons of Sceva

---

28. I provide such a reading in my *Who is the Holy Spirit?*.

29. That Luke is no mere historian but is also a theologian in his own right is now established, the picture of Luke the theologian emerging, interestingly, during a similar period of time as that of modern pentecostal scholarship; see Bovon, *Luke the Theologian*, and Johnson, *Prophetic Jesus, Prophetic Church*.

30. See Shelton, *Mighty in Word and Deed*, and Penney, *The Missionary Emphasis of Lukan Pneumatology*.

31. As noted also by Green, "'Tell Me a Story'"; Green proceeds to extrapolate from the Acts narratives a theology of discipleship and formation. The following aspires to extend Green's considerations from a pentecostal and pneumatological perspective.

(19:14), and the daughters of Philip (21:9).[32] Children are also rarely referred to: once metaphorically with regard to the people of Israel (13:33) and then at Paul's departure from Tyre to Jerusalem. Interestingly, on this latter occasion, it is said: "When our days there were ended, we left and proceeded on our journey; and all of them, with wives and children, escorted us outside the city. There we knelt down on the beach and prayed" (21:5). Luke the narrator is obviously present, but so are entire households in saying goodbye to Paul.

But while children are seldom mentioned, households appear quite frequently. Cornelius's household is said to have feared God (10:2), and entire households are visited with the salvation of the Spirit (Cornelius's in 11:14), and then initiated into faith through baptism (Lydia's and the jailer's in Philippi, in 16:15 and 16:31–34; and Crispus's in Corinth, in 18:8). So although children are not talked about explicitly in these accounts, some understanding the social structure of first-century Mediterranean families helps us to realize that they were included in these households. Children travelled with their parents (the father being the head of household); they often participated in the faith practices of adults in the home; and it was not surprising that when the head of household—who could be a woman (like Lydia)—converted from one religion to another, the children also would follow suit.

More importantly for our purposes: the universal scope, eschatological reach, and soteriological promises of God—that all flesh, including sons and daughters, would be visited by and receive the gift of the Holy Spirit—are anticipated in the Third Gospel and find their fulfillment even in the Acts narrative within the context of the household.[33] Children are saved and baptized, just as Peter indicated would happen in this assuring response to the anxious crowd on the Day of Pentecost. Now nowhere does Luke mention that children, as toddlers or what not, received the fullness of the Spirit. However, it is said of Philip the deacon that he "had four unmarried daughters who had the gift of prophecy" (21:9). We are not told how young they were at the onset of these gifts, but for Luke's pneumatological and eschatological theology of salvation history, when that happened is not as important as that such happened. Whereas during the Second Temple period the major formative rites for children were in the synagogue, for the earliest Christians, these events, particularly those associated with the coming and even present reign of God, happened within households as heads of

---

32. All scriptural references here and in these next few paragraphs are to the book of Acts, unless otherwise noted.

33. Matson, *Household Conversion Narratives in Acts*.

households and their families responded to the presence and activity of the Spirit of God.³⁴

From this overview of households in Acts, then, I wish to turn to Luke's account of the life of Christ. A number of noteworthy references to children immediately surface.³⁵ First, John the Baptist, the forerunner of Jesus, is also said to be pneumatically empowered to prepare the way for the salvation-historical events to come. More precisely, it is said of John: "With the spirit and power of Elijah he will go before him, to turn the hearts of parents to their children, and the disobedient to the wisdom of the righteous, to make ready a people prepared for the Lord" (1:17). What is the issue here—intergenerational conflicts? Perhaps. More probably, the "disobedience" of the fathers needs to be aligned with the holiness of God the Father, so that redemption might be affected for all, parents and children, the latter in all of the innocence with which they are taken up into the reign of God.³⁶ The goal is clear: that the renewal and restoration of Israel can occur and that the people of God can be revitalized and reinvigorated as the dwelling place of the Spirit. Hence, John "grew and became strong in spirit, and he was in the wilderness until the day he appeared publicly to Israel" (1:80). This should not be surprising: both of his parents also experienced charismatic visitations of the Spirit (Elizabeth: 1:41; Zechariah: 1:67); should not the son of two Spirit-filled parents also be nurtured in the ways of the Spirit, especially one with his own charismatic vocation before him? Should not one whose task it was to effect a ministry of reconciliation between parents and children also be bonded together with his parents, even from his mother's womb (1:41, 44)?

Second, Jesus' childhood certainly deserves comment. Conceived through the Holy Spirit (1:35), he was recognized, even as an infant, through the revelation of the Spirit, as symbolically representing and even embodying the promised salvation not only of Israel but also of the world (2:25–32). Alongside his cousin John, Jesus "grew and became strong, filled with wisdom; and the favour of God was upon him" (2:40). At the age of twelve, Jesus had already developed spiritually enough to recognize that while he needed to remain obedient to his parents, Mary and Joseph (2:51), he had also at least become sufficiently sensitive to spiritual and religious matters that he sought out the teachers of Israel to learn more about God as

---

34. See Elliott, "Temple versus Household in Luke-Acts."

35. Now, unless otherwise noted, all scriptural references in the remainder of this section are to the Gospel of Luke.

36. See Green, *The Gospel of Luke*, 76–77.

the Father of Israel (2:46-49).³⁷ This divine fatherhood is later revealed as merciful (6:36), as a caretaker and provider (12:30-32), and as patient and long-suffering (the parable of the Prodigal Son), although it is unclear at this point if Jesus recognized all of these theological qualities. Yet clearly the Spirit was with Jesus, even during these years, as he "increased in wisdom and in years, and in divine and human favour" (2:52). Yet he honored his earthly parents so that his mother "treasured all these things in her heart" (2:51b)—one wonders to what degree his mother was able to recognize and be supportive of her son's youthful mission since she herself was probably not much more than a teenager when she responded to the divine call and even prophesied then (see what we now call the "Magnificat"; 1:46-55), as if anticipating the Pentecost unleashing of the Spirit's "prophesying daughters—even as he related to his heavenly Father as one intent on fulfilling, rather than falling short of, his vocational call.³⁸ Jesus' stepping into his vocational calling at the age of twelve anticipates the Spirit-filled younger generation of Acts, when young men shall see visions and shall prophesy in the power of the Spirit.

Third, then, Jesus as the Spirit-empowered agent of redemption clearly also is recorded as having uttered some hard sayings that set off, rather than reconciled, parents with children and vice-versa. Representative of these are the following:

- "Whoever comes to me and does not hate father and mother, wife and children, brothers and sisters, yes, and even life itself, cannot be my disciple" (14:26);³⁹

- "And he said to them, 'Truly I tell you, there is no one who has left house or wife or brothers or parents or children, for the sake of the kingdom of God'" (18:29);

---

37. Hannam, *In the Things of My Father*, 45-49, reminds us that Jesus was not only answering his teachers but also asking questions and inquiring of them (2:46-47). If we are unclear about the precise nature of Jesus' relationship to the God of Israel, so also were Jesus' parents (Luke 2:50); on this point, see the informative discussion of Byrne, *My Father's Business*, 38-40.

38 Adrienne von Speyr's beautiful book, *The World of Prayer* has a short section (290-91) on Jesus' sonship being shaped as a child through pneumatic participation in the divine love; in other words, Jesus was able to pursue his father's will without deviation because of his own Spirit-filled life.

39. To "hate" means not to abhor, detest, or loathe, but to love less in comparison to something else, in this case, to the call of discipleship, so notes Bruce, *The Hard Sayings of Jesus*, 120. Yet this way of alleviating the sting of this "hard saying"—not to mention the others cited here—should not numb the force of the challenges involved in responding to the call of the reign of God.

- "You will be betrayed even by parents and brothers, by relatives and friends; and they will put some of you to death" (21:16).

From a child theological perspective, these pericopes might appear to suggest that Jesus advocated not honoring one's parents, or that he exonerated parents for neglecting their children for the sake of the reign of God. However, keep in mind that: 1) Jesus was aware of the commandment to honor one's parents (18:20), and there is no clear indication that his way of life was dishonoring to them. 2) More importantly, from within the eschatological horizon of the outpouring of the Spirit, these texts bear witness consistently to Jesus' commitment to do the work of establishing the reign of God to restore, renew, and redeem Israel. From this perspective, there can be no partial allegiances since the oppression of Israel has persisted for far too long and any stragglers will simply perpetuate the wilderness wandering of the people of God.

Fourth and most importantly as a counter to more fundamentalist readings of the previous litany of texts related to family relationships, Jesus' explicit teachings about children as well as his dispositions toward, behaviors regarding, and treatments of children are all positive.[40] For instance, when Jesus was aware of the disciples' bickering among themselves about who was the greatest, he said: "But Jesus, aware of their inner thoughts, took a little child and put it by his side, and said to them, 'Whoever welcomes this child in my name welcomes me, and whoever welcomes me welcomes the one who sent me; for the least among all of you is the greatest'" (9:47–48). Later in rejoicing with his disciples about their experiencing the manifestation of God's saving power in their itinerant ministries, he exclaimed in the Holy Spirit: "I thank you, Father, Lord of heaven and earth, because you have hidden these things from the wise and the intelligent and have revealed them to infants; yes, Father, for such was your gracious will" (10:21). The reference to "infants" here is, of course, metaphorical, but the metaphor works precisely because of the point that was being made: that the reign of God would arrive not among the wise or intelligent, but to and through those who were most intimate with and dependent upon the goodwill of the Father. Then, on the road to Jerusalem, it was said of him: "People were bringing even infants to him that he might touch them; and when the disciples saw it, they sternly ordered them not to do it. But Jesus called for them and said, 'Let the little children come to me, and do not stop them; for it is to such as these that the kingdom of God belongs. Truly I tell you, whoever does not receive the kingdom of God as a little child will never enter it'" (18:15–17). In these in-

---

40. See Ibita and Bieringer, "(Stifled) Voices of the Future," 90. See also Weber, *Jesus and the Children*, and Hull, *When You Receive a Child*.

stances, Jesus established children, even infants, as being the central citizens of the reign of God.[41] The "least of these" are thus neither merely tolerated nor only recognized as only potential contributors to the divine will and work. Instead, they are part of the people of God whom God promises to care for as God's own, even to the point of promising (24:49) to give them fully of God's own self in the Holy Spirit (11:11–13).[42]

Space constraints prevent any more analysis of Luke's accounts of Jesus' responses to other children like the son of the widow of Nain (7:11–17), Jairus's daughter (8:41–56), and the demon-possessed son (9:37–45), even as any more complete recognition of child theological considerations in dialogue with Lukan perspectives will need to consider these as well as other aspects of the above materials that we have only scratched the surface about. Suffice to say for the moment that Jesus' interactions with children as well as his teachings about them are all messianic activities accomplished under the inspiration and empowerment of the Holy Spirit (4:1, 14, 18). Put more forcefully, Jesus' understanding of children was thoroughly soteriological and eschatological, having to do with the coming reign of God inaugurated with his charismatic and messianic-prophetic life and ministry. If the outpouring of the Spirit in Acts serves to herald the present realities of the coming reign of God, then the words and deeds of the Spirit-filled Christ in Luke prefigure and precipitate this eschatological event to the point that some— i.e., the son of the widow of Nain—experienced the ultimately power of the Spirit of the last days, the coming to life from the dead!

Children and the Coming Kingdom: Aspects of a Third Article Theology

In this last section we can do no more than briefly outline some of the broader implications from the preceding discussion for and from the child theological enterprise. I will comment on four topics or areas—the

---

41. For further explication of this passage in Luke 18 by Peruvian pentecostal theologian, see Rodriguez, *The Liberating Mission of Jesus*, ch. 7; note that the focus on López Rodriguez's work is on an evangelical liberation theology of mission, not at the interface we are focused at where Lukan pneumatology and pentecostal theology of children meet.

42. Jeremy Worthen calls attention to the fact that Jesus' willingness to welcome children, even infants, as expressions and mediations of the reign of God was itself anticipated by Simeon's reception of the reign of God in and through the infant Jesus; see Worthen, "Babes in Arms," 56–57.

eschatological, pneumatological, theological, and practical—as they gesture toward a child theology.[43]

Thinking about theology of children in dialogue with the Lukan narrative as turning on the Day of Pentecost event invites, as we have seen above, an eschatological perspective. From this "last-days" vantage point, the normal lives of children persist to some degree: they are shown as being cared for by parents and thus in submission to parental authority (i.e., being present with their parents for Paul's departure to Jerusalem). On the other hand, there is nothing conventional about life in the reign of God. The activation and enablement of sons and daughters by the Spirit, and the presence of children, even infants, at the heart of the coming kingdom, signals that Jesus in the power of the Spirit is bringing about another form of sociality, one oriented not around the values of the world but that of the reign of God. This is a world, as was noted of the apostles, turned upside down (Acts 17:6).[44] It was an in-between time, during the last days inaugurated by the Spirit-filled Christ and his outpouring of the Spirit on all flesh, but yet awaiting the final consummation. In this time and space, children symbolized both the innocence and the potential of a new order, one redeemed from sin and not contaminated by fallen conventions.

It might be thought then that Luke (in his two-volume work) has nothing to say about children in the "real world." After all, it seems to be too far-fetched to think that children only live in the eschatological time and space of the Spirit of God. But perhaps it is adults who have been habituated into the systems of this world that need to be awakened to the possibilities of the present experience of God's eschatological reign. Perhaps instead it is looking again at the lives of children that will help Christians recover eschatological relationality in terms of how children can or should interact with each other, relate to their parents, and go about being in the world. In other words, rather than measuring Luke's eschatological reality according to contemporary conventions of family and child life, why not rethink the latter in light of the images of children associated with the coming reign of God? It may well be that the world is incapable of accepting Jesus in part because we have conformed children to adulthood rather than entering into the eschatological horizon of children to receive them on their own terms and participate with them in the Spirit-filled life. Pentecostals have as much to gain from thinking about on these matters as others.

43. The following takes off my reflections on theology of the family in the previous chapter.

44. Luke's not only believes in an upside-down world but also an "inside-out world of reversal that is God's dominion" in which children "will be specially honored guests"; see Carroll, "What Then Will This Child Become?," 194.

What then about pneumatology? That the Spirit is poured out upon young and old highlights the freedom of the Spirit to give of herself as she wills. St. Paul perceived as much in his thinking about the charismatic dimensions of ecclesial life and congregational worship: "All these are activated by one and the same Spirit, who allots to each one individually just as the Spirit chooses" (1 Cor 12:11). A further refrain throughout Paul's interactions with the Corinthians is that the Spirit empowers not the strong but the weak; the Spirit elects not the elite but the marginalized; the Spirit works through not the wise but the foolish, etc.[45] This is consistent with how Luke understands the central role of young men and young women in the eschatological work of the Spirit. In short, the workings of the Spirit highlight the normativity of prophesying daughters as well as visionary adult males, although perhaps the former more clearly depicts the Spirit's unconventional methods in bringing about the reign of God.

I would also note, though, that in Luke, the divine Father not only wants to give good gifts, but desires also to give of deity itself. In Jesus' words, as recorded by Luke, "If you then, who are evil, know how to give good gifts to your children, how much more will the heavenly Father give the Holy Spirit to those who ask him!" (Luke 11:13).[46] The Spirit actually becomes the promise of the Father (Luke 24:49, Acts 1:4) that begins to be fulfilled on the Day of Pentecost (Acts 2:33, 39). In other words, the promise of the Father and the outpouring of the Spirit on all flesh — sons and daughters, young and old — is not only what enables the reconciliation of parents and children but also restores their relationship to YHWH. From this pentecostal, eschatological, and pneumatological perspective, then, children become central to the salvation historical intention of God to renew Israel and to redeem the world; it may even be that children are the most receptive of the human species to the dawning of the reign of God.

This leads also to more systematic theological considerations. To be sure, there is no space for a full consideration across the loci, much less any in depth reflection in any one locus. Nevertheless, let me suggest two strands of inquiry: the christological and the methodological. Christologically, thinking about children ought to return us, again and again, to Jesus.[47] Both Jesus' teachings about children and his reception of them are theologically potent. My point is to emphasize those aspects of the Gospel accounts

---

45. I discuss aspects of these unconventional moves in my "Disability and the Gifts of the Spirit"; see also Yong, *The Bible, Disability, and the Church*, ch. 4.

46. See also my *Spirit of Love*, esp. ch. 6.

47. Besides the earlier discussion, see also Gundry-Volf, "The Least and the Greatest."

regarding these matters: the pneumatological and, especially for Luke, the eschatological. Jesus' teachings and actions are Spirit-anointed, precisely the meaning of his messiahship; as such, what is said of children is just as much pneumatological and christological. What we need, then, is a Spirit-christological theology of children followed by teasing out implications for the child-theological project. Further, as already intimated, Jesus' teachings about and interactions with children must be understood in an eschatological plane. In that case, then, his salvific message and actions bring about the reign of God, at the center of which are the children of the world.

Perhaps this means that at the heart of the reign of God is both vulnerability and play. I will return in a moment to the former; for the time being, I want to concentrate on the latter. If children are the point of entry into the reign of God and if the reign of God is characterized at its core by children, what does this tell us about how God not only sees but wishes to structure the world? What children do is play, at least if they are healthy, cared for, and properly nurtured.[48] In that case, the reign of God is also characterized fundamentally by play rather than by any pragmatism, utilitarianism, or even instrumentalism. If play reigns, then, calculative and instrumental logic do not. The image of God then becomes most deeply manifest in the playful nature of *homo ludens*.

Pentecostal theologian Wolfgang Vondey has recently argued at length that the pentecostal spirit—in effect the Spirit of Pentecost—is essentially and primarily playful.[49] For Vondey, the work of the Spirit is liberative, creative, and playfully unpredictable. Children exhibit these qualities; adults, however, have been "trained" to grow up, and play is transformed into work. Not that work is bad, but human rationality in the case of work without or apart from play becomes rationalism when driven by calculative goals. Instead, the imagination ought to be given permission and encouraged to be engaged in and exercise imaginative play, even amidst our work. What Vondey's argument does not factor in is the perspective of children. When that is added into the mix, then, reason is directed toward creative play and a playful kind of creativity is nurtured and even unleashed. Children reason imaginatively and intuitively in their playful interactions with one another. Child theologizing would also similarly emphasize the proper role of creativity, spontaneity, and novelty in the work of reason. The theological imagination, then, would not work first and foremost deductively or inductively, but perhaps abductively—by provisionally drawing and exploring affective sensibilities and instinctively formulated hypotheses and

---

48. Even the Lukan Jesus expects this (7:22); see also Privett, "Play."
49. See Vondey, *Beyond Pentecostalism*.

inferences—in a creative hermeneutical circle that connects the dots in an attitude of playful reverence.

That said, we must still and finally attend to the practical dimension of child theologies. While play ought to be central to theology of children and even to the theological task, we must also be vigilant because of the vulnerability of children. As noted by practical theologian Joyce Ann Mercer, when talking about children, "it's not 'child's play'!"[50] Children are vulnerable to all kinds of threats, from poverty to war. Their needs are manifold—physical, economic, social, educational, and spiritual—and they are reliant on the provision of adults. But they are even more at risk because of the asymmetry between adults and children. Hence they are susceptible to adults who have power and authority over them, and are defenselessly exposed to those who might prey on their unsuspecting nature. Child abuse happens in many forms, and each time it happens, the child's capacity to play, create, and imagine a better world is compromised.[51]

Adults, we theologians included, have the moral obligation to look out and care for the vulnerable in our midst, children included. Practical theologian Adrian Thatcher has insisted: "the Christ Child is the foundation of children's rights! God became a Child."[52] I would further add that is it not just the Christ child who symbolizes our state of being obligated to children but that the Sprit-Christ child exemplifies what it means to be people who abide according to the dictates of the reign of God: the young Jesus of Nazareth who was doing his father's work because he was full of the wisdom, grace, and leading of the Spirit. In that case, the Spirit of the last days is the Spirit who empowers young men and young women—sons and daughters—to prophetically call the church to her moral responsibility for these same children. With regard to the life of the church or the ecclesial community, how then can we not just make accessible to children our formative liturgies but also incorporate and involve children in them? The former would only train them to be no more than "consumers" of these central Christian rites;[53] as important as these are, it is more important that children also come to experience how their lives, actions, and words contribute to the constitution of these Christian practices, and that adults also come to expect this as a normative part of Christian celebration. Put another way: if the Spirit is poured out indiscriminately upon all flesh, our children included, then they also become the prophetic witnesses—some-

---

50. Mercer, *Welcoming Children*, ch. 3.
51. See the moving account of Pais, *Suffer the Children*.
52. Thatcher, "Beginning Again with Jesus," 159.
53. As unfolded in Nelson, "Christian Formation of Children."

times using words, other times not, perhaps simply in and through the way they are present in our midst—to the eschatological judgment, renewal, and salvation of God. To involve children in the central Christian practices is to allow their presence to be felt, their voice (to the degree possible) to be heard, and their lives to be a conduit of the Spirit's work in the ecclesial community. This in turn will have practical ramifications for how the church engages the issues pertaining to the vulnerability of children in our society, whatever its context, today.

Transitions

There can be no conclusions to this programmatic set of reflections at the interface of pentecostal theology, pneumatology, and theology of children. What I have attempted to consider is the shape of the child theology project, particularly within a pneumatological and eschatological framework. In turn, we have also observed how thinking specifically from a child theological perspective also impacts other theological loci. Much more work needs to be done, for example, exploring in more detail the implications of St. Paul's charismatic theology for family life in general and for child theology especially, or thinking about how the references to children function in the passages discussing the Day of YHWH in the Hebrew prophets or in the eschatologically-dominated message of the Apocalypse. In the meanwhile, we will not too soon exhaust ourselves in thinking about children as being at the center of what the Spirit of God wishes to continue to accomplish in these last days.

PART III

Pneumatological Soteriology: The Lukan Imagination II

CHAPTER 7

The Social Psychology of Sin

A Pentecostal Perspective[1]

The following attempts to bring together two conversations: one, on pentecostal theology in dialogue with the sciences, in its embryonic stages, and the other, on a distinctively pentecostal theology or perspective on sin, heretofore underdeveloped.[2] One might wonder about the wisdom of attempting such a transdisciplinary exploration, not only in that the engagement of pentecostal theology and the sciences is still its gestational period, which presses the concern that there is insufficient traction at this nexus to take up yet another contested theological topic, that of hamartiology (the doctrine or theology of sin), but more so that, to my knowledge, there has been little to no critical reflection on the Christian teaching about sin from the pentecostal academy, which begs further the question of how to extend such a non-existent enterprise into the theology and science arena. Obviously, the plausibility of this seemingly bold and even brash exercise can only be

1. I am grateful to Michael Tenneson for the invitation to present a previous version of this paper at the Faith & Science Conference, Evangel University, Springfield, Missouri, on September 23, 2016; thanks also to my colleagues Veli-Matti Kärkkäinen, Thomas J. Oord, and Wolfgang Vondey for their critical feedback on an earlier draft of this chapter that saved me from various confusions. I alone am responsible for the final product.

2. The most substantive original reflection on the doctrine of sin engaged with contemporary scientific perspectives by someone from a pentecostal background I know is the recently ordained Lutheran Finnish systematician, Kärkkäinen, *A Constructive Christian Theology for the Pluralistic World*, vol. 3, ch. 15. As his five-volume opus is intended to be a contribution to ecumenical theology, he does not foreground his pentecostal vantage point. The following is intended to complement Kärkkäinen's massive achievement from a distinctively pentecostal site.

discerned after the fact (at the end of the discussion), but two preliminary comments are in order. First, it is not that pentecostal theologians have not considered hamartiology at all, but that the various forays into this arena, as will be clear below, have traversed well-worn tracks carved out by evangelical tradition rather than being guided by specifically pentecostal perspectives. The following thus seeks to press more deeply into the achievements of the emerging pentecostal theological academia in order to reconsider sin from such a more particular horizon, and yet simultaneously envision how the unfolding efforts might also further explorations in the interdisciplinary domain where theology and the sciences continue in cross-fertilization.

Second, although barely underway, there is every indication that the pentecostal theology and science interface even it its very short term has been generative of insights and debate, both indicators of the fertility of the conversation so far and inviting of further inquiry.[3] This essay seeks to press further into this node via attentiveness to the doctrine of sin not only to see how scientific viewpoints might be informative but to forge distinctive pentecostal reflection that may have broader ecumenical purchase. More precisely, following the paths charted so far from the intersection where pentecostal theology and science have converged, we will inquire more specifically into hamartiology from a specifically pneumatological perspective, one that begins with Christian understandings of the person and work of the Holy Spirit.

We will proceed first to map discussions in theology and science on the topic or theme of sin, and then, second, suggest how pentecostal vantage points might fare amidst that discussion. I will urge in part II that the Day of Pentecost narrative in Acts chapter 2 provides springboards toward what might be considered a pneumatological theology of sin, albeit one that includes also an eschatological and Trinitarian theology of redemption and salvation from the effects of sin that inhibit conformity with the ideals of the coming reign of God. Our goal given the present state of the discussion cannot be a fully developed pentecostal theology of sin; instead, we will sketch

---

3. Besides my own monograph—*The Spirit of Creation*—I have edited a collection of articles in one of the foremost scholarly journals devoted to the theology-and-science dialogue and two other books in this area. The former is introduced by my "Pentecostalism, Science, and Creation." The two edited volumes are *The Spirit Renews the Face of the Earth*, and (with Smith) *Science and the Spirit*. There have been over two dozen reviews of these works, including roundtables of critical engagements in online scholarly platforms such as the *Cyberjournal for Pentecostal-Charismatic Research* 20 (April 2011) [http://www.pctii.org/cyberj/cyber20.html], the *Australasian Pentecostal Studies* 15:1 (2013) [http://aps-journal.com/aps/index.php/APS/issue/view/13], and the *Canadian Journal of Pentecostal-Charismatic Christianity* 3:1 (2012) 89–129 [https://journal.twu.ca/index.php/CJPC/issue/view/7].

first steps toward such an interdisciplinary and ecumenical harmartiology that nevertheless attends to, rather than ignores, pentecostal instincts and commitments.

Sin: Interdisciplinary Formulations

This section does not presume to provide an exhaustive discussion of the doctrine of sin whether theologically or as covered in the theology and science literature. Instead our goal is to overview contemporary understandings of the notion of sin, particularly as such have been informed by a scientific worldview. Here is not the place for defending the viability of such an enterprise. Suffice it to say that I have elsewhere argued that theology should be formulated with awareness of developments in the sciences even as the distinctiveness of these domains of inquiry and methods ought not to be confused.[4] Put alternatively, theology can be illuminated by advances in other spheres of human knowledge (the sciences included) even as the goal is never to revise orthodox understandings for the sake of novelty or to "keep up with the times," so to speak. Instead, truth will prevail no matter where such may be found, and, from a faith-seeking-understanding posture, Christian theologians can proceed interactively with other branches of knowledge, drawing from them but also speaking from their own stance as appropriate. When talking about sin, then—which is first and foremost, we ought to be reminded, a *theological* notion of homo sapiens not being aligned with, or falling short of, the will and glory of God—the question is how twenty-first-century understandings can be helpfully illuminated from scientific outlooks. We begin here with the literature on sin assessed in empirical and scientific perspective, step back to overview broader theologies of sin informed by the sciences, and then relate such with the current state of pentecostal understandings of sin.

Sin in Empirical Perspective

Although from two generations ago, Reinhold Niebuhr's claim, "the doctrine of original sin is the only empirically verifiable doctrine of the Christian faith,"[5] remains with us today. Even if Niebuhr meant no more than the tru-

---

4. See Yong, *Renewing Christian Theology*, ch. 10.4; cf. my essay, "Pentecostalism and Science."

5. Niebuhr, *Man's Nature and His Communities*, 24. Note that Odegard, *Sin and Science*, is not quite applicable to the task of the present essay in desiring to explore the theology of sin in dialogue with the sciences as it is an effort to discredit the

ism that sin is easily observable all around us, the recent interface between theology and the sciences has generated unexpected empirical perspectives extending the discussion. My awareness of the nascent literature at this intersection where sin and science meet suggests that we can grasp the convergences at least at three interrelated levels: the genetic-sociobiological, the neuropsychological, and the sociocultural.

At the *genetic* level, if Augustinian notions of original sin and hereditary guilt (whatever else these extremely complex notions may have meant and continue to mean) have been predominant in the Latin or Western theological tradition, recent proposals may, intended or not, instigate a retrieval and restatement of the bishop of Hippo's ideas, albeit in conversation with the evolutionary sciences.[6] In its most basic form, scientists and theologians working amidst the foundations of the discussion presume the evolutionary history of the world and the concomitant set of ideas about random mutation at the genetic level and natural selection of the fittest traits at the level of organic populations. Although the author of the notion of the "selfish gene" has been particularly hostile to theism and its religious matrices,[7] that fundamental idea has been quite productive at the science and theology intersection, urging formulations such as *original selfishness*, the notion that the genetic drives toward replication generate self-preservational instincts, tendencies, and behaviors in living organisms at every level of the evolutionary chain, including that of homo sapiens.[8]

The *sociobiological* perspective deepens the analysis of what happens at the level of organisms. Here, reductive egocentrism, as opposed to reciprocating behaviors, actually is maladaptive for the organism within its population group in the long run. Hence, altruistic relations emerge selectively first among kin as adaptive strategies competing over and against out-groups.[9] The "fittest" groups survive and reproduce on the basis of their cooperative behaviors albeit not without struggle and competition internally and vis-à-vis outsiders.

Neuroscientific perspectives shed further light on the sinful dispositions and behaviors of homo sapiens. Proper functionality of the mammalian brain nurtures trust, even as a healthy limbic system facilitates memory and fosters meaning-making. The neocortex organizes thinking and funds

---

Niebuhrian vision from a contrasting sociopolitical perspective.

6. Peters, *Sin*, 320–27, for example, asks if original sin is now understandable as "hereditary sin."

7. Dawkins, *The Selfish Gene*.

8. Domning, with Hellwig, *Original Selfishness*.

9. Williams, *Doing without Adam and Eve*.

inquiry, while the frontal lobes and forebrain cultivate intentionality and provide orientation and direction (teleology). From this vantage point, one way to understand sin is in terms of the brain's functions "'falling short' of potentialities and demands,"[10] in that its various parts or systems work improperly (malfunction) or do not provide the needed checks (defenses) and balances (for safety) for defining in binary terms what is beneficent (helpful) and what is maleficent (harmful) essential for harmonious relationship of human persons within their wider social environment.[11]

From this, correlations can be specified among the genetic, biological, and neurological domains and the psychological profiles of sinful dispositions and behaviors. Psychologist and neuroscientist Matthew Stanford, for instance, argues that rage (so-called *intermittent explosive disorder*) is undergirded by a dysfunctional prefrontal cortex that fails to restrain an over-activated amygdala; that irresponsible sexual behaviors are driven by dysfunctional or neurochemically misfiring attraction and attachment systems; that impulsive, aggressive, and even criminal behaviors (stealing for example) are often the result of personality disorders, including *borderline personality disorder*, impairing the regulation of social and interpersonal relations; and that addictions derive from *reward deficiency syndrome* that require greater and greater stimulants in order to restore organismic equanimity or equilibrium.[12] What needs to be emphasized is that such underlying neurological factors are understood not deterministically but dispositionally, preserving the psychological dimension of human moral decision-making, albeit as operating within its neuro-genetic constraints.

Last (for our purposes) but not least is the *sociocultural* level. Here human interactions work in, through, and with the genetic, neurological, and physiological "hardware" of the human body, whether initially through nurturing by parents and caregivers or later through culture-making activities, with the result that some dispositional pathways are perpetuated and opened up and others marginalized or neutralized through social learning and practices.[13] One route of inquiry observes how biologically rooted experiences of anxiety, pride, and concupiscence generate distrust, scapegoating, and cruelty in relationship to others—not in any one-to-one causal sense but through the webs of interpersonal and social exchange—such that

10. Ashbrook and Albright, *The Humanizing Brain*, 157.

11. Tsakiridis, *Evagrius Ponticus and Cognitive Science*, is an interesting neuroscientific account of experiences of the demonic as related to the brain's binary operations.

12. Stanford, *The Biology of Sin*.

13. van den Toren, "Human Evolution and a Cultural Understanding of Original Sin," 16–17; cf. Wilcox, "A Proposed Model for the Evolutionary Creation of Human Beings."

we talk about a spectrum of sin and evil from and between the human soul and the social sphere.[14] Another perspective, going back to Niebuhr himself during the time between the two world wars, emphasizes that personal human virtuousness is undermined by societal relations and dynamics.[15] Human persons and their self-understandings are themselves constituted by society even as their behaviors are shaped into conformity with social roles and conventions, so that in this framework we would need to talk about *social sins* like slavery or racism that is "rooted, embodied, and perpetuated in social institutions."[16] Recognition and critical analysis of such societal sinfulness requires an intersubjective "structural epistemology" that identifies the interwovenness of the personal (in all its bio-physiological, cognitive, and psychological complexity) and the social.[17]

Theologies of Sin: Scientifically-Informed Understandings

How might the preceding more empirically oriented inquiries be related to understandings of sin operative in the theological tradition more generally and in the theology-and-science dialogue more specifically? Two trajectories of responses might be charted, one more inclined to reconsider received theological understandings of sin in light of scientific advances and the other less sure that there is enough consensus on the science side to warrant major theological adjustments. It may be unsurprising to note that the central point upon which critical discussion has turned has been the traditional Christian doctrine of original sin.

Focus on original sin has been particularly urgent given that historical versions of this teaching appear irreconcilable at least on the surface with an evolutionary understanding of human life and origins. A literal twenty-four–hour understanding of the days of creation certainly is incompatible with the billions of years on the evolutionary time scale. Even if some might be willing to read the "days" of Genesis as referring to ages of time in natural history and thereby embrace an ancient (rather than young) earth, the biblical implications are that Adam and Eve are not just historical but the first human creatures, and such notions seem rather arbitrary within the framework of contemporary evolutionary biology and anthropology. There

---

14. This is the argument of Peters, *Sin*, although his discussion is less linear than I have characterized here.

15. Famously argued in Niebuhr, *Moral Man and Immoral Society*.

16. O'Keefe, *What Are They Saying about Social Sin?*, 3.

17. See Arokiasamy, "Sinful Structures in the Theology of Sin, Conversion and Reconciliation," 91.

are also biblical passages such as Romans 5 that suggest creaturely death came into the world through Adam's sin, and this would be impossible in an evolutionary world wherein death is part and parcel of the circle of life.

The majority doing work in the theology-and-science arena accept the more or less mainstream consensus about an evolving universe and hence adopt a variety of hermeneutical and methodological strategies to reformulate the notion of sin, original and otherwise. The most common versions presume a dynamic or organic ontology that in turn facilitates interpretation of the biblical and theological traditions from such developmental perspectives.[18] More evangelically committed proposals have also appeared in this vein and these are usually more biblically and theologically concerned than they are philosophically or metaphysically oriented. The most standard versions in the evangelical tradition tend to emphasize that Genesis ought to be read literally and theologically as dictated by its genre as an ancient Near Eastern document rather than historically or scientifically, and such moves usually minimize if not eliminate conflict with scientific theories, models, and interpretations.[19] While the arguments are distinct, the results in general hold forth the compatibility of an evolutionary universe with the scriptural traditions even if there is little agreement on the details of how to think about death, Adam and Eve, and the age of the cosmos. With regard to original sin, the diversity of models prompt a variety of reconceptualizations: Adam as a historical creature whom God elected from out of the evolutionary stream of history, but who failed to live in relationship with the divine; Adam as symbolic of an evolved population group confronted with its morality, and then mortality, in resisting divine overtures; or no primordial fall but a recognition of sin's universality, following upon the moral and spiritual choices of each member of the evolved species of homo sapiens.[20] These scientifically informed articulations would map, more or less, on to the various theories of original sin found in the Christian faith—none definitively accepted or dogmatically defined by the main lines of the ecumenical tradition—whether effected via genetic transmission (through a

---

18. At the head of the conversation is Francoeur, *Perspectives in Evolution*—with the third chapter of part II dealing with original sin—with more recent versions being Edwards, "Original Sin and Saving Grace in Evolutionary Context," and Korsmeyer, *Evolution and Eden*.

19. See, for instance, Collins, "Evolution and Original Sin," who teaches in the religion department at Messiah College, an institution in the Anabaptist, Pietist, and Wesleyan streams of the evangelical tradition; cf. my essay, "God and the Evangelical Laboratory."

20. The basic outlines of these views can be extrapolate from, among other sources, Caneday and Barrett, eds., *Four Views on the Historical Adam*.

primordial human being), via Adamic representation, or via divine judicial or forensic declaration.

Conservative Protestants, however, are a bit less enthusiastic about so-called mainstream science perhaps as much because of the oftentimes prominent atheistic scientism within those circles that is dismissive of religion generally as because of the sense that an ancient earth, but more so the evolutionary theory of common descent jeopardizes the scriptural witness especially regarding Adam and Eve as created in the image of God. While one expression of such views are in the young earth creationist camp,[21] others may be found among the intelligent design movement or even advocates of the old earth position buttressed by the view that human beings were divinely and specially formed rather than evolved creatures. The reasons are both biblical but also theological, particularly concerns regarding what is received as the orthodox tradition's embrace of a historical Adam and Eve.[22] Within this frame of reference, the instinct is that to privilege the historic consensus of the church's dogmatic teachings about the human fall from grace rather than bend ecclesial confessions to the shifting views of modern science that lead us to biologize, psychologize, or sociologize the phenomenon of sin.[23]

While my own leanings are to work with the current scientific consensus,[24] I am also of the firm conviction that the theology-and-science *dialogue* ought to mean that there is communication and impact moving in both directions. Rather than correcting the theory of evolution, however (which, if undermined at all in the long run will be accomplished not by theology but by the advance of science, which has built into its methods the capacity to correct itself), the theological voice can be sounded variously: more technically in shaping scientific hypotheses and research projects, or morally in chastening scientific hubris and shaping epistemic attitudes, for instance.[25] In addition, the specifically theological character of Christian teaching means that such truth, if sustainable over time, will be plausible in any context, properly interpreted and understood therein. Sin is such a

---

21. This would be the fourth view represented in the Caneday and Barrett, eds., *Four Views* volume referred to in the preceding paragraph and footnote.

22. As represented, e.g., in Madueme and Reeves, eds., *Adam, the Fall, and Original Sin*.

23. Campbell, *The Doctrine of Sin*.

24. Yong, "The Spirit of an Evolving Creation."

25. Coleman, *Eden's Garden*, for example, warns that religion and theology can check scientific overreach. An excellent example of how theology's input can guide scientific inquiry is Russell, *Time in Eternity*.

theological notion: science can perhaps help to illuminate its realities in a scientific age, but not overthrow the notion altogether.

Traditional Pentecostal Views of Sin

What then about pentecostal perspectives on sin? How has pentecostal theology understood the doctrine of sin, how have these related to the received doctrines of sin in the theological tradition, and how might such inform the opportunities and challenges before us? As already indicated, so far pentecostal scholars have not taken up the theology of sin in dialogue with the sciences, but what are the contours of the more-or-less received pentecostal hamartiology that would frame such efforts?

If the broader theology-and-science conversation's ruminations on the topic have focused on the doctrine of original sin more specifically, such emphases are also consistent with heretofore pentecostal forays in this area. Traditional pentecostal perspectives—or classical viewpoints related to a view of modern Pentecostalism's origins from out of the Azusa Street revival at the beginning of the twentieth century—foreground analysis of the origins, nature, universality, transmission, and consequences of sin.[26] The origins of sin, whether through Adam or the serpent in the garden (representing Satan), is related to original sin, which elucidates the mysterious but yet all-encompassing nature of sin that binds all persons into sinful solidarity with each other and inclines all toward sinful acts and behaviors. The consequences of sin—its results and effects—are destruction (personal, social, cosmic), suffering, and death, ultimately alienation from God, which perpetuates the suffering due to sin in the present life to eternity.

Parallel treatments can be found among charismatic theologians, those informed by the Neo-Pentecostal movement within the mainline Protestant denominations since the 1960s. One account, unfolded out of a three-volume *Systematic Theology from a Charismatic Perspective* frame of reference, situates the hamartiology in the first volume amidst the broader discussion of the doctrine of creation. Two chapters totaling over fifty pages (of a 415-page book and a 1375-page tri-volume systematics) also expound on the origins, nature, and consequences of sin,[27] including further elabora-

---

26. See from a Church of God (Cleveland, Tennessee) perspective, Arrington, *Christian Doctrine*, vol. II, part II (in three chapters); and from an Assemblies of God perspective, Marino, "The Origin, Nature, and Consequences of Sin," a one chapter version of what Arrington covers in forty pages; both are denominationally authorized theological textbooks.

27. See Williams, *Renewal Theology*, vol. 1., chs. 10–11, on sin and the effects of sin, respectively.

tion in the last part on the guilt and punishment demanded by sin alongside the separation, estrangement, and bondage sin initiates and effects. This work, developed from out of a Presbyterian or Reformed perspective, is also careful to specify how a sovereign God can nevertheless create a world with freedoms that allow for sin's tarnishment, which is minimized in another, more baptistic approach. The latter discussion of the nature and consequences of sin transitions also between theological anthropology (the *what* that needs saving) and Christology (the *who* that brings salvation),[28] while discussing the fall, Adam and original and inherited sin, the nature and universality of sin, and the results of sin.

Two summations are in order. First, if the science-and-theology conversation (above) has by and large focused on understanding the nature of original sin, pentecostal spirituality appears to spotlight the personal character of sin, how the fall has resulted in sinful inclinations within each and every person.[29] There is a sense in which this is expected: if pentecostal spirituality lifts up the saving work of Jesus Christ through the person and work of the Holy Spirit, then it also makes sense that its general understanding of sin revolves around what is wrong in the world such that the intervention of the triune God is redemptive. Second, then, pentecostal theologians have not spent much time thinking about the doctrine of sin in scientific terms. Following their evangelical counterparts, much of pentecostal hamartiology is shaped by the received dogmatic tradition, especially as mediated through conservative Protestant streams. Within this venue, if science appears at all in the discussion, it would be in the chapter on the doctrine of creation, and in that context, the focus is usually on (or against) the theory of evolution and its (disastrous) implications for Christian theology of creation.[30]

Although any attempt to develop a scientifically informed theology of sin within such a pentecostal discursive environment would be like a fish out of water, not asking theological questions in the present milieu would also be intellectual suicide for the church. While evangelical—and hence

---

28. Hart, *Truth Aflame*, ch. 6 on sin.

29. Warrington, *Pentecostal Theology*, 35.

30. Williams, *Renewal Theology*, I.112–13, is clearly against the evolution of species, hinging his position on the Genesis narrative's indication regarding creatures being formed according to their own *kinds*, but Hart, *Truth Aflame*, 168–78, is more of a progressive creationist, albeit one open to arguments from a theistic evolutionary point of view. Munyon, "The Creation of the Universe and Humankind," 222–35, also rejects macroevolutionary ideas, but does say that "the Scriptures simply do not speak in support of [any creationist] models with the degree of specificity [we] would like" (235).

pentecostal—engagements with science ought not to be confronted frontally given the historical suspicions and polemics,[31] I think it is possible to make some headway if explorations were grounded within ecclesially defined traditions, in this case according to pentecostal spirituality and its sensibilities. For instance, if an evolutionary cosmology might also suggest that sin could be similarly understood as the distortions or disruptions introduced into the world by primordial selfishness, then how might the Spirit-empowered struggle against sin at the personal level illuminate the brokenness that exists due to sin at the various creaturely levels and domains? In other words, might the alien character of sin in an evolutionary cosmos be better grasped when viewed from the perspective of the historical and existential struggles of homo sapiens with what seems to be wrong with the world? The following thus seeks to delineate first steps toward such an hamartiology from specifically pentecostal starting points while being mindful of the scientifically delineated understandings of sin sketched above.

Sin: A Pentecostal Interpretation

In another essay, I have explored in preliminary fashion, with the assistance of scholars within that tradition, a Wesleyan theology of sin and sanctification.[32] My strategy in that venture was to probe more deeply into the anthropological assumptions, in dialogue especially with the cognitive and psychological sciences, undergirding the Wesleyan theology of sanctification given the latter's centrality in Wesleyan self-understanding. Similarly, here, I think a productive way forward is to press more deeply into the Day of Pentecost message in the book of Acts that has been generative for modern pentecostal piety and practice and has thus operated loosely as a canon within the canon for theologizing within the pentecostal movement.[33] The following thus gestures toward a preliminary hamartiology from out of the Pentecost account, situates such within the broader Lukan theological framework, and then attempts to reconnect to the preceding scientifically elaborated notions of sin. Our goal is to outline a distinctively pentecostal but no less ecumenical platform for a theology of sin for a scientific world, one that views sin in terms of the potencies countering human acceptance, cooperation, and response to the redemptive works of the Spirit.

---

31. Some of which is charted by Elbert and Yong, "Christianity, Pentecostalism."
32. See Yong, "Sanctification, Science, and the Spirit."
33. See part I of this book.

Sin—In, through, and after Pentecost

An initial pause might be to address the concern that Acts 2, whatever else it might discuss, is not intended to develop a theology of sin.[34] Yet we begin here since the second chapter of Acts provides the basic arc for understanding the promised Spirit-empowered witness "to the ends of the earth" (Acts 1:8), culminating in the arrival of the gospel to Rome in the final chapter, even as those from Rome were already found gathered in Jerusalem and recipients of the Spirit's outpouring at Pentecost (2:10).[35] Hence every endeavor to think theologically in dialogue with this book will be forged in light of its pentecostal witness to the good news of Jesus Christ.[36] Our approach therefore asks a twofold set of questions from this Day of Pentecost starting point: first, what is it that the Spirit does in the Day of Pentecost outpouring, and second, how might such activities of the Spirit provide insight into what is wrong with human beings and their world? Conceptualizing the latter will provide a springboard, I will argue, for outlining a pentecostal theology of at least the effects of sin.[37]

---

34. Sin appears only once in Acts 2, in Peter's response to the crowd's querying about how they should receive his message: "Repent, and be baptized every one of you in the name of Jesus Christ *so that your sins may be forgiven*; and you will receive the gift of the Holy Spirit" (2:38, italics added). This call to repentance resulting in the expiation of sin is repeated in Peter's message to the crowd gathered around the healing of at the Beautiful Gate in the next chapter (3:19) even as it is consistent with the passing references to *sin* in the rest of Acts, mostly in relationship to the preaching of the good news regarding the availability of forgiveness through Christ (5:31, 10:43, 13:38–39, 26:18). The only other reference is to Stephen not holding the sin of his murderers against them (7:60). For broader perspective on the Lukan notion of forgiveness of sins see Moessner, "The 'Script' of the Scriptures in Acts."

35. For argument regarding Acts 2 as central to any theology of Acts, much less a pentecostal theological reading of the book, see my *The Spirit Poured Out on All Flesh*, ch. 4.

36. Here following Macchia, *Baptized in the Spirit*, which provides a pentecostal vision for theology, not just in terms of unfolding modern pentecostal perspectives but in terms of going back to the scriptural witness via the Day of Pentecost point of entry in order to re-envision a coherent articulation of a theology framed pneumatologically, as if via the Third Article of the creed.

37. Insightful and exemplary in this respect is Welker, *God as Spirit*, whose exposition rightly connects the accomplishments of the Spirit at Pentecost with the work of the divine *ruah* detailed in the First Testament, observing that the constraining work of the Spirit in ancient Israel is consistent with that inaugurated on the Day of Pentecost; I would suggest also, however, that Welker can just as easily be read backward, as unfolding how the pentecostal achievements of the Spirit also illuminate the previous workings of the divine *ruah* as recorded in Israel's sacred texts.

We begin by noticing that the Spirit descends on human "flesh" (Acts 2:17a). This summarizes what the author describes earlier in these terms: "... suddenly from heaven there came a sound like the rush of a violent wind, and it filled the entire house where they were sitting. Divided tongues, as of fire, appeared among them, and a tongue rested on each of them. All of them were filled with the Holy Spirit and began to speak in other languages, as the Spirit gave them ability" (2:2–4). Note here that there is a carnal dimension to the Spirit's coming: human ears resound, human bodies are perceptive, human heads are touched, and human tongues are activated. The Spirit's arrival registers itself across the full human sensorium. One might thus ask what it is about human embodiment that is targeted by the Spirit's gift and giftings?[38] Might it be that human perceptibility, epistemology, and renewal are being accomplished in the Spirit's redemptive work?

Next, the author wants us to understand that "there were devout Jews from every nation under heaven living in Jerusalem" (2:5), and that these include alongside local Galileans other representative groups from around the Mediterranean world (2:7–11). As important, amidst the bewilderment, amazement, astonishment, and perplexity (2:6, 7, 12a) of the multitude of tongues and languages unleash at the event, there is an unfathomable intelligibility: the exclamation that, "in our own languages we hear them speaking about God's deeds of power" (2:11b) proceeds alongside and simultaneous with the cacophonous, "What does this mean?" (2:12b). Many others have commented on what is here obscurely understood: that whatever else Pentecost means, it somehow reunifies what the Tower of Babel dispersed, but achieves such harmony not by silencing but by harmonizing in pneumatological key the many tongues and languages of the world.[39] One might thus ask how such divine redemption is responsive to the plight of human sociocultural and transnational alienation, not least the demarcation between Jew and Samaritan, much less Jew and Gentile, both segregations clearly reconciled in the rest of Acts. Could the pentecostal miracle, in other words, be addressing the sin of human ethnocentrism, the biased preferences for the in-group over and against all other (out-) groups?[40]

---

38. I develop these ideas further in my pentecostal (Acts 2) theology of diverse (dis)abilities; see Yong, *The Bible, Disability, and the Church*, ch. 4.

39. E.g., González and González, "Babel and Empire, Pentecost and Empire," Green, "'In Our Own Languages,'" and Davis, "Acts 2 and the Old Testament." From a pentecostal perspective, see Macchia, "Babel and the Tongues of Pentecost—Reversal or Fulfilment?," best represents the basic thrust upon which this essay proceeds.

40. I began my scholarly research program asking about the implications of the Pentecost narrative for intercultural and interreligious theological tasks; more recently, I have turned my gaze to political theological enterprises, forging deeper into

Peter's exposition in response to the wonderment of the crowd provides additional clues to the problems Pentecost might be directed at. Here, Luke records Peter's appeal to the book of Joel, effectively providing an authoritative (scriptural) explanation of the pentecostal outpouring as justifying egalitarian prophesying from out of the mouths of women, youth, and slaves (2:17–18), groups of persons traditionally not viewed as recipients of divine favor or authorization. Yet another way to read Peter's (and Luke's) use of sacred writings is to inspire the overcoming of hierarchical divisions or other chasms—between male and female, young and old, slave and free—prevalent in the ancient world but no longer relevant in the community of the redeemed. It might even be further speculated from the apocalyptic themes in the Joel text preserved here in Acts 2 that the division between the human-cultural world and its/their natural environments (2:19–20) is also minimized. That the witness of the gospel comes through those on the margins and through cosmic signs and wonders suggests that it is the work of the Spirit to eliminate the hierarchies of being, both those conventionally erected and those presumed to be natural to the created order, not in order to instantiate anarchism but to renew human community and relationality in its various domains.

Yet central to the pentecostal message proclaimed by Peter is Jesus' resurrection from the dead (2:24), understood also through the witness of ancient Israel's scriptures (2:25–28, 31). If David the prophet of resurrection remains dead and buried (2:29–30), then Jesus shows himself to be Messiah through his exaltation to the right hand of the Father (2:33–36). Death and bodily corruption, in other words, are part of the pentecostal witness of the Spirit, consistent in this regard with the broader apostolic claim that Jesus "was declared to be [the] Son of God with power according to the spirit of holiness by resurrection from the dead" (Rom 1:4). So if elsewhere the evangelists witness to death being the crucible from out of which life flows (e.g., John 12:24),[41] it is worthwhile asking here about what kind of death the pentecostal arrival of the Spirit overcomes.

Finally, Acts 2 concludes with the instantiation of the pentecostal community, one characterized by mutuality and gratuitous reciprocity (2:42–47). Herein is epitomized pneumatic koinonia and sharing, made possible through an economy of grace dispersed through the Spirit's residing upon carnal human bodies and transforming their self-centeredness and

---

the challenging questions that exist in the pluralistic and antagonistic public square in Yong, *In the Days of Caesar*.

41. This would be central to an evolutionary universe (see my discussion in *Renewing Christian Theology*, ch. 10).

greed into communal flourishing.[42] The Pentecost chronicle thus convincingly registers the counter-effects of the Spirit vis-à-vis human behaviors of hoarding, greed, or self-preservation.[43]

An Implicit Lukan Theology of Sin

I now want to situate briefly the present discussion against the broader Lukan message, especially as portrayed in his Gospel account. Again, one would be hard pressed to insist that the Third Gospel includes within it a developed theology of sin.[44] Yet it will be clear that there is no denying the presence of a Lukan ethical vision that provides orientation to what the evangelist considered as plaguing the human condition,[45] even as there are major thematic threads connecting the two books he wrote that I suggest sustain the incipient harmartiology distilled above. Four lines of inquiry provide cues for a Lukan understanding of sin relative to our quest.

First, if Acts 1:8 provides the outline for that book and Acts 2 frames its overarching horizons, then Jesus' Nazareth message provides orientation for his ministry and message in the Third Gospel.[46] Here, the Isaianic text serves as the blueprint:

> The Spirit of the Lord is upon me,
> because he has anointed me

---

42. Which explains why the economic sins of Ananias and Saphira in Acts 5:1-10 were judged so harshly; see Kuecker, "The Spirit and the 'Other', Satan and the 'Self.'"

43. I argue this theme of the economy of the Spirit in my monograph, *Spirit of Love*.

44. The word *sin* appears in Luke's gospel much more often than in his sequel, but again, is associated with the good news of forgiveness made available through or proclaimed by and in relationship to Jesus (mostly although not exclusively): 1:77, 3:3, 5:20-24, 11:4, 17:3-4, 24:47. The few other references include confessions of sinfulness (5:8, 18:13), comparisons between perceived sinner and the presumed just (6:32-34), Galileans who were political martyrs (13:2), the story of the sinner who kissed and washed Jesus' feet with her hair (7:36-50), the parables of the lost sheep, coin, and son (15:7, 10, 18, 21), and Jesus being put to death at the hands of sinners (24:7). For our purposes, the repeated observation of Jesus eating with sinners (5:30-32, 7:34, 15:2, 19:7) is suggestive and will be commented on further momentarily.

45. Thus Conzelmann, *The Theology of St. Luke*, 228, writes: "The conception of sin [in Luke], compared with Paul's has a strong ethical colouring, and the same is true also of deliverance from sin." Other than passing statements such as this one and with one exception (to be referred to below), I have not otherwise been able to locate any substantive or focused treatment of the doctrine of sin in the Lukan writings. We thus proceed cautiously.

46. See, e.g., Prior, *Jesus the Liberator*.

> to bring good news to the poor.
> He has sent me to proclaim release to the captives
> and recovery of sight to the blind,
> to let the oppressed go free,
> to proclaim the year of the Lord's favour (Luke 4:18–19; cf. Isa 61:1–2a).

Clearly, the gospel according to the Third Evangelist is concerned with the poor and even more so for those marginalized and oppressed in general, and Jesus' consistent teaching in the rest of the gospel is that people should put their trust not in their wealth but be open to giving to others following the heart of the Father God.[47] That Jesus intends to inaugurate the "year of the Lord's favour" also hearkens back to the Jubilee message of the First Testament and is consistent with the community of sharing and mutuality formed through the Pentecost outpouring of the Spirit.[48] The correspondence between this primary feature of Jesus' mission and what was instantiated, however short lived, in the early followers of the messianic message supports a social understanding of sin that divides oppressor from oppressed, the affluent from those in poverty, the political elite from those on the margins of society.[49] A pentecostal perspective emphasizes the central role of the Spirit who accomplishes this delivering work through the anointing of Jesus in the Gospel and then within the egalitarian community in Acts.[50] For our hamartiological purposes, then, we can observe that the missions of the triune God, in the incarnation of the Son and in the pentecostal gift of the Spirit, counters the structural and systemic sinfulness of socioeconomic oppression pervasive in a fallen world.

Second, note that the unveiling of Jesus' public ministry passes through his Spirit-enabled wilderness sojourn where he is tempted, attacked even, by

---

47. The themes of poverty and wealth are palpable throughout the Third Gospel: e.g., 4:16–18, 16:1–15, 18:9–11, 19:1–10, 19:11–27, 20:9–26, 21:1–4; see Pilgrim, *Good News to the Poor*, Johnson, *Sharing Possessions*, Gillman, *Possessions and the Life of Faith*, and Phillips, *Reading Issues of Wealth and Poverty in Luke-Acts*.

48. See Ringe, *Jesus, Liberation, and the Biblical Jubilee*. Note also in this connection both Sanders, "Sins, Debts, and Jubilee Release," and Sri, "Release from the Debt of Sin," which are arguably the only sustained discussions of the Lukan notion of sin, albeit framed vis-à-vis the good news of the cancellation of debt that foregrounds the poverty-wealth ways of categorizing the issues in the Third Gospel.

49. See further the discussion of Jesus' "social stance" in Cassidy, *Jesus, Politics, and Society*, ch. 2.

50. Argued by Wenk, *Community Forming Power*. Relative to liberation theology's famous "preferential option for the poor," see also the recognition of "God's special love for the poor and marginalized" by pentecostal theologian, Rodriguez, *The Liberating Mission of Jesus*, ch. 10.

the devil (Luke 4:1-13). Recognition that this is surely a spiritual encounter does not mean denying its materially constituted, politically charged, and environmentally situated character. The point is that if the Joel passage defines the pentecostal outpouring as having apocalyptic and cosmic dimensions (see above), then nothing less would be anticipated from Jesus' own mission in the Spirit. The brokenness of humanity's social world here finds its symbolic counterpart in the barrenness of the wilderness, and in its hostility toward full human flourishing.

Third, and consistent with the initial point, Luke also identifies one of the major features of the gospel as what might be called an *upside-down world*. I get this from the reputation the apostles earned as those who were "turning the world upside down" (Acts 17:6), but this is the Acts rendition of what John York describes in the Third Gospel as the "rhetoric of reversal" that begins with Mary's Magnificat, the humbling of the exalted and vice-versa (Luke 14:11, 18:14), and Jesus' teaching that, "some are last who will be first, and some are first who will be last" (13:30).[51] The point is that the perspective of the coming reign of God, heralded in Jesus' life and teachings contrasts with the conventions of the world that are hierarchically organized (sinful) and that privilege certain groups while subordinating others. If, as indicated earlier, the Joel text undergirding the significance of the Day of Pentecost event overturns the anti-gospel hierarchies of the world, then the Third Evangelist's theology of reversal suggests the dismantling of socially structured systems that disempower the masses. The implications for a Lukan hamartiology are further extrapolatable: that the contributions, voices, and perspectives of those otherwise socially excluded and sin against are restored and redeemed, especially but not only the women, beginning with Mary and continuing with prophesying young women.[52] Sinful realities in a fallen world are thus those forces that perpetuate the conditions of those socially marginalized by authoritarian powers and those on the underside of history. The coming of the Spirit confronts, unmasks, and subverts these destructive schemes and arrangements.[53]

---

51. See York, *The Last Shall Be First*, ch. 2. Part of Mary's song includes these lines:
He has brought down the powerful from their thrones,
   and lifted up the lowly;
he has filled the hungry with good things,
   and sent the rich away empty (1:52-53).

52. See in this regard Arlandson, *Women, Class, and Society in Early Christianity*, ch. 5, "The Fall of Men and the Rise of Women."

53. This said, our discussion here ought not to be read as a commendation of a simplistic social agenda since Luke's focus—as Twelftree, *People of the Spirit*, ch. 13,

Last but not least for our purposes, the "to the ends of the earth" motif structuring Acts is clearly anticipated in the universalistic arch of Luke's gospel. The crucial role of the later portions of Isaiah already seen reemerge along this front, now in the form of Deutero- or Second Isaiah's universalistic message of Israel as "light to the nations" (Isa 42:6, 49:6) that is cited not only in Acts (13:47) but also as part of Simeon's announcement regarding the arrival of Jesus:

> my eyes have seen your salvation,
> which you have prepared in the presence of all peoples,
> a light for revelation to the Gentiles
> and for glory to your people Israel (Luke 2:30–32).

The universality of Jesus' significance is reiterated at the end of the Third Gospel in Jesus' commissioning the disciples—"that repentance and forgiveness of sins is to be proclaimed in his name to all nations, beginning from Jerusalem" (24:47)—even is such is symbolized in the genealogy that traces his lineage not through David to Abraham as in Matthew but back to "Adam, son of God" (3:38),[54] and is promoted through inclusion of Jesus' intentional journeying through Samaria (9:52).[55] The point is unmistakable: the good news of Jesus is not just for the Jews but for all humanity, for the nations to the ends of the earth, in Lukan parlance.[56] The Gospel account thus provides a ramp toward the pentecostal baptism of all flesh, those from every tongue, tribe, and nation, by the Spirit. For hamartiological purposes, the saving purposes of God in Christ overcomes the ethnocentrism dividing people groups from one another via the pneumatological visitation starting in Jesus' mission in Judea and intending from the beginning the inclusion of the Gentiles.[57]

---

reminds us—remains on nurturing the redemptive practices of the Spirit *within* the community of faith, rather than is directed outwardly to society; yet surely, there are social implications, as I argue also in my *Who is the Holy Spirit?*

54. See González, *Luke*, 54–55.

55. Other distinctive Lukan references to the Samaritans are in 10:25–37, 17:11, which in turn anticipate the apostolic witness into Samaria in Acts (1:8, 8:2–25); see also Yong, *Who is the Holy Spirit*, part IV (on Samaria).

56. The contours of which are superbly portrayed in Mittelstadt, *Reading Luke-Acts in the Pentecostal Tradition*, ch. 4.5.

57. This would be the Lukan version of "salvation history" that goes to "the ends of the earth"; see Jervell, "The Future of the Past."

Toward a Pentecostal and Scientific Theology of Sin

The goal of this essay is to initiate discussion about the possibility of a pentecostal theology of sin engaged with and perhaps even informed by the sciences. Our investigation, forged in dialogue with St. Luke's pentecostal theology, intimates a view of sin that resists the pentecostal work of the Spirit, inclinations and behaviors that are oppressive rather than liberative, selfish rather than other-concerned, xenophobic rather than hospitable to and embracing of outsiders, etc. To be sure, we are still far from any final word on this topic, so our concluding remarks ought to precipitate further inquiry. On theological and one methodological comment are intended to provide the impetus.

Theologically, we must begin as Pentecostals, even as Christians, with our theological commitments. Hence, if at the center is pentecostal spirituality as normed by the Day of Pentecost story, then it is not just generic theistic questions that emerge but specific pneumatological, soteriological, and eschatological concerns. Starting with the Spirit of Pentecost thus ensures that the Christian dialogue with the sciences is never theologically neglectful and also not ignorant of the sinful realities that the gift of the Spirit is designed to correct and redeem. More pointedly, a pneumatological perspective in conversation with the sciences shifts our gaze from the primordial past with its obsessiveness on origins to the eschatological future and its concerns about how the coming reign of God can be grasped given what science anticipates about how a fallen and finite cosmos will come to an end.[58] What emerges might be an eschatological theology of sin, not one that talks about sin's evolution—although there is a sense in which the emergence of higher and higher levels of complexity involves intensification of sinful propensities over deep time—but one that recognizes how the alien intrusiveness of sin in a good creation is being perpetually countered by the triune God seeking reconciliation with all creation.[59] Obviously this is not meant to bar the path to inquiry about the cosmic past, but it is to say that a pentecostal orientation will ask other, equally important but yet heretofore neglected questions in dialogue with the sciences, and do so in ways that are consistent with its theological ideals and even guided and normed by them.

Methodologically, our observations thus far suggest that any pentecostal theology of sin that springs off the heart of the pentecostal experience grounded in the Day of Pentecost narrative is ill-equipped to take on the major questions related to evolution and human origins that pentecostal

---

58. I argue for this shift of perspective in *The Spirit of Creation*, esp. chs. 3–4.
59. See here Bradnick, "A Pentecostal Perspective on Entropy."

scholars (parallel to their evangelical counterparts) have focused on at the theology-and-science interface. While these matters are not unimportant, I suggest they are not the initial site from which pentecostal engagement with the sciences ought to ensue. Rather, if we attended to the working of the Spirit launched at the Day of Pentecost and regarding which modern pentecostal believers are most keen to experience and participate in, it is discovered that the Spirit's redemptive activity is explicable in anthropological, cultural, sociological, and environmental terms, and that this therefore invites, I urge, consideration of scientific perspectives in these domains.[60] Christians can thereby understand what science has to contribute at these levels first, and what its limitations are therein—particularly as impeded by the effects of sin, which is after all our primary topic—and then perhaps later they can devote effort to comprehending the issues that others have been concerned about. So the anthropological and biological sciences can help us understand the effects of sin, even the biological death that is intertwined with biblical claims, and may hence even enable our cooperation with the redemptive work of the Spirit in and through the suffering of our personal lives and also death of our bodies.[61] The social sciences can illuminate how human individualism and self-centeredness and our group predilections, behaviors, and structures have all been defaced by sin and perhaps thereby inspire human repentance and concomitantly corrective attitudes and behaviors in the social sphere.[62] Then, the natural sciences can clarify how fallen human relations impact and are shaped by their environmental situatedness, not only on our planet but within our solar system and beyond, and could even facilitate our reorientation from paths of self-destruction toward activities that herald the coming reign of God.[63] How these scientific perspectives can illuminate human creaturely and sinful realities at their proper levels without undermining theological (and pneumatological, soteriological, and eschatological) perspectives will need to be a matter of

---

60. That the effects of sin are multidimensional corresponds with the way in which I developed a Lukan soteriology in an earlier work: *Spirit Poured Out on All Flesh*, ch. 2.

61. The essay by biologist Mitchell, "Let There Be Life!," is instructive with regard to understanding death in both scientific (biological) and theological (pentecostal) terms.

62. The Godly Love research project focused on studying altruism among pentecostal-charismatic exemplars from social scientific perspectives carves out venues for such explorations; see Lee and Yong, eds., *The Science and Theology of Godly Love*.

63. I have attempted to outline a pneumatological theology of the environment in dialogue with the sciences (and in dialogue with other faiths traditions) in my *The Cosmic Breath*, part III.

ongoing research and reflection.[64] None of this is to say that science becomes salvific—far from it. Instead, science can be a helpful handmaid within a broader theological quest, perhaps even guided by the Spirit.[65]

The result thus far is not any scientific theology of sin that trumps other perspectives but the much more modest proposal about the possibility of pneumatological and scientific perspectives converging toward a harmartiology that in turn complements the dogmatic tradition in this regard, particularly proposals that have sought to formulate and develop sin in interpersonal and social terms. I hope other pentecostal theologians can build on these insights, but more importantly, I wish that such discussions would benefit not just pentecostal communities of faith but the broader ecumenical conversation. Does this exercise generate optimism regarding how an apostolic, pentecostal, and pneumatological approach could push the discussion forward? I submit such to be one promising venue in quest of a theology of sin in a scientific age.

---

64. Tanner, "Workings of the Spirit," urges that on the theological plane, the workings of the Spirit are simple—i.e., asserted by faith—but that in the horizontal plane, they might be understood as appropriately complex, to be discerned perhaps even with the help of the sciences at their different levels; my own argument along these lines is in *The Spirit of Creation*, ch. 2.

65. This exceedingly brief sketch is consistent with what is elaborated on much more substantively by physician, psychotherapist, and theologian Warren, *Cleansing the Cosmos*.

CHAPTER 8

Jubilee, Pentecost, and Liberation

The Preferential Option of the Poor on the Apostolic Way[1]

Recent trends in liberation theology show remarkable diversification compared with the perceived Marxist underpinnings of the first generation's efforts. In the meanwhile, although it was said that liberation theologians opted for the poor, it was also noted that the poor were opting for Pentecostalism.[2] This chapter considers how pentecostal spirituality which has served the poor across the majority world can *both* gain further theological traction and specification *and* expand evangelical thinking on this topic via sustained engagement with the "many tongues" of liberation theology in the present global context as refracted through the apostolic witness, particularly of the Third Gospel and its sequel volume.[3] The argument, unfolded in the three sections that follow, begins with contemporary liberationist impulses in global and evangelical theological discourses, continues with developments of pentecostal liberationist thought, and concludes with scriptural reflections, focused particularly on Luke-Acts.

1. Thanks to Mae Elise Cannon for initiating this paper via inviting my contribution to her book on evangelical theologies of liberation. I am grateful to PhD and ThM students in my informal seminar in Mission and Theology in the Spirit, especially Christopher The, for the careful reading and vigorous discussion of the paper and response to it. All errors of fact and interpretation remain my own responsibility.

2. A saying that goes back decades; for one version, see Miller and Yamamori, *Global Pentecostalism*, 215.

3. Most immediately in the background of this essay is my book *The Future of Evangelical Theology*, esp. chs. 5–6; the direct focus on liberation theology in this essay is a relatively new area for me, although much of my work in disability theology (two books and many essays) engages such emphases variously.

The Preferential Option for the Poor: Global and Evangelical Developments

Liberation theology burst onto the scene not too long after the Latin American Catholic Bishops conference in Medellin, Colombia in 1968.[4] In the first decade plus after Medellin, the dominant liberation voices (e.g., Gutiérrez, Bonino, Segundo, and the Boff brothers, among others) drew from a wide range of critical theories, most prominently neo-Marxist social analysis, and brought such into dialogue especially with the tradition of Roman Catholic social thought (these were mostly Catholic theologians) vis-à-vis the contexts of poverty widespread across the Latin American hemisphere. The point about liberation was that the gospel was historically, politically, economically, and socially relevant, and this also impacted the nature and mission of the church as the people of God and the body of Christ. Methodologically, liberation theology emphasized the hermeneutical starting point of solidarity with the poor: the Scriptures and the Christian tradition were received from those perspectives and in relationship to those realities and the challenges identified therein, and the goal was not armchair speculation but—here consistent with Marx's own commitments—to change the world.

Within two decades, reactions came in hard and fast, not only from the Roman Catholic magisterium—with concerns about the role of Marxist analyses and implications of such for mobilizing uncritical participation in class struggles even to the point of violence[5]—but also from evangelical quarters. Like the Roman Catholic hierarchy, evangelicals among others also perceived that Marxist tools would precipitate revolutionary violence,[6] so even if liberationists were rightly and justifiably driven by motivations regarding the alleviation of poverty, liberation theology ought to be approached very reservedly.[7] So although the liberationist option for the poor was recognized by some evangelicals to have biblical moorings, the concern was that as a hermeneutical principle it would compromise evangelical convictions about allowing Scripture to interpret itself, thus subjecting the

---

4. The impact of the Medellin conference was felt within a few years, as exemplified in O'Connor, *Liberation*; cf. Quigley, ed., *Freedom and Unfreedom in the Americas*.

5. The Roman curia was and remains concerned about the poor but attends less to the structural causes of poverty than Latin American liberation theologians have focused on; cp. the Congregation for the Doctrine of the Faith, "Instruction on Certain Aspects of the 'Theology of Liberation,'" and Curnow, "Which Preferential Option for the Poor?"

6. Thus arguments emerged—e.g., Wan-Tatah, *Emancipation in African Theology*—that explicitly eschewed violence as defensible means to liberative ends.

7. Hundley, *Radical Liberation Theology*; McGlasson, *Another Gospel*.

message of the Bible to biased perspectival lenses or other ideological commitments.[8] Within these main lines of the evangelical theological tradition, then, liberation theology, even if useful thematically, could not provide the primary framework even to engage the concerns of Latin America and the challenges of global poverty; instead, liberationist perspectives could make their contribution only when resituated within a more biblically-oriented paradigm such as that provided by contextual theological approaches.[9]

Part of the challenge was that the emerging postcolonial world since the 1960s inspired theological thinking from those outside the traditional theological orbit of the Euro-American West. Hence one way to read the tradition of liberation theology is as an expression of non-Western experiences, frustrations, and aspirations. One early evangelical commentator recognized this aspect of the liberation theological enterprise and hence sought to engage its multifariousness.[10] In Andrew Kirk's reading, the central biblical themes of the Exodus and Jesus Christ as liberator and herald of the coming reign of God emerged from out of the Third World context and hence registered the needs and challenges at the forefront of undeveloped and underdeveloped regions around the globe. Kirk rightly put his finger on the so-called Third World context that was birthing liberationist momentum, and clarified the underlying hermeneutical and methodological issues for consideration.

Evangelical theology at large, however, has been ill equipped to grapple seriously with such hermeneutical and methodological pluralism. Although Kirk's important contributions were made almost four decades ago, evangelical biblicism and theological method challenge any dialogical approach that takes seriously contextual realities in relationship to the scriptural traditions.[11] So even when evangelicals labor to propose a holistic theology that is Jesus-centered, poor/marginalized-oriented, directed toward the reign of God, and communally engaged[12]—each of which themes are central to liberation theologies—these have remained marginal to rather than received by the center of the evangelical theological tradition. The result is that when contemporary evangelical thinkers have embraced the liberationist vision,

---

8. Núñez C., *Liberation Theology*.

9. This is the argument of Heaney, *Contextual Theology for Latin America*.

10. Kirk, *Liberation Theology*.

11. See for instance my "Restoring, Reforming, Renewing," which documents these issues in relationship to Larsen and Treier, eds., *The Cambridge Companion to Evangelical Theology*.

12. E.g., Pope-Levison, *Evangelization from a Liberation Perspective*.

such has to be parried under a *postconservative* label rather than being defensible as belonging to the heart of evangelical thought and action.[13]

The putatively global character of liberation theology needs further elucidation. Although there is no denying the central role played by Latin American theologians, particularly those inspired by the Medellin gathering, one might argue that these Roman Catholic impulses were part of a wider transcontinental wave that crested toward the end of the 1960s. In fact, alongside and rather oblivious to developments outside of the North American context, one of the first books on liberation theology was by James Cone, in 1970.[14] Cone's dialogue partners were theological rather than only sociotheoretical: it was Karl Barth and the neo-orthodox theology in the Barthian train that provided for Cone language to bridge the worlds of black suffering and that of the gospel.[15] This tradition of black theology in North America spawned a range of chords and accents (e.g., books by Deotis Roberts and Major Jones, among many others) even as it confirmed that liberation theology deployed a diversity of theological and analytical tools, not to mention derived from similar but yet contrasting life perspectives, across the Americas.

Meanwhile, Kirk's assessment in the late 1970s was itself possible only because of the flurry of so-called Third World theologies of liberation that multiplied in the preceding decade. If Marxist and sociotheoretical analyses were dominant (although not exhaustively so) in Latin America, indigenous spiritualities were more prominent across sub-Saharan Africa and the dialogue between political theology and world religious traditions more substantive in Asian theologies of liberation.[16] One is struck within this context of a kaleidoscope of claims and positions, each constituted by a multiplicity of converging perspectives and interests since the point is not only that liberation theology in the 1970s was effectively global in its chorus, but also that each harmony was formed out of otherwise dissonant notes. No

---

13. For instance, Chaves, *Evangelicals and Liberation Revisited*; Chaves is a Brazilian theologian at the Baptist University of the Americas in San Antonio and he attempts to forge what he calls a postconservative liberation theology that brings into conversation Gustavo Gutiérrez and Anabaptist theologian William James McClendon Jr.

14. At least this was the first book in English with that title: Cone, *A Black Theology of Liberation*.

15. The preface to the 1986 edition of Cone's book, reprinted in his *A Black Theology of Liberation: Fortieth Anniversary Edition*, xv-xxiv, documents these matters.

16. Ferm, *Third World Liberation Theologies*; cf. Anderson and Stransky, eds., *Third World Theologies*, Torres and Fabella, eds., *The Emergent Gospel*, Appiah-Kubi and Torres, eds., *African Theology En Route*, and Amaladoss, *Life in Freedom*.

wonder evangelical theologies, even the ones forged by those sympathetic to liberationist aims, were unable to account for the multivocality of the conversation. If it was difficult enough to hear clearly the voices of the poor, now these were sounded through the tones of indigenous and other faith traditions, and from out of the complexity of contested matters abounding within the public squares of the majority world.

Two case studies of particularizing trends in liberation theology into the 1980s accentuate our point. On the one arc was that represented by South African theologians like Allan Boesak, who sought to think liberatively about the realities of Apartheid; if black theologians like Cone engaged with dominant theological traditions such as neo-orthodoxy, black South Africans like Boesak sought to retrieve aspects of the Reformed Calvinist tradition (which was prevalent in Dutch Afrikaner theological discourse), especially those emphasizing social justice.[17] Another distinct course was that represented by the Minjung theologians of South Korea; like their friends from Latin America and Africa, these theologies of the people (the *minjung*) sought to appropriate cultural and ritual realities for liberationist enterprises, but the influence and legacy of conservative Protestant missions meant that such arguments had to be unfolded biblically as well.[18] The point is that these are complementary projects—in South Africa and in South Korea—but they were urged along contrasting sociocultural, ethnic, hermeneutical, and methodological venues. If evangelicals could embrace Boesak's Calvinism, they were much less certain about how to respond to his reappropriation of that tradition for the purposes of liberating South Africa from apartheid, even as evangelicals generally could only engage the Minjung theologies polemically and apologetically, at best with guarded hesitation.[19]

The present ferment in liberation theology shows no signs of abatement on the global stage, but even further complexification. A number of trajectories are worth noting. First, liberation theology is needed not only for so-called Third or underdeveloped world contexts but also in the first- and second-world regions wherever there are marginalized groups;[20] in

17. See Boesak, *Black and Reformed*; there were also Roman Catholics involved in the South African apartheid context: Nolan and Broderick, "To Nourish Our Faith."

18. These dual streams are represented in Bock, *Minjung Theology*, and Moon, *A Korean Minjung Theology*.

19. I have not found any published responses by evangelicals to Boesak's work in the periodical literature; the one article on the South Korean conversation by and large rejects the viability of the *minjung* approach as legitimately evangelical—see Kim, "The Concept of God in Minjung Theology."

20. Part IV of Van Nieuwenhove and Goldewijk, eds., *Popular Religion, Liberation*

fact, on that score, even the Western world needs liberation from its own oppressiveness (its tendencies toward exploitation and victimization of those less fortunate). Second, and along this same line of inquiry, there are now urban liberation theologies focused particularly on the slums and ghettos of the cosmopolitan centers of the world, arguably all developed environments but stratified socioeconomically and in many other ways;[21] here, because of the systemic networks that constitute twenty-first–century global cities, liberation must operate in multiple directions, addressing different and many layers of systems that generate urban flows. Third, liberation theology in the last two decades faces fundamentally different circumstances than before 1989–1991 and can therefore no longer merely oppose capitalism with socialism but has to envision global capitalism not as a monolithic whole but as a set of dynamic and constructed systems that is thereby also open to piecemeal democratization, transformation, and redemption; this means that socioeconomic theory itself needs to be updated in order to engage neoliberal capitalism with global poverty in its many twenty-first-century guises.[22] The point is that liberation theology in the twenty-first century is pluriform not only in its regional, ethnic, and cultural diversity but also in its interdisciplinarity and in its multiple layeredness moving between and within the grassroots and the theoretical elite.[23] The constant refrain, however, is the preferential option for the poor, albeit increasingly the mantra is being developed along multiple registers and availing itself of a myriad of analytical tools.[24]

What hope is there for an evangelical theology of liberation in this ever more diverse and convoluted phenomenon? A traditionalist evangelical hermeneutic that simply insists on scriptural priority too easily dismisses or ignores liberationist claims that might be uncomfortable. A range of holistic missiological models are emerging within evangelical circuits that seek to incorporate liberationist perspectives, but inevitably these are elements

---

and Contextual Theology, is on Eastern Europe with two chapters on Czechoslovakia and Hungary, and which calls attention to liberation theologies among Native North Americans and among the Roma across the continent as operative, ostensibly, in the so-called First World.

21. Representative here is Shannahan, *Voices from the Borderland*.

22. Leading the discussion here is Ivan Petrella; see Petrella's *The Future of Liberation Theology, Latin American Liberation Theology*, 147–72, as well as his *Beyond Liberation Theology*.

23. Cooper, ed., *The Reemergence of Liberation Theologies*.

24. See further Groody, ed., *The Option for the Poor in Christian Theology*, and Groody and Gutiérrez, ed., *The Preferential Option for the Poor beyond Theology*.

sanitized of whatever intercultural, trans-ethnic, or racialized features in order to be compatible with the traditional evangelical imagination.

It is here that I suggest we look at an evangelical spirituality—that of modern Pentecostalism—for resources with which to engage liberationist concerns. If liberation theology opted for the poor, it would appear that the poor in the last generation has opted for Pentecostalism.[25] As Harvey Cox, Philip Jenkins, and many other observers have noted, world Christianity has been growing largely due to the vibrancy of pentecostal and charismatic renewal movements across the global South.[26] My claim in the next section is that pentecostal spirituality can assist evangelical theology precisely because its "many tongues" sensibility provides theological and not just pragmatic justification for attending to the voices of the poor and many others in a pluralistic and needy world.

The Preferential Option of the Poor: Liberationist Routes in Global Pentecostalism

Let us not naively think that classical forms of Pentecostalism, the kinds closest to evangelicalism in various respects, have been enthusiastic about liberation theology from the beginning. In many ways, traditional pentecostal thinkers, especially within white pentecostal movements and churches, would not object to the evangelical prioritization of Scripture and even subordination of perceived liberationist ideological constructs within that biblical frame. Even within the African American pentecostal community, dispensationalist and premillennialist eschatology, traditionalist demonology, and rigid holiness stances impede whatever impulses might be present toward liberationist initiatives and projects, and this is the case even though black Pentecostals are often much more sociopolitically alert and even engaged than their white counterparts.[27] We can only proceed, then, fully cognizant that there are significant hurdles to be overcome in any efforts to craft a liberation theological platform from pentecostal sources.

Yet granting the above, there has also been a substantive compulsion toward dialogue with liberation theology from the pentecostal sector. Already within the early years of the emergence of pentecostal academic theology

---

25. E.g., Chesnut, *Born Again in Brazil*, and Corten, *Pentecostalism in Brazil*, are representative of global Pentecostalism at the grassroots even if they are focused on the Brazilian context.

26. Cox, *Fire from Heaven*, and Jenkins, *The Next Christendom*.

27. E.g., Ware, "On the Compatibility/Incompatibility."

(ca. 1990),[28] Miroslav Volf, by now a renowned theologian, had written about the "Materiality of Salvation: An Investigation in the Soteriologies of Liberation and Pentecostal Theologies."[29] Volf's article has been repeatedly cited as signaling the confluence of pentecostal and liberation theological efforts by others who over the last two-plus decades have attempted to press further into this vein from a variety of locations, particularly across the Americas.[30] In the following I attempt to summarize particularly those who have attempted book-length contributions at this interface, and focus especially on the diversity of pentecostal voices across the majority world.

We begin with Latin American contributions not least because the impact of Medellin has been felt even within the emerging pentecostal academy first within this segment. The 1990s featured two substantive contributions: by Hispanic American social ethicist Eldin Villafañe and by Puerto Rican theologian Samuel Solivan.[31] The approach of the former (Villafañe) sought to triangulate around the Hispanic American social realities, its religious dimensions (including the interwoven narrative of Roman Catholicism in Hispanic America life), and the urban pentecostal experience within those communities, but promoted a congruence amidst this plurality through the work of the Spirit that enabled these various voices to speak toward a spirituality of social justice without insisting that they all said the same thing. The latter (Solivan) attempted a parallel strategy of harmonizing (without homogenizing) the many Hispanic American hermeneutical sensitivities but entwined these around the felt presence of the Spirit, identified in terms of suffering, thus opening up to considerations of the mutuality between human anguish and divine pathos (*orthopathos* in the latter case). The goal in each case was to register Hispanic Pentecostal hermeneutical and methodological approaches to the Christian tradition and to push liberative pathways forward.

It was quickly becoming recognized that pentecostal spirituality provided an alternative paradigm for liberation theology that while consonant with the main thrusts of classical liberationist approaches could not be reduced to sociotheoretical or Marxist frameworks.[32] In the meanwhile,

28. For periodization of pentecostal theology in the late 1980s and into the 1990s, see Yong, "Pentecostalism and the Theological Academy."

29. Volf, "Materiality of Salvation."

30. E.g., Sepúlveda, "Pentecostalism and Liberation Theology," Melander, "'New' Pentecostalism Challenges 'Old' Liberation Theology?," Martins and de Pádua, "The Option for the Poor and Pentecostalism in Brazil," Wilkinson and Studebaker, "A Liberating Spirit," and Santiago-Vendrell, "Not By Words Alone!"

31. Villafañe, *The Liberating Spirit*, and Solivan, *Spirit, Pathos and Liberation*.

32. See the observations of non-pentecostal observers like Schaull and Cesar,

Hispanic and Latin American pentecostal theologians have pressed on. Peruvian pentecostal mission theologian Darío López Rodriguez has proffered a biblical and even Lukan liberation theology, even as Hispanic systematic theologian Sammy Alfaro has recommended a spirit-christological vision that connects the struggle of Jesus amidst the Roman imperialism of his day with the struggles of Hispanic immigrants with the American empire of the current era.[33] The former provides grassroots pentecostal readings of the biblical text while the latter mines pentecostal *coritos* and *hymnos* for liberative purposes. This next generation of Latin American pentecostal scholars, as it were, unveils how the voices of the pentecostal poor read for and sing about the liberation of the gospel by the power of the Spirit.[34]

Asian pentecostal theology is a bit less developed along the liberation axis than their Latin American counterparts. Korean American pentecostal systematician Koo Dong Yun has written books about Spirit baptism and pneumatology in interreligious perspective, but framed neither in liberative terms.[35] Yet he has also begun to propound an Asian pentecostal liberation theology in conversation with *minjung* sources along the way, advocating that pentecostal perspectives lift up the affective and emotive aspects of the indigenous Korean *minjung* (or the poor) spirituality and connect these to biblical themes of the Spirit's converting, sanctifying, and saving work.[36] If this more East Asian vantage point connects to the *minjung* poor, then South Asian theologian Shaibu Abraham starts with the Indian context to formulate a liberation theological option from this vantage point.[37] Yet the latter does not re-engage Indian Pentecostal sources (reliant primarily on Shaul and Cesar's work—see above), which leaves much space for next steps in this discussion. Pointing the way forward here would be Indian Pentecostals engaging with Dalit traditions, although a full-fledged Dalit pentecostal liberation theology still is on the horizon.[38] Yet the point is that

---

Pentecostalism and the Future of the Christian Churches, and Bahmann, *A Preference for the Poor*, esp. ch. 12.

33. Rodriguez, *The Liberating Mission of Jesus*, and Alfaro, *Divino Compañero*.

34. See also the range of proposals in Medina and Alfaro, eds., *Pentecostals and Charismatics in Latin America and Latino Communities*.

35. Yun, *Baptism in the Holy Spirit* and *The Holy Spirit and Ch'i (Qi)*.

36. Yun, "Pentecostalism from Below." More traditionally pentecostal, and in that sense more consistent with conservative evangelical approaches, is Sung, in his "Response" to efforts to bring pentecostal thought more fully in line with *minjung* theology elaborated by Korean Presbyterian theologian, Jung, "Minjung and Pentecostal movements in Korea."

37. Abraham, *Pentecostal Theology of Liberation*.

38. An initial foray is Pulikottil, "Ramankutty Paul." More recent developments

Asian Pentecostalism is vast and the available resources are strewn across various spectra, so the emergence of organically Asian commitments is just a matter of time.[39]

On the African front, the liberation accents are more on the development and socioeconomic than other fronts, and the literature is being produced by those studying pentecostal activities as much as by those crafting pentecostal ideas or doctrines in relationship to their practices.[40] While the focus here is surely not on liberation as understood in the Medellin "tradition," what is being described and categorized in this related field of literature concerns liberative developments within pentecostal churches, communities, and movements especially in the sub-Saharan region. African theologians like David Ngong are attempting to articulate liberative soteriological visions for African societies in dialogue with pentecostal spirituality, but African pentecostal theologians themselves have yet to produce full-blown liberation theological treatises.[41] Two instances in the wider Afro-pentecostal diaspora, however, deserve mention at this juncture.

First, Redeemed Christian Church of God missionary and Walter Muelder Professor of Social Ethics at the Boston University School of Theology (since 2015) Nimi Wariboko has been at work on what might be called a pentecostal or charismatic theology of economics. With background on Wall Street and a commitment to thinking through the Nigerian pentecostal experience for a global pentecostal theology and social ethics,[42] Wariboko's contributions related to liberative initiatives include at least the following: reflections on pentecostal spirituality for ecclesial public life; extensions of charismatic piety and practices sensibilities for urban formation; and reappropriations of pentecostal-charismatic entrepreneurship for engag-

---

include Thomas, *Dalit Pentecostalism*, and Rapaka, *Dalit Pentecostalism*, both of which are historically rather than theologically oriented, albeit with possibilities for extension in liberation directions. M. Stephen is an Indian pentecostal ethicist, but his work circles around rather than engages liberation discourse explicitly; yet see, e.g., Stephen's *A Christian Theology in the Indian Context*, ch. 23, that includes discussion of subaltern, Dalit, tribal, women's, and eco-theology, which can resource Indian pentecostal liberationist efforts.

39. Chan's *Grassroots Asian Theology* features distinctive pentecostal resonances, but does not embrace liberation theological verbiage or agendas; more promising for the latter trajectory are the chapters by Finny Philip, Ekaputra Tupamahu, and Iap Sian-Chin, among others, in Synan and Yong, eds., *Global Renewal Christianity*, vol. 1.

40. For instance: Akoko, "Ask and You Shall Be Given," Lounela, *Mission and Development*, and Freeman, ed., *Pentecostalism and Development*.

41. Ngong, *The Holy Spirit and Salvation in African Christian Theology*; see also Zalanga and Yong, "What Empire? Which Multitude?"

42. E.g., Wariboko, *Nigerian Pentecostalism*.

ing with the volatility of the global market.[43] Obviously Wariboko is not writing liberation theology in its traditional or classical style. Yet it would be a mistake to ignore his contributions toward what might be considered a distinctive pentecostal modality of formulating a liberative theological praxis, one that is just at home in, albeit resisting and subverting variously, the neoliberal global economy in its destructive guises. Wariboko's major contribution in this direction, one that emphasizes cultivation of what he calls the *pentecostal principle* that creatively innovates so as to always be able to begin again, is applicable to liberative theological projects since the challenge is always how to imagine a more just and shalomic alternative to the sociopolitical status quo. So if the poor have opted for Pentecostalism since the rise of liberation theology, arguably more recently the poor have been opting for specifically prosperity forms of pentecostal spirituality,[44] those more conducive to being operationalized in unpredictable market economy,[45] and it is here that Wariboko's socioeconomic praxis can potentially intervene to engage and temper, if not redirect, glocal systems.

On the British front, in some respects twice-removed from the Afro-pentecostal diaspora because of mediations through the Caribbean, Robert Beckford has been long at work on a Dread pentecostal and liberation theology.[46] On multiple fronts—e.g., theology of cultural transformation, political theology, theology of social transformation[47]—Beckford has consistently pressed through the black pentecostal experience, in dialogue with especially Jamaican ideological and cultural resources, to explore the possibilities of an authentic pentecostal vision for the British public square. If Beckford's focus on race is unique and practically single-handed within the global pentecostal theological landscape,[48] its implications for liberation

---

43. Respectively, Wariboko, *The Pentecostal Principle*; *The Charismatic City and the Public Resurgence of Religion*; and *Economics in Spirit and Truth*.

44. Here it is important to heed the point made by Noble, *The Poor in Liberation Theology*, that the poor ought not to be objectified, even into an idol, but that their agency ought to be foregrounded, so that the category of "the poor" becomes an icon to their activity and efforts; hence we need help from pentecostal social ethicists like Wariboko to understand how liberation is necessary to address not just situations of dire poverty but transitions into and faithful living amidst the global market economy.

45. As documented in Attanasi and Yong, eds., *Pentecostalism and Prosperity*.

46. The following summarizes an earlier discussion of Beckford's work in Yong, "Justice Deprived, Justice Demanded," 134–40.

47. E.g., Beckford, *Jesus is Dread*; *Dread and Pentecostal*; *God of the Rahtid*; and *Jesus Dub*.

48. Although see here the theme of "Race and Global Renewal: Mulattic Tongues and Hybridic Imaginations to the Ends of the Earth," which was a special issue of *Pneuma: The Journal of the Society for Pentecostal Studies* 36:3 (2014), the final issue

theology are palpable. One might argue that Beckford's is the most obvious sustained contribution to liberation theology from a pentecostal perspective even as the radicality of his proposals, particularly due to its Dread credentials, means that its reception within pentecostal circles, even among pentecostal academia, is gradual at best and contested (even if not so much in print).

The preceding survey of pentecostal contributions to liberation theology reflect their cross-cultural, transnational, and interdisciplinary character. Western contributions are emerging precisely on the heels of their majority world colleagues, and these efforts engage with the full range of sociopolitical issues related to the liberation of the poor and oppressed including but not limited to race and ethnicity, class, gender, globalization, and ecology and creation care.[49] If liberation theology opted for the poor and the poor opted for Pentecostalism, then pentecostal scholars, theologians, and academics are slowly but surely also reflecting on the prospects for a pentecostal liberation theology from out of these realities on the ground.

Divine Preferences and Options? Apostolic Liberation Today

In this final section, then, I would like to build constructively toward what might be called a pentecostal-evangelical theology of liberation and do so in ways that addresses the pluralism inherent in the many levels of the conversation. Our argument will suggest that the preferential option *of* the poor is one that empowers their voices toward liberation. I will briefly unpack this thesis hermeneutically and develop the normative arguments, both via scriptural engagements within the corpus of Acts-Luke.[50]

I begin with Acts 2 not only because I am adopting a modern pentecostal perspective that derives its name from the Day of Pentecost narrative, but because the Pentecost event is arguably the other side of Easter and locates the situatedness of all followers of Jesus as Messiah. What I mean is that all Christian reflection proceeds not just after Easter (the resurrection and, relatedly, ascension) but also after Pentecost. As such a proper Christian hermeneutical stance and posture is not only incarnational—after and

---

that I oversaw as coeditor (with Dale Coulter) before turning the journal over to a new editorial team.

49. Wilkinson and Studebaker, *A Liberating Spirit*.

50. The reasons for my saying Acts-Luke in contrast to the usual Luke-Acts is that, as will be unfolded in the next few paragraphs, I begin with Acts 2 and work backward from there through Luke's two volumes; see for instance my *Who is the Holy Spirit?*

through Jesus' life, death, and resurrection—but also pentecostal: informed primordially and in the life of each believer by the gracious gift and outpouring of the Spirit "upon all flesh" (Acts 2:17).[51]

There are two interrelated consequences to this claim: one more theological and the other more methodological. Theologically, Christian theology in general is Trinitarian, but an authentic and robust Trinitarianism links incarnation and Pentecost, Christology and pneumatology in ways that foreground the import of the Acts narrative. For our purposes in this essay, Christian (and evangelical, and pentecostal) liberation theology thereby also ought to be Trinitarian, and begins to achieve this aspiration when pneumatology is intrinsic rather than incidental to the theological enterprise.[52] This leads to the second, methodological claim: that the Acts narrative should be read not just historically, as it has been traditionally, but theologically, so that the content of pneumatology in the Day of Pentecost outpouring has hermeneutical force. For the purposes of Christian—and evangelical and pentecostal—liberation theology, Acts 2 provides hermeneutical warrant for thinking about how many tongues opens up to many liberative beliefs and practices.[53]

The Acts 2 narrative identifies that the witness of and to "God's deeds of power" (2:11) arises exactly through the many languages spoken around the Mediterranean world. In other words, the witness of the gospel emerges *through* the cacophony, bewilderment, and perplexity of the plurality of tongues. Whether such is a miracle of speech or of hearing—it is recorded of the crowd that "each one heard them speaking in the native language of each" (2:6), leading them to ask: "how is it that we hear, each of us, in our own native language?" (2:8)—is immaterial since Luke's communicative intent is that God's redemptive purposes are achieved via the multivocity of the known world's cultures and languages, not apart from such.[54]

The result, it ought to be noted, is the formation of a new community (that of the 3,000 who were baptized on that day; 2:41), a new political economy ("All who believed were together and had all things in common;

---

51. I have done a good deal of work on the Acts narrative, starting with a Day of Pentecost hermeneutic that reads not only Acts but also Luke from the apostolic experience of the Spirit; see, e.g., ch. 2 in this book.

52. This thesis is argued extensively—some might say in an exhausting manner—in my *Spirit-Word-Community*.

53. This is an extension of my prior theses regarding *many tongues many modalities of interfaith engagement*, *many tongues many political practices*, and *many tongues many disciplinary modes of inquiry*, argued respectively in my *Hospitality and the Other*; *In the Days of Caesar*; and *The Spirit of Creation*.

54. See Welker, *God as Spirit*, ch. 5.

they would sell their possessions and goods and distribute the proceeds to all, as any had need"; 2:44–45), and in effect, a new liberative way of life.[55] There is plenty of argument about how to understand Luke's admittedly idealized description of this nascent messianic community, how such relates to modern and late modern forms of collectivities, and how long or short it persisted and why it did not have much staying power despite being of divine provenance. Any thorough response exceeds the scope of this essay, but suffice to say for the moment that the redemptive outpouring of the Spirit at Pentecost had concrete liberative consequences. The implications for contemporary liberation theology of whatever guise—remember that the Day of Pentecost belongs to all followers of Jesus as Christ, not to pentecostal believers only—have yet to be realized.

As important is the interconnectedness between Acts and the Gospel of Luke. Clearly, the many tongues of Pentecost (2:1–21) spawned a liberative community (2:41–47) through the proclamation about Jesus (2:22–40). More specifically, the Spirit-inspired and empowered work among the apostolic community followed the paradigm of the Spirit-led and anointed Jesus of Nazareth. Thus, when Luke writes of Peter's message to the Cornelius household that "God anointed Jesus of Nazareth with the Holy Spirit and with power; how he went about doing good and healing all who were oppressed by the devil, for God [the Holy Spirit] was with him" (10:38), this calls attention to how the first of these two Lukan volumes provides the prototype of the Spirit-filled life.

The Day of Pentecost event and its outcomes are further clarified when we turn to the Gospel narrative. If Acts 1:8—"But you will receive power when the Holy Spirit has come upon you; and you will be my witnesses in Jerusalem, in all Judea and Samaria, and to the ends of the earth"—provides the outline for the apostolic community in book two, then Luke 4:14–21 provides the table of contents for the life and ministry of Jesus in the first volume:

> Then Jesus, filled with the power of the Spirit, returned to Galilee, and a report about him spread through all the surrounding country. . . . When he came to Nazareth, where he had been brought up, he went to the synagogue on the sabbath day, as was his custom. He stood up to read, and the scroll of the prophet Isaiah was given to him. He unrolled the scroll and found the place where it was written:

---

55. Other of my essays touch on these themes, albeit without accentuating the liberation theological thrust: Yong, "Salvation, Society, and the Spirit"; "Glocalization and the Gift-Giving Spirit"; and "Informality, Illegality, and Improvisation."

> *"The Spirit of the Lord is upon me,*
>   *because he has anointed me*
>   *to bring good news to the poor.*
> *He has sent me to proclaim release to the captives*
>   *and recovery of sight to the blind,*
>   *to let the oppressed go free,*
> *to proclaim the year of the Lord's favour."*
> And he rolled up the scroll, gave it back to the attendant, and sat down. The eyes of all in the synagogue were fixed on him. Then he began to say to them, "Today this scripture has been fulfilled in your hearing."[56]

More particularly, the Isaianic quotation (italicized above, from Isaiah 61:1–2) provides the basic template for the ministry and message of Jesus unfolded in the remainder of the Gospel account, all accomplished via the work of the Holy Spirit.[57] Thus we see Jesus evangelizing, healing, and delivering people, those who are poor not only in the socioeconomic sense alone, but in terms of their being marginalized outside the centers of imperial power, in the power of the Spirit.[58]

Yet Jesus' efforts were directed ultimately to heralding—not just proclaiming but inaugurating—"the year of the Lord's favour." In Isaianic terms, such amounted to the messianic installation of the Day of the Lord announced by the prophets, which in turn relied upon the Pentateuchal message regarding the liberative year of Jubilee.[59] Thus when Jesus heals the sick, or cleanses lepers, or delivers the oppressed widow, he is not only speaking about the coming reign of God but instantiating its presence by the power of the Spirit: "For, in fact, the kingdom of God is among you" (Luke 17:21).[60] From this vantage point, then, Jesus is not just a liberation theologian in the abstract, but one who charismatically embodies the liberative good news.

It is thus no wonder that the poor, those most in need of liberation from the yoke of imperial Rome, flocked to Jesus (see Luke 7:22b), and it is also therefore not unexpected that those variously oppressed from the countryside flocked to join the apostolic community in Jerusalem (Acts

---

56. This passage is central to the thesis of pentecostal New Testament scholar Beers, *The Followers of Jesus as the Servant*, esp. ch. 5. See also the previously mentioned Rodriguez volume, *The Liberating Mission of Jesus*.

57. Prior, *Jesus the Liberator*.

58. See Green, "Good News to Whom?"

59. Ringe, *Jesus, Liberation, and the Biblical Jubilee*.

60. Thus did Baptist charismatic New Testament scholar Ervin write *Healing*.

5:16).⁶¹ Jesus ministry of empowerment for the poor in Luke is followed by his pouring out of the Spirit in Acts (2:33) so that they (the poor) are given their own voice, and surely through that vocality, enabled to also further herald and inaugurate the redemptive and liberative message of Jubilee in the first-century, imperial context. The Spirit-empowered ministry of the apostolic community was not identical with that of Jesus (in Luke) but there are fundamental continuities amidst the differences. For our purposes, Jesus' ministry of liberation of the poor in the Gospel was transformed into the liberative ministry in Acts by many who were themselves poor (fishermen, widows, and others), but all by the power of the Spirit.

Central to this essay is that liberation theology's preferential option *for* the poor is one side to—and the other side of—pentecostal theology's preferential option *of* the poor. If the former focuses on identification and repair of systems and structures of oppression, the latter enables faithful perseverance against the life-destroying principalities and powers. It is within such a complementary framework, then, that I have suggested the Day of Pentecost narratives provides theological legitimation not only for the many voices, but also for the many tongues of the poor. Pentecostal theology thus asserts a liberative theology, spirituality, and praxis *of* the poor via its multivocality.⁶² Its contribution to evangelical theology then is to underwrite the plurivocity of liberative witnesses and testimonies, not only from the majority world but wherever people find themselves marginalized and oppressed by dominant cultures.⁶³

More generally, and here beyond the evangelical horizon toward the wider ecumenical frontiers, pentecostal perspectives provide pneumatological resources for revitalizing liberation theology, at least in terms of empowering the impoverished in faithful witness *in* the world. If at this intersection the role of pneumatology has already been recognized,⁶⁴ the contemporary pentecostal contribution seeks to renew such tasks within

---

61. See also Harms, *Paradigms from Luke-Acts for Multicultural Communities*, ch. 3 on "Good News to the Poor (Luke 4:18)" as explicating the central thrust of this Lukan mission paradigm; Harms presents an evangelical-Catholic-liberationist paradigm as an Episcopal priest who works with Hispanic communities in Puerto Rico, Texas, and California.

62. Johns, *Pentecostal Formation*, chs. 4–5.

63. The perennial question of course has to do with how to discern among the many voices; the christological criterion is always indispensable—see my *Spirit of Love*, esp. ch. 9, and *The Missiological Spirit*, part IV—but oftentimes, the Spirit empowers prophetic witness un recognized at the time; for the challenges and opportunities pertaining to the latter, see Hill, *Prophetic Rage*.

64. E.g., Comblin, *The Holy Spirit and Liberation*; Yoo, *The Spirit of Liberation*.

a global context of many tongues and many cultures. As the Spirit indeed gives many gifts (1 Cor 12:4), then the gift of the Spirit empowers many witnesses to the liberative gospel of Jesus Christ. It is perhaps the charism of pentecostal spirituality to the church catholic that it renews liberation theology indeed from the underside of history as the poor are enabled to speak and act in the power of the Spirit.

CHAPTER 9

Apostolic Evangelism in the Postcolony

Opportunities and Challenges[1]

There is no doubt that mission in general and evangelism in particular are problematic in our postcolonial world.[2] The colonial legacy has left a palpable distaste for Eurocentrism and its ideologies, and this has impacted the evangelistic efforts of the church to the degree that the gospel it sought to proclaim was associated with the Christendom that supported the colonial enterprise. Thus Christian evangelism is understood as a subversive tool of Westerners to undermine local, native, and indigenous ways of life, as an imperialistic means of displacing other cultural and religious understandings, and as a monological activity that marginalizes, ignores, or silences the language and aspirations of non-Christians. Christians hence find themselves in a dilemma: either continue with evangelism and risk being viewed as intolerant, aggressive, and antagonistic to others, or replace evangelistic

---

1. Thanks to Al Tizon and Bob Whitesel, who invited me to give the plenary address of the annual meeting of the Academy for Evangelism in Theological Education, on the theme "Postcolonial Critique of Evangelism: Demands and Hopes," at the University of Northwestern in St. Paul, Minnesota, June 16–17, 2016. I appreciate the feedback given to the paper at the meeting. I am grateful also to Tony Richie for his comments on an earlier version of the paper, and to PhD and ThM students in my informal seminar in "Mission and Theology in the Spirit" for the vigorous discussion of the paper, especially Daniel Topf for his stimulating questions prompting some revisions to the text. Last but not least, two anonymous reviewers for *Mission Studies* provided important feedback that helped me bring the essay to a more appropriate conclusion. Nevertheless, all errors of fact and interpretation remain my own responsibility.

2. The crisis of evangelism is not new, being announced in the evangelical world as far back as a half century ago: Henry, *Evangelicals at the Brink of Crisis*.

proclamation with other forms of non-verbal witness, or withdraw into the ecclesial enclave and share the good news only with those who wander into its sacred spaces. Is it possible to formulate a theology of evangelism that is faithful to its historic practice and yet viable for a postcolonial world?

I suggest a pentecostal theology of evangelism, one informed less by modern Pentecostalism and more by the Day of Pentecost narrative that inspires the name of the contemporary movement, that can potentially chart a path forward for Christian evangelism in the twenty-first-century global context. The three parts of this essay explore the contours of a pentecostal hermeneutic for theology of evangelism, develop the bases for such a theological vision in Luke-Acts, and correlate apostolic evangelism amidst imperial Rome with contemporary evangelism in a postcolonial century. We shall see that the plurality of evangelistic practices constituting apostolic resistance to the Pax Romana can inform evangelistic variation and faithful Christian witness across the public square of the global postcolony.

One caveat before proceeding, on my use of the neologism *postcolony*. It appears in the title of Marion Grau's book as descriptive of our postcolonial situation.[3] In this essay, *postcolony* could be taken as the noun form of our postcolonial condition, but I am also linking to Stanley Hauerwas and William Willimon's reference to ecclesial existence *within*, but certainly not *of*, the world and its dominant cultures so that the church as the body of Christ and the fellowship of the Spirit consists in some senses as enclaves—as colonies, even—within nation states or other sociocultural contexts.[4] I would emphasize, however, that such Christian postcolonial existences are not silos or islands isolated from the world, even if they are havens of fellowship that nurture evangelistic engagement with the broader culture.[5]

Toward a Pentecostal Theology of Evangelism

There is an extensive literature on modern pentecostal missiology and mission theology,[6] but, surprisingly, few book-length treatments devoted specifically to pentecostal theology of evangelism. There may be a few reasons for this—for instance, that little distinction is made between mis-

---

3. See Grau, *Rethinking Mission in the Postcolony*, which is a dense, but valuable, contemporary discussion of what might be called a postcolonial missiology.

4. Hauerwas and Willimon, *Resident Aliens*.

5. I will say more about this throughout the rest of this essay, even as further discussion of what I have in mind can be found in my "The Church and Mission Theology in a Post-Constantinian Era," and *In the Days of Caesar*, ch. 5.

6. Most of the scholarly work on pentecostal missiology is referenced in my *The Missiological Spirit*, esp. part II.

sion and evangelism in pentecostal circles or that the former is understood expansively to include the latter, thus minimizing the need for its more specific discussion[7]—but even if we were to lament the situation, it is what it is. The one scholarly volume with the word *evangelization* in the title refers to the Brighton Conference on World Evangelization held in 1991,[8] but even within it, the topic of evangelism proper is absent, subsumed under other discussions on human rights advocacy among refugees, Christian relationships with and approaches to the world religious traditions, notions of power evangelism (involving charismatic signs and wonders), the urgency of evangelism in connection with the apocalyptic worldview of the New Testament, and the then (and still) conflicted matters of pentecostal proselytism vis-à-vis the established, especially ecumenical, churches.[9]

When we turn to the periodical literature, we will find many more sources. In many cases, evangelism is synonymous with mission so that what is discussed—not too much different from what we find in books on the topic—is as much if not more a theology of mission or missiology than specifically a theology of evangelism. Yet there are some common themes, four of which deserve comment to set the stage for our own constructive efforts.

First, pentecostal evangelism is well-known for its aggressive style. This reputed aggressiveness has as much if not mostly to do with the fact that there is a zealousness to pentecostal faith-sharing that "God is no respecter of persons"—to use a well-known phrase from the King James Version (Acts 10:34b)—so that anyone who is not of (pentecostal) faith is fair game for the evangelist. This means that pentecostal proclamation is directed oftentimes to those who are perceived to be no more than nominal Christians—which would include for most Pentecostals those in non-pentecostal churches[10]— and certainly those in other faiths also. The latter is particularly combustible, especially in Islamic and Hindu contexts, although some Pentecostals

7. Case in point is Shibley, *A Force in the Earth*, which is more a book on charismatic missiology than on evangelization, technically understood, although power evangelism is discussed in ch. 3.

8. Hunter and Hocken, eds., *All Together in One Place*.

9. See the chapters by Luis Segrada, Clark Pinnock, Norbert Baumert, Paul Bechdolff, and (tri-authored) Philippe Larère, Theodore Jungkuntz, and Roger Cabezas in the Hunter and Hocken volume.

10. Proselytism as a concern is evidenced in "Evangelization, Proselytism, and Common Witness—Final Report of the Dialogue between the Roman Catholic Church and Some Classical Pentecostal Churches: 1990–1997," included in Vondey, *Pentecostalism and Christian Unity*, 159–98, although anxieties on this issue are widespread among mainline Protestant and also Eastern Orthodox churches and not limited to Catholic circles.

have ameliorated their approaches where evangelism of religious others is illegal.[11] The point is twofold: that pentecostal zeal for spreading the gospel is widely directed, and that in some cases, felt "targeting" of those perceived as more vulnerable within their faith communities has fostered "bad blood" both in intra-Christian and wider interfaith arenas.[12]

There is a second aspect to pentecostal evangelism that contributes to its negative reputation: the emphasis persisting in some areas under the label of *power evangelism*. Popularized three-plus decades ago by so-called Third Wave pastor and teacher, John Wimber (a leader in the Vineyard movement),[13] this feature of pentecostal evangelism has taken on multiple forms, especially across the majority world. In most cases, the focus is on healing, signs and wonders, and miraculous displays of the Holy Spirit's power as accompanying means of confirming the evangelistic message.[14] In some instances, especially in the African context, the focus is on power encounters, especially rites of exorcism through which people are delivered from oppression by demonic, evil, or other malignant spirits.[15] Last but not least, power evangelism entails what some advocates and practitioners call strategic level spiritual warfare that seeks to discern or map the spiritual forces that dominate certain geographic regions of the world and then conduct exorcisms against these so-called territorial spirits so that local inhabitants can be delivered from their grip and opened up to the gospel message.[16] The goal is that the evangelistic message can have a chance of reception that is otherwise spiritually hindered by these demonic strongholds. In the process, pentecostal rhetoric often labels, albeit in insider terms, not usu-

---

11. Yet Pentecostals have been part and parcel of the mix that has perpetuated the so-called "clash of civilizations" thesis in their encounter with Islam, not least in Muslim-dominated northern Nigeria and in Hindu South Asia; for discussion, see Yong, *Hospitality and the Other*, 15–29, and Bauman, *Pentecostals, Proselytization, and Anti-Christian Violence in Contemporary India*.

12. The work of Church of God (Cleveland, Tennessee) bishop Tony Richie has been especially directed toward developing a more dialogical albeit no less pentecostal approach to evangelism; see, e.g., Richie, "On 'Christian Witness in a Multi-religious World,'" and "A Discerning Theology of Christian Evangelism in a Multi-faith World," among other pieces.

13. See Wimber and Springer, *Power Evangelism*.

14. So much so that most pentecostal converts around the world attribute their conversion to the experience of healing in their lives or that of family members or close friends; see Brown, ed., *Global Pentecostal and Charismatic Healing*.

15. See discussion in Asamoah-Gyadu, *Sighs and Signs of the Spirit*, ch. 10; cf. Collins, *Exorcism and Deliverance Ministry in the Twentieth Century*.

16. E.g., Holvast, *Spiritual Mapping in the United States and Argentina*; cf. Jorgensen, "Third Wave Evangelism and the Politics of the Global in Papua New Guinea."

ally publicized, such mapping in terms of other religions—e.g., the spirit of Islam or the spirit of specific Hindu gods or goddesses—but these inevitably leak out, thereby exacerbating whatever relations may exist with religious others in these regions.

A third element of pentecostal evangelism that further compounds its public relations problem is its use of various forms of the latest technologies to facilitate its evangelistic activities. Where mass crusades are organized, these are amplified through the use of loudspeakers that not just infiltrate but penetrate public spheres and soundscapes.[17] Aside from these boosts to pentecostal audibility, evangelists of this movement have from the beginning availed themselves of advancing telecommunicative media to spread the message. Usage of radio and then television waves has now expanded to the Internet, where pentecostal evangelism continues around the world.[18] Thus the pentecostal message is coming across not only loud and clear but from many directions and via multiple media.[19] This further solidifies the public perception that pentecostal evangelists are out to make converts of them, their family members and friends, and their ethnic, cultural, or religious groups.

Yet if such apparent pentecostal aggressiveness is linked to Western missionaries and their tactics, as much ought to be said about what is happening evangelistically at the grassroots. On the ground, Pentecostalism is a popular religion that spreads through relational networks. Those initiated into pentecostal churches and piety are taught that as was promised to the earliest disciples of Jesus—e.g., "you will receive power when the Holy Spirit has come upon you; and you will be my witnesses in Jerusalem, in all Judea and Samaria, and to the ends of the earth" (Acts 1:8), which translated maps directionally onto the convert's immediate locality and opens up to the wider region and nation, and beyond that internationally—so also is the Spirit available to empower their witness to friends, in their neighborhoods, and to non-believers wherever they are. This is relational evangelism that occurs organically within the friendships and interpersonal connections that Spirit-filled believers have with others, and unfolds naturally in local events (like festivals) or through social activities (like community projects).[20] In short,

17. As documented by Gifford, "'Africa Shall Be Saved.'"

18. See Coleman, *The Globalisation of Charismatic Christianity*; cf. Thomas, *Strong Religion, Zealous Media*, and James, *McDonalisation, Masala McGospel and Om Economics*.

19. Onyinah, "New Ways of Doing Evangelism."

20. See Manriquez, "Religion of the People and Evangelism," Santiago-Vendrell, "The Gospel in a New Tune!," and Alfaro, "Expressions of Evangelism in Latin America."

pentecostal evangelism on the ground manifests itself in many forms, as many as their evangelists pursue in relationship to their loved ones, friends, acquaintances, and others in their spheres of influence.

What should be emphasized at this juncture is that regardless of the variety of means and modes of pentecostal evangelism in reality, the faithful are motivated from their own experience of the transforming work of the Spirit in their lives, and they have been provided scriptural reasons to expect such manifestations of the Spirit in the lives of those they care for around them. In other words, they themselves have been recipients of the Spirit's outpouring and, beyond that, the gift of the Spirit has also been personalized through the Bible: "For the promise is for you, for your children, and for all who are far away, everyone whom the Lord our God calls to him" (Acts 2:39). Thus what was pledged to the first apostles remains available to those who follow in their footsteps as the body of Christ and the fellowship of the Holy Spirit so that the "that" of the first-century believers correlates to the "this" of Spirit-filled followers of Jesus in any subsequent age.[21] Contemporary pentecostal believers can therefore expect that the Spirit will enable their witness to others with similar results as with the apostolic generation.

Stepping back for a moment from the assumptions undergirding pentecostal understandings of evangelism, note the fundamental pneumatologically oriented theology that is operative. Pentecostals engage in evangelism because this is what the Holy Spirit enables. This work of the Spirit was inaugurated on the Day of Pentecost, and continues by and through the power of the Spirit. Hence within such a framework, Christian theologies of evangelism are thoroughly pneumatological (empowered by the Spirit) and pentecostal (initiated through the Day of Pentecost gift of the Spirit by Christ, from the right hand of the Father; Acts 2:33). As such, pentecostal Christians read the book of Acts not just historically as concerning what happened to the earliest followers of the Messiah but as theologically normative in providing a template for what Jesus-disciples do in any and every age.[22]

Since our task is a theology of evangelism for a postcolonial world, I suggest, following these pentecostal instincts, to return to the apostolic way for insights. The next section examines evangelism in Acts in relationship to its companion volume, the Gospel of Luke, and looks also specifically at

21. For more on such a "that" is "this" of pentecostal hermeneutics, see ch. 12 below.

22. Thus in my own work, I have developed from the book of Acts such a pneumatological and pentecostal theology of interfaith relations, of the political, and of disability, among other topics; see my books, *Hospitality and the Other*, ch. 4, *Who is the Holy Spirit?*, and *The Bible, Disability, and the Church*, ch. 4, respectively.

Jesus as the paradigmatic or prototypical Spirit-filled evangelist, before the final section returns to read evangelism in Acts against the imperial backdrop of the first-century Mediterranean world for purposes of sketching a postcolonial theology of evangelistic praxis. Our goal is to resource current thinking about evangelism from the apostolic and Day of Pentecost storyline in order to articulate a more robust pneumatological and pentecostal theology of evangelism for the postcolony.

Toward a Lukan Theology of Evangelism

There are a number of studies on evangelism in Luke-Acts, so the preceding does not pretend to be exhaustive or to engage extensively with the existing literature.[23] One significant proposal has not been received as widely as its author may have hoped. Pedrito Maynard-Reid suggests a model, quite consistent with recent calls for holistic mission in the wider missiological conversation, he calls "complete evangelism" that is both socially and kerygmatically intertwined (so that there is no prioritization of the two) because it is incarnational and thereby based on following in the evangelistic footsteps of Jesus' ministry.[24] The response has been less than enthusiastic in some quarters, with even pentecostal and charismatic scholars questioning whether Maynard-Reid has demonstrated his thesis due to selective and arguably unbalanced exegesis that does not recognize the poor as metaphoric in the gospels, particularly given Luke's emphasis on the proclamation of the word and the Spirit's empowerment for verbal witness.[25] As Maynard-Reid does not intend to minimize the centrality of proclamation, I think the debate becomes more semantic than real. More importantly, as we shall see, complementing the incarnational rationale with the pentecostal and pneumatological perspective makes it even more difficult to dismiss his (and others') call for a more holistic or "complete" (to use Maynard-Reid's terminology) missiological approach.

---

23. Scholarship on evangelism in the New Testament or on mission more broadly in Luke-Acts—e.g., Green, *Evangelism in the Early Church*, and Rogers, *Holistic Ministry and Cross-cultural Mission in Luke-Acts*, respectively—both include discussion of evangelism in the Lukan materials.

24. Maynard-Reid, *Complete Evangelism*, esp. 150–58.

25. See pentecostal New Testament scholar, Menzies, "Complete Evangelism," who responds directly to Maynard-Reid, and compare with the argument of charismatic historical Jesus scholar Twelftree, *People of the Spirit*, ch. 13, who concludes, quite apart from Maynard-Reid's argument, that social witness is subordinate to evangelism, if relevant at all, for Lukan missiology.

Before unpacking the pneumatological framework, a few preliminary remarks are in order regarding evangelism in Luke-Acts. First, our study will be limited to two key verbs and their cognates: *kerusso* (to preach or proclaim) and *euangelizo* (to evangelize or to announce the good news). The former appears about eight times each in Luke and Acts, while the latter appears with similar frequency in the first volume but includes thrice as many references in the second Lukan book. On occasion, they occur together (Luke 8:1).

Second, *kerusso* as a verb can stand on its own (e.g., Luke 4:44) or include many objects. John preached "a baptism of repentance for the forgiveness of sins" (Luke 3:3; cf. Acts 13:38); the man from whom many evil spirits had been cast out proclaimed "how much Jesus had done for him" (8:39); the disciples were sent out "to proclaim the kingdom of God and to heal" (9:2; cf. 20:25, 28:31); Philip "proclaimed the Messiah" to the Samaritans (Acts 8:5); the converted Saul preached "Jesus in the synagogues, saying, 'He is the Son of God'" (9:20); Peter recounts that he and the others were commissioned to "preach to the people and to testify that [Jesus] is the one ordained by God as judge of the living and the dead" (10:42); and even the Jews proclaim Moses (15:21). In short, one can preach or proclaim various messages, even if they are related. In contrast, *euangelizo* includes its object, good news, so that the activity of evangelizing or of evangelization is always of the gospel. In all cases this is assumed, although in some instances, it is added that the apostolic evangelists went about "proclaiming the word" (8:4), or that they "proclaimed the word of God" (13:5; cf. 17:13) or "the word of the Lord" (15:35–36). Here the "word" is equivalent to the good news, so that evangelism throughout the book of Acts includes the annunciation of the gospel word.

Last but not least by way of preliminary comments, note also that there are various evangelistic agents in Luke-Acts. It has already been noted that even the Jews are evangelists, of Moses, to be clear (Acts 15:21). Besides the famous prophesying daughters (21:9) of Philip the evangelist (8:5), and the preaching of the key protagonists in the second volume—both Peter and Paul—the good news or gospel is declared by angels (Luke 2:10, or Gabriel in 1:19), John the Baptist (3:3, 18; cf. 13:24), "some men of Cyprus and Cyrene" at Antioch (11:20), Barnabas (13:5, 32, 38, 14:7, 15, 21), and even Luke himself (among whoever else may have been Paul's traveling companions: 16:10). Intriguingly, Luke also tells about "a slave-girl who had a spirit of divination and brought her owners a great deal of money by fortune-telling. While she followed Paul and us, she would cry out, 'These men are slaves of the Most High God, who proclaim to you a way of salvation'" (16:16–17). In effect, this spiritually oppressed girl evangelizes by calling attention to the apostolic preaching. None of this is surprising in light of the outpouring of the Spirit on all flesh (2:17), including male and female servants (2:18).

In the remainder of this section, I want to develop the first step of our constructive proposal related to Spirit-empowered apostolic proclamation as a model for contemporary evangelism in the postcolony, and this involves consideration of Jesus as Spirit-filled evangelist.

Recall that our focus is derived from understanding the Day of Pentecost account as central to Luke's portrait and theological vision of evangelism.[26] Although the main thrusts in our reading are consistent with the themes highlighted in the preceding, the pneumatological accent underscored here establishes a distinctive framework for thinking through the intersection of the spiritual and the imperial domains. More precisely, I will urge that Luke's understanding of Jesus as Spirit-filled evangelist within the colonized region of Judea will be especially important for our own constructive theology of evangelism for the postcolony.

If Acts 2 provides the hermeneutical key to the early apostolic community, then Luke 4 serves a parallel function for the gospel story. For Luke, the Spirit-empowered apostolic ministry in Acts is possible only because they are recipients of the Spirit of and from Jesus (Acts 2:33), who was himself Spirit-anointed: "God anointed Jesus of Nazareth with the Holy Spirit and with power; how he went about doing good and healing all who were oppressed by the devil, for God was with him" (10:38). The Lukan narrative thus not only presents Jesus as one who was conceived by the Spirit (Luke 1:35) and who received the Spirit afresh at his baptism by John (3:33), but also introduces his public ministry by going into the wilderness "full of the Holy Spirit" (4:1) and returning from the desert temptations still "filled with the power of the Spirit" (4:14). Thence Jesus came into the synagogue at Nazareth and read from Isaiah the prophet:

> "The Spirit of the Lord is upon me,
>   because he has anointed me
>   to bring good news [*euangelisasthai*] to the poor.
>   He has sent me to proclaim release to the captives
>   and recovery of sight to the blind,
>   to let the oppressed go free,

---

26. No study of evangelism in Acts can overlook the pneumatological thrust of the early Christian community's proclamation; even cessationist publications have articles — e.g., Rainer, "Church Growth and Evangelism in the Book of Acts" — that recognize the role of the Spirit in apostolic prayer, spiritual warfare, and indigenization efforts related to the preaching of the gospel. For a preliminary discussion of Acts evangelism otherwise by a reputed pentecostal scholar, see Warrington, *The Message of the Holy Spirit*, ch. 10.

to proclaim [*kēryxai*] the year of the Lord's favour" [cf. Isa
61:1–2].
And he rolled up the scroll, gave it back to the attendant, and
sat down. The eyes of all in the synagogue were fixed on him.
Then he began to say to them, "Today this scripture has been
fulfilled in your hearing." (Luke 4:18–21)

Three sets of comments about this passage and its role in the Gospel of Luke deserve comment at this juncture. First, the announcement of Jesus' public ministry via declaration of scriptural fulfillment invites us to read this passage as summarizing and providing the theological warrants for the rest of Luke's first book. From the perspective of theology of evangelism, then, Jesus' entire life and ministry is evangelistic, variously proclaiming, heralding, and inaugurating "the year of the Lord's favour."[27] Second, although those evangelized by Jesus—the poor, captives, blind, and oppressed—can be understood variously, including in literal terms in at least some respects from how the Jesus story unfolds in the rest of the Gospel,[28] what is clear is that the good news makes a liberative difference to those who existed under the yoke of imperial Rome.[29] After all, Jesus' life and ministry unfolded in the days of Augustus and then Tiberius Caesar, as Luke himself frames it (2:1, 3:1),[30] and it is within this context that we can appreciate how the Isaianic "day of the Lord" now addresses the yearnings of the people of Israel and their longing for the renewal and restoration of the nation's fortunes under the Messiah.[31] Last but not least, Jesus is the prototypical evangelist precisely as filled with the Spirit. Put alternatively, the liberative good news of, by, and through Jesus is pneumatically enabled and pneumatologically constituted, thereby setting up the same dynamic in his followers in Acts.

27. If Teng, "Evangelism and the Teaching of Acts," 17–19, argues that the good news is intended for all in Acts (cf. 19:10, 22:15), then this applies also in Luke in the sense that all of Jesus' ministry is evangelistic. In fact, even after his death, resurrection, and ascension, Jesus' evangelistic ministry and mission continue; as Paul indicated in his message to Agrippa: "the Messiah must suffer, and that, by being the first to rise from the dead, he would proclaim light both to our people and to the Gentiles" (26:23).

28. E.g., Sabourin, "Evangelize the Poor (Lk 4:18)," and Green, "Good News to Whom?," among other discussions;

29. Thus Costas, *Liberating News*, urges a liberative theology of evangelism that is contextual in various ways: at the Galilean periphery rather than the Roman center and vis-à-vis the needs of specific groups of people; see also the previous chapter.

30. Which provides the rationale for my book, *In the Days of Caesar*; see the discussion in its ch. 3.

31. For further discussion of Isaiah 61 in the broader context of the messianic message, see my *The Spirit and the Missio Dei* (manuscript in progress), ch. 4.3.

Jesus thus addresses the range of physical, spiritual, and other needs by the power of the Holy Spirit. How do these facets of his evangelistic vocation inform an apostolic theology of evangelism for the postcolony?

Toward an Apostolic and Pneumatological Theology of Evangelism for the 21st Century

In this final section, I extend the preceding discussion from Luke's Gospel to the book of Acts in order to tease out the rudiments of an apostolic theology and praxis of evangelism for the present time. If in the gospel story Jesus' entire evangelistic ministry is empowered by the Spirit, so also in Acts, the witness of the apostles is initiated only "when the Holy Spirit has come upon [them]" and from there proceeds from Jerusalem through "all Judea and Samaria, and to the ends of the earth" (Acts 1:8). Within this Spirit-led evangelistic initiative, then, there are at least three interrelated aspects of evangelism that complement and extend the liberative proclamation of Jesus against the backdrop of the Roman imperium: that related to his messianic identity, his lordship, and the coming reign of God.

The early apostolic community proclaimed Jesus as Messiah or anointed one (the Christ) in many different contexts. Early on, indeed even after being imprisoned for their evangelism, it is said that, "every day in the [Jerusalem] temple and at home they did not cease to teach and proclaim Jesus as the Messiah" (5:42). Later Philip preaches the Messiah in Samaria (8:5), Saul in Damascus (9:22), Paul in Thessalonica (17:3) and Macedonia (18:5), and Apollos in Ephesus (18: 28), among other occasions (e.g., 26:23). Public declaration of Jesus' Spirit-anointed Messiahship extolled him as the hope and deliverer of Israel from its enemies—in this case, the Roman imperium—and the extent of this message is corroborated from Jerusalem through Samaria to the rest of the imperial domain. Jesus is Messiah, the Christ, not only to the Jews but also to the Gentiles across the Mediterranean world.[32]

Consistent with the preceding observation, Jesus is also proclaimed as *kyrios*, or Lord. Although this has become an honorific title in Christian worship, in the first-century Mediterranean world, there was only one lord, Caesar, and elevation of anyone else with that title was seen to be politically subversive.[33] No wonder Jesus was executed and his followers persecuted as

---

32. See also Best, "The Revelation to Evangelize the Gentiles."

33. See for instance discussion by Andrew Walls of what he calls "The Ephesian Moment," an analysis of how the declaration of Jesus lordship was cosmically envisioned in ways that challenged the lordship of Caesar, in Walls's *The Cross-Cultural*

his lordship was proclaimed far and wide amid the Roman rule: Peter and other Jews to Gentiles in Caesarea (10:35); those from Cyprus and Cyrene engaging Hellenists in Antioch (11:20); and Paul before philosophers at the Areopagus (17:24), among other venues. Early on, even in Jerusalem, it was already discerned that the principalities and powers would not easily recognize Jesus' lordship and messiahship, as indeed lamented in Israel's Scriptures: "The kings of the earth took their stand, and the rulers have gathered together against the Lord and against his Messiah" (4:26; cf. Ps 2:2). Now clearly there is a sense in which Luke's two-volume account is presented in ways that ameliorates rather than exacerbates imperial anxieties about another revolutionary uprising from the Judean outpost.[34] Nevertheless the undertone of the early Christian proclamation is clear: as much as they might attempt to be model citizens who paid their taxes and respected their governmental authorities, their ultimate allegiances were not to Caesar but to Jesus the Messiah (cf. Acts 4:17–20).[35]

Along this evangelistic arc, then, the earliest messianists proclaimed Jesus as Lord in relationship to the coming kingdom or reign of God (*basileia tou theou*).[36] Jesus' final message before his ascension, consistent with his preaching and teaching throughout his public ministry prior to his death, was about the reign of God (1:3), and although his followers then still thought the reestablishment of this divine reign would involve kicking the Romans out of Palestine (1:6), the promise of the Spirit was designed to empower witness to that already-in-some-respects but also not-yet-and-still-coming-in-other-respects reality. So again, we find the reign of God proclaimed as part of the good news to the ends of the earth: Philip in the colonial backwaters of Samaria (8:5, 12); Paul and Barnabas at other Hellenistic cultural centers Lystra, Iconium, and Antioch (14:21–22); and Paul at Ephesus (20:25) and at the heart of the imperial order: Rome (28:31). Although much talk about the reign of God twenty centuries removed from the apostolic endeavors is spiritualized, there is no evading the sociopolitical dimensions of such "kingdom" evangelism that countered the ideology of the Pax Romana.[37]

Process in Christian History, ch. 4.

34. See Walaskay, *"And so we Came to Rome."*

35. For further reflection on this theme from a pentecostal perspective, see Reid, "Spirit-Empowerment as Resistance Discourse."

36. I prefer *reign* over *kingdom* given the latter's patriarchal connotations.

37. See also del Agua, "The Lucan Narrative of the 'Evangelization of the Kingdom of God.'"

What is important in transitioning to implications and applications for the contemporary postcolony is both the unity and diversity of apostolic evangelism and witness to the living Christ as Lord of the here-and-yet-still-to-come reign of God. The diversity of early Christian Spirit-inspired proclamation surely has something to do with the fact that evangelism occurs in concrete historical situations, and the means and message thus has local flavors. In the Samarian region, for instance, we see Philip evangelizing the masses at the level of popular religiosity by declaring Jesus' lordship through signs and wonders, healings and exorcisms, and other manifestations of the Spirit. In the Hellenistic and pagan context of Lystra, on the other hand, while involving the healing of a man crippled from birth (14:8–10), Paul and Barnabas witnessed to the reign of God via natural theological references and ideas (14:15–18, 21–22).[38] Then at the Areopagus (17:22–34), when engaging with the intellectual literati and philosophical elite, Pauline proclamation cited and sprang off Greek poets and Stoic sources.[39] From a pentecostal perspective grounded in the Day of Pentecost horizon regarding the outpouring of the Spirit on all flesh, this should not be surprising: there are as many forms and modes of evangelistic proclamation as there are contexts and audiences, and in each case, inspirited witnesses is borne through many tongues, not only in their distinctive languages but also in their unique discursive genres, their range of attitudes and affective dispositions, and various types of performative praxes (whether involving healings, exorcisms, congregational or synagogue ministry, conversational interactions, etc.).[40]

We are now ready to think, at least in a preliminary way, about apostolic evangelism in the twenty-first century postcolony. Our contemporary global context is postcolonial in the technical sense of following independence of majority world colonies, but nevertheless we still live with the legacy of colonialism in the present time. Beyond that, some might argue that the current postcolony is dominated either by the American empire or

---

38. The evangelization of pagans at Lystra thus proceeded within to their rhetorical (structural), semiotic (linguistic), and theological (God, not Jesus, focused) frame in contrast to the midrashic character of evangelism of Jews in the previous chapter (Act 13:16–41); for comparative discussion, see Fournier, *The Episode at Lystra*, ch. 5.

39. Gibson, "Paul and the Evangelization of the Stoics," observes that Paul's Areopagus evangelism involved theological (rather than Jesus-specific), philosophical, and cosmological elements in conversation with Stoic sources but concludes with the call to repentance and includes warning of judgment, both of which are distinctive to the kerygma; see also Losie, "Paul's Speech on the Areopagus."

40. For further discussion and then contemporary application, see George, *Meeting Your Neighbor*.

by the imperial regime of the neoliberal global market.[41] Yet others could counter-argue that there are totalitarian, authoritarian, and oppressive "regimes" across a range of majority world contexts, whether in patriarchal societies prevalent within the global South, in varying contexts of civil war, or in dictatorial or corrupt states resisting democratic governance. The point is that the church as colony exists in faithfulness to Jesus lordship *in* but not *of* the political forces of the present age. How might faithful Christian witness and evangelism be sustained by those inhabiting the Spirit-filled colony amidst and across the broad spectrum of this postcolonial but yet variously imperialistic world? More precisely, what do the many tongues of Christian proclamation say in the third millennial postcolony?

A postcolonial pneumatology of evangelism can be charted along the following parameters. First, the means of evangelism is pneumatic, by the Spirit, and the content of evangelism is pneumatological: concerning the Spirit-anointed and empowered Messiah. The former is premised on the pluralism of tongues through which the Spirit enables witness and this refers both to the linguistic vernacular media of evangelization in many cultures and also to the diversity of gospel witness in many modes and forms.[42] Here the many tongues of the Spirit arouses worshipful witness, for instance, whereby the gospel and message of the reign of God is advanced through the liturgical life of the apostolic community.[43] In a postcolonial context that is suspicious of abstract metanarratives, for instance, Spirit-empowered witness grounded in the concrete praxis and *poiesis* of a worshipping community communicates more effectively the gospel in a world of bad news.[44] The other side of this point is that pluriformity of Spirit-empowered witness proceeds in attentiveness to the diversity of postcolonial situations and audiences of the evangelistic message.[45]

But if the Spirit facilitates apostolic witness, the content of the good news is also pneumatological, more precisely about the living Spirit-anointed Messiah. Evangelistic christocentricity, in this respect, is not apart from

---

41. See for instance Studebaker, *A Pentecostal Political Theology for American Renewal*.

42. The vernacularization thesis is argued classically by Sanneh, *Translating the Message*, and has yet to be applied, to my knowledge, to a theology of evangelism; for more on the vernacular in relationship to worship and witness, see my articles, "Worship in Many Tongues," and "The Power of Language."

43. The notion of *worshipful witness* is mine, elaborated in my and Anderson's *Renewing Christian Theology*, ch. 12.

44. See Pickard, *Liberating Evangelism*.

45. Wesleyans call this *relational evangelism*, a notion that is pneumatologically substantive; see Knight and Powe Jr., *Transforming Evangelism*.

the Spirit, and hence the gospel is thoroughly Trinitarian, including Son and Spirit, from beginning to end.[46] Yes, the message of the Spirit-empowered Christ includes the reign of God that he announced and inaugurated. The good news thus proclaimed by the body of Christ and the fellowship of the Spirit—the church of gathering of Jesus' followers by the power of the Spirit—thus renews the church, according to the form of the reign of God, in its various local socioeconomic and political contexts in and across the postcolony.[47] There is one body but many members constituted by the many gifts of the Spirit (cf. 1 Cor 12), and these bear witness to the lordship of Jesus amidst the multiple polis that dot the postcolonial geoscape. To be clear: nothing argued here is intended to minimize the import of personal conversion to Jesus' lordship as central to the goal of evangelism, but it is also the case that especially evangelical theologies of evangelism have made little of this political dimension of apostolic proclamation. Attentiveness to the pneumatological aspects of apostolic messianism alerts us to how such can be understood politically in Jewish versus Roman contexts, and this in turn invites discernment about the political implications of how the good news of Jesus as Christ and Lord may, or not, be received within the many nodes of the global postcolonial network.

The other major trajectory to be charted for a postcolonial pneumatology of evangelism concerns the message and reality of the reign of God proclaimed by Jesus under the unction of the Spirit throughout his public ministry. In the end, the good news of the divine reign is that the oppressive powers of death and destruction have been overcome through the resurrection of Jesus (see Acts 1:22, 4:33, 17:18, 32), and this has not just spiritual but material consequences. The earliest Spirit-empowered evangelists realized the socioeconomic significance of the gospel message even if their efforts to shape such a community of mutuality (2:44–46, 4:32–37) did not persist as long as we, or they, might have hoped for. The point is that Jesus' evangelistic message was meaningful for the many dimensions of human need—"holistic" in today's missiological parlance[48]—and this remains central to any annunciation about the coming divine reign. If evangelism in the present postcolonial regime does not enable realization of gospel for the poor, oppressed, and marginalized in their many dimensions—one thinks

---

46. Keener, "Power of Pentecost," unfolds this pneumatological Christocentrism as foundational to the theology of Acts.

47. The relationship between evangelism and ecclesial renewal is central to Holmes, *Turning to Christ*; see also McDonnell, ed., *Toward a New Pentecost for a New Evangelization*, to Keum, ed., *Together towards Life*, for other ecumenical developments of these intersecting and intertwining themes.

48. See Pope-Levison, *Evangelization from a Liberation Perspective*.

today of refugees, victims of the war on terror, the ongoing trafficking of children and women, among so many other transnational crises—then it ceases to be the good news of the Spirit of Jesus as Messiah.

In all of this, apostolic evangelism in the post-colony proceeds not with the haughty aggressiveness of the colonial era or via colonialist aspirations and triumphalism but as tempered by the eschatological posture of humility that "see[s] in a mirror, dimly" (1 Cor 13:12). Yet such dispositional modesty also does not merely defer to the powers but attends to the full scope of the messianic message across the socioeconomic and political domains of human life and works in the patient power of the Spirit to instantiate the divine reign. In short, apostolic evangelism in the present time both declares and attempts to embody the proper attitudes and practices reflective of Jesus' life and message so that good news is manifest in the global post-colony. May the Spirit be poured out afresh to instigate many tongues, empower their concomitant liberative practices, and deliver the captives for effective evangelistic witness within their respective postcolonial times and spaces, for the sake of the coming reign of God.

PART IV

Theological-Scriptural Interpretation in the Spirit: Apostolic Pathways

CHAPTER 10

The Light Shines in the Darkness

Johannine Dualism and the Challenge of Christian Theology of Religions Today[1]

Exclusivistic theologies of religions have long been prevalent in the history of Christian thought.[2] In this tradition, a pretty clear-cut division between believers and unbelievers exists that undergirds both the traditional ecclesiocentric soteriology—e.g., as expressed in the classical motto, *extra Ecclesiam nulla salus* ("there is no salvation outside the church")—and the contemporary evangelical conviction that, generally speaking, salvation is impossible for those who have neither heard nor confessed belief in Jesus Christ.[3] The core of such a dualistic conception between believers and unbelievers can be traced, at least in part, to Christian Testament claims regarding salvation

---

1. The original version of this paper was given at a special topics forum, "Christian Theology's Engagement with Religious Pluralism: Biblical Texts & Themes," at the American Academy of Religion, Philadelphia, Pennsylvania, November 2006. I am grateful to the questions from the audience that helped to sharpen some aspects of my argument in this paper. Thanks to John Christopher Thomas, Gerald R. McDermott, and Jonathan W. Rice for their critical comments as well, and to the editors of the *Journal of Religion* and two anonymous referees whose insightful remarks and questions have helped clarify the thrust of my paper. My former graduate assistant, Doc Hughes, helped ensure a smoother read of the manuscript. All errors of fact and interpretation remain my own.

2. See the survey in Plantinga, *Christianity and Religious Plurality*, esp. parts II–IV.

3. The Protestant version of the Roman Catholic *extra Ecclesiam nulla salus* derives largely from Romans 10:9–13, which is taken to mean that there is no salvation outside of hearing and confessing Jesus as Lord; see Race, *Christians and Religious Pluralism*, 10–37.

as a process of coming out of darkness into the light.[4] It seems clear that the first Christians understood themselves to have undergone this conversion while adherents and devotees of other religious traditions remained deceived and in the dark. Hence the light-darkness motif in the early church has translated into a theological stance that viewed people in other religions to be in need of deliverance into the light of Christ and the Christian faith.

I want to argue, however, that things are not so obvious under the surface. To do so, I focus on the light-darkness motif in the Gospel of John. Even though it is arguable that the Fourth Gospel was not written to address questions raised by contemporary theology of religions, yet as part of the canon of Scripture, its contents inevitably inform Christian theological reflection in general, and, as I will show, the construction of an exclusivistic approach to theology of religions in particular. Thus, precisely because the light-darkness motif is not on the margins of the evangelist's account, it needs to be squarely confronted. My thesis is that while the light and darkness application has traditionally been used defend an exclusivistic Christian theology of Judaism, there are other ways to understand this motif specifically and the Johannine narrative as a whole that belie such a theological conclusion. If I can make the case even in the face of the pervasiveness of this theme in the Fourth Gospel for a less exclusivistic approach to Christian theology of religions, then this will open up to the possibilities of a more dialogical and hospitable set of postures and practices vis-à-vis those in other faiths.

The respective sections of this chapter will a) survey the light-darkness theme in the Fourth Gospel (FG) and observe how it has come to inform discussions in Christian theology of religions; b) assess this theme as related to the early Christian polemic against the Jews; c) explore this theme at the intersection of recent studies of Qumran and early Christian sectarianism; and d) identify other trajectories in the FG which complicate attempts to develop a theology of religions from the Johannine understanding of light and darkness. I will conclude with some suggestions for a contemporary

---

4. Representative texts include: "to open their eyes so that they may turn from darkness to light and from the power of Satan to God" (Acts 26:18); "Do not be mismatched with unbelievers. For what partnership is there between righteousness and lawlessness? Or what fellowship is there between light and darkness?" (2 Cor 6:14); "For once you were darkness, but now in the Lord you are light" (Eph 5:8); "But you, beloved, are not in darkness, for that day to surprise you like a thief; for you are all children of light and children of the day; we are not of the night or of darkness" (1 Thess 5:4–5); cf. Matt 4:16, Luke 1:79, Col 1:13, and 1 Pet 2:9, among other texts. For explication of this light-darkness motif in the NT vis-à-vis early Christian understandings of conversion, see Green, "'To Turn from Darkness to Light,'" and Gaventa, *From Darkness to Light*.

theology of religions that go beyond the traditional framework by asking how the FG can enable the performing of hospitable interfaith practices instead.

One caveat before proceeding: I am neither a biblical studies scholar nor an expert in the voluminous scholarship on the FG.[5] My background and training is in constructive and systematic theology, the study of religion, and theology of religious pluralism.[6] Yet since Christian theology will go only so far as biblical interpretation will allow, systematicians and comparative theologians must inevitably deal with the "hard texts" of Scripture. Needless to say, my argument is therefore vulnerable to correction from both the theological and the exegetical side. Hence I submit these thoughts in trepidation, but also in eager anticipation of responses from scholars in both arenas.[7]

Light and Darkness in John: Aspects of a Classical Christian Theology of Religions

Any impartial reading of the FG will immediately notice the centrality of the light-darkness motif to its plot, characterization, and rhetoric.[8] From the beginning, the Prologue presents the Logos in contrast to the darkness— "The light shines in the darkness, and the darkness did not overcome it" (1:5)—and says that the Baptist (like the evangelist) "came as a witness to testify to the light, so that all might believe through him" (1:7). Further, Jesus identifies himself as "the light of the world," saying also, "Whoever follows me will never walk in darkness but will have the light of life" (8:12; cf. 12:46). And as the light, Jesus admonishes his listeners: "The light is with you for a little longer. Walk while you have the light, so that the darkness may not overtake you. If you walk in the darkness, you do not know where you are going. While you have the light, believe in the light, so that you may become children of light." (11:35-36)

---

5. For this reason, I do not deal with questions of authorship, source redaction theories, and other such convoluted issues in Johannine interpretation. For a widely referenced discussion on these issues, see Brown, *The Community of the Beloved Disciple*.

6. My work in theology of religions has been, by and large, in the genre of constructive theology; see Yong, *Discerning the Spirit(s)*; *Beyond the Impasse*; and *Hospitality and the Other*.

7. [This paragraph is obviously written prior to my awareness of developments in the area of theological interpretation of Scripture, certainly before I thought of myself as participating in such inquiry.]

8. See, e.g., Kent, *Light in the Darkness*.

From this, it is clear that the fourth evangelist is concerned not only about describing Jesus as the light, but also with ensuring that his listeners and readers walk in Jesus' light rather than allow the darkness to overtake them. But John is worried because the light of Jesus also brings about judgment on the world: "And this is the judgement, that the light has come into the world, and people loved darkness rather than light because their deeds were evil. For all who do evil hate the light and do not come to the light, so that their deeds may not be exposed. But those who do what is true come to the light, so that it may be clearly seen that their deeds have been done in God." (3:19–21)[9] To remain in the dark not only risks coming under the judgment of God, it also transforms those in darkness into lovers of evil and haters of the light. For this reason, whereas those who are in the light are doers of the truth and believers in and followers of Jesus,[10] the world of darkness hates Jesus and his followers (7:7, 15:18–24, 17:14).

Taken at face value, these and many other passages in the FG represent the "darkness" as unbelief in and rejection of the revelation of Jesus, who is the light. Hence those who are in darkness remain in the state of not knowing God and of being spiritually separated from God.[11] In this way, the light-darkness motif functions in the FG to demarcate between the saved and the lost, between the elect and "the world."[12]

Given this clear opposition between believers and unbelievers, it should not be surprising that Christian thinking about the religions has long been dominated by a similar logic. The traditional exclusivist position developed along these lines, reasoning at least in part from this New Testament idea that only believers in Jesus were in the light to the conclusion that members of other religious traditions remained in darkness. Colonial and missionary expansions from the eighteenth through the twentieth centuries were justified in part as the necessary work of reaching the multitudes of lost "heathen" in the non-western world with the light of the gospel.[13] Insofar

9. On darkness as a symbol of judgment in the Hebrew Bible, see Achtemeier, "Jesus Christ, the Light of the World."

10. See Hodges, "Coming into the Light—John 3:20–21."

11. Arguably, one could make the argument that the gospel is an extended elaboration of the Johannine claim, "If we say that we have fellowship with him while we are walking in darkness, we lie and do not do what is true" (1 John 1:6); cf. Baylis, "The Meaning of Walking."

12. See Barrett, *Essays on John*, ch. 7 on "Paradox and Dualism." Note also that the "world" is constructed negatively throughout the FG: 8:12, 23; 9:39; 12:31, and 13:1.

13. Representative of missionary literature during the colonial period is Godbey and Godbey, *Light in Darkness*. For a more comprehensive analysis, see Pakenham, *The Scramble for Africa*.

as such "heathen" were adherents of other religions and members of non-Christian communities, they were undoubtedly lost in darkness without the light of Christ. In this scheme of things, the light-darkness motif provided the church throughout much of its history with a fairly stable theological frame of reference for locating and defining the religions of the world as lying "outside" the light of God in Christ.

In the rest of this essay, however, I wish to complicate this reading of the light-darkness dualism in John in light of efforts to wrestle afresh with the topic of theology of religions in our late modern context. My approach will attempt to understand how the light-darkness motif functions in John against the backdrop of early Jewish-Christian relations, of dualism at Qumran, and of other Johannine references to the world and to the Gentiles. In each case, I hope to show that any simplistic application of the light-darkness motif that contrasts the light of Christian faith with the darkness of other religions is problematic on exegetical, hermeneutical, and theological grounds.

John and the Jews: Reconsidering Implications for Theology of Religions

Jesus' claim, "I am the light of the world" (8:12), sets the context for his confrontation with the Pharisees in particular (8:13) and "the Jews" in general (8:22 and passim). Now the Jewish context of this self-revelation of Jesus should not be underestimated. Based simply on textual considerations, once the passage about the woman caught in adultery (7:53–8:11) is recognized to be a later interpolation, Jesus' claim is seen to be made in the Temple courtyard in the context of the climactic day of the Jewish celebration of the Feast of Tabernacles (7:10-11, 14, 37; cf. 8:20). Whereas Jesus had claimed to be "living water" earlier, perhaps on the occasion of the water-drawing ceremony on the last day of the festival (cf. 7:37-38), here he claims to be the "light of the world," perhaps on the occasion of the lighting of the lamps ceremony concluding the Feast.[14] This piece of detail reminds us that we need to understand Jesus' declaration to be the light of the world in its original Jewish context.

When this contextual background is factored in, the light of the world is seen to pass judgment not only on darkness in general, but on Jewish disbelief in particular. Following this proclamation, Jesus engages in a heated

---

14. For commentary, see Beasley-Murray, *John*, 27-28, and Schnackenburg, *The Gospel according to St. John*, 2.189-90. Keener, *The Gospel of John*, vol. 1, discusses the entirety of 7:1–10:42 under the section titled "Tabernacles and Hanukkah."

exchange with the Jews (*hoi Ioudaioi*[15]), during which he denies that they know either him or his father (8:13–20), condemns them to death in their sins unless they believe in him (8:21–26), and rejects their claim to being legitimate children (*tekna*) of Abraham because they neither know nor accept him (8:31–42). When the Jews respond that they are both children of Abraham and of God, Jesus counters, "You are from your father the devil, and you choose to do your father's desires. He was a murderer from the beginning and does not stand in the truth, because there is no truth in him. When he lies, he speaks according to his own nature, for he is a liar and the father of lies." (8:44) Existing tensions between Jesus and the Jews (5:18, 7:1–9, 44) are here exacerbated, with the Jews charging that Jesus was demon-possessed (8:48, 10:19) and being even more motivated than ever to silence him (8:59, 10:31, 39, 11:53–57).

Jesus' exchange with the Jews should be understood also against the background of the ejection of believers in Jesus from the synagogue (9:22; 12:42; 16:2; cf. 7:12–13). It is possible that these expulsions had persisted during the time of the composition and even final redaction of the gospel. Even if this were not the case,[16] still many believe that the *Sitz im Leben*

15. There seems to be no consistent reference for *hoi Ioudaioi* in the fourth gospel. In some contexts, they refer to Christian Jews who are outside the Johannine community, while in others they refer to Jewish neighbors in the Johannine community who are not disciples of Jesus, residents of Judea, or—what many scholars seem to agree upon today—Jewish religious leaders in Jerusalem. The debate involves decisions about the provenance of the gospel as well as the date(s) of its (various) redaction(s), although there is no denying the increasingly pejorative connotations regarding *hoi Ioudaioi* as the narrative progresses (into the passion). While for our purposes no definitive resolution is necessary, I think that even if it could be demonstrated beyond a shadow of a doubt that John meant to refer only to the Jewish religious leaders with this title, that would still not completely resolve our problem since such leaders are, by definition, representative of the Jewish tradition then and now. In other words, we would still have the problem regarding a Johannine theology of Judaism and, by extension, of the religions in that case—which is precisely why we are undertaking this task of revisiting the FG in light of this question.

16. Schnelle, *Antidocetic Christology in the Gospel of John*, 31–36, registers a minority opinion among contemporary scholars in suggesting that the Gospel of John was written at some remove from earlier polemics with Judaism, with the references to synagogue expulsion being more retrospective (even functioning as a literary designation for unbelievers) than concerning contemporary historical realities. Schnelle argues instead that the central contrast in the fourth gospel is between law and gospel rather than between Jews and Christians. Going beyond Schnelle, Hakola, *Identity Matters*, ch. 2, argues against the conflict-expulsion thesis, claiming that there was insufficiently strong leadership among the post-70 CE Jewish communities that could have articulated and then defended a new orthodoxy; rather, the early Jewish-Christian communities slowly came to distance and alienate themselves from their Jewish

of the FG reflects the painful process through which the earliest Christian community emerged out of and began to separate from its Jewish roots.[17] Now to be sure, any hypothesis about the history of the Johannine community text remains speculative at some level. Nevertheless, even if we cannot prove that hostilities between Jews and Jewish-Christians are behind the text of the FG, the evangelist is still understood as motivated to both encourage and admonish those who were less mature in their Christian faith to persevere in the face of persecution.[18] The Jews are portrayed as opponents of Jesus who were self-opinionated (chs. 7–8), foolish (ch. 9), disloyal to God (19:15), and deceived and ignorant regarding their rejection of Jesus (7:49). Hence they represent the adversaries of the gospel and serve to persuade the nascent Christian community to stand fast amid whatever circumstances might come upon them.[19] Further, this sociohistorical background also illuminates the rationale for the evangelist's preserving Jesus' words to walk and work while it is still day, before the night falls (9:4, 34; 11:9–10; 12:35–36). Whereas the "night" that is coming refers first to the passion of the Christ (cf. 13:30), yet Jesus' admonitions become for the Jewish-Christian readers of the Gospel urgent "summons to do what is required at any particular time, to hear the voice of God here and now."[20] At the end of his extended presentation of Jesus as the light who brings judgment on the Jews, the evangelist brings to a culmination his argument that the unbelief of the Jews can be explicated in part by God's having blinded their eyes on the one hand, even as the Jews are responsible for their own obstinate rejection of the light on the other (12:37–46).[21]

---

backgrounds as they embraced Gentiles.

17. Hence, there are those who now argue that the debate is really between Jews committed to the Torah and Jews committed to following Jesus. If so, then this is less a case of Jewish-Christian polemics than it is an intramural Jewish disagreement; on this point, see preface to Evans and Hagner, eds., *Anti-Semitism and Early Christianity*, xix. But consult also the now standard study on this complex issue, Sanders, *Schismatics, Sectarians, Dissidents, Deviants*, which suggests that the inter- and intra- distinction is too blurred to allow for us to neatly compartmentalize the one from the other. Hence the challenge before us.

18. Hence Schnackenburg comments in light of the heated debate in John 8 that "the evangelist has in mind Jewish Christians of his time who—perhaps as a result of Jewish counter-propaganda—are in danger of lapsing from faith in Christ" (*Gospel according to St. John*, 2.204).

19. See further, Freyne, "Vilifying the Other and Defining the Self."

20. Schnackenburg, *Gospel according to St. John*, 2.242.

21. See Painter, "'The Quotation of Scripture and Unbelief in John 12.36b–43.'" Similarly, the man born blind (ch. 9) nevertheless truly sees, not only because his eyes were opened by Jesus, but because he recognized and accepted Jesus as Lord (9:38), in

While much more can and should be said about the light-darkness motif in relationship to the Jews, time and space constraints require that we move on to ask theological questions regarding the religions. The major issue to be confronted here, I suggest, is that the light-darkness motif has contributed to a Christian theology of Judaism that has in turn shaped, both implicitly and explicitly, Christian reflection on the broader question of theology of religions. In the case of Christian theological reflection on Judaism, two developments require attention. First, there is the question about whether or not the negative portrayal of the Jews in John's Gospel in particular and in other portions of the New Testament in general becomes a normative guideline for how Christians should think about Jews, Jewishness, and Judaism. Some would argue that once we locate the anti-Judaic rhetoric—which should clearly be distinguished from "anti-Semitism," since "anti-Judaism" is more geographically and historically delimited in contrast to the loaded language of "anti-Semitism—in its original sociohistorical context, we realize, as Luke Timothy Johnson has argued, that "the slander of the New Testament is typical of that found among rival claimants to a philosophical tradition and is found as widely among Jews as among other Hellenists."[22] Building on Johnson's argument, Stephen Motyer proposes that while John might be considered "anti-Jewish" in terms of seeking to delegitimate Jewish beliefs and practices and to legitimate belief in Christ, John is not hostile toward the Jews; rather, even the polemical claim in 8:44 "serves not merely to *denounce* but more particularly to *warn*, to *persuade*."[23] Thus, "far from 'demonising' the Jews, this charge [8:44] is part of a strategy, rooted in the conditions of late first-century Judaism, which is designed to appeal to Jews to see Jesus as the Messiah, and is motivated by a deep commitment to the good of Israel."[24]

But even if we grant the original *Sitz im Leben* of an intramural debate, other scholars are convinced that the plain surface reading of the FG has

---

contrast to the seeing Pharisees who nevertheless remained spiritually blind because of their incapacity (unwillingness?) to receive the Messiah. I will return to this episode later.

22. Johnson, "The New Testament's Anti-Jewish Slander," 429. Johnson suggests that there is stronger anti-Gentile rhetoric in the New Testament—he cites Matt 6:7, 32; Rom 1:18–32; 1 Cor 6:9–10; Eph. 2:11–12; 1 Thess 4:5, 13; Tit 1:12; 1 Pet 1:14, 18, 4:3–4, etc. (441n66)—and that by comparison, the anti-Jewish rhetoric is actually fairly mild.

23. Motyer, *Your Father the Devil?*, 212; italics Motyer's.

24. Ibid., xii. This is an extension on John Koenig's argument that the earliest Christians understood themselves as Jews and were, in that sense, more pro-Jewish when read on their own terms than through the lens of the history of anti-Semitism and the Shoah; see Koenig, *Jews and Christians in Dialogue*.

played its part in nurturing later Christian anti-Semitism toward Jews.[25] Now to be sure, the sources of anti-Semitism are by no means fully derivative from early Christianity.[26] At the same time, even if scholars can agree that the New Testament as a whole or the FG in particular are not inherently theologically anti-Semitic, it is certainly the case that later generations of Christians far removed from the original context have developed an anti-Semitic Christian theology of Judaism by drawing from these texts, and some have even proceeded to act upon those beliefs.[27] In other words, the assumption that Jews are those who remain in darkness in the service of their father the devil has not only fostered certain Christian attitudes and postures toward Jews,[28] but has even served to justify oppressive Christian practices against Jews over the centuries. Unfortunately, it is no simple matter to distance Christian texts from their interpretations, reception, and effects.[29]

What then about Christian theology of religions in terms of the light-darkness theme in John? At one level, it might be argued that no conclusions can be drawn since the FG identifies those in darkness as Jews, and this permits us to extract only a Christian theology of Judaism rather than a full-blown Christian theology of religions. In this case, the special relationship between Christianity and Judaism—either in terms of covenant connectedness or in terms of intramural hostilities—may mean that the division between light and darkness in John has no bearing on Christian theological views regarding other religious traditions. But of course things are never that easy since the fact that Judaism falls under the category of a "non-Christian religion" itself has implications for Christian theological reflection about the religions.

---

25. E.g., Kysar, "Anti-Semitism and the Gospel of John," revised in Kysar, *Voyages in John*, ch. 9, and many of the authors of Bieringer, Pollefeyt, and Vandecasteele-Vanneuville, eds., *Anti-Judaism in the Fourth Gospel*. The more radical thesis—that is, that the New Testament is anti-Semitic rather than that the New Testament only nurtures later Christian anti-Semitism—has been widely accepted in some circles since the publication of Ruether's *Faith and Fratricide*.

26. See Sevenster, *The Roots of Pagan Anti-Semitism in the Ancient World*, and Gager, *The Origins of Anti-Semitism*.

27. One of the standard historical accounts is Flannery, *The Anguish of the Jews*.

28. Arguably, such attitudes made possible the Holocaust. After identifying a number of reasons why America did not do more to save the Jews, historian David Wyman concludes, "The real obstacle was the absence of a strong desire to rescue Jews"; see Wyman, *The Abandonment of the Jews*, 339.

29. See Culpepper, "The Gospel of John as a Threat to Jewish-Christian Relations."

But given the connections between Christian theology of Judaism and Christian theology of religions, we can also pursue the implications of Christian rethinking the light-darkness theme that is central to the FG's theology of Judaism. As the rupture of the Holocaust has led Christians to reconsider the relationship between Christianity and Judaism from the ground up, might this also open up theological space to rethink the simplistic division between Christian faith and non-Christian religions? The way forward may be along any number of trajectories. For example, one might stay at the level of the Johannine narrative, and note that not every Jew is an unbeliever. Here we are referring not only "to the Jews who had believed in him [Jesus]" (8:31), but also to individuals like Nicodemus (of which more later) and Nathanael. The last mentioned was called by Jesus "truly an Israelite" (1:47) even before they met, and then also declared to Jesus, "you are the Son of God! You are the King of Israel!" (1:49). In these cases, we observe that even within the darkness of "the Jews," there appear to be lights among individuals who had true faith before meeting Jesus. The problem with this approach for theology of religions, however, is that we risk identifying and naming the light(s) in the darkness of the religions in a manner similar to the way in which Karl Rahner talked about the "anonymous Christian" over a generation ago. Even if we grant that such language represents more that of the Christian faithful attempting to be more inclusive of those in other faiths, in today's climate any such posturing is at best ignorant of how people of faith identify themselves and at worst another imperialistic Christian act in a postcolonial world.[30]

Perhaps more fruitful may be the now widespread attempts to develop a non-supersessionistic theology of Judaism.[31] If Christian faith can at least run parallel with if not include (without displacing) Judaism, is it possible also to formulate a more inclusive rather than exclusive Christian theology of religions? More precisely, if Judaism is associated not with the category of darkness but recognized instead as the "elder brother" of Christianity—with not only responsibilities, but also the rights (e.g., respect) thereof[32]—then might other religious traditions also serve in their own way as *praeparatio evangelica* to the Christian faith?[33] The potential problem with such an approach is the risk of understanding the *praeparatio* in a quasi-supersession-

---

30. Precisely this criticism is articulated by Dube, "Reading for Decolonization."

31. The most sustained efforts so far have been made by Van Buren, *A Theology of the Jewish-Christian Reality*, Williamson, *A Guest in the House of Israel*, and Moore et al., *Toward a Dialogical Community*. See also Novak, "From Supersessionism to Parallelism in Jewish-Christian Dialogue."

32. As recently proposed by Inch, *The Elder Brother*.

33. See Kemp, "'The Light of Men.'"

ist way since the arrival of Christianity could be understood as dispensing with the previous dispensation. But if the *praeparatio* means not "being succeeded by" but rather "opening up to" a parallel way of religious faithfulness, then might it not be possible to reconstruct a positive Christian theology of Judaism despite the FG's categories of light and darkness, and to reconfigure Johannine-inspired Christian theology of religions also in other terms?

These possibilities, however, presume that Christian theology of religions informed by John has to be extrapolated from a Christian theology of Judaism. Rather than this indirect approach, some will argue that the light-darkness motif is applied by the evangelist not only to the Jews, but also to the world at large. Hence we must now turn our attention to this more comprehensive understanding of light and darkness in the FG.

The Light Shines in the Darkness: John's Prologue and Sectarianism at Qumran

The Prologue to John sets the world as the stage for the incarnation. The cosmic frame of reference is unmistakable: "All things came into being through him, and without him not one thing came into being" (1:3). So when the evangelist proceeds to declare that "in him was life, and the life was the light of all people," and "The light shines in the darkness, and the darkness did not overcome it" (1:4-5), two observations are pertinent. First, if the Logos is the light, then the world lies in darkness. But secondly, the darkness is not summarily dispersed by the light; rather, the darkness attempts (even if it fails) to resist—"overcome" is from *katelaben*, which could be translated "apprehend," "comprehend," or "overtake"[34]—the light. Schnackenburg thus concludes, "The Enemies of God do not merely walk in darkness . . . , they are themselves 'darkness.'"[35] In this case, all unbelievers, which include not only "the Jews" but also, by extension, those in other faiths, are by definition those who are in the darkness.

There are, however, other exegetical, contextual, and theological considerations. Most textually pertinent is when John goes on to say "The true

---

34. Keener, *The Gospel of John*, 387, asks: "Does katelaben mean that darkness could not apprehend the light intellectually (so Cyril of Alexandria), that darkness did not accept the light, or that darkness could not conquer the light (Origen and most Greek fathers)? More than likely John, whose skill in wordplays appears throughout his Gospel, has introduced a wordplay here: darkness could not apprehend or overtake the light, whether by comprehending it (grasping with the mind) or by overcoming it (grasping with the hand)."

35. Schnackenburg, *Gospel according to St. John*, 1.246.

light, which enlightens everyone, was coming into the world" (1:9). There are a number of separate issues here, of which I will mention three. First, it appears the light that enlightens the world also offers salvation to the world, and rather than give up in the face of rejection, the Logos became flesh precisely in order to be received by humankind.[36] In this case, the light pursues the darkness, even if the darkness does not understand the light. Second, and building on the first, there is the question of whether or not the light of the Logos was available to all people before or only after the incarnation of the Logos. If before, then clearly the light of the Logos was nevertheless available to humankind apart from its being manifest in the flesh. But even if so, although the Logos "was in the world, and the world came into being through him; yet the world did not know him" (1:10). Finally, there is also the question about whether or not the "everyone" of 1:9 refers comprehensively to the world—after all, grammatically, "was coming into the world" could connect just as well to "the true light"—or only to the Logos's own people. If the latter, then "He came to what was his own, and his own people did not accept him" (1:11). So on the one hand, 1:9 could be the basis for a more optimistic theology of religions if indeed it were understood that at least potentially, the light of the Logos offers salvation to all human beings.[37] On the other hand, 1:10 seems to take back what 1:9 gives away and 1:11 suggests that the scope of "everyone" in 1:9 may be restricted to the Jews, but whoever is being referred to nevertheless rejects the Logos.[38] Still, there seems to yet remain the opportunity for any and even all to believe and receive the Logos, and to these are given the right and power to become children of God (1:12).

But what is the wider context within which these claims regarding the light of the Logos and the darkness of the world can be further understood? This is an especially crucial issue given the increasingly accepted hypothesis that the Prologue (and the FG itself) is itself shaped by dualistic assumptions

---

36. For a defense of this reading, see Haenchen, *John*, 1.118. I should mention that some interpreters believe 1:9 constitutes not God's special or saving revelation, but God's general revelation. But even here, some understand such general revelation to be subjectively endowed in each heart (the dominant view throughout Christian history), while others argue that such general revelation is objectively present to all people (a version of the doctrine of prevenient or common grace). For an overview of these debates, see Miller, "The True Light Which Illumines Every Person," 69–78.

37. 1:9 is the most quoted text in defense of a more inclusive Christian theology of religions by Dupuis, *Toward a Christian Theology of Religious Pluralism*.

38. Hence while the Logos perseveres in revealing himself to the world, the world rejects him. In this case, the offer of salvation intimated in 1:9 functions more as a judgment on an unrepentant world; see Philip, "The Light of Glory," 119–23.

that were "in the air" during the first century.[39] What a previous generation of researchers had suggested were features of Gnosticism—e.g., the dualisms of light and darkness, truth and falsehood, and life and death[40]—have more recently come to be seen as characteristics of a pervasive first century Jewish-Hellenistic milieu that included "the dualism of Qumran and other Jewish apocalyptic texts, *hekhalot* mysticism, Hermeticism, Philo and Neoplatonism."[41] Here, the discovery of the Dead Sea Scrolls and the community at Qumran suggests both comparisons and contrasts between the dualism of the FG and that of Qumran. Generally speaking, whereas Qumranic dualism is both cosmic and metaphysical, Johannine dualism, while not excepting these features—including the blanket claims regarding the world being in darkness and in bondage to the devil (12:31, 14:30, 16:11)—is more straightforwardly soteriological and ethical, especially in terms of requiring moral decisions and personal commitments of its readers (and community members).[42] Yes, the Qumranic Community Rule more explicitly distinguishes between the Spirit of Truth versus the Spirit of Perversity, and the Sons of Light versus the Sons of Darkness; still both in the Rule and John, "light symbolically represents life, truth, knowledge, and eternal life; conversely darkness represents death, falsehood, ignorance, and annihilation."[43] Now even if Johannine dependence on Qumran is rejected,[44] it is arguable the fourth evangelist had adopted a Greek philosophical idea, the Logos, but at the same time reshaped it according to the dualistic sensibilities of Jewish Hellenism prevailing in the first century.

39. See Hakola, *Identity Matters*, 197–210.

40. See Bultmann, *Theology of the New Testament*, ch. 2, esp. 17–21. Bultmann's Mandean Gnostic source theory for the origins of the FG never achieved consensus among Johannine scholars; see Yamauchi, *Pre-Christian Gnosticism*, 29–34. For a more recent discussion of the difficulties related to associating the FG with Gnosticism, especially the more definitively heterodox versions characteristic of the later second century, see Lieu, "Gnosticism and the Gospel of John."

41. Hengel, *The Johannine Question*, 113.

42. Here I am following the work of Qumran scholars like Charlesworth, "A Critical Comparison of the Dualism in 1QS 3:13–4:26," and Dimant, "Dualism at Qumran."

43. Charlesworth, "A Critical Comparison," 100. Other parallels cited by Charlesworth include: Fragment of Book of Noah 108:11–15; Test Zebulun 9:8; Test. Levi 2:8–3:1; 1 Enoch 58:5ff; and 2 Baruch 17:4–18:2, 48:50; 59:2.

44. Against Charlesworth's argument that there is mutual dependence between John and the Community Rule, David Aune suggests that at best there is "indirect dependence" and more probably simply a vague overlap based on the composition of both documents during a similar time period; see Aune, "Dualism in the Fourth Gospel."

Why and how did this reshaping occur? I suggest the similarity of their sociohistorical contexts may cast some light on this question: both the Qumran community and the Johannine community were sectarian groups, the former resisting the Roman rule (among other dominant forces) and the latter "the world" in general and "the Jews" in particular.[45] There are hence at least two aspects to what we might call Johannine sectarianism: the social and the rhetorical. From the perspective of recent social scientific research, the Johannine community has many of the features of a sectarian movement: with beginnings in protest against the establishment view of reality; an egalitarian ethos and a voluntary association; love and acceptance promised to community members; and total commitment commanded from its members.[46] In this framework, Johannine exclusivism is a direct offshoot of its being a sectarian, first-century Jewish movement parallel to, if not overlapping with, other Jewish sects such as the Essenes at Qumran.[47] It should not be surprising, then, that the FG adopts the kind of rhetoric prevalent among other sectarian groups of its time. Dualistic categories serve the purposes of crafting a "resocializing story" that protests against the sociopolitical-religious establishment through the articulation of an "anti-language." In the cases of John, Qumran, and other first-century Jewish and Jewish-Christian sectarian movements then, spirit, above, life, light, not of the/this world, freedom, truth, and love—all of which are essential features of the Logos now revealed in the flesh in Jesus—contrast with flesh, below, death, darkness, this/the world, slavery, lies, and hate.[48] From this socio-rhetorical perspective, "The social experience of John and his people engendered a fear that made life in this world hateful because it had become untenable. Having been hated by the world, they came to hate the world, which is yet another special language inversion."[49] The Johannine duality of light and darkness (among other contrasts) has the effect, "for the insider who accepts them, of demolishing the logic of the world, particularly the world of Judaism, and progressively emphasizing the sectarian conscious-

---

45. Here and throughout the rest of this essay, I use "sectarian" and its cognates descriptively rather than pejoratively, at least in the sense in which the Johannine community understood themselves as alienated from other groups in the wider society, if not in the contemporary sociological sense of its being a formally organized sect. On this point, see the discussion in Brown, *The Community of the Beloved Disciple*, 89–90; cf. also Segovia, "The Love and Hatred of Jesus and Johannine Sectarianism."

46. Scroggs, "The Earliest Christian Communities as Sectarian Movement."

47. Nickelsburg, "Revealed Wisdom as a Criterion."

48. The concepts of "resocializing story" and "anti-language" are described in Malina and Rohrbaugh, *Social-Science Commentary on the Gospel of John*, 11–14.

49. Petersen, *The Gospel of John and the Sociology of Light*, 86.

ness. If one 'believes' what is said in this book, he is quite literally taken out of the ordinary world of social reality."[50] Hence the FG is sectarian not only in terms of its original social climate (Jewish-Christian polemics), but also in terms of its rhetorical strategies, with the latter either derived from Qumran or mutually partaking with the Qumranic community of a common dualistic worldview.[51]

What do all these ideas have to do with Christian theology of religions today? Three sets of questions emerge from the preceding. First, while some have rightly questioned why some aspects of Johannine sectarian theology have been historically subordinated to other New Testament voices,[52] from a socio-sectarian perspective the dualism of the FG has and will always continue to speak to Christian communities on the margins of their respective societies. But does that mean that a Johannine-inspired theology of religions is necessarily limited in relevance only to marginal communities on the "underside" of the dominant forces of their societies? Is the light-darkness motif only appropriate for Christians who are being persecuted by other faith communities (as the Johannine Christians were arguably being persecuted by the Jews), and is such a theological perspective (that is dualistic and exclusivistic) valid only in the "world" of those Christians under similar interreligious conditions and circumstances? On the flip side of this question, is the ascription of darkness to other religious communities a (subjective) socio-rhetorical expression of the feelings of a persecuted and beleaguered group rather than an (objective) account of how God actually sees non-Christian religious people? In his discussion of John 8:44, for example, Raimo Hakola comes close to suggesting this point of view when he says, "Dualistic polemic in John is not written with the outsiders in mind but tries to confirm the insiders who are faced with the world's rejection; this polemic aims at justifying the decision to turn their backs on central aspects of Jewish traditions."[53] In other words, the Fourth Gospel is as much, if not more, an active attempt to develop a sectarian

---

50. Meeks, "The Man from Heaven in Johannine Sectarianism," 71.

51. On the other side, such a sociological interpretation of John would need to be balanced by a more theological approach which would insist that it is not social dualism that produces metaphysical (cosmic) and theological (mythological) dualism but the other way around; see Dokka, "Irony and Sectarianism in the Gospel of John," 100, and Gundry, *Jesus the Word according to John the Sectarian*, 53.

52. For example, O'Day, "Johannine Theology as Sectarian Theology," 199–203, wonders why none of the dominant theories of atonement—ransom, substitutionary or moral influence—register John's relationship model of reconciliation as recorded in 10:17–18 and 12:23–36.

53. Hakola, *Identity Matters*, 210.

identity as it is a response to actual "demonic" enemies. But while the Jews were not actually demonic, it is nevertheless true that the Johannine community perceived their opponents as such. Extrapolated to contemporary theology of religions, exclusivism may be more about Christian self-identity than it may be a theological description about religious others in the eyes of God. (Those interested in making this argument can still defend the veracity of Scripture in a similar way to how biblical infallibility—and inerrancy, in some circles—is preserved through emphasizing the scriptural authors' perspective in any biblical claim.)

This line of response raises a second set of theological questions. If Johannine dualism arises out of a certain early Jewish-Christian-sectarian matrix, to what extent is the applicability of its central categories, including the light-darkness motif, constrained by that original context? For example, inasmuch as scholarly research has observed the FG presents a distinctively soteriological and ethical dualism (in contrast to Qumran's more cosmic and metaphysical dualism) emphasizing response to the light, should not contemporary applications of the light-darkness distinction also jettison dichotomistic ontological understandings of this motif in favor of a more ethical framework?[54] Insofar as a rigorous absolutism cannot but divide "the world" into the light of Christian faith and the darkness of Judaism and other religions, such a distinction can neither account for the various spheres of "the world"—e.g., the political, the economic, and the cultural,[55] all of which are intertwined with the religious—nor recognize the various degrees of truth, beauty, and holiness that are manifest in the religions (as affirmed by Vatican II). An ethical rendition of the light-darkness motif, on the other hand, opens up theological space for a more nuanced understanding of the complexity of "the world," and requires instead a discerning posture toward the various spheres of human life as they intersect with the religious dimension.

This ethical criterion also requires contemporary Christians to be self-critically reflective and honest about Christian practices vis-à-vis those in other faiths, especially in light of the historical track record of the church. Even if it is the Synoptic Gospels and not John that commands us to love our enemies (a point to which I will return momentarily), a canonical reading of the New Testament requires us to examine the fruits of our beliefs (doctrines and theological ideas) as they are manifest in our practices. Hence

---

54. To be sure, an epistemic criterion is also present in John, but we will postpone until the next section the question about how this is related, if at all, to the issue of theology of religions. Suffice to say at this point that the ethical criterion of responding to the light will need to be qualified as that which is "available to them."

55. On these aspects of "the world," see Salier, "What's in a World?," 106–17.

we need to ask about the practical implications of framing Christian theology of religions in terms of light and darkness. On this question, whereas anti-Judaic (and, by extension, anti-Islamic, anti-Buddhist, etc.) rhetoric in the hands of marginalized Christian communities could be understood as essential to the formation and preservation of developing Christian identities (as social-scientific readings of the New Testament confirm), the same in the hands of socially and politically mainstreamed Christians could be oppressive for those in other faiths. The problem is not that minority disenfranchised groups identify themselves as being in the light over and against all others; rather, the problem accrues when groups have the power to act on their convictions about those who they believe are in darkness.[56] Hence Christians need to be cognizant of the performative dimension of theology of religions, and this raises the question of the proper posture and practices that Christian beliefs about the religions should inculcate and foster. Before doing so, however, we must engage with a few other questions that need to be taken into account in any attempt to think through a theology of religions against the background of the light-darkness motif in the FG.

At Dawn and at Dusk: Ambivalence regarding a Johannine Theology of Religions

In this section, I want to pursue briefly three sets of additional questions: a) the tension in the FG between the believing community and the world; b) the dynamic characterizations that blur any fixed lines between light and darkness in John; and c) the question about the unevangelized. Together, I suggest these considerations give us further pause about any simplistic dichotomy between "Christian light" and "other religious darkness."

We have already mentioned the Prologue identifies the mission of the Logos's coming into the world as intended to offer salvation (light and life) to the world. This theme of God's concern and love for the world is not a marginal one in the FG. The evangelist records, "For God so loved the world that he gave his only Son" (3:16a). Clearly there is a sense that while the Logos came first to his own people, the Jews, his salvific mission also encompasses the whole world. Other putative references to the salvific efficacy of the incarnational mission as including but reaching beyond the Jews are the

---

56. As David Rensberger puts it, "In a culture where Christianity has been the established religion, such statements have the ring of oppression.... Sweeping claims such as these could have been ignored [in the first century], laughed at, or given some consideration, but they could not have been enforced." See Rensberger, "Sectarianism and Theological Interpretation in John," 145; cf. Charlesworth, "The Gospel of John."

Samaritan realization that Jesus "is truly the Saviour of the world" (4:42), Jesus' statements that "the bread that I will give for the life of the world is my flesh" (6:51) and "I have other sheep that do not belong to this fold" (10:16a), and the (inadvertent) "prophecy" of Caiaphas the high priest that "Jesus was about to die for the nation, and not for the nation only, but to gather into one the dispersed children of God" (11:51–52).[57] To be sure, the assumption is that the salvation of these Gentiles constitutes their conversion (believing and receiving the Christ). At the same time, we now understand conversion to include the transformation and not necessarily displacement of whole life histories. People do not lose their ethnicity, culture, and language totally in conversion to Christ. Is it not then also true that prior religious identities may not be entirely negated but rather transformed in Christian conversion, and if so, would not the cosmic reach of God's love be redemptive of ethnicity, culture, language, and *religion* rather than threaten their eradication?[58]

At the same time, however, even granting the cosmic scope of God's love in the FG, there is nevertheless a tension between this "outward" reach and the "inward" focus on the believing community. In his study of Jesus' "High Priestly Prayer," Fernando Segovia suggests the this-world/otherworld dichotomy is much more porous than at first glance when we consider that the prayer is not for the world but for believers (17:9), but yet the goal is that the world of non-believers will believe that Jesus has been sent by the Father (17:21); further, there is a radically privileged distinction of the believers over and against the world (17:14–16) but yet they are also being sent out into the world (17:18).[59] To be sure, the rhetoric of John 17 is designed to console, edify, encourage, and admonish the believers in their minority stance and posture toward a hostile world. Segovia hence concludes:

> Behind such consolation, I would argue, lies an unmistakable but unspoken fear of loss, of seepage across that ultimately porous barrier between the given dichotomies of the world-at-large and the circle of disciples. Indeed, one could even argue that it is such fear above all that is ultimately responsible for the collapse of the prayer as an ideological product: if such a superior group [who know, are in the light, are loved by God, etc.] cannot be altogether trusted to deliver on its assigned "task" [in

---

57. This leads R. Culpepper, "Inclusivism and Exclusivism in the Fourth Gospel," 102, to "caution against setting any limitations on the Johannine vision of God's redemptive purpose."

58. Elsewhere—*The Spirit Poured Out on All Flesh*, §4.3—I argue for the interrelationality of language, culture, and religion.

59. Segovia, "Inclusion and Exclusion in John 17."

the world], then a fundamental revision of such a conception of chosenness and privilege is clearly in order.[60]

Now Segovia's own agenda is to destabilize the text so as to break down dichotomies that might otherwise be used to justify certain destructive practices against those on the margins. My preliminary response, to be expanded on in our concluding comments, is to remind us that Christians on the margins are nevertheless precisely those who will continue to find encouragement from this text, especially in situations where they are suffering persecution. At the same time, I agree with Segovia that the tensions between concerns for the believing community and emphasis on the importance of their engaging the world render dichotomistic views of Christianity and the world, including the "worlds" of other religious traditions, problematic. Put in other words, the motifs of God's love for the elect and God's love for the world at large in the FG serve to check and balance triumphalistic exclusivism on the one hand and sentimental inclusivism on the other.[61]

The permeability of the boundaries between Christian light and non-Christian darkness in John can also be seen in the dynamic characterizations of the evangelist. Very quickly, we can note that the depictions of Nicodemus, Judas, and the man born blind (John 9) caution us against any simplistic once-for-all assignment of them either to the light or to darkness. Nicodemus initially comes to Jesus at night, perhaps "lest his deeds be exposed" (3:20 [cf. 19:38]),[62] and his status as a follower of Jesus is uncertain until much later in the Gospel when he "who had at first come to Jesus by night, also came, bringing a mixture of myrrh and aloes, weighing about a hundred pounds" (19:39). Judas is identified as chosen by Jesus (6:70), although he is never under suspicion among the twelve—hence the narrator's interpolation in 6:71 that Judas was to later betray Jesus—not even after Jesus identified him at the Passover supper and he went out into the night (13:30).[63] Finally (for our purposes), the man born blind was assumed (and

---

60. Ibid., 206.

61. Sectarian or liberal readings of the FG, of course, would attempt to collapse the tension. Robert Gundry is at least honest in his own proposal for a contemporary sectarian interpretation of John that the Gospel speaks of God's love for the world, whereas even Jesus' love is limited to the circle of the disciples; see Gundry, *Jesus the Word according to John the Sectarian*, 57–64 and 105–6.

62. See Keener, *The Gospel of John*, 573. Insofar as in the context of Qumranic dualism "Darkness and night symbolize the realm of evil, untruth, and ignorance" (Brown, *The Gospel According to John (xiii-xxi)*, 130), E. C. Hoskyns rightly suggests that the darkness in which Nicodemus stood hints at his "dangerous position betwixt and between" (cited in Beasley-Murray, *John*, 47)

63. Not coincidentally, Judas goes into the night only after "Satan entered into him"

would have been assumed by the original readers of the FG) to have been suffering the consequences of sin, either that of his own or that of his ancestors (9:3). Yet it is he who had spiritual sight and understanding, whereas the seeing Pharisees who threw him out of the synagogue were those who were ultimately blind.[64] In each of these cases, Johannine characterization reveals that the lines between light and darkness are fluid, with people moving in both directions, sometimes in the same life, and it is not always easy to discern, except retrospectively, where a person is on the spectrum. Most (apart from the Jewish opponents of Jesus) are in some sort of transition at dusk or dawn, rather than being stationary at either midnight or noonday.[65]

The same ambivalence applies also to "religious traditions," if we factor in the characterization of the Samaritans in John 4. Elsewhere, I have suggested the Jewish-Samaritan (non-) relations in the first century were equivalent in many ways to interreligious (non-) relations in our time.[66] But whereas Jews of that time did not "share things in common with Samaritans" (4:9), Jesus chose to interact with the Samaritan *woman!*[67] Further, he also announced that true religion transcends both Judea and Samaria and that "the hour is coming when you will worship the Father neither on this mountain nor in Jerusalem" (4:21). And finally, whereas "the Jews" in the FG were those who rejected Jesus, the Samaritan "outsiders" "believed in him" and even "asked him to stay with them" (4:39–40). The strict lines between

---

(13:27). Schnackenburg (*Gospel according to St. John*, 3.32) comments: "'Night,' after all, has its own symbolism in the fourth gospel. For Judas, 'night' represents the sphere of darkness into which he has fallen and, what is more, of which he has become a definitive part. It is, moreover, the zone in which man is ruined (cf. 11.10). For Jesus, it is the hour which marks the end of his work among men (cf. 9.4). This brief statement, closing the account of the traitor's departure, gathers into itself all the darkness of this event."

64. See Staley, "Stumbling in the Dark, Reaching for the Light."

65. For a more extended argument regarding the ambiguity of many of the characters in the FG, which in turn subverts the rigid dualism of the gospel, see Conway, "Speaking through Ambiguity."

66. See Yong, *The Spirit Poured Out on All Flesh*, 241–44; cf. de Klerk, "Through Different Eyes," 168–70, for another reading of the Samaritan woman pericope as applicable to the contemporary interreligious encounter.

67. Maccini, "A Reassessment of the Woman at the Well," downplays the gender aspect of this interchange, but nevertheless rightly retrieves the idea prevalent especially in early Church interpretations of this text that in the larger structure of John, the Samaritan woman is an "outsider"—someone from another faith, I would now add—who bears unique witness and testimony to Jesus.

light and darkness presumed in the first-century Palestinian context to have applied between Jews and Samaritans were in this case obliterated.[68]

Still the Samaritan contrast was that unlike the Jews who were presented with the gospel and rejected it, they responded in belief to the Messiah's self-presentation. But what about the unevangelized?[69] Does the fourth evangelist's assignment of unbelievers and evildoers to the realm of darkness include all those who have never heard the gospel? This may be a legitimate inference from John's division between "Christian light" and "non-Christian darkness," but any such rigid demarcation regarding the unevangelized sits uneasily with the Johannine narrative itself. Rather than make an extended exegetical argument, I focus instead on a crucial text:

> Indeed, God did not send the Son into the world to condemn the world, but in order that the world might be saved through him. Those who believe in him are not condemned; but those who do not believe are condemned already, because they have not believed in the name of the only Son of God. And this is the judgement, that the light has come into the world, and people loved darkness rather than light because their deeds were evil. For all who do evil hate the light and do not come to the light, so that their deeds may not be exposed. But those who do what is true come to the light, so that it may be clearly seen that their deeds have been done in God. (3:17–21)

Two comments suffice. First, in contrast to Gnostic and Qumranic dualism, Schnackenburg rightly points out that in 3:17 (and 3:16 before that), "John affirms that God wills the salvation and not the destruction of the 'world', the well-being of all men and not just that of a privileged section."[70] It seems that only those who hear and nevertheless love their darkness remain condemned. Jesus himself later states, "Very truly, I tell you, *anyone who*

---

68. So this point I am making would hold even if this text were read not as regarding interreligious relations but as one involving a vision for the restored and renewed nation of Israel (and her "relatives") from under Roman rule; see Kim, *Woman and Nation*, ch. 4.

69. By "unevangelized" and "those who have never heard," I am referring to any and all who lack proper knowledge to believe and receive Jesus. This would include those who have literally never been evangelized as well as those only partially evangelized and even those evangelized by groups who hold to non-orthodox theological (or christological) positions. Of course, there is always the question of what constitutes sufficient knowledge of Jesus in order to believe in or reject him, and if there is ever any human being that has attained such a level of understanding, but we'll leave that question for another occasion. I discuss many of these questions in my "The Spirit, Christian Practices, and the Religions."

70. Schnackenburg, *Gospel according to St. John*, 1.401.

hears my word and believes him who sent me has eternal life, and does not come under judgement, but has passed from death to life" (5:24), and then again, "This is indeed the will of my Father, that *all who see the Son* and believe in him may have eternal life" (6:40; emphases added).

Second, and perhaps as important, is that the ethical dualism of the FG is clearly pronounced in this text. The dividing line between light and darkness is less what people do or do not know, and more so what they do. Craig Keener observes "that the contrast between faith and unbelief can also be expressed in terms of obedience points again to the practical rather than merely theoretical nature of genuinely salvific faith in the Fourth Gospel. Whereas the Spirit 'abides upon' Jesus (1:33) and Jesus will abide in his disciples (15:4, 7), wrath 'abides upon' those who disobey him through unbelief (3:36)."[71] This distinction seems to be further confirmed by Jesus when he later says, "Whoever believes in the Son has eternal life; *whoever disobeys* the Son will not see life, but must endure God's wrath" (3:36), and "Do not be astonished at this; for the hour is coming when all who are in their graves will hear his voice and will come out—those who have done good, to the resurrection of life, and *those who have done evil*, to the resurrection of condemnation" (5:28-29; italics added). In the Johannine scheme of things, then, light and darkness are most clearly manifest in what people do, even as faith (*pistis*) is a matter not only of knowledge but also practices. If so, the unevangelized, including those who are also members of other faith traditions, are judged to be in light or darkness just as are followers of Jesus: according to their deeds.

Pressing the Question: Performing Johannine Theology in the Interreligious Encounter

What then can we conclude about Christian theology of religions today in light of the preceding discussion? On the one hand, our discussion of the light-darkness motif in John suggests that the classical categories of exclusivism, inclusivism, and pluralism are less pertinent.[72] There is simply

---

71. Keener, *The Gospel of John*, 583. Raymond Brown writes with regard to this passage: "Notice the present tenses, 'believes,' 'disobeys'; John is not thinking of a single act but of a pattern of life. Notice too that the contrast to believing is disobeying; we saw in 18-21 the strong connection between the way a man lives, acts, and keeps the commandments and his belief in Jesus. Evil deeds and disobedience to God's commands express themselves in refusal to believe in Jesus; and since God's commandment means eternal life . . . , 'whoever disobeys the Son will *not see life*'" (*The Gospel According to John (xiii-xxi)*, 162 , emphasis Brown's).

72. Two recent surveys conclude just that, proposing in turn more sophisticated

not much that is said about other religions in John, unless we attempt to develop a theology of religions out of the fourth evangelist's views regarding the Jews. But going down that road is problematic both on account of the very particular sociohistorical circumstances "behind" the text and on account of the undeniable special relationship between Judaism and Christianity within the broader history of religions. If this were not enough to complicate matters, there is also as much darkness amidst the "Christian" camp as there may be light in the "other religions."

On the other hand, our study in no way requires the rejection of the light-darkness motif for Christian theology of religions, only a more nuanced application. Hence I propose that a Christian posture toward the religions in general and the interreligious encounter in particular informed by the FG will be flexible, contextual, and multi-faceted, featuring at least the following three mutually related modes of engagement. First, in view of the high Johannine Christology and its attendant soteriological and ethical dualism, there is abundant theological rationale for explicit evangelism, kerygmatic preaching, and interreligious apologetics in the appropriate contexts.[73] This would be the case not only for marginal or persecuted Christian communities, but also for those who are socially and even politically established. Inasmuch as Jesus invites everyone out of darkness into fellowship with the light (himself), and inasmuch as human beings do persist in unbelief and wrongdoing, there will always be occasion for the invitation to repent, convert, believe, and follow after him.

But second, and this not in subordination to but in conjunction with the first, the Christian mission is also dialogical. John's transmutation of the Hellenistic philosophical concept of the Logos and Jesus' dialogue with the Samaritan woman are but two examples in the FG of this more dialogical approach. There is a time for proclamation even as there is a time for listening and understanding. We should not underestimate the dialogical power of the FG especially for the religiously plural world of the twenty-first century.[74]

---

categories and typologies; see Knitter, *Introducing Theologies of Religions*, and Kärkkäinen, *An Introduction to the Theology of Religions*.

73. See also Griffiths, *An Apology for Apologetics*.

74. In her account of the reception of the FG in Japan, Bonnie Thurston conveys that Japanese Buddhists have been attracted to Christianity and even converted to Christ through the Gospel of John at least in part because of the "experiential" approach of the gospel (which invites readers to come and examine the applicability of the gospel message for themselves); see Thurston, "The Gospel of John and Japanese Buddhism."

Beyond dialogue and proclamation, however, might be the demonstration of love and the expression of hospitality.[75] Here the ethical dualism of the FG demands that followers of the way of Jesus first ask themselves whether or not they are performing their faith and loving one another that the world may know that the Father has sent the Son. Alan Culpepper notes that in today's religiously plural world, "John's circumscribed love command—that you love one another, that is, fellow Christians—is no longer adequate. To paraphrase Matthew rather ironically, 'Do not even the Gentiles do the same?' (Matt 5:47)."[76] While Culpepper's claim overlooks other Johannine texts that insist that loving and embracing those who do not hold to the truth would be to participate in their evil deeds (cf. 2 John 11 and 3 John 8), it is also important to remember that the whole point of loving fellow believers is for the purpose of bearing an adequate witness to the world. And in some contexts—i.e., that in which Jesus and the Samaritan women interacted with one another—it may even be appropriate to show hospitality to those "outside the fold." To be sure, the offering of such hospitality may be more difficult in some sociopolitical contexts than others, but such discerning responses may be what the Word made flesh is seeking. The fourth evangelist indicates as much when he says, "But to all who received him, who believed in his name, he gave power to become children of God" (1:12), with the word "receive" here meaning to welcome and embrace in intimate relationship.[77] The Word will remain a stranger in a strange land until the world sees his followers embracing one another and, by extension, inviting others into a mutual embrace. And the believers in Jesus have been commissioned into the world for precisely such a task. Hence, "the church as a community [is] always located 'outside the gate,' at home with other outsiders, distrustful of any impulse to set itself apart yet faithful in proclaiming the unique but paradoxical Lordship of Jesus."[78]

My goal in this essay has been to reappropriate the "hard texts" of the FG, including its light-darkness motif, in quest of a less exclusivistic theology of religions for a time when demonizing those in other faiths will not do. I have suggested that if we better understand how the light-darkness theme functions in the FG, this will help us to see the limitations of its applicability to a theological understanding of religious pluralism while simultaneously

---

75. See Yong, *Hospitality and the Other*, esp. chs. 4–5; cf. also my "The Spirit of Hospitality," and "Guests, Hosts, and the Holy Ghost."

76. Culpepper, "The Gospel of John as a Document of Faith," 116.

77. On this point, see Schnackenburg, *Gospel according to St. John*, 1.260, and Morris, *The Gospel according to John*, 97.

78. Breidenthal, "Reconstructing Christianity before Supersessionism," 347.

enabling us to identify other more helpful and hopeful Johannine ideas for our thinking about and interacting with others in a religiously plural world. There is much more work that needs to be done on many fronts—e.g., that of the FG, that of theology of religions, and that of Christian approaches to the interfaith encounter—but I hope that the preceding has contributed in some small measure to these tasks.

CHAPTER 11

Running the (Special) Race

New (Pauline) Perspectives on Disability and Theology of Sport[1]

This essay attempts to speak into the intersection where theology of disability and theology of sport meet. Our primary interlocutor will be the Apostle Paul, although I should admit that my training is in systematic theology rather than in New Testament or Pauline studies. In any case, I have argued elsewhere for seeing St. Paul as at least the first theologian *of* disability, if not the first theologian *with* a disability,[2] and in this study extend that claim to understand him as the first disability theologian of sport. The following unfolds in three sections, beginning with the broader context where contemporary culture, sport, and disability meet, and with the problems that have emerged at that juncture. The middle and longest part unfolds the implications of St. Paul's use of athletic imagery in 1 Corinthians 9 against the backdrop of his theology of weakness in the letter in order to tease out the rudiments of what might be called a Pauline theology of sport. The concluding section drives toward the thesis that from a disability perspective, a Pauline theology of sport would challenge the dominant mentality, attitudes, and practices of contemporary sport. Practical implications of this thesis will be sketched in a hypothetical address of St. Paul's to an audience consisting of the commissioners of the Olympics, Paralympics, and Special Olympics.

---

1. Thanks to Nick Watson for inviting my contribution to this special issue of the *Journal of Religion, Disability & Health*.
2. As I suggest in my *The Bible, Disability, and the Church*, ch. 4.

I ought to register three caveats about what follows. First, I am neither a scholar nor theologian of sport. I therefore come to this field as a novice, seeking only to register disability perspectives on theology of sport. I make no claims that the following amounts to an exhaustive theology of sport. Suffice it to say that I attempt to provide some critical perspectives on theology of sport looked at from its "underside," through the lens of disability theology, and in the effort to do so, add to the growing number of other scholars working at this emerging interface.[3] Second, I am also neither a biblical scholar nor an expert on the Pauline literature. As a systematician, however, engaging the scriptural horizon is important for theological reflection. In particular, any effort to articulate a theology of disability needs to return to the scriptural sources. I do not claim that the following is either the correct or only way to read St. Paul or the focused-upon passage in the First Epistle to the Corinthians. I do offer it as part of a reading of St. Paul's theology of disability that I have begun to consider elsewhere.[4] What is new in this text is consideration of this Pauline material in light of theology of sport. Finally, I approach the theology of disability not as a person with disability but as a brother of a man with Down Syndrome. The following reflects this perspective of intellectual disability, which often includes a range of physical disabilities as well. However, I am in no position to speak for all people with disabilities. I only believe that it is important to factor in the disability perspective both in reflection on Scripture and on Christian faith in the late modern context.[5]

Contemporary Culture, Sport, and Disability

Given how pervasive sport is across contemporary culture in general and contemporary Christianity, especially in the Anglo-American West, in particular, it may come as a surprise to some that this wedding of sport and Christianity is a fairly recent development in the broader historical landscape. Up until the twentieth century, Christians did not routinely participate in formal or organized sport.[6] Even before the 1950s, at least some in conservative Christian circles also eschewed sport because of its long history of questionable associations with nationalism, emperor worship, and leisure activity—understood as useless and as being the "devil's playground."

3. E.g., Brock, "Discipline, Sport, and the Religion of Winners," and Watson, "Sport, Disability and the Olympics" and "Special Olympians."
4. See Yong, "Disability and the Gifts of the Spirit."
5. Yong, *Theology and Down Syndrome*.
6. See Hoffman, *Good Game*, chs. 1–3.

Yet beginning in the late nineteenth century, the tide began to turn.[7] There were both internal and external motivations, with the former driven by the discovery that the religious pursuit of perfection involved the kind of physical, moral, and character training afforded by sport participation, and the latter involving the concomitant realization that sport could also be an arena for and means of Christian evangelism. Over the course of the twentieth century, sport not only emerged, but came to establish a pervasive presence across American Christian culture.[8] Even conservative Christians came to see that sport competition could develop virtue, model exemplary character, and nurture self-control.[9] Indeed, at the turn of the twenty-first century, there is a veritable marriage between Christianity and sport, as witnessed to by phenomena such as self-identified "God's teams," slogans like "winning for Jesus," and church or "faith days" at the ballpark.[10]

Amidst and in the aftermath of World War II, certainly accelerated by the civil rights movement in the 1960s, people with disabilities and their advocates also began to enter into the mainstream of American educational, economic, and sociopolitical life.[11] This was no different in the domain of sport.[12] Rehabilitation programs for war veterans on both sides of the Atlantic provided the initial impetus. The Paralympics itself began in 1960, followed by the Special Olympics in 1968. These international events build, of course, on elaborate national, regional, state, and local structures. Children and youth with disabilities are now socialized from a very young age to participate in sport, including integration into inclusive physical education environments in their schools.[13] Disability sport is a growing commercial market. It is just as competitive as mainstream sport culture.[14] People with disabilities are no more or less engaged in the training, competition, and enjoyment of sport. Yet old stereotypes and prejudices persist about people with disabilities, despite the increased media coverage, since all too often, what is projected are athletes with disabilities that perform at the elite level

---

7. Putney, *Muscular Christianity*.

8. Baker, *Playing with God*.

9. Ladd and Mathisen, *Muscular Christianity*.

10. Krattenmaker, *Onward Christian Athletes*.

11. I have discussed this further in see Yong, *Theology and Down Syndrome*, chs. 3–4.

12. Doll-Tepper, "Disability Sport"; DePauw and Gavron, *Disability Sport*, ch. 2; and Thomas and Smith, *Disability, Sport and Society*, ch. 2.

13. See Fitzgerald, *Disability and Youth Sport*, and Stoccino, "Full Integration in Italian School."

14. Gard and Fitzgerald, "Tackling *Murderball*."

and whose aesthetic and embodied forms map well with those of "normal" bodies.[15]

There is certainly much good that has emerged in contemporary sport, including the development and expression of virtues such as self-discipline, self-cultivation, courage, justice, trust, and honesty, its provision of a social context for leisure, enjoyment, and community enhancement, and its eliciting human creativity, spontaneity, and zest for the trivial yet important aspects of life. This plurality of goods can also be observed to have touched the lives of people with disabilities.

At the same time, there are also some worrisome features. At the top of this list is the ambiguous notion of competition. There are certainly healthy modes of competition that contribute to sport as wholesome personal and community-building activity.[16] On the other hand, competition also spurs personal animosity against opponents, particularly within the "win-at-all-costs" climate and environment that characterizes at least the professional sport circuits.[17] All too often, sport competition is featured as a zero-sum gain: there are winners (perhaps only one) and others are losers. The result is that the competitive nature of sport generates attitudes to opponents are un-Christian at best if not anti-Christian at worst. The goal of competitive sport becomes the exaltation of the self at the expense of others. Egoism emerges as well as a devalued perspective on others who are reaching for the same accolades and achievements as oneself.

Second, associated with but distinct from the drive to win at all costs is that ethical corruption is insidious especially within the professional sporting arena. Such corruption extends in multiple levels. There is certainly the level of athletic cheating and doping. Supplying these performance-enhancing drugs are dealers, agents, and even coaches.[18] There is also the gambling that exists at all levels of organized sport, certainly at in the professional circuits but also in the college and even lower levels.[19] Sport aficionados might say that such activities cannot be controlled or that they do not touch on the nature of the game, per se. However, it cannot be denied that corruption in these domains exists because sport is a huge money-making machine.

This leads, third, to the commercial aspects of sport. Sport is big business. Precisely because of its capacity to generate revenue, sport generates

---

15. Thomas and Smith, *Disability, Sport and Society*, ch. 7.
16. E.g., Walker, *Winning*, and Newman, *Competition in Religious Life,*.
17. Watson and White, "'Winning at All Costs.'"
18. McNamee, *The Ethics of Sports*.
19. Forrest, "Sport and Gambling."

large investments and is awash with commercialization.[20] Performance enhancement is thus caught up in the commerce of sport. As Beamish and Ritchie summarize:

> World-class sport systems today include the systemic use of pure and applied scientific research to enhance physical performance; the early identification, streaming and specialization of athletic talent; professional coaching, the use of professional nutritionists, biomechanicians, exercise physiologists, and sport psychologists; carefully organized training facilities with state of the art equipment and instructional technologies; and financial reward systems and incentives for athletes and sport associations ... [H]igh-performance sport in the contemporary era is a complex whole with performance enhancement as one of its most central features.[21]

The plain "thrill of the game" is now inextricably tied into the global market economy. And this commercial element infects not only athletes but also the institutions that organize sport at all levels, including and perhaps especially at the highest level of Olympic competition.[22]

There is also a darker side to competition, one deserving separate comment, which has to do with the prevalence of violence in sport. Of course, sport attitudes do not begin with violence, but aggression is certainly nurtured during the teenage years and beyond. It is true that violence could be profitably channeled in sport.[23] In many cases, unfortunately, violent aggression is managed improperly, and in some contact sports, the violence is simply sanctioned as part of the athletic experience. What is also noteworthy is that even sport spectators are drawn to the violence. Many will pay to watch and observe violent interactions in the name of competition.[24] Violence is part of the attractiveness and fascination that keeps us tuned in.

Last, but not least, from a Christian perspective, note the degeneration of sport into idolatry. Here I am not only referring to the dangers of the uncritical admiration and idolization of athletes by the masses. More problematically, given the preceding overview of challenges regarding misguided competition, ethical and financial corruption, and its larger-than-life quality, there is a very real danger that what some have called an "unholy

---

20. Walsh and Giulianotti, *Ethics, Money and Sport*.
21. Beamish and Ritchie, *Fastest, Highest, Strongest*, 138.
22. Barney, Wenn, and Martyn, *Selling the Five Rings*.
23. See Kerr, *Rethinking Aggression and Violence in Sport*, and Young, *Sport, Violence and Society*.
24. Goldstein, ed., *Why We Watch*.

alliance" between sport and religion has been broken decisively by the triumph of sport over religion.[25] If the gist of idolatry involves the captivation of human ultimate concerns, then sport is indeed idolatrous.[26] Nick Watson thus identified modern sport as a "surrogate religion," a "'Tower of Babel' alongside other cultural idols such as scientism, healthism, intellectualism, unhealthy perfectionism, commercialism and materialism."[27] This trenchant critique does not assume the irredeemability of sport but rather seeks to be honest about the seamier underbelly of its contemporary expressions.

Truth be told, when disability sport is factored in, things are not much improved. There is as much, if not more, egoistical competitiveness, corruption, commercialization, and violence to disability sport.[28] In fact, in some cases, things may even be exacerbated if people with disabilities attempt to overcompensate for their condition and establish their sporting credentials, and this also, ironically, perpetuates ableist notions of athleticism.[29] Disability sport is certainly not free from the challenges that plague sport in general.

Things are a bit more ambiguous, however, in turning to intellectual disability and sport. Research on Special Olympians uncovers, perhaps not surprisingly, that there less focus is placed on winning.[30] Athletes are motivated more to meet people, build relationships, and travel. Yet even if winning is deemphasized, the competitive spirit is not necessarily entirely absent. While young women with intellectual disabilities minimized competition and winning, "males with mental retardation scored higher on competitiveness than their male counterparts without mental retardation."[31] Regardless of what athletes with intellectual disability desired to accomplish, athletic events nevertheless are just as anxiety-generating as for those without intellectual disabilities.[32] Therefore, even if corruption and violence are minimal in environments involving athletes with intellectual disability, the pressure of competition is no less palpable for them.

Stepping out of the competitive arena, however, it should be noted that people with intellectual disabilities enjoy sport on their own terms. Organizations like L'Arche, for example, sponsor various kinds of physical and

25. Higgs and Braswell, *An Unholy Alliance*.
26. White, "Idols in the Stadium."
27. Watson, "Special Olympians," 170,
28. Jespersen and McNamee, eds., *Ethics, Dis/Ability and Sports*.
29. E.g., Cherney and Lindemann, "Sporting Images of Disability."
30. Farrell et al., "The Driving Force."
31. Zoerink and Wilson, "The Competitive Disposition," 40,
32. Boeschen, "Examining the Cognitive and Somatic."

sporting activities that combine interpersonal, social, intellectual, and spiritual/emotional engagement. In this framework, "leisure is centered not on the activity itself but on the joy of being together no matter what the activity is."[33] Nevertheless, is what happens at places like L'Arche such an exception to the rule that it no longer should be called sport?

I will return to this question at the end of this essay. For the moment, however, it is only important to note from the preceding that the melding of sport and contemporary Christianity is well nigh complete. Yet it is also fair to say that this merger of sport and religion has not averted many of the troublesome features of contemporary sport. This applies also to disability sport. How might Christian theologians respond?

Running the Race: St. Paul as Disability Theologian of Sport?

In the final few verses of the ninth chapter of 1 Corinthians, Paul suggests he was familiar with and maybe even endorsed the sporting culture of his day and time:

> [24] Do you not know that in a race the runners all compete, but only one receives the prize? Run in such a way that you may win it. [25] Athletes exercise self-control in all things; they do it to receive a perishable garland, but we an imperishable one. [26] So I do not run aimlessly, nor do I box as though beating the air; [27] but I punish my body and enslave it, so that after proclaiming to others I myself should not be disqualified. (1 Cor 9:24–27)

Abstracted from its broader context, it is certainly plausible to understand this affirmation as legitimating Christian participation in and enjoyment of sport. Yet such retrieval of Paul is improbable if we paid closer attention to his first-century Jewish and Greco-Roman context.[34] I will argue the contrary: that Paul would be critical of the values that prevail over the contemporary culture of sport.[35] More precisely, when read across the Corinthian letters, Paul's model athlete is less the champion of the Isthmian games than today's Special Olympian.

While there are many other references and allusions throughout the Pauline corpus to athletics, focusing on 1 Corinthians 9 provides us with plenty for consideration. Commentators have long noted that this passage

---

33. O'Keefe, "Leisure at L'Arche," 112.

34. Pfitzner, *Paul and the Agon Motif*; cf. Pfitzner, "Was St Paul a Sports Enthusiast?"

35. Here I am largely complementing the thesis of Brock, "Discipline, Sport, and the Religion of Winners."

makes a good deal of sense against the backdrop of not only the Olympics at Olympia, the Pythian Games at Delphi, and the pan-Hellenic games at Nemea, but of the Isthmian games that were held biennially at Corinth from the sixth-century BCE.[36] At Corinth, there would be only one winner at any event, who received a relatively worthless wreath of celery leaves. What mattered then was the honor bestowed upon the victor, which came to rest also on his city. Thus, "Victory, *nikē*, is the aim of every fight," as well as of every race or event.[37]

It is possible that Paul was present for the Isthmian games in 49 or 51 CE.[38] Although it was unlikely that the Jews among the Corinthian congregation would have been too deeply involved with the games (because of its close associations with the cult of the emperor), some of the Gentiles may have been avid supporters of the event, at least until their Christian conversion. They would have appreciated that Paul trained himself to engage the apostolic task just as athletes prepared to compete in the Games, whether in running or fighting events. For Paul, disqualification would have meant dishonor, as it would have for the athletes coming in after the winner. Of course, for Paul, the goal was an imperishable and everlasting prize, rather than the honor that accrued to the winning athlete.

Over time, however, the metaphorical power of the athletic imagery came to stand on its own, in some senses quite apart from the original apostolic argument. Certainly, the Constantinian settlement of the fourth century alleviated the stigma associated with the games. In this context, the spiritual, moral, and metaphorical character of the allusions would have taken on more concrete application.[39] That Paul originally intended to motivate apostolic perseverance could be understood now also as simply urging development of moral character shaped by vigorous athletic training. Over time, the soteriological, evangelistic, and eschatological goals targeted by the apostle would have receded from the horizon,[40] and they did.

However, things would be worse. The athletic imagery of the ancient world was intertwined deeply with the nationalism and militarism of the Greco-Roman games.[41] Military language was implicit in this text and diffused throughout the Corinthian letters (e.g., 1 Cor 9:7, 14:8, 15:57–58, 16:13; 2 Cor 2:14, 7:7, 10:3–6) as well as other of Paul's epistles. When the

36. Garrison, *The Greco-Roman Context of Early Christian Literature*.
37. Ringwald, "Fight, Prize, Triumph, Victory," 644.
38. See Hullinger, "The Historical Background of Paul's Athletic Allusions," 346.
39. Combes, "Nursing Mother, Ancient Shepherd, Athletic Coach?"
40. Henderson, "The Athletic Imagery of Paul."
41. Krentz, "Paul, Games, and the Military."

early Christians were being martyred for their faith, the consequence of such military motifs was minimal. After the fourth century, however, the overlap between military/warfare and athletic imagery led to the latter being interpreted according to the dominance of the former.[42]

The result was that gradually the athletic imagery of St. Paul came to be viewed in dualistic and antagonistic terms. If there is only one winner of the prize, then the rest are losers; or there are only a few, those who exercise self-control, and who punish and enslave their bodies, who gain the imperishable reward, while others who do not win the prize are disqualified. Applied militaristically, the Christian soldier is to be on his guard against the wiles of the devil and anyone who opposes the ongoing march of the gospel of Christ. Those hostile to the gospel ought to be engaged with all of one's might, following the exemplary model of the apostle. There would be no room for failure since none wanted to risk disqualification.

In short, focused commitment to the apostolic task, the central message of what Paul wrote about in 1 Corinthians 9, translates into an antagonistic mentality. Either "we" are successful and prosperous against "them," or we also will be disqualified. Believers then are led to think that they cannot afford not to "win" or be victorious in the spiritual war they are engaged. After all, as the centuries unfolded, eternity was at stake, not only for the lives of others, but also for themselves.

It is no wonder, then, that by the time of the apostle's reception in the twentieth century, such Pauline imagery was believed to underwrite the agonistic enterprise of sport. Athletic training trains us for life in general and for spiritual warfare against the enemies of God more specifically. Amidst these life-and-death circumstances, we cannot afford to be lax. The Pauline imagery of eschatological reward is experienced proleptically in sport. Winning or losing in sport anticipates how we will fare in the arenas that really matter. Hence, these "training grounds" are just as important for inculcating the habits, virtues, and skills needed to avoid disqualification and attain the ultimate prize.

Yet when situated within the broader context of the Corinthian letters, I suggest that this plain sense reading of the text is mitigated by other themes. In particular, the major theological motif of "weakness" across the Corinthian letters invites an alternative, more expansive, understanding of Paul's use of athletic imagery. In what follows, I re-situate Paul's allusions to athletic competition within the broader context of his soteriology (1 Cor 1) and his ecclesiology (1 Cor 12).

---

42. See Pfitzner, "We are the Champions!," 63–64.

One of the central aims of Paul's Corinthian correspondence is to shape and form a new people of God. The Corinthians certainly had high estimations of themselves. Some of their members were highly educated and had attained a certain level of social status within the community.[43] Thus, Paul begins with what might be considered a frontal assault on the elevated Corinthian self-understanding. Rather than exalting the wisdom, learning, and status of the Corinthians, he rhetorically asks, "Has not God made foolish the wisdom of the world?" (1 Cor 1:20b). His claim, of course, is that God saves not through human exploits or achievements but through Christ crucified, a symbol of foolishness to Gentiles. "God chose what is foolish in the world to shame the wise; God chose what is weak in the world to shame the strong; God chose what is low and despised in the world, things that are not, to reduce to nothing things that are" (1 Cor 1:27–28).

In another place, I have argued that Paul's opening salvo invites reading from the perspective of disability in general and intellectual disability in particular.[44] The foolishness of the world is articulated in terms of the root *mōron* and its cognates, which appears five times in this passage (1 Cor 1:20, 21, 23, 25, 27). Paul insists God has chosen not only the foolish (*mōra*) and weak (*asthene*) of the world (1:27), but also "the low and despised in the world, things that are not" (1:28). People with intellectual disabilities are not only at the bottom of the social ladder but their lives also signify the foolishness and weakness of the world, at least as conventionally understood. Read from this disability vantage point, then, St. Paul challenges the normate sensibilities of the Corinthians by pointing to those on the opposite end of the social spectrum. God's redemptive work in the world is most evident not in the abilities of the Corinthians—which in turn are prejudiced against those less able, this being the gross expression of an ableism and is oppressive of people with disabilities!—but in the lives of those who are otherwise considered weak and foolish. Participation in and knowledge of "Christ, and him crucified" (1 Cor 2:2) is most naturally enabled and accessed by the weak and foolish of this world, and this then provides an exemplary model for avoiding disqualification and attaining the imperishable prize.[45]

This conjunctive reading of the opening part and the end of the ninth chapter of this first Corinthian letter finds further traction when we shift to Paul's ecclesiology in the twelfth chapter. In this latter context, Paul is not satisfied merely to affirm an ecclesial body of many members; instead, he also insists that "the members of the body that seem to be weaker are

---

43. Dutch, *The Educated Elite in 1 Corinthians*.
44. See Yong, *The Bible, Disability, and the Church*, ch. 4.
45. See also Brock, "Discipline, Sport, and the Religion of Winners."

indispensable" (1 Cor 12:22), and that "God has so arranged the body, giving the greater honour to the inferior member" (1 Cor 12:24b). It is important here to guard against the presumption that "weakness" or "inferiority" automatically correlates with disability. Yet the point is precisely that Paul is undermining the social conventions and presuppositions of an ableist Corinthian congregation, and he has sought to do so by rendering those who are "weak" or thought to be "inferior" as being central to the new people of God that is being constituted by the Spirit. Instead, the body of Christ values each of its members, regardless of how they are socially perceived. "If one member suffers, all suffer together with it; if one member is honoured, all rejoice together with it" (1 Cor 12:26). Read from a disability perspective, then, the norms of power, achievement, and success are undermined. God's evaluative scheme is the opposite of the Corinthians'.

Some might wonder if reading Paul through a disability lens distorts his meaning. I suggest, following scholars like Martin Albl,[46] that there is very good reason to think, from the internal evidence of his authentic letters, that Paul suffered from some kind of debilitating physical or ophthalmological condition. Even if it could be shown conclusively that he did not (no one should be holding their breath for this), it is also clear that he experienced stigmatization related to his physical appearance. These considerations, along with his advocacy on behalf of the foolish and the weak, invite a reading of Paul in disability perspective.

Setting the passage of athletic competition next to Paul's new social order and ecclesiology of weakness results in a new perspective on what it means to compete, win, or be disqualified. The rules of the games certainly stipulated only one winner. Yet the Christian race, engaged with by all members of the body of Christ, did not amount to a social competition. Rather, all were to strive for the approval of Christ, for participation in the victory of Christ, as signaled by being crucified with him (1 Cor 2:2; cf. Gal 2:19–20). In this context, "when the Christian runs the race he does not win by making someone else a loser. There is no competition for the crown in this running."[47] In other words, the Pauline race looks out for the welfare and success of all, with those who appear to be the least able in engaging the task being the most indispensable and honored.

Set within the broader context of the challenges Paul encountered among the Corinthians, then, his athletic allusions in the ninth chapter takes on a different hue. Yes, within the broader landscape of that chapter, Paul is attempting to justify his own apostolic calling and mission. Yet this

46. Albl, "For Whenever I Am Weak."
47. De Vries, "Paul's 'Cutting' Remarks about a Race," 116.

involves also the shaping and forming of the Corinthian missional self-understanding.[48] More importantly, for our purposes, the ultimate goal of building up the body of Christ at Corinth had to do with the common good, the edification of all, including and especially those who were otherwise socially (and ecclesially) marginalized because of their foolishness or weakness. The result was a revision of values according to the gospel of the crucified Christ. This applied also to the role of athletic imagery and allusions as they functioned in the Pauline letter: "Paul undermines the aesthetic and social canons of athleticism in antiquity: the strong, the beautiful, and the honourable. The cruciform weakness of God had triumphed over the strength of human beings (1 Cor 1:25b). God's intention, instead, was to destroy the Graeco-Roman agonistic spirit that led to discord in the body of Christ (1 Cor 12:18, 25a) and to replace the Stoic ethos of self-sufficiency (1 Cor 12:15–16, 26) with mutual care (1 Cor 12:25b)."[49] If this is the case, then we cannot "use" Paul to legitimate our participation in sport, especially not if the values of sport are antithetical to the values of the gospel as he understood it.

Running the Special Race: Pauline Proposals for Theology of Sport

The race that St. Paul urges Christians to engage is not a zero-sum game that pits human beings against one another. If it is competitiveness that, arguably, motivates the aggression, violence, commercialization, and corruption marring contemporary sport, then is it possible to sketch a differently considered theology of competition in dialogue with St. Paul? In Galatians 5:15, for instance—"If, however, you bite and devour one another, take care that you are not consumed by one another"—Paul "casts a clear eye on the pathological dimension of competitiveness between males in this culture and condemns it."[50] How else might thinking about the edification of all and about the common good be registered in a contemporary theology of sport?

Part of the challenge certainly emerges from approaching Paul in particular and the Bible in general from an egocentric perspective. Any theology of sport and of competition will necessarily have to confront the implications of such assumptions. But what if, as we have already seen in 1 Corinthians, the horizon is not the advancement of the self but the

---

48. Seesengood, *Competing Identities*, ch. 2.
49. Harrison, "Paul and the Athletic Ideal in Antiquity," 104.
50. Esler, "Paul and the *Agon*," 377.

formation of a new people of God constituted at its center by those who are weak and otherwise socially ignored or marginalized? St. Paul urges us to adopt such an other-centered ethic and perspective. Most starkly framed of these invitations is his subordinating his own welfare and well-being to that of others, especially his people, the Jews. In thinking about the ongoing relevance of the covenantal promises of God to the Jews, Paul writes, "I have great sorrow and unceasing anguish in my heart. For I could wish that I myself were accursed and cut off from Christ for the sake of my own people, my kindred according to the flesh" (Rom 9:2–3). What is clear here is a compassion for others—his Jewish brothers and sisters—that overrides any self-centered notion of salvation. Even the entire concept of witness, related in the early church to martyrdom, was for the sake of others.[51] In this Pauline framework, winning as an individualized achievement is not everything; it is certainly not the only thing—in fact, it is nothing!

Reading St. Paul from a disability perspective urges reconsideration of how to understand the metaphors of winning and achievement of the imperishable prize. Within this Pauline framework, winning does not come at the expense of losers. On the contrary, those who are most successful are shaped by norms of competition that foster the well-being of others, that honors and respects those who are otherwise deemed weak and inferior, and that seeks to edify the whole rather than the individual self. Is it possible for us to develop a Pauline theology of sport from this platform?

In these last few pages, I want to sketch the basic parameters of such a Pauline proposal by teasing out some recommendations in a thought experiment. Imagine St. Paul having an audience with the commissioners of the Special Olympics, the Paralympics, and the Olympics. What might he say to them today in light of a perspective that is sensitive to the experiences of those who are weak in our midst?

Dear commissioners, he would begin. Rather than having the Special Olympics or Paralympics mimic the "real" Olympics, how about we consider evaluation of the latter according to the values of the former? What would happen if the Special Olympics were to set the framework for thinking about and engaging in sport? Two principles would emerge at the fore in this case. First, all people, regardless of differing abilities, deserve the opportunity to participate. Such participation involves skill development (practice) within an inclusive environment that includes not only accessibility variously considered but also a sense that all people are welcomed regardless not only of ability but also of economic circumstance.[52] Yet, second, such participation

---

51. Compare Acts 1:8 and Pfitzner, "Martyr and Hero," 16.
52. See further see Yong, "Disability from the Margins to the Center."

ought to foster community in ways that also recognize the differing levels of ability. None should feel left out,[53] although none should also be pressured, implicitly or otherwise, to conform in order to be or feel included. Instead, any competition is valid that supports the formation of a differentiated community, one that does not overlook the unique particularities that follow all bodies (able or not), and does not stigmatize such because of their diversity. These are the hallmarks of the Special Olympics.[54] Is it too far-fetched to think that these values can also be adapted for sport across the range of abilities?

Discussing the virtues and values related more directly to those with intellectual disabilities is particularly challenging when addressing those with non-intellectual disabilities. In many respects, the inclusion sought by people with disabilities related to their exclusion from mainstream culture, not from the circles of intellectual disability. The chasm between those with intellectual disabilities and those with non-intellectual disabilities is maybe wider than between the latter and non-disabled people.[55] Invariably, disability sport culture seeks to adapt almost all of mainstream sport so that many if not all of the issues at the latter level can also be found within the former domain.[56]

Yet within the Pauline framework, there is not much difference between foolishness and weakness. Both are conventionally stigmatized aspects of the human identity. So if people with intellectual disabilities can shine forth what some call a prophetic light on the world through the power of the Holy Spirit,[57] then why would not the Spirit of God similarly challenge the normate biases of the world through the lives of people with disabilities in general? Can disability sport cultivate a competitive spirit that does not subscribe to the "win-at-all-costs" attitude? How might disability sport foster community across the lines of ability, whether physical, intellectual, or otherwise? Athletes and people with non-intellectual disabilities should be drawn into a conversation to talk about the ideals of disability sport in terms of how to promote competition without undermining participation, and how to integrate people with disabilities into sport without simply endorsing and seeking to adapt everything that happens in mainstream sport.

53. See Dinn, *Hearts of Gold*, ch. 3.
54. Sawyer, Bodey, and Judge, *Sport Governance and Policy Development*, 288–89.
55. Corr, "From the Outside Looking In and the Inside Looking Out."
56. See, e.g., Doll-Tepper, Kröner, and Sonnenschein, *New Horizons in Sport for Athletes with a Disability*.
57. E.g., Harshaw, "Prophetic Voices, Silent Words," and Trevett, "Asperger's Syndrome and the Holy Fool," 137.

Do the above recommendations remove the heart and soul of competition that make sport what it is? Is the nature of sport itself threatened by the imposition of values derivative from and congenial to a rather small minority segment of the population? Can we imagine sporting events without winners and losers? The theological counter to this question has to do precisely with what kinds of winners and losers result. Is it not possible for us to acknowledge winners without perpetuating the ancient Greek ideal that second place (or worse) is unacceptable? Is it possible to nurture a spirit of sportsmanship that seeks the common good of all, including those who have been otherwise excluded and marginalized? How might we need to reconceive sporting organizations, networks, and events that emphasize differentiation in community and that seek to realize what Christians believe to be the goals and values of the coming reign of God? Is it possible to pursue the imperishable prizes of God in ways that qualify and include (rather than leave out) many others along the way? Ought not the commissioners of sport at this most elite level collaborate to discern how to shape a less violent and more just world that simultaneously promotes the common good that sport has to offer?

My goal throughout has been to look back to St. Paul, arguably the first theologian of and perhaps with disability, to see if we might be able to tease out some additional insights of his use of athletic imagery. My intention is not to disparage sport. There are healthy expressions of sport in many contexts. Yet I have wondered what St. Paul might say about our contemporary culture of sport, in particular about its abuses and excesses. Further, how would Paul address the tendency in Christian culture that marries his thinking about athletics with the world of sports in order to legitimize the latter? The preceding ruminations suggest that Paul would intone some cautionary admonitions about the various manifestations of sport. In particular, he might suggest that in this domain, we might still be able to learn a thing or two if we adopted the perspectives of those with disabilities. After all, if foolishness and weakness are at the heart of what means to be the people of God, might we not also take these as ordering principles that structure how we compete alongside one another for the ultimate prizes that truly matter?

CHAPTER 12

Reading Scripture and Nature

Pentecostal Hermeneutics and Their Implications for the Contemporary Evangelical Theology and Science Conversation[1]

Many conservative evangelicals are concordists when it comes to their views regarding how the Bible relates to modern science.[2] What this means is that they assume the plain sense of Scripture, rightly understood, should be confirmable by and be in concord with rather than contradict the findings of modern science, correctly interpreted. When applied to the creation narrative in the book of Genesis, however, such expectations are challenged,

---

1. I am grateful to my colleagues Wolfgang Vondey and Dale Coulter, for their feedback on an initial draft of this essay. I also appreciate my (former) graduate assistant, Tim Lim, for his comments. Most importantly, thanks to Darrel Falk for inviting me to write something for the BioLogos Foundation, then for his careful reading of an earlier version of this paper, which has since been published on the Foundation website, and finally for permission to submit a slightly revised and expanded version of the essay to *PSCF*. *PSCF* editor Arie Leegwater encouraged me to revisit the theme of the two books metaphor in light of previous articles in the journal of the topic, and that also has improved this essay. Needless to say, I remain fully responsible for the views expressed herein.

2. I use "conservative evangelicals" in this essay to include fundamentalists, fully recognizing that there are differences between evangelicalism and fundamentalism. For purposes of this essay, however, the ideological, theological, and presuppositional divergences are less germane than are the similarities and what binds folk in this arena together (against common perceived enemies). This is especially the case in terms of how many pentecostals would understand themselves vis-à-vis the wider cultural issues. Still, for an overview of the spectrum of conservative evangelical views about science, see my "God and the Evangelical Laboratory," and "Science and Religion."

and many conservative evangelicals feel as if they have to opt for what the Bible says (that God created the world in six days) rather than what science says (that the world has evolved over a long period of time). This explains, in large part, the popularity of creationism—the idea that scientific evidence can be marshaled in support of the biblical account—among conservative evangelicals not only in North America but also, increasingly, around the world.[3]

Insofar as many pentecostals consider conservative evangelicals their allies and agree with them about the authority, infallibility, and even inerrancy of the Bible, to the same degree many pentecostals also presume a concordist hermeneutic along with the accompanying young earth view of the world. This explains, at least in part, why many pentecostals are creationists who are suspicious, at best, about the theory of evolution. But what if concordism is itself a modern concoction, developed by modernists—including conservative evangelicals—who feel as if they need to adapt the explanatory power of modern science to interpret the Bible, resulting, paradoxically and ironically, in a scriptural method of interpretation that is itself at odds with a biblical self-understanding? What if the concordist privileging of modern scientific modes of reference and causality is out of sync with the way that Scripture presents itself? Might application of concordist assumptions about science to the Bible do violence to (at worst) or miss the point of (at best) the Scriptures in general and the Genesis creation narrative in particular?

Others have provided very convincing responses urging against adoption of such concordist presuppositions.[4] In this chapter, I want to add to these arguments from a specifically pentecostal perspective. In brief, I will suggest, negatively, that pentecostal hermeneutical instincts and sensibilities should lead them to question, even reject, concordism, especially in its creationist manifestations since that is inconsistent with their own instinctive approaches to Scripture; put positively, I will present a rudimentary argument for a pentecostal theological hermeneutic that reads the book of Scripture soteriologically—i.e., primarily as a theological book focused on God's redemptive work in the world—while remaining capable of acknowledging and even benefitting from modern disciplinary perspectives, including modern science. If this is true, then evangelical Christians can seek to engage existentially with the realities pointed to by the Scriptures while be-

---

3. For the growth and expansion of creationism worldwide, see Roberts, *Evangelicals and Science*, 167–77.

4. E.g., Seely, "The First Four Days of Genesis," and Lamoureux, *Evolutionary Creation*.

ing less concerned about what the relevant secular or scientific disciplines may or may not say about such matters.

I will make my case in three steps, corresponding to the three major sections of this essay, by arguing: 1) that pentecostal biblical interpretation (hermeneutics), our case study, is fundamentally soteriological and pneumatological, that is, focused on the ongoing redemptive work of the Holy Spirit, rather than merely historical; 2) that such a soteriological and pneumatological way of reading the Bible can be appropriately applied to the Genesis narrative as well, resulting in a more expansive theology of creation than that produced by concordism in its creationist guises; and 3) that the result will be a distinctive contemporary contribution to the Christian understanding of the "two books" of God's revelation, Scripture and creation/nature, one that preserves the integrity of both the life in the Spirit and the modern scientific enterprise but yet provides an overarching theological narrative that can hold the two together.[5] We will conclude with some brief reflections on how such an approach to Scripture might be helpful especially for evangelicals who wish to make peace with modern science.[6]

This is That! Pentecostal Biblical Hermeneutics—A Case Study

In order to appreciate pentecostal hermeneutical views, let us focus first on how pentecostals have read the book of Acts. Modern historical criticism, of course, has debated about the historicity of Acts. Since Luke presents the Acts narrative as derivative from consultation with the relevant eyewitnesses (Luke 1:1–4; cp. Acts 1:1), on modernist historiographical terms, the reported events either happened as indicated or they did not. Modernist readings thus are presented either *in faith*, believing that since the Bible is the inspired word of God Acts is accurate regardless of its believability, or *in skepticism*, countering that there are too many inconsistencies in the text or that the fantastic nature of what is described suggests there are ideological

---

5. My colleague Wolfgang Vondey rightfully reminds me that pentecostals generally are less interested in books, metaphorically understood—whether of Scripture or of nature—than in engaging a living and self-revealing God (whether through the Bible or the creation). Yet I also think the ancient and venerable two books metaphor is helpful for pentecostals to negotiate their own hermeneutical options vis-à-vis modern science, and thus will retain that verbiage and conceptualization in this essay. For Vondey's own considerations about a pentecostal theology of revelation, see his *Beyond Pentecostalism*, ch. 2.

6. Here, I am playing off the title of, and thereby see my essay as an ally to, Darrell R. Falk's excellent *Coming to Peace with Science*.

motivations or other reasons for what now appears as a largely mythic or legendary, rather than more strictly historical, document.

On this issue, at one level, pentecostals are modernists and read their Bibles in faith as the inspired, infallible, and, often, inerrant word of God, even if they may never have heard of these terms. This is in part because the earliest pentecostals at the turn of the twentieth century came mostly from the Holiness movement and carried over their commonsense realist approach to the Scriptures.[7] Yet at the same time, if their other commonsense realist cousins, the fundamentalists, were interested in defending the historical veracity of the biblical claims, pentecostals were more motivated pragmatically by what the Bible meant for their day-to-day lives.[8] Hence it was not so much that pentecostals dismissed the historical dimensions of the biblical accounts, but that they collapsed the presumed distinction between the scriptural text and its contemporary readers. For them, what was important was not so much what happened back then as it was how the back then and the here and now were connected.

Pentecostal scholar Rickie Moore has highlighted the difference this pentecostal approach makes for biblical interpretation.[9] Whereas the historical-critical methodology long prominent in the guild of biblical scholarship measures the historicity of the Bible against modernist canons of plausibility, a pentecostal hermeneutics highlights instead the uniqueness of biblical history vis-à-vis any contemporary generation of readers or interpreters. So whereas modern historical criticism emphasizes the objectivity of the text over and against the interpreter, pentecostals observe instead the "this is that"—our or my experience (this) is equivalent to the reality accomplished in the lives of the biblical characters or anticipated by them (that)—character of the Bible in relationship to its readers. If modern interpreters approach the Bible as a historical document containing objective truths (facts) about the world (the past, in the case of historical references), pentecostals view the Scriptures as a narrative that invited its readers (and hearers) to receive, inhabit, and participate in the world of God. And while modern approaches emphasize the critical distinction between what the text meant in its original context (which was the task of the biblical critic to uncover), as opposed to how such meanings might be applied to our con-

---

7. McCall, "A Contemporary Reappropriation of Baconian Common Sense Realism."

8. The pragmatic character of pentecostal spirituality is richly portrayed by Wacker, *Heaven Below*.

9. The following summarizes Moore, "Deuteronomy and the Fire of God," a must-read for any pentecostal reflection on biblical hermeneutics; see also Moore, "Canon and Charisma in the Book of Deuteronomy."

temporary lives (the task of the homiletician), pentecostal approaches see first and foremost the *rhema* or living and revelatory word of God making demands on each generation of readers in a way that collapsed the horizons of what the text pointed to and that of the text's later readers.

In short, pentecostal hermeneutics emphasizes not the historicity of the biblical accounts but its capacity to open up possibilities for contemporary readers and hearers by the power of the Spirit.[10] Scripture's purpose is not primarily to give us truthful or factual knowledge about the past (pentecostals assume this commonsensically without making much of it); rather, it "is useful for teaching, for reproof, for correction, and for training in righteousness, so that everyone who belongs to God may be proficient, equipped for every good work" (2 Tim 3:16-17). The goal, thus, is not merely "head knowledge" about what happened but "heart knowledge" that leads to sanctification, participation in the divine life, union with God—in short, reception of the salvation of God made available through Christ by the Holy Spirit. None of this is to deny that the historical dimensions of the Acts narrative are unimportant; it is simply to affirm that pentecostals read Acts not merely as history but as *salvation history*, i.e., not merely as a historical document about what happened but as a literary-theological document about what may and even should happen.

Of course, the wider theological academy has also been discovering that the Bible can and should be read theologically and soteriologically rather than merely historically and that the line between history and theology is much more blurred than assumed within the modernist framework. Thus many other scholars have come to recognize, even appreciate, the theological nature of the Acts narrative.[11] But pentecostals have, from the very beginning, read Acts as having ongoing and contemporary relevance, as seen in the doctrine of initial evidence of the baptism in the Holy Spirit, which the first pentecostal generation found as normatively portrayed in the second Lukan volume.[12] While the details of this doctrine can be debated, my point is that it has been precisely this specific interpretive approach that historically has set apart pentecostal readings of Acts in particular and of the Bible in general from those in non-pentecostal and non-charismatic

---

10. This is both a historical claim about the now century-old pentecostal movement and a normative claim about how pentecostals understand their relationship to the Bible going forward, as summarized in Archer, *A Pentecostal Hermeneutic for the Twenty-First Century*.

11. A summary of the trends over the last half century has been provided by Bovon, *Luke the Theologian*.

12. This story is told by Goff Jr., *Fields White unto Harvest*, esp. ch. 3; see also some of the chapters in part I of McGee, ed., *Initial Evidence*.

ecclesial traditions. And it has been precisely such a "this-is-that" hermeneutic which nurtured pentecostal contributions the theological reading of the Acts narrative.[13]

Now modernists might cringe that such an approach does violence to the Bible simply because it allows for the interpreter to assert too much of his or her own self-understanding into the biblical narrative. Pentecostals can respond at least at three levels. First, modernist interpreters should not presume that their own rationalistic, positivistic, and historicistic perspectives do not influential their readings of Scripture. Second, it is not so much that our subjectivities are inserted into the biblical narrative—after all, a hard-and-fast distinction between *exegesis* (a taking out of the text) and *eisegesis* (a reading into the text) is a modern concoction anyway—but that our subjectivities are themselves interrogated directly by the Spirit's witness through the biblical text. Last but not least, such an approach is consistent with the broader apostolic witness, for whom the events narrated in the Bible are never mere facts of what happened, but always signs of God's intentions and purposes in the world.

The Johannine notion of miraculous signs, for example, supports this understanding.[14] From a modernist perspective, the implausibility of such accounts as historical events demands other explanations. Yet this ignores the Johannine self-understanding, which insists that the miraculous works of Christ were recorded for the explicit purposes that the Gospel's readers "may come to believe that Jesus is the Messiah, the Son of God, and that through believing you may have life in his name" (John 20:31). Pentecostals have approached the Acts narrative precisely in that spirit. The focus has thus never been on a historical apologetic for the textual accounts happening in all particulars as described. Rather, the motivation has always been to invite hearers (pentecostals are people who privilege the oral testimony) of the word to experience the power of God for themselves. It is not so much what God has done in the past that matters, but that the past intersects with the present that counts.

Critics might insist that such a pentecostal hermeneutic presumes the historicity of the events described in Acts, otherwise why might pentecostals assume that such remains possible in their lives today?[15] At one level,

---

13. E.g., Stronstad, *Spirit, Scripture, and Theology*. My own proposals are in the following books: *The Spirit Poured Out on All Flesh*, and *In the Days of Caesar*.

14. E.g., Morris, *Jesus is the Christ*, ch. 2, and Collins, *These Things Have Been Written*, ch. 10.

15. This has been most forcefully registered by John C. Poirier in his articles (with B. Scott Lewis) "Pentecostal and Postmodernist Hermeneutics," and (independently), "Narrative Theology and Pentecostal Commitments." While I am appreciative of

this is true: insofar as Acts purports to be about what did happen, as we have earlier noted that author himself tells us, to that degree the pentecostal commonsense realist presumes the historicity of the narrative fairly. At this level, I would go further to affirm, the various historiographical methods can be helpful in illuminating the nature of the world behind the text, even to the point of supporting—complementing, to use my term—pentecostal faith.[16] However, the presumption of historicity is not equivalent to embracing a historical-critical hermeneutic as the sole or major interpretive lens for understanding Acts in particular or the biblical narrative in general. Instead, as I have suggested, pentecostals have often ignored (at worst) or at least had a diffident relationship with (at best) historical criticism in favor of literary and narrative models focused less on what the Bible meant then on its present application.[17] In short, they have never privileged a historical approach to the Bible, opting always instead for a salvation history reading that locates them in relationship to the saving and eschatological work of God.

In the end, however, my claim is that such a "this-is-that" approach to the Bible is not really distinctive of pentecostalism.[18] As a restorationist

---

Poirier's concerns, I find his emphases on historicity puzzling in light of the above discussion. Further, he neither engages substantively with pentecostal scholars who have discussed the contested issues (e.g., Rickie Moore, Walter Hollenweger, Scott Ellington, Mark Cartledge, James K. A. Smith, myself) nor with the wider hermeneutical debates on especially narrative hermeneutics, resulting in a very monolithic and inaccurate understanding of the latter. Most problematic, Poirier makes too many false assumptions—i.e., about authorial intention as being central to hermeneutics, about hermeneutics being either objective or subjective, about narrative hermeneutics being opposed to the historical-critical method or being based on opposed ontologies, about the links between quantum physics and postmodern hermeneutics—with the result that his discussions of the scientific, philosophical, or theological issues are inconsistent and not coherent. A more substantive response to Poirier's arguments, however, will have to await another occasion.

16. For example by Gordon Fee, Robert Menzies, Max Turner, or many other pentecostal and charismatic exegetes working in the wider biblical studies arena. My colleague, Graham Twelftree, has long engaged in critical dialogue with the Jesus Seminar scholarship, and deploys historical critical tools to argue for fairly traditional pentecostal conclusions with regard to miracles and exorcisms, among other classical pentecostal phenomena.

17. This is, of course, a very general claim, given, as indicated in the previous footnote, the many that have expertly deployed historical critical tools in their exegetical work. Yet I believe that literary and narrative methods resonate more with pentecostal sensibilities than do historical-grammatical approaches. Scholars as widely divergent as Walter J. Hollenweger, Roger Stronstad, Clark Pinnock, John Christopher Thomas, Larry McQueen, among many others, have argued these points.

18. One might argue that the earliest followers of the Messiah also read their

movement, pentecostals have long participated in Reformation traditions that have sought to return to and retrieve the apostolic example for Christian life. Pietist movements of all sorts, baptistic traditions, and Wesleyan-Holiness Christians in all of their various streams—each of these and more have established hermeneutical practices that focus on the relevance of the apostolic experience for contemporary Christian faith.[19] What pentecostals add to the mix, more specifically, is the emphasis on the work of the Holy Spirit, in particular how the Spirit empowered the people of God as recorded in the Scriptures and how that same empowerment is available to Christians in all post-biblical times. Might this pneumatological twist that highlights how the Holy Spirit enables our participation in the biblical message be helpful for a reading of the Bible as a whole and perhaps even the Genesis narrative more particularly?

That is This! A Pneumatological Hermeneutics of the Creation Narratives?

I now want to suggest that the pneumatological "this-is-that" hermeneutic as applied to the Acts narrative can also profitably illuminate a reading of the creation narrative that helps conservative evangelicals overcome the concordist assumptions behind the scientific creationist model. To do so, we will need to see first what best describes the genre of the creation narratives, and then how amenable Genesis 1–2 is to such a rereading.

There are probably three dominant types of interpretations of the creation narratives, which I call the scientific, mythological, and literary-theological views.[20] There are inevitably overlaps between these views even as there are profound differences among those who may be classified within each type. But in brief, the first two are both modern approaches, the former insisting that the inerrancy of the Bible means that the book of Genesis, rightly interpreted, must be compatible with modern science, rightly understood, and the latter countering that the incompatibility between the

---

"bibles" (what we call the Old Testament) pneumatically, convinced that they were charismatically led to interpret the Scriptures unto salvation and that what had been spoken of before was being fulfilled in their time; see Aune, "Charismatic Exegesis in Early Judaism and Early Christianity."

19. For more on the complementary hermeneutics of Baptists, pietists, Wesleyans, and pentecostals, see Yong, "The 'Baptist Vision' of James William McClendon, Jr."

20. These do not map very well onto the three views in Hagopian, ed., *The G3n3s1s Debate*, which is limited to conservative evangelical options: 24-hour day view, day-age view, and framework view.

plain sense of first chapters of the Bible and modern science means that the former cannot be understood literally or scientifically, and thus should be interpreted either spiritually or mythically (with, except on occasions, no pejorative intentions behind the last designation). These two views often characterize conservative evangelicals or scientific creationists on the one side who view the first book of the Bible as ancient science, and liberal Christians or theistic evolutionists on the other side who view this same text as ancient myth.

The third approach, however, is both the most elastic and perhaps also inclusive of the most ancient readings of Genesis, under my definition. This would include not only moral, spiritual, and allegorical interpretations of Genesis prevalent during the first Christian millennium, which inevitably read the Hebrew Bible in general figuratively and typologically in light of New Testament or christological revelation, but also literary interpretations increasingly popular across the broader theological academy. I would locate my own inclinations within this last trajectory of interpretation, especially its emphasis on how the Genesis narrative should be understood in its ancient near Eastern context on the one hand, and from a salvation history perspective on the other.[21] With regard to the former, Genesis should be understood as presenting ancient Israel's theology of the one creator God who, in contrast to the pagan deities of the Mediterranean world, overcomes the primeval chaos (the *tohuwabhohu* of Gen 1:2) by the word of his *ruah*.[22] The latter refers to the broader theological horizons of the biblical canon, first the covenantal framework within which God the creator enters into relationship with Israel,[23] and then the founding incarnational and pentecostal events of the Christian Scriptures.

While widely divergent in many ways, interpreters and exegetes who hold to a literary-theological approach to Genesis 1—2 in general reject attempts to render as concordant the creation accounts—there are two accounts: 1:1–2:4, and the rest of Genesis 2—with modern science. Instead of telling us *how* the world was created, Genesis informs us *that* the world

---

21. Narrative is a type of literature that includes a wide range of genres, as described by Coats, *Genesis*, 5–10. My claim is that pentecostals in particular, and Christians in general, inhabit such texts theologically rather than merely observe them discursively.

22. Predominant here is Niditch, *Chaos to Cosmos*. See also O'Brien and Major, *In the Beginning*.

23. E.g., Walke, with Fredricks, *Genesis*, 55–78; Collins, *Genesis 1–4*; and Walton, *The Lost World of Genesis One*. Note that for Walton, the seven days of creation functionalize and inaugurate the cosmic temple within and upon which YHWH sits enthroned. A recent book that grapples seriously with the theological nature of Genesis is Moberly, *The Theology of the Book of Genesis*.

was made by a God who seeks to enter into covenant with human creatures. Thus, this ancient text need not be made to conform to modern scientific theories; instead, it is about human existence, history, spirituality, and relationality—i.e., it is thus more anthropological, theological, and soteriological rather than scientific.[24] Put narratively and canonically, Genesis is also about the God who redeems and renews the creation as a whole, as well as its creatures, in spite of its fallen character.

I suggest, then, that pentecostals in particular and Christians in general can read the creation narratives of Genesis as they do the historical narratives of Acts: in light of the soteriological work of the Holy Spirit. While Acts presents itself as a history of the early Christian movement, the historicity of the narrated events is less the point than the invitation to enter into, receive, and inhabit the saving work of God in Christ through the Spirit. Similarly, while Genesis presents itself as a story of the creation of the world, its historicity—or, in this case, its scientific accuracy—is also less the point than its invitation to enter into a covenantal relationship with the creator God. If the pneumatological this-is-that hermeneutic enables readers to participate in God's redemption of the world through the church, then might this not also hold forth promise for a pneumatological reading of the Genesis story that enables participation in God's creative activity as well? Now while modern scholarship would differentiate the genre of Acts from that of Genesis—an important distinction in various respects—theologically and soteriologically both are narratives of divine activity in the past that have relevance for faithfulness to the divine covenant and to participation in the salvation history of God's work in the present.

Paul Elbert is a pentecostal scholar who has begun to provide such a reading of the Genesis narrative that highlights the work of the Holy Spirit.[25] Elbert observes that the *ruah* of God "swept over the face of the [primordial] waters" (Gen 1:2), and from there correlates the Spirit's work in divine creation with the Spirit's communication through ancient near Eastern linguistic patterns and rhetorical conventions. At one level, Elbert's is a sophisticated reading of the Genesis account in its ancient near Eastern context; at another level, however, his interpretation depends to some degree on concordist presuppositions. The result, refracted through Elbert's pentecostal lenses, is a prophetic view of Genesis 1 that both anticipates contemporary experimental scientific findings and provides apologetic confirmation for the truthfulness of the Bible's creation story. While not necessarily opposed to Elbert's reading, I am also not enthused about it since I think that pente-

24. As argued, e.g., by Brodie, *Genesis as Dialogue*.
25. Elbert, "Genesis 1 and the Spirit."

costals, in particular, are motivated intuitively less by scientific apologetics than by personal testimony.[26] Put otherwise, pentecostal sensibilities are dependent not on correlating Scripture with scientific data (or Scripture with historical research) but on identifying the "that" of what the Bible points to as anticipating the "this" that the Spirit of God continues to accomplish today.[27]

Given these commitments, I suggest a more viable theological reading of Genesis would register participation in the creative and redemptive work of the Spirit along at least the following lines. First, the pneumatological "this-is-that" recognizes that the Spirit empowers the creation's response. The Spirit not only hovers over the watery chaos but also enables the word of God to be spoken that in turn brings forth the creation's responses. Thus, "God said, 'Let the earth put forth vegetation: plants yielding seed, and fruit trees of every kind on earth that bear fruit with the seed in it.' And it was so. The earth brought forth vegetation: plants yielding seed of every kind, and trees of every kind bearing fruit with the seed in it" (Gen 1:11–12). Then later, "God said, 'Let the earth bring forth living creatures of every kind: cattle and creeping things and wild animals of the earth of every kind'" (1:24). What happens next is that the biblical author says first, "And it was so," before saying, "God made the wild animals of the earth of every kind, and the cattle of every kind, and everything that creeps upon the ground of every kind. And God saw that it was good" (1:25). In short, these jussive and passive imperatives throughout the Genesis 1 account invite participation of the earth and its creatures, and they actively respond to that invitation.[28] These aspects of the creation narrative resonate with contemporary experiences of the Spirit's empowering work.

Secondly, Genesis 1—2 is meant not to provide scientific details about the formation of the earth but to illuminate the purposes for which God created the world. These include, of course, humanity as the apex of

26. My main question concerns Elbert's claim (if I understand him correctly) that the Genesis creation narrative has a prophetic character, one anticipating the experimental findings of modern science that in effect confirm the truthfulness of the creation myths. But this is like saying that after I reconstructed a historical event based on very few original sources, my descendents later find other sources that corroborate my reconstruction, and this then leads me to label my original reconstruction as prophetic. I don't think this is the best way of treating the Genesis narratives.

27. Is pentecostal hermeneutics thereby fideistic? No more or no less than other Christian approaches to the Bible. But whereas the faith of conservative evangelicals would be compromised if Genesis were not vindicated by modern science, I would say that pentecostal hermeneutics is falsifiable if the works of the Spirit described in the Scriptures were to cease and no longer occur as part of pentecostal spirituality.

28. See Welker, "What is Creation? Rereading Genesis 1 and 2."

creation—in which the breath of God is given (Gen 2:7)—now charged to care for the world. Thus do human beings participate not only as co-creators with God, in the sense of responding to God's creative image, but also to be partners with the divine providence over all things.[29] Thus also did God say to *ha adam*: "have dominion over the fish of the sea and over the birds of the air and over every living thing that moves upon the earth" (1:28). Read theologically and soteriologically, then, the creation narratives invite humanity to exercise moral responsibility, even a degree of spiritual oversight, over the creation and its creatures, in relationship to God.

Last but not least, read also canonically, the original creation narrative provides a template for and foreshadows the redeemed creation that is promised later in the Hebrew Bible (as the day of YHWH) and in the New Testament (the new heavens and earth).[30] Read from the perspective of the active work of the Spirit in the world, we now live between the times—between the original creation and the new creation—albeit yet still imbued with the same *ruah* of God. The difference here, amidst the fallen yet already-but-not-yet-fully-actualized new creation, is that now we "who have the first fruits of the Spirit, groan inwardly [with the creation] while we wait for adoption, the redemption of our bodies" (Rom 8:23). In short, the creative work of the divine *ruah* begun prior to the appearance of *ha adam* continues to the present and anticipates the sanctifying and redemptive work of the Spirit of Christ in the future. While declared good, the creation is still incomplete, and human creatures are not only part of what needs renewal, but potentially also the ones who herald, through their groans, cries, and prayers inspired by the Spirit, that renovative work.[31]

These brief considerations invite us to think theologically about the creation instead of scientifically. So just as Acts tells us what happened in order to enable us to inhabit the eschatological gospel story in the footsteps of the earliest Christians, Genesis tells us what happened in order for us to participate in the creative-redemptive work of the *ruah* of God amidst the chaos and sin of the world. Further, if Acts provides a theological perspective on salvation history that neither requires nor denies historical-critical scholarship, then Genesis similarly provides a theological perspective on the creative and redemptive works of God that is neutral with regard to the various modern scientific analyses, theories, or conclusions (all of which, by the way, are still being negotiated within the scientific community). There is

---

29. See Hefner, *The Human Factor*, esp. ch. 2.

30. See Gage, *The Gospel of Genesis*.

31. A much more lengthy discussion of the preceding paragraphs can be found in my *The Spirit of Creation*, ch. 5.

a difference: with regard to Acts, while there is a literary dimension to Acts, it still presents historical perspectives on what happened with the earliest Christian communities so much so that historical-critical scholarship has more direct relevance for understanding the earliest followers of the Messiah; but with regard to Genesis, the literary dimension is predominant with that result that the historical events behind the text are minimally accessible, if not excluded altogether, so much so that the results of modern science are not immediately correlatable with the biblical account. But still in either case, the concerns are less about how God has created, orchestrated, or ordered the world and its events than on what God has intended to accomplish through the divine creative and redemptive activity.

Thus Christians in general and conservative evangelicals in particular are free to allow historical-critical scholarship to run its course or even to adopt or adapt historical-critical methods vis-à-vis Acts to understand first century Mediterranean history on the one hand, even as they are free to allow scientific inquiry to proceed or to engage in scientific inquiry themselves—although not so directly vis-à-vis the Genesis narrative—to understand the history of the world on the other hand. However, Christians certainly do not have to master the methods or results of historical criticism or the natural sciences, nor do they have to adjudicate the disputes within these fields of inquiry, in order to hear from, receive, or participate in the word of God as mediated through the Scriptures in general or Genesis and Acts in particular. In fact, we need historical critics and natural scientists precisely in order to provide some perspective on these texts so as to prevent any of us from reading into the Bible or making it say whatever we want. And especially when issues are still contested, this should give us pause that any particular interpretation tied to such debates needs to be held loosely, rather than dogmatically.

The Books of Scripture and of Nature: Toward a Hermeneutics of Science

The preceding prepares the way for seeing how a pneumatological perspective can contribute to the ancient tradition that came to distinguish between the books of Scripture and of nature as two complementary sides of the same coin.[32] By this, I mean that Scripture read in faith provides us with the

---

32. This complementarity between the two books is associated, in my mind, to that which goes under the same label as applied to explaining the relationship between theology and science. Complementarity in the theology and science arena refers to the idea that each provides valid insights into the one world in which we inhabit which

theological significance of nature, understood on its own terms. Thus there are two levels of importance, although each level has its own integrity. So if concordism insists that Scripture and science are or should be about the same thing, the scripture-nature complementarity I am suggesting says that the Scriptures provide a higher level set of meanings for scientific findings without undermining the integrity of science or its methods. In order to see this, we will briefly overview highlights in the history of the two books idea before turning to more contemporary applications.

While Augustine was one of the first of the early church fathers to call nature a book,[33] the basic idea goes back even behind him and certainly has seen major developments since the fifth century.[34] The Christian tradition has perennially appealed to the Scriptures with regard to thinking about the revelatory power of the creation: "The heavens are telling the glory of God; and the firmament proclaims his handiwork" (Ps 19:1), and, in the New Testament, "since the creation of the world his eternal power and divine nature, invisible though they are, have been understood and seen through the things he has made" (Rom 1:20). There are other scriptural allusions, for example, to the sky being like a scroll (Isa 34:4 and Rev 6:14), which have lent themselves to the emergence of the metaphor of the book of nature.

During the patristic and especially medieval periods, then, Scripture and nature were interpreted in light of each other. Following the dominance of Augustine and the neo-Platonic worldview, however, the visibility of the natural world was thought to point clearly toward the invisible things of the spiritual world. Hence the interpretation of nature's symbolism was multi-leveled, parallel to that of Scripture, although both were considered revelatory instruments of the character and works of God. Hugh of St. Victor (1078–1141) thus understood that nature revealed God's power, wisdom, and goodness, and that attendance to the message of nature enabled participation in the sanctification and redemption of nature itself, so that in Christ, the world would be completed, reconciled with, and returned to God.[35]

---

should at least be non-contradictory, if not also convergent in some respects. My use of the term is informed by, among other sources, Loder and Neidhardt, *The Knight's Move*, esp. sect. 1; Mackinnon, "Complementarity"; and (a succinct exposition) McGrath, *Science and Religion*, 165–74.

33. Augustine, *Contra Faustum Manichaeum*, 32.20, in Augustine, *Answer to Faustus*, 422.

34. The most complete discussion, and certainly now the standard account, is the four-volume work edited by van der Meer and Mandelbrote, *Nature and Scripture in the Abrahamic Religions*.

35. On Hugh's theology of nature, see Mews, "The World as Text."

The Renaissance, Reformation, and early modern periods, however, saw some major shifts in the Christian understanding of the book of nature.[36] First, the medieval conviction about nature's revelatory powers was expanded so that nature illuminated not just theological truths (like Scripture) but also could be expected, if properly mined (or interpreted), to disclose the secrets of the creation itself.[37] Second, the medieval fourfold sense of interpretation—literal, moral, allegorical, and spiritual—was increasingly abandoned in favor, especially among the magisterial Reformers, of the literal sense;[38] correspondingly, the clarity of nature was understood not in terms of its universal accessibility (as this was held during the first millennium) but as enabled by the emergence and use of the empirical methods of early modern science which brought the causal mechanisms of nature into plain view.[39] Third, the Reformers' insistence on interpreting Scripture directly rather than relying on authorities also favored the growing class of elite scientists, who also urged the importance of engaging nature directly (experientially and experimentally) rather than relying on the discoveries of their ancestors. Last but not least, if Jesus' mentioning of the Scriptures and the power of God (Matt 22:29) were oblique references to the two books, as Francis Bacon (1561–1626) took them to be,[40] then not only did the book of nature require its own distinctive methods of interpretation, but the identification of the powers of nature also suggested that nature was less a set of facts to be uncovered than a web of processes and potentials to be mastered and deployed.[41]

The result during early modernity, at least in part, was the emergence of the scientific method as the key to unlocking the book of nature. If the medieval schoolmen distinguished ontological and divine causality from cosmological or creaturely causality—for instance, that God is first or primary cause of all there is, while creatures are valid secondary causes,

36. A book-length discussion is Harrison, *The Bible, Protestantism and the Rise of Natural Science*.

37. Howell, *God's Two Books*.

38. This despite the strategic protestations of Galileo, in his letter to the grand duchess Christina, that Scripture remained ambiguous, subject to various interpretations (when compared with nature); see Drake, trans., *Discoveries and Opinions of Galileo*, esp. 181–81 and 196.

39. With regard to the transformation of the two books metaphor in the early modern period, I have been helped by the overview of Tanzella-Nitti, "The Two Books Prior to the Scientific Revolution"; but the interpretation is mine and Tanzella-Nitti should not be held responsible for it.

40. Matthews, "Reading the Two Books with Francis Bacon," 61–77, at 67.

41. See Harrison, "Reinterpreting Nature in Early Modern Europe," esp. 33–38.

viewing these in compatibilist terms—the early modern scientists began to focus their expertise on tracing the efficient and material causes operating in nature. As the scientific enterprise has continued to unfold over the last few hundred years, various disciplines have attempted to secure primacy of place, but each has defended itself against the encroachments of others. Contemporary science is thus characterized by a vigorous interdisciplinarity (in which the lines between disciplines are blurred) and multidisciplinarity (featuring collaborative inquiry between two or more disciplines), both of which combine to illuminate the natural world.

Non- or anti-religious scientists might conclude that the revelatory power of the book of Scripture has been entirely eliminated by that of the book of nature and its scientific methods. Concordists who insist on the literalistic harmonization of the Bible and science have sought to restore the authority of the book of Scripture but go about it erroneously: by legitimating its credentials on the basis of modernist assumptions about science. On the one hand, this is understandable given the explanatory power of modern science: who would not want to affirm truths consistent with the most powerful fount of knowledge produced by the modern world? But on the other hand, concordists overlook the fact that the scientific method's focus on the book of nature means that its purview is by definition limited to the natural world. This means that science is not equipped to make metaphysical or religious claims, and it is only by transgressing these boundaries that science (or book of nature experts) can render or adjudicate such claims. In short, concordists have to stretch science beyond its boundaries in order to harmonize Scripture with it.

I suggest that pentecostals can contribute to a contemporary theology of the two books by developing its pneumatological imagination in ways that adapt both premodern and modern understandings.[42] In the following, I sketch two basic trajectories for a pentecostal reconsideration of the relationship between the books of Scripture and of nature. First, recognizing that the *ruah of God* both hovered *over* the primeval chaos and yet was dynamically at work as the breath *within* the creatures of the world, so also does a pneumatological theology of creation emerge that understands the Spirit to be present and active *over* and *within* history and creation, even while illuminating both worlds to human minds. Such illumination, however, is by nature theological, soteriological, and eschatological (related to God's final salvation of the world), providing a perspective on history's

---

42. I present the details of such a pneumatological imagination in my book, *Spirit-Word-Community*, part II. Many of my claims in this essay are grounded in my views about epistemology and interdisciplinarity argued at (some would say exhausting) length in this earlier volume.

and nature's ends as intended by God. Second, what dominant history of Christian thought has called the interpretation of nature, pentecostals call discernment; but while theologians or scripturalists will discern (exegete) the books of Scripture and nature theologically and soteriologically, others also discern (interpret) the nature and history of the world from their respective disciplinary perspectives. The theological discernments (readings) inevitably will go beyond the non-theological interpretations, but that neither delegitimizes the latter nor does it undermine the possibility for complementary perspectives to emerge.[43]

The preceding discussion invites us to think analogically about the relationship between theology, concerned with the book of Scripture, and contemporary science, concerned with the book of nature. The multi- and interdisciplinarity character of the sciences are discursive practices that depend on peculiar methodological presuppositions, cultural practices, and institutional arrangements.[44] If the work of the Spirit was to harmonize the many tongues on the Day of Pentecost so as not to eliminate their differences but to declare the wonders of God (Acts 2:11), then might it not be possible for the same Spirit today to harmonize the many discursive practices of the various theological, natural, and human sciences so as not to eliminate their differences but to exalt the glory, power, and goodness of God?[45]

This means, then, that Christians can proceed in faith to suggest overarching theological interpretations of both books, while recognizing that the many disciplines also have their integrity, methods, and contributions. Thus historians might interpret the events of history (i.e., early Christianity of the book of Acts) in ways that complement pentecostal and Christian understandings, even as scientists might interpret the events of nature (i.e., the events of natural history behind the Genesis account) in ways that complement theological and soteriological perspectives. Concordism would insist that theological, historical, and scientific interpretations all proceed at the same level, and I believe this is a mistake. Instead, I suggest that the view

---

43. I see my theological approach to the two books as consistent with what is suggested by others who have contributed to this journal—e.g., Menuge, "Interpreting the Book of Nature"; Thorson, " Hermeneutics for Reading the Book of Nature"; and Murphy, "Reading God's Two Books." Menuge and Thorson agree that nature is also interpreted but differ over whether intelligent design is to be read scientifically (Menuge) or theologically (Murphy). I tend to agree that contemporary intelligent design is by and large a theologically funded project (here standing with Murphy, who sees ID as a natural theology) while also seeing that in some cases, discussion of some of the corollary issues like function are more strictly scientific (so here, open to Menuge's claims about the scientific engagement of nature).

44. See Grinnell, *Everyday Practice of Science*, esp. part I.

45. See Yong, "Academic Glossolalia?"

of the two books as complementary is distinctively theological and does not need to claim either historical or scientific expertise in these respective domains. Thus historical critical approaches and natural scientific methods can proceed to do their work. From a theological point of view, the truth will ultimately be complementary, even if, "For now we see in a mirror, dimly" (1 Cor 13:12). This is based on nature of historical and scientific inquiry, which revises itself in the long run as each engages in the honest search after the truth and deploys the methods at its disposal.

Of course, biblical and theological interpretations should be consistent with the various historical and scientific consensuses[46]—that is what we would expect if all truth is ultimately theologically funded. But given the fallibility and finitude of all human knowing—in things theological as well as in things historical and scientific—it may be that the aspired complementarity does not arrive, either because of a lack of consensus in one or more fields of inquiry or because of contradictory perspectives within or across disciplines. In the case of the former, when no consensus has been achieved, biblical and theological accounts should be tendered provisionally, perhaps sufficiently vaguely so as to be consistent with alternative historical or scientific theories under adjudication (regardless of what happens),[47] or with the recognition that later findings may warrant revisitation of the issues. In the case of the latter, if contradictions persist, this simply means that those working on contrary sides of the issue need to be open to further researching the matter and to revising their position as appropriate (while being cognizant that the complexity of some disagreements may not yield complementary resolution even in their lifetime). Yet in all of these cases, those interested in the theology and science dialogue or those working in

---

46. Clayton, *Adventures in the Spirit*, esp. ch. 3, argues convincingly about how theology's engagement with the sciences needs to recognize what can be said within scientific constraints. Thus, for example, the spherical nature of the earth confirmed by science dictates that intimations of a flat earth in the scriptural accounts need to be reinterpreted. I take this as meaning that not that science is supremely authoritative, but that when engaging specifically with the sciences, theologians need to understand that specific context and thus have to accommodate themselves, at least in part, to that field of discourse.

47. Thus, for example, theological interpretations should be potentially compatible with both intelligent design and theistic evolution, perhaps even with progressive and young earth creationisms, all of which are currently being negotiated within evangelical Christianity. To affirm this of *theological* interpretation is not to say that each of these are equal options in the science classroom—in that arena, other experts with more than just theological interests need to adjudicate the issues. This is in part what it means to retain the integrity of disciplines rather than to either reduce any to others or subsume all under theology, as it was during the medieval period. For further discussion of these matters, see my *The Spirit of Creation*, esp. chs. 2 and 5.

the sciences can rely on the Spirit's illumination in their endeavors, which is negotiated variously in their immediate confessional community, in wider communities of faith, amidst their disciplines, and within the backdrop of the broader scientific community.[48]

* * *

My goal in this chapter has been twofold: to encourage fellow pentecostals to develop their own hermeneutical approach both to the book of Genesis and to the book of nature, and to show how such an approach informed by their own interpretive instincts as derived from reading their canon-within-the-canon, the book of Acts, can contribute to the wider (especially evangelical) discussion about the relationship between the Bible and science, between the book of Scripture and that of nature. Such will be a narrative and theological approach that sees the work of the Spirit in history and in creation without denying the validity and even helpfulness of other interpretive methods. If this is possible, then conservative evangelicals can extricate themselves from the kind of concordism that requires harmonization of a literal reading of Genesis 1—2 with modern science. Instead, evangelicals should mine their "this-is-that" view of the Bible as God's living word so that the goal is not merely an intellectual understanding of what happened (which is illuminated by historiographical and scientific inquiry) but a practical and saving knowing of how we can inhabit the eschatological world of God in Christ, by the power of the Holy Spirit.

In short, a pneumatological view of the books of Scripture and of nature sees both books as comprehensible in faith, by the Spirit. Yet while such a pneumatic or pneumatological hermeneutic reads both Scripture and nature in Christ according to the saving intentions of God, it also leaves space for "natural"—i.e., scientific and historical—renditions of the same realities. But as the realities of the first century cannot be exhausted by historical-critical analysis, so neither can the realities of the formation of the world be exhausted by scientific analyses. In fact, it is also inevitably the case that such "natural" approaches will always be subject to what Paul Ricoeur calls the "conflict of interpretations," since it is in the nature of historical and scientific inquiry to revise continually its conclusions as more and more data come into clearer light.[49] On the other hand, light is, however gradually

---

48. For instances of such inter-confessional and interdisciplinary inquiry, see Yong, "Pentecostalism, Science, and Creation"; Yong, ed., *The Spirit Renews the Face of the Earth*; and Yong and Smith, eds., *Science and the Spirit*.

49. Ricoeur, *The Conflict of Interpretations*.

and inexorably, being shed, so that historical critical analysis can certainly enlighten the realities of the first century, even as science can also just as certainly elucidate the realities of the history of the world. Yet amidst the ongoing inquiries, evangelicals can expect that the "this" of our experiences relates to the soteriological "that" of the realities described in Scripture, even while the latter are being studied either with historical-critical tools (Acts) or scientific ones (Genesis).

This takes away nothing from such scientific and historical investigations since these unveil the natural mechanisms and historical conditions operative in the long formation and history of the world. Simultaneously, evangelicals believe that they are in but not merely of the world, so that whatever else science and history might suggest, there is also the saving work of the Spirit that is present and active. Of course, in this scenario, there is minimal possibility for apologetics as traditionally conceived in either direction: it is impossible to either verify or to falsify Christian faith except eschatologically. On the other hand, it may also be practically impossible to either verify or falsify some historical claims or some scientific theories, even in the long run. But that devalues neither historical nor scientific work, even as the implausibility of classical apologetics does not minimize evangelical commitments. This curiously paradoxical situation is, however, indicative of the life of the Spirit, whose "wind blows where it chooses, and you hear the sound of it, but you do not know where it comes from or where it goes" (John 3:8).

Conclusion

Theological Interpretation of Scripture after *Pentecost: Trinitarian Hermeneutics for the 21st Century*

The cumulative argument of the preceding is intended as a contribution to contemporary *theological interpretation of Scripture* (hereafter TIS) discussions. As a theologian rather than a biblical scholar, I am intrigued with the prevalence of Trinitarian rhetoric and reference in the TIS arena. My pentecostal sensibilities and perspectives have precipitated the hypothesis that such Trinitarianism can be more robustly conceptualized via fresh attentiveness to apostolic spirituality and practice in relationship to the narrative of the Day of Pentecost outpouring of the Holy Spirit.

Four general types of scriptural interpretation are presented in support of the book's thesis. The chapters in part I focus on the readings of Acts 2 for hermeneutical purposes, in particular bringing the many tongues and many cultures thesis embedded in the text into dialogue with contemporary (Asian and African, for instance) pentecostal thinking about hermeneutics and theological method. The second section of chapters each spring off the Day of Pentecost narrative toward a broader Lukan theological—and even pneumatological, eschatological, and pentecostal—anthropology, engaging in an ad hoc manner along the way with disability studies, and extant theologies of the family and theologies of children. Chapters 7–9 build from theological anthropology to pneumatological soteriology via a Pentecost-al perspective on what is wrong with the world (the doctrine of sin: hamartiology), the response of the good news (in the Spirit-anointed mission of Jesus and those he commissioned) and its means of dissemination (through Spirit-empowered evangelism). The fourth part presumes that apostolic interpretation starts with the Spirit of Pentecost and from there reads the rest of the Christian Testament both in its wholes (the Fourth Gospel) and in its parts (1 Corinthians 9:24–27) as well as the First Testament (Genesis

1–2). There are certainly other viable theological readings of all of the texts read in this book, and my interpretations are not intended to displace or delegitimize the alternatives. I am claiming that any efforts in TIS at least presume something like what I am proposing here: Christian engagement with Scripture proceeds *after* Pentecost and hence is not only christological and incarnational but pneumatological and pentecostal.

This concluding set of reflections provides a synthesis of what such a pentecostal TIS involves. We will discuss the hermeneutical, theological, and teleological dimensions of the proposed *pneumatological interpretation of Scripture*. As has been repeated above and will be clear here, a deeply Christian TIS cannot but be a pentecostal TIS, that less because of the modern pentecostal movement than because of the Spirit of Pentecost poured out on all flesh.

The *Hermeneutical* Spirit

Reading Scripture *after* Pentecost means reading with and through the many tongues of Pentecost.[1] Such a post-Pentecost-al approach (see chapter 1 above) thus invites, one the one hand, an ad hoc manner that reads Scripture *in* even if not *of* the world, and thus is never removed from the many voices of the world, even as this context-dependent and contingent process does not preclude the emergence of a more systematic articulation over time, precisely because of its pentecostal character. In this section, I elucidate this improvisional hermeneutic vis-à-vis the ecumenical, intercultural, interreligious, and interdisciplinary horizons of contemporary scriptural reading.

First, the many tongues of Pentecost include, obviously and foremost, the many members of the body of Christ, not only in terms of individuals but also in terms of ecclesial traditions. Here, I read pentecostal plenitude in ways that correlate Luke's universal or cosmic vision—that reaches to the ends of the earth (Acts 1:8) inclusive of its many generations to the ends of time (2:38)—with St. Paul's charismatic and ecumenical ecclesiology (1 Cor 12; cf. chs. 4 and 11 above), resulting in a pneumatological and Trinitarian rationale for attending to the diversity of ecclesial voices. My proposal

---

1. My colleague here at Fuller Seminary and leading TIS architect, Joel Green, discusses from his New Testament perspective, "Reading the Scriptures at Pentecost," in terms of the apostolic reading of the Hebrew scriptures (Green, *Seized by the Truth*, 27–33); my proposal presumes his but, from my systematician's point of view, proceeds from and since Pentecost, reading with, through, and after the apostles, without ever leaving them behind (Christian interpretation cannot do so, actually).

here clearly presumes a pneumatological ecclesiology that understands the church not only as the people of God and the body of Christ but also as the fellowship or "communion of the Holy Spirit" (2 Cor 13:13), and as such highlights less the institutional character of the ecclesia (although not ignoring this aspect) than its charismatic dimension.[2] As such, what is important about the church is not so much its established mechanisms and traditions as its improvisational capacities in the effort to follow the Spirit's leading over space and time. Here, the many voices of the church resounded in different contexts is essential to her self-understanding and also witness. Not that every ecclesial claim is sacrosanct, but discernment of which is which follows, rather than precedes, attending to the putative witness.

The polyvocality of the Spirit-imbued church resonates in part through its being constituted amidst many cultural-linguistic contexts. This is the Pentecost message central to the Lukan narrative, and it has become axiomatic for pentecostal interpreters confronted with the transcultural explosion of global pentecostal-charismatic Christianity in the present time.[3] To be sure, in a Western contextual time of multicultural political correctness, we ought to be wary about embracing enculturated forms of Christianity that have been seduced by the *Zeitgeist* (the spirits of the age), and in these cases, the charismatically empowered fellowship of the Holy Spirit is a prophetic voice advocating countercultural postures and resistant practices.[4] Still the scriptural witness is clear that the coming reign of God includes many peoples and nations speaking not homogeneously but through the diversity of their languages.[5] Reading Scripture *after* Pentecost grounds such interpretive pluralism theologically, in the Spirit's gift to and outpouring upon all flesh.

Intercultural hermeneutics includes, rather than is easily distinguishable from, interreligious hermeneutics. This is in part because of their interrelationality and interdependence—only in the evangelical West are the domains of *culture* and *religion* conceptually demarcated—and in part because each can be comprehended as encompassing the various spheres

---

2. Kärkkäinen, *Toward a Pneumatological Theology*, part II, and Yong, *Spirit Poured Out on All Flesh*, ch. 3, and *Renewing Christian Theology*, chs. 4–7, develop this idea of the church as fellowship of the Spirit.

3. Beginning with Hollenweger, *Pentecostalism*; see also Solivan, *Spirit, Pathos, Liberation*, 112–18, for more explicit theologizing (or pneumatologizing) about cultural plurality in light of the Pentecost narrative.

4. Billings, *The Word of God for the People of God*, ch. 4, discusses the Spirit's illuminating work across varying cultural contexts but also admonishes that there needs to be a critique of cultural idols in order to ward off cultural captivity.

5. See Yong, "The Spirit Says Come."

of human life and thereby giving such meaning and significance. The many languages of Pentecost are thus not only culturally suffused but also religiously infused. This is thereby not to accept uncritically the claims of those in other religions but it is to ask if and how truth, goodness, and beauty might be witnessed to by other faiths and thereby be redeemed for the witness of the Spirit.[6]

Last but not least for our hermeneutical considerations, reading Scripture *after* Pentecost proceeds amidst the cacophony of the many realms of knowledge. In the twenty-first-century academic context, these are constituted interdisciplinarily, involving multiple domains of scholarly and scientific inquiry. The many tongues of Pentecost, to the degree that they reverberate from many forms of life, also anticipate the many discursive practices of the disciplines as diverse epistemic quests. Again, this is not to baptize the academy and its many guilds wholesale, but it is to say that TIS proceeds amid, rather than oblivious to, the advance of human knowledge across many fronts. If it was said by Barth—and then widely repeated—that Scripture is to be read in one hand alongside the newspaper in the other, then TIS in this century is attentive to rather than unmindful of scientific journals and other scholarly ventures.[7]

As in a post-Gadamerian frame there is no interpretation that is not a fusion of horizons between that of the text and that of the reader,[8] then the pneumatological TIS on offer here embraces the hermeneutical circle. Interpretation all the way down can be grounded in an incarnational ontology,[9] but also, and here in a complementary rather than exclusive manner, in the pentecostal outpouring of the Spirit to the ends of the earth. My point is that TIS is part of the work of the church as a charismatic fellowship, and in this sense, theological and Trinitarian interpretation is funded by the hermeneutical Spirit.

---

6. Much of my constructive theological efforts have been forged amidst the nexus of the interfaith encounter; see Yong, *Hospitality and the Other*, *The Cosmic Breath*, and *Pneumatology and the Buddhist-Christian Dialogue*, among other works.

7. "Take your Bible and take your newspaper, and read both. But interpret newspapers from your Bible" (Karl Barth, *Time Magazine*, 1 May 1966). Relatedly, Lowther, *Spirit and Life*, talks about the multimedia manifestations and expressions of the Spirit in relationship the multidimensionality of human existence, thus inviting, if not requiring, engagement with many forms of knowledge; see also Yong, *The Spirit of Creation*, ch. 2, on pentecostal interdisciplinarity.

8. E.g., Thiselton, *The Two Horizons*.

9. See Smith, *The Fall of Interpretation*.

The Hermeneutical *Spirit*

Yet if the Spirit is hermeneutical, the interpretive process is also not arbitrary and relativistic in the nihilistic sense. There is a plurality of voices related to the many environments of TIS—and in that sense, TIS is relative in terms of related to and situated within many contexts—but sometimes these voices are inconsistent if not contradictory. How are the many tongues to be discerned? How are the many voices determined to be of the Holy Spirit as opposed to some other spirit? I suggest the most important pneumato-theological criteria for adjudication are christological, Trinitarian, and canonical, respectively.

First, then, the hermeneutical Spirit is, first and foremost but also ultimately, the Spirit of Jesus Christ. Hence any final identification of the Spirit is normed by what is manifest in the life and ministry of Jesus of Nazareth, and any contrary expression cannot be of the Holy Spirit. Acts is thus inseparable from the Third Gospel, even as the narratives of the Spirit's outpouring ought to be comprehended in light of the Spirit-filled mission of Jesus. Yet as already indicated, Jesus is *the Christ*, the *anointed Messiah*, only in and through the Spirit, and recognition of him as such is also via the Spirit (1 Cor 12:13), so herein is also another dimension of the hermeneutical circle: we recognize the Spirit through Jesus, but we also acknowledge Jesus through the Spirit. Such a hermeneutical and pneumatological Christology, then, involves an eschatological horizon: we understand Jesus now through a glass dimly (1 Cor 13:12) although "when he is revealed, we will be like him, for we will see him as he is" (1 John 3:2). It is in this respect that the hermeneutical Spirit enables us to delve deeper into the mystery of Christ via ecumenical, intercultural, interfaith, and interdisciplinary engagement, in anticipation of Christ's full glory to be unveiled eschatologically.

Further, the hermeneutical Spirit is the Spirit of the Father of the Son. This is not just the Father recognized and addressed by the Son, but the Father who those baptized into the Son by the Spirit also call *abba* (Father; Rom. 8:15-16). This is also, by extension, the God of Israel, the covenant-making deity revealed in the First Testament as the creator of the world. Hence, the hermeneutical Spirit of the Father has a Trinitarian shape, now also in relationship to the witness of ancient Israel's Scriptures.[10] The continuity-in-discontinuity, or discontinuity-in-continuity, exhibited between the God of Israel and the God of Jesus the Spirit-anointed Christ reflects already the hermeneutical circle of many (scriptural) voices, inviting reflection, debate,

---

10. See also Studebaker, *From Pentecost to the Triune God*, and Atkinson, *Trinity after Pentecost*.

and contestation.[11] Nevertheless, this Trinitarian criterion is non-negotiable in the pentecostal and pneumatological interpretation-of-Scripture model suggested in this book. This is because the Spirit of Pentecost in and after which all scriptural reading ensues is the Spirit of the Father of the Son and the Spirit of the God of Israel.

Effectively, then, the hermeneutical Spirit—the triune Spirit of Jesus and the Father—is discerned precisely through the canonical narrative of Scripture comprising both Old and New Testaments. Herein we confront most starkly the hermeneutical circle of TIS and, by extension in light of the argument of this book, PIS—pneumatological interpretation of Scripture: that we read Scripture in light of the Spirit poured out at Pentecost even as we discern the Spirit of Pentecost in light of the Scriptures. Put hermeneutically, we read Scripture with the apostolic Christians who wrote what we now have as the New Testament in response to their experience of the risen Christ in the power of the Spirit.[12] Hence we attend both to how they read their Scriptures (the Hebrew Bible) in the light of their incarnational and pentecostal experience even as we are now invited to read the canonical script from our own encounter of the ascended Christ made present in and through the Spirit.

If Scripture itself is the norming norm for discerning the hermeneutical Spirit, then does this not undermine the prioritization of Luke-Acts as a kind of canon within the canon apparent in the preceding pages?[13] Not initially but potentially affirmative in the long run, I would say. This is because, for starters, no one is merely canonical or biblical *simpliciter*; instead,

---

11. The prospects for a biblical pneumatology derived from both testaments are no less convoluted and contested than efforts to generate a coherent biblical theology in general, given not only the diversity within each Testament but also the major questions regarding the relationship between the two. Levison, *Filled with the Spirit*, and Welker, *God as Spirit*, exemplify the trends in biblical pneumatology of cohesive differentiatedness and diversified convergence respectively. My own pneumatology—better: *ruahology*—of the Old Testament is in progress, in a manuscript tentatively titled, *The Spirit and the Missio Dei*, part I.

12. Beldman and Swales, "Biblical Theology and Theological Interpretation," 155–64, describe the "apostolic method" of interpretation as involving saturation in the scriptures of ancient Israel albeit via Jesus Christ as fulfilling its prophecies (either directly or subtly/typologically), and hence by way of a christological hermeneutic; note that my apostolic hermeneutic takes nothing away from theirs but, precisely by making explicit the pneumatological and pentecostal reality in and through which Christ is revealed—both to the first century messianic believers and to those in the last two thousand years—fulfills the Trinitarian aspirations that can only be latent in their christocentric formulation.

13. Dempster, "The Canon and Theological Interpretation," 143, is one who cautions against canon-within-the-canon approaches for TIS.

we all begin somewhere, as socialized through our ecclesial traditions or communities of reading. I make no apologies for my formation within the modern pentecostal movement, even as this book suggests one way (a Lukan version) of coming to terms with the implications of such discipleship for TIS. This leads to the larger point that any TIS will inevitably feature confessional or ecclesial distinctives, whether Catholic, Orthodox, Lutheran, Reformed, Baptistic, Wesleyan, or, in the case of this book, pentecostal. My point is that recognizing such situatedness and owning such dynamically shifting traditions can be productive for engaging the *theological* specifics of TIS. The argument of this book is that the pentecostal starting with the Spirit of Pentecost (and Luke-Acts) foregrounds pneumatological sensibilities, instincts, and commitments conducive to a more fully Trinitarian vision of TIS. But finally and yes, remaining at the level of tradition specificity in the long run is unhealthy since critical checks and balances most often derive from perspectives outside of the home community. The point about the hermeneutical Spirit is the goal of a more expansively catholic/ecumenical and Trinitarian interpretation of Scripture, and remaining with Luke-Acts as the be-all and end-all of TIS would be counterproductive. That is not, however, what is being recommended here. Yet clearly, there remains at this time more work that needs to be done, even in Lukan theology, which is precisely the point.[14]

Trinitarian and Teleological Interpretation of Scripture for the Third Millennium Global Context

The Lukan narration of Pentecost was not for the purpose of focusing on the Spirit in and of itself but on telling the bigger story about what the Spirit does for followers of Jesus, for those in the community of faith, and for heralding the coming reign of God. Apostolic praxis then and now, hence, is also oriented toward these objectives. Therefore, TIS and PIS with it are also teleologically in soteriological, ecclesiological, and missiological directions. Soteriologically, scriptural reading and interpretation is not just informative but also formative, reformative, and transformative in the Spirit. This is what Kevin Vanhoozer, as discussed in the introductory chapter at the beginning of this book, identifies as the illocutionary goal of Scripture (to

---

14. Those unconvinced about the viability of a strategically adopted Lukan priority for TIS/PIS at the present historical moment or era ought to ask themselves about the need for ongoing biblical and theological scholarship on Luke-Acts specifically; I might suggest that the day in which such efforts are no longer needed will be the day when canon-within-the canon approaches have run their course.

mediate the experience of salvation in some way) and the perlocutionary effects of Scripture via the Holy Spirit.[15] Scripture hence might be initiative and formative in discipleship for those nurtured in the Christian faith and its communities from a young age, or be reformative for those who come to (new) faith later in life and need reorientation toward the divine; but in all cases, there is a transformative dimension of scriptural reading through which the Spirit sanctifies human souls so as to enable, here and now but also ultimately, participation in the triune life.[16]

Ecclesiologically, then, scriptural reading and interpretation ought to be emphasized as liturgical or corporate activity that facilitates the formation-reformation-transformation of human hearts and lives. Most renewal movements, modern pentecostal-charismatic Christianity included, never intended to start a new tradition or denomination. Instead, the goal has usually been—in the case of the early pentecostal believers assuredly—that of renewing their own spiritual lives and, more importantly, revitalizing their existing churches. PIS thus receives the sacred writings as divinely pneumatized—"inspired" or "God-breathed," as the *theopneustos* (θεόπνευστος) of 2 Timothy 3:16 says—for ecclesial regeneration and empowerment. The church—the people of God, the body of Christ, and the fellowship of the Spirit—embraces Scripture as the word of God even as that reception shapes the community's beliefs and practices in a multiplicity of ways relevant to its various contexts. If for Protestantism the church is *semper reformanda* (reformed and always reforming), then in the PIS purview, the fellowship of the Spirit is *semper renovation* (renewed and always renewing),[17] particularly and definitively in and through its reading and interpreting of Scripture.

Missiologically—which is last for our immediate purposes but certainly not by any stretch of the imagination any final word—TIS in light of Pentecost is positioned and turned toward nothing less than bearing witness to the gospel of Jesus Christ to the ends of the earth (Acts 1:8).[18] Scripture communicates the love of the Father for the Son in the Spirit and invites

---

15. See also Work, *Living and Active*, for more on Scripture as a soteriological means of grace; cf. Goheen and Wright, "Mission and Theological Interpretation," 190–91.

16. *Theosis* is the goal of holiness and sanctification, for which Scripture is the medium, according to pentecostal theologian Chris Green, *Sanctifying Interpretation*.

17. See Yong, "Renewed and Always Renewing."

18. TIS scholars Goheen and Wright, "Mission and Theological Interpretation," 186–88, recognize the importance of the book of Acts for missiological interpretation of Scripture; my contribution is to fill out the pneumato-Trinitarian dimension pointed to in the Acts narrative for the missiological telos of TIS.

creatures to receive and participate in that love.[19] To be sure, there are a multitude of ways through which human beings bear witness to the divine love, and these are pneumatologically and theologically funded as well vis-à-vis the many tongues of Pentecost that speak distinctively and perform variously in the multitude of missional contexts. Yet the point of PIS is the interrelatedness of personal formation-reformation-transformation within the community of faith—the fellowship of the triune Spirit—that is in turn performative of the triune love in and for the world so that others can experience and be invited into the fullness of life in the Spirit.

In the end, of course, the missional reading and interpreting of Scripture in the power of the Spirit in the present life and world heralds the reign of God that is in some respects present but in other respects yet still to come. The message of the divine administration proclaimed and inaugurated by Jesus' Spirit-empowered life and ministry now resounds through the lives of other Spirit-filled disciples, rejoicing in the glimpses of peace and joy that are signs of the Spirit's sway (Rom 14:17), but yet also anticipating the glorious governance of the time to come. My point is that in this time between the times—betwixt-and-between the first and second coming of Christ—there can be no TIS that is not "in the last days" (Acts 2:17), and hence pneumatologically funded to announce and instantiate the triune reign.

It is in this liminal space longing and yearning for the Parousia and return of the Messiah that scriptural interpretation arises. Hence although normatively encoded in the biblical canon, PIS emphasizes, perhaps in ways TIS does not, the provisionality of our understanding and, given the dynamic nature of life in the Spirit, the improvisationalty of our beliefs and practices. Pentecostal and pneumatological TIS repeatedly asks, "What does this mean?" (Acts 2:12), as those on the path of the Spirit attempt to discern the whence and whither of the divine breath. This is not to say that there can be no decisions along the way, yeses or nos in response to specific circumstances, questions, and challenges, authorized from out of the hermeneutical circle wherein it is deemed in the light of a fresh reading of Scripture that "it has seemed good to the Holy Spirit and to us [the people of God]" (Acts 15:28) and that this is the word of God for such a time as this. It is to say that every such decision's reception at a later moment will have to be discerned anew, through return to Scripture in light of the contemporary situation. PIS holds forth rather than recoils from such openendedness in expectation that the depths and riches of God's work in Christ will continue

---

19. Levering, *Participatory Biblical Exegesis*, writes first and foremost about the reader's participation in the biblical world, but the point of that, he recognizes as a systematician, is participation in the triune life and love.

to be unveiled through the Spirit, in expectation of the final revelation that transcends creaturely space and time.

References

Abraham, Shaibu. *Pentecostal Theology of Liberation: Holy Spirit and Holiness in the Society*. Christian Heritage Rediscovered 6. New Delhi: Christian World, 2014.

Acheampong, Joseph Williams. "'I Will Pass over You': The Relevance of the Passover to the Understanding of Salvation in Contemporary Ghanaian Pentecostalism—A Critical Reflection from an Akan Perspective." DTheo diss., Universität Hamburg, 2014. http://d-nb.info/1076359868/34.

Achtemeier, Elizabeth R. "Jesus Christ, the Light of the World: The Biblical Understanding of Light and Darkness." *Interpretation* 17.4 (1963) 439–49.

Adam, A. K. M., et al. *Reading Scripture with the Church: Toward a Hermeneutic for Theological Interpretation*. Grand Rapids: Baker Academic, 2006.

Adamo, David Tuesday. *Reading and Interpreting the Bible in African Indigenous Churches*. Eugene, OR: Wipf & Stock, 2001.

Akoko, Robert Mbe. *"Ask and You Shall Be Given": Pentecostalism and the Economic Crisis in Cameroon*. African Studies Collection 2. Leiden: African Studies Centre, 2007.

Albl, Martin. "For Whenever I Am Weak, Then I Am Strong: Disability in Paul's Epistles." In *This Abled Body: Rethinking Disabilities in Biblical Studies*, edited by Hector Avalos, et al., 145–58. Atlanta: Society of Biblical Literature, 2007.

Albrecht, Daniel E. *Rites in the Spirit: A Ritual approach to Pentecostal/Charismatic Spirituality*. Sheffield: Sheffield Academic Press, 1999.

Alexander, Estrelda Y. *Black Fire: One Hundred Years of African American Pentecostalism*. Downers Grove, IL: IVP Academic, 2011.

———. *The Women of Azusa Street*. Cleveland, OH: Pilgrim, 2005.

Alexander, Estrelda Y., and Amos Yong, eds. *Afro-Pentecostalism: Black Pentecostal and Charismatic Christianity in History and Culture*. Religion, Race, and Ethnicity Series. New York: New York University Press, 2011.

Alexander, Kimberly E. *Pentecostal Healing: Models in Theology and Practice*. Journal of Pentecostal Theology Supplement series 29. Blanford Forum, UK: Deo, 2007.

Alfaro, Rubén (Tito) Paredes. "Expressions of Evangelism in Latin America." *International Review of Mission* 103.2 (2014) 334–47.

Alfaro, Sammy. *Divino Compañero: Toward a Hispanic Pentecostal Christology*. Eugene, OR: Pickwick, 2010.

Althouse, Peter. *Spirit of the Last Days: Pentecostal Eschatology in Conversation with Jürgen Moltmann*. Journal of Pentecostal Theology Supplement series 25. London: Continuum, 2003.

Althouse, Peter, and Robby Waddell, eds. *Perspectives in Pentecostal Eschatologies: World Without End.* Eugene, OR: Pickwick, 2010.

Amaladoss, Michael. *Life in Freedom: Liberation Theologies from Asia.* Maryknoll, NY: Orbis, 1997.

Anderson, Allan. *An Introduction to Pentecostalism: Global Charismatic Christianity.* Cambridge: Cambridge University Press, 2004.

———. *Spreading Fires: The Missionary Nature of Early Pentecostalism.* London: SCM, 2007.

Anderson, Allan, and Edmond Tang, eds. *Asian and Pentecostal: The Charismatic Face of Christianity in Asia.* London: Regnum International, and Baguio City, Philippines: Asia Pacific Theological Seminary, 2005.

Anderson, Gerald H., and Thomas F. Stransky, eds. *Third World Theologies: Asian, African and Latin American Contributions to a Radical Theological Realignment in the Church.* Mission Trends 3. New York: Paulist, 1976.

Anoka, Victor Ahamefule. *African Philosophy: An Overview and a Critique of the Philosophical Significance of African Oral Literature.* Frankfurt am Main: Peter Lang, 2012.

Appiah-Kubi, Kofi, and Sergio Torres, eds. *African Theology En Route: Papers from the Pan-African Conference of Third World Theologians, December 17–23, 1977, Accra, Ghana.* Maryknoll, NY: Orbis, 1979.

Archer, Kenneth J. *The Gospel Revisited: Towards a Pentecostal Theology of Worship and Witness.* Eugene, OR: Pickwick, 2011.

———. *A Pentecostal Hermeneutic for the Twenty-First Century: Spirit, Scripture and Community.* Journal of Pentecostal Theology Supplement series 28. New York: T & T Clark, 2004.

———. "The Spirit and Theological Interpretation: A Pentecostal Strategy." *Cyberjournal for Pentecostal-Charismatic Research* 16 (2007). http://www.pctii.org/cyberj/cyber16.html.

Archer, Melissa L. *'I Was in the Spirit on the Lord's Day': A Pentecostal Engagement with Worship in the Apocalypse.* Cleveland, TN: CPT, 2015.

Arlandson, James Malcolm. *Women, Class, and Society in Early Christianity: Models from Luke-Acts.* Peabody, MA: Hendrickson, 1997.

Arokiasamy, S. "Sinful Structures in the Theology of Sin, Conversion and Reconciliation." In *Social Sin: Its Challenges to Christian Life*, edited by S. Arokiasamy and F. Podimattom, 90–115. Bangalore: Claretian, 1991.

Arrington, French L. *Christian Doctrine: A Pentecostal Perspective.* 3 vols. Cleveland, TN: Pathway, 1992–1994.

Asamoah-Gyadu, J. Kwabena. *Contemporary Pentecostal Christianity: Interpretations from an African Context.* Oxford: Regnum, 2013.

———. "Pulling Down Strongholds: Evangelism, Principalities and Powers and the African Pentecostal Imagination." *International Review of Mission* 96.382–383 (2007) 306–17.

———. *Sighs and Signs of the Spirit: Ghanaian Perspectives on Pentecostalism and Renewal in Africa.* Oxford: Regnum, 2015.

Ashbrook, James B., and Carol Rausch Albright. *The Humanizing Brain: Where Religion and Neuroscience Meet.* Cleveland: Pilgrim, 1997.

Asumang, Annang. "Powers of Darkness: An Evaluation of Three Hermeneutical Approaches to the Evil Powers in Ephesians." *Conspectus: The Journal of the South African Theological Seminay* 5 (2008) 1–19.

Atkinson, William P. *Trinity after Pentecost*. Eugene, OR: Pickwick, 2013.

Attanasi, Katherine, and Amos Yong, eds. *Pentecostalism and Prosperity: The Socioeconomics of the Global Charismatic Movement*. Christianities of the World 1. New York: Palgrave Macmillan, 2012.

Augustine. *Answer to Faustus, a Manichean*. The Works of Saint Augustine: A Translation for the 21st Century I.20. Translated by Roland Teske. Hyde Park, NY: New City, 2007.

———. *Confessions*. Translated by E. B. Pusey. Accessed May 13, 2016. http://www.sacred-texts.com/chr/augconf/aug06.htm.

Aune, David E. "Charismatic Exegesis in Early Judaism and Early Christianity." In *The Pseudepigrapha and Early Biblical Interpretation*, edited by James H. Charlesworth and Craig A. Evans, 126–50. Journal for the Study of the Pseudepigrapha Supplement Series 14 / Studies in Scripture in Early Judaism and Christianity 2. Sheffield: Sheffield Academic Press, 1993.

———. "Dualism in the Fourth Gospel and the Dead Sea Scrolls." In *Noetestamentica et Philonicai: Studies in Honor of Peder Borgen*, edited by David C. Aune et al., 281–303. Supplements to *Novum Testamentum* 106. Leiden: Brill, 2003.

Avalos, Hector. "Introducing Sensory Criticism in Biblical Studies: Audiocentricity and Visiocentricity." In *This Abled Body: Rethinking Disabilities in Biblical Studies*, edited by Hector Avalos, et al., 47–59. Atlanta: Society of Biblical Literature.

Badcock, Gary D. "Holy Spirit, Doctrine of the." In *Dictionary for Theological Interpretation of the Bible*, edited by Kevin J. Vanhoozer, 302–5. Grand Rapids: Baker Academic, 2005.

Baer, Jonathan R. "Redeemed Bodies: The Functions of Divine Healing in Incipient Pentecostalism." *Church History* 70.4 (2001) 735–71.

Bahmann, Manfred K. *A Preference for the Poor: Latin American Liberation Theology from a Protestant Perspective*. Lanham, MD: University Press of America, 2005.

Baker, Robert O. "Pentecostal Bible Reading: Toward a Model of Reading for the Formation of the Affections." *Journal of Pentecostal Theology* 7 (1995) 34–38.

Baker, William J. *Playing with God: Religion and Modern Sport*. Cambridge, MA: Harvard University Press, 2007.

Barnes, Colin. *"Cabbage Syndrome": The Social Construction of Dependence*. London: Falmer, 1990.

Barnes, Kim. *In the Wilderness: Coming of Age in Unknown Country*. New York: Anchor, 1996.

Barney, Robert K., Stephen R. Wenn, and Scott G. Martyn. *Selling the Five Rings: The International Olympic Committee and the Rise of Olympic Commercialism*. Salt Lake City: The University of Utah Press, 2004.

Barrett, C. K. *Essays on John*. Philadelphia: Westminster, 1982.

Barth, Karl. *Church Dogmatics*, Vol. III/4, *The Doctrine of Creation*. Edited by G. W. Bromiley and Thomas F. Torrance, translated by A. T. Mackay, et al. Peabody, MA: Hendrickson, 2010.

Bartholomew, Craig G. "Listening to God's Address: A *Mere* Trinitarian Hermeneutic for the Old Testament." In *Hearing the Old Testament: Listening for God's Address*, edited by Craig G. Bartholomew and David J. H. Beldman, 3–19. Grand Rapids: Eerdmans, 2012.

Bartholomew, Craig G., Colin Greene, and Karl Möller, eds. *After Pentecost: Language and Biblical Interpretation*. Scripture and Hermeneutics series 2. Carlisle, UK: Paternoster, and Grand Rapids: Zondervan, 2001.

Bartholomew, Craig G., and Heath A. Thomas, eds. *A Manifesto for Theological Interpretation*. Grand Rapids: Baker Academic, 2016.

Bauman, Chad M. *Pentecostals, Proselytization, and Anti-Christian Violence in Contemporary India*. Oxford: Oxford University Press, 2015.

Baylis, Charles. "The Meaning of Walking 'in the Darkness' (1 John 1:6)." *Bibliotheca Sacra* 149 (1992) 214–22.

Beamish, Rob, and Ian Ritchie. *Fastest, Highest, Strongest: A Critique of High-Performance Sport*. London: Routledge, 2006.

Beers, Holly. *The Followers of Jesus as the Servant: Luke's Model from Isaiah for the Disciples in Luke-Acts*. Library of New Testament Studies 535. New York: Bloomsbury/T & T Clark, 2015.

Beasley-Murray, George R. *John*. 2d ed. Word Biblical Commentary 36. Nashville: Thomas Nelson, 1999.

Beckford, Robert. *Dread and Pentecostal: A Political Theology for the Black Church in Britain*. London: SPCK, 2000.

———. *God of the Rahtid: Redeeming Rage*. London: Darton, Longman, and Todd, 2001.

———. *Jesus Dub: Theology, Music and Social Change*. New York: Routledge, 2006.

———. *Jesus is Dread: Black Theology and Black Culture in Britain*. London: Darton, Longman, and Todd, 1999.

Belck, Jack, ed. *The Faith of Helen Keller*. Kansas City: Hallmark Cards, 1967.

Beldman, David J. H., and Jonathan Swales. "Biblical Theology and Theological Interpretation." In *A Manifesto for Theological Interpretation*, edited by Craig G. Bartholomew and Heath A. Thomas, 149–70. Grand Rapids: Baker Academic, 2016.

Bell, Richard H. *Understanding African Philosophy: A Cross-cultural Approach to Classical and Contemporary Issues*. London: Routledge, 2002.

Bernard, David K. *The Glory of God in the Face of Jesus Christ: Deification of Jesus in Early Christian Discourse*. Journal of Pentecostal Theology Supplement Series 45. Blandford Forum, UK: Deo, 2016.

Berryman, Jerome W. *Children and the Theologians: Clearing the Way for Grace*. New York: Morehouse, 2009.

Bertone, John A. "The Experience of Glossolalia and the Spirit's Empathy: Romans 8:26 Revisited." *Pneuma: The Journal of the Society for Pentecostal Studies* 25 (2003) 54–65.

Best, E. "The Revelation to Evangelize the Gentiles." *Journal of Theological Studies* NS 35.1 (1984) 2–30.

Betcher, Sharon. "Monstrosities, Miracles, and Mission: Religion and the Politics of Disablement." In *Postcolonial Theologies: Divinity and Empire*, edited by Catherine Keller, et al., 79–99. St. Louis: Chalice, 2004.

———. "Rehabilitating Religious Discourse: Bringing Disability Studies to the Theological Venue." *Religious Studies Review* 27.4 (2001) 341–48.

———. *Spirit and the Politics of Disablement*. Minneapolis: Fortress, 2007.

Bielo, James S. *Words upon the Word: An Ethnography of Evangelical Group Bible Study.* New York: New York University Press, 2009.

Bieringer, R., D. Pollefeyt, and F. Vandecasteele-Vanneuville, eds. *Anti-Judaism in the Fourth Gospel: Papers of the Leuven Colloquium, 2000.* Assen, The Netherlands: Royal Van Gorcum, 2001.

Billings, J. Todd. *The Word of God for the People of God: An Entryway into the Theological Interpretation of Scripture.* Grand Rapids: Eerdmans, 2010.

Billingsley, Scott. *It's a New Day: Race and Gender in the Modern Charismatic Movement.* Tuscaloosa, AL: The University of Alabama Press, 2008.

Blumhofer, Edith. "The Role of Women in the Assemblies of God." *Assemblies of God Heritage* (Winter 1987–1988) 13.

Bock, Darrell L. *Acts: Baker Exegetical Commentary on the New Testament.* Grand Rapids: Baker Academic, 2007.

Bock, Kim Yong, ed. *Minjung Theology: People as the Subjects of History.* Singapore: The Commission on Theological Concerns, 1981.

Boersma, Hans, and Matthew Levering. "Introduction: Spiritual Interpretation and Realigned Temporality." In *Heaven on Earth: Theological Interpretation and Ecumenical Dialogue*, edited by Hans Boersma and Matthew Levering, 1–10. Malden, MA: Wiley-Blackwell, 2013.

Boesak, Allan. *Black and Reformed: Apartheid, Liberation and the Calvinist Tradition.* Edited by Leonard Sweetman. Maryknoll, NY: Orbis, 1984.

Boeschen, E. S. "Examining the Cognitive and Somatic Manifestation of Competitive State Anxiety in Special Olympics Athletes." PhD diss., University of North Dakota, 2010.

Bongmba, Elias Kifon. *African Witchcraft and Otherness: A Philosophical and Theological Critique of Intersubjective Relations.* Albany, NY: State University of New York Press, 2001.

Borgman, Paul. *The Way According to Luke: Hearing the Whole Story of Luke-Acts.* Grand Rapids: Eerdmans, 2006.

Bovon, François. *Luke the Theologian: Fifty-five Years of Research (1950–2005)*, 2d ed. Waco, TX: Baylor University Press, 2006.

Bradnick, David. "A Pentecostal Perspective on Entropy, Emergent Systems, and Eschatology." *Zygon: Journal of Religion and Science* 43.4 (2008) 925–42.

Breidenthal, Thomas. "Reconstructing Christianity before Supersessionism." *Cross-Currents* 49.3 (1999) 319–48.

Brock, Brian. "Discipline, Sport, and the Religion of Winners: Paul on Running to Win the Prize." *Studies in Christian Ethics* 25.1 (2012) 4–19.

Brodie, Thomas L. *Genesis as Dialogue: A Literary, Historical, and Theological Commentary.* Oxford: Oxford University Press, 2001.

Brown, Candy Gunther, ed. *Global Pentecostal and Charismatic Healing.* Oxford: Oxford University Press, 2011.

Brown, Raymond E. *The Community of the Beloved Disciple.* New York: Paulist, 1979.

———. *The Gospel According to John (xiii–xxi).* Garden City, NY: Doubleday, 1970.

Browning, Don S. *Equality and the Family: A Fundamental, Practical Theology of Children, Mothers, and Fathers in Modern Societies.* Grand Rapids: Eerdmans, 2007.

Bruce, F. F. *The Hard Sayings of Jesus.* Downers Grove, IL: InterVarsity, 1983.

Brusco, Elizabeth E. "The Peace that Passes All Understanding: Violence, the Family and Fundamentalist Knowledge in Colombia." In *Mixed Blessings: Gender and Religious Fundamentalism Cross Culturally*, edited by Judy Brink and Joan P. Mencher, 11–24. London: Routledge, 1997.

———. *The Reformation of Machismo: Evangelical Conversion and Gender in Colombia*. Austin, TX: University of Texas Press, 1995.

Bultmann, Rudolf. *Theology of the New Testament* vol. 2. Translated by Kendrick Grobel. New York: Charles Scribner's, 1955.

Bunge, Marcia J. "Theologies of Childhood and Child Theologies: International Initiatives to Deepen Reflection on Children and Childhood in the Academy and Religious Communities." *Dharma Deepika: A South Asian Journal of Missiological Research* 12.2 (2008) 33–53.

Butler, Anthea D. *Women in the Church of God in Christ: Making a Sanctified World*. Chapel Hill, NC: The University of North Carolina Press, 2007.

Byrne, Matthew. *My Father's Business: St. Luke's Narrative of the Ministry of Jesus*. Dublin: Columba, 2009.

Cadbury, Henry J. *The Style and Literary Method of Luke*. Harvard Theological Studies 6. New York: Kraus, 1969.

Campbell, Iain D. *The Doctrine of Sin*. Ross-shire, UK: Mentor, 1999.

Caneday, Ardel B., and Matthew Barrett, eds. *Four Views on the Historical Adam*. Grand Rapids: Zondervan, 2013.

Carlson, Licia. "Rethinking Normalcy, Normalization, and Cognitive Disability." In *Science and Other Cultures: Issues in Philosophies of Science and Technology*, edited by Robert Figueroa and Sandra Harding, 154–71. New York: Routledge, 2003.

Carroll, John T. "'What Then Will This Child Become?': Perspectives on Children in the Gospel of Luke." In *The Child in the Bible*, edited by Marcia J. Bunge, 177–94. Grand Rapids: Eerdmans, 2008.

Cartledge, Mark J. *Practical Theology: Charismatic and Empirical Perspectives*. Carlisle, UK: Paternoster, 2003.

———. *Testimony in the Spirit: Rescripting Ordinary Pentecostal Theology*. Burlington, VT: Ashgate, 2013.

Cassidy, Richard J. *Jesus, Politics, and Society: A Study of Luke's Gospel*. Maryknoll, NY: Orbis, 1978.

The Center for Development and Enterprise, South Africa. "Under the Radar: Pentecostalism in South Africa and Its Potential Social and Economic Role." In *Pentecostalism and Prosperity: The Socioeconomics of the Global Charismatic Movement*, edited by Katherine Attanasi and Amos Yong, 63–86. Christianities of the World 1. New York: Palgrave Macmillan, 2012.

Chan, Simon. *Grassroots Asian Theology: Thinking the Faith from the Ground Up*. Downers Grove, IL: IVP Academic, 2014.

Charlesworth, James H. "A Critical Comparison of the Dualism in 1QS 3:13–4:26 and the 'Dualism' Contained in the Gospel of John." In *John and Qumran*, edited by James H. Charlesworth, 76–106. London: Geoffrey Chapman, 1972.

———. "The Gospel of John: Exclusivism Caused by a Social Setting Different from That of Jesus (John 11:42 and 14:6)." In *Anti-Judaism in the Fourth Gospel: Papers of the Leuven Colloquium, 2000*, edited by R. Bieringer, et al., 479–513. Assen, The Netherlands: Royal Van Gorcum, 2001.

Chaves, João B. *Evangelicals and Liberation Revisited: An Inquiry into the Possibility of an Evangelical-Liberationist Theology*. Eugene, OR: Wipf & Stock, 2013.

Cherney, James L., and Kurt Lindemann. "Sporting Images of Disability: *Murderball* and the Rehabilitation of Masculine Identity." In *Examining Identity in Sports Media*, edited by Heather L. Hundley and Andrew C. Billings, 195–216. Los Angeles: Sage, 2010.

Chesnut, R. Andrew. *Born Again in Brazil: The Pentecostal Boom and the Pathogens of Poverty*. New Brunswick, NJ: Rutgers University Press, 1997.

Chitando, Ezra, Masiiwa Ragies Gunda, and Joachim Kügler, eds. *Prophets, Profits and the Bible in Zimbabwe: Festschrift for Aynos Masotcha Moyo*. Bible in Africa Studies 12. Bamberg: University of Bamberg Press, 2013.

Clarke, Clifton R., ed. *Pentecostal Theology in Africa*. Eugene, OR: Pickwick, 2014.

Clayton, Philip. *Adventures in the Spirit: God, World, Divine Action*. Minneapolis: Fortress, 2008.

Coats, George W. *Genesis, with an Introduction to Narrative Literature*. Grand Rapids: Eerdmans, 1983.

Coleman, Joyce. *Public Reading and the Reading Public in Late Medieval England and France*. Cambridge: Cambridge University Press, 1996.

Coleman, Richard J. *Eden's Garden: Rethinking Sin and Evil in an Era of Scientific Promise*. Lanham, MD: Rowman & Littlefield, 2007.

Coleman, Simon. *The Globalisation of Charismatic Christianity: Spreading the Gospel of Prosperity*. Cambridge Studies in Ideology & Religion 12. Cambridge, UK: Cambridge University Press, 2000.

———. "Textuality and Embodiment among Charismatic Christians." In *Reading Religion in Text and Context: Reflections of Faith and Practice in Religious Materials*, edited by Elisabeth Arweck and Peter Collins, 157–68. Aldershot, UK: Ashgate, 2006.

Colker, Ruth. *The Disability Pendulum: The First Decade of the Americans with Disabilities Act*. New York: New York University Press, 2005.

Collins, C. John. *Genesis 1–4: A Linguistic, Literary, and Theological Commentary*. Phillipsburg, NJ: P & R, 2006.

Collins, James Michael. *Exorcism and Deliverance Ministry in the Twentieth Century: An Analysis of the Practice and Theology of Exorcism in Modern Western Christianity*. Milton Keynes, UK: Paternoster, 2009.

Collins, Raymond F. *These Things Have Been Written: Studies on the Fourth Gospel*. Louvain Theological & Pastoral Monographs 2. Grand Rapids: Eerdmans, 1990.

Collins, Robin. "Evolution and Original Sin." In *Perspectives on an Evolving Creation*, edited by Keith B. Miller, 469–501. Grand Rapids: Eerdmans, 2003.

Combes, Isoble H. "Nursing Mother, Ancient Shepherd, Athletic Coach? Some Images of Christ in the Early Church." In *Images of Christ: Ancient and Modern*, edited by Stanley E. Porter et al., 113–25. Roehampton Institute London Papers 2. Sheffield: Sheffield Academic Press, 1997.

Comblin, José. *The Holy Spirit and Liberation*. Translated by Paul Burns. Maryknoll, NY: Orbis, 1989.

Cone, James H. *A Black Theology of Liberation: Fortieth Anniversary Edition*. Maryknoll, NY: Orbis, 2010.

Congregation for the Doctrine of the Faith. "Instruction on Certain Aspects of the 'Theology of Liberation.'" 6 August 1984. Accessed March 30, 2016. http://www.vatican.va/roman_curia/congregations/cfaith/documents/rc_con_cfaith_doc_19840806_theology-liberation_en.html.

Conway, Colleen M. "Speaking through Ambiguity: Minor Characters in the Fourth Gospel." *Biblical Interpretation* 10.3 (2002) 324–41.

Conzelmann, Hans. *The Theology of St. Luke*. Translated by Geoffrey Buswell. Philadelphia: Fortress, 1961.

Cooper, Thia, ed. *The Reemergence of Liberation Theologies: Models for the Twenty-First Century*. New York: Palgrave Macmillan, 2013.

Corr, Peter. "From the Outside Looking In and the Inside Looking Out." In *The Paralympic Games: Empowerment or Side Show?*, edited by Keith Gilbert and Otto J. Schantz, 126–33. Maidenhead, UK: Meyer & Meyer, 2008.

Corten, Andre. *Pentecostalism in Brazil: Emotion of the Poor and Theological Romanticism*. New York: Palgrave Macmillan, 1999.

Costantino, Antonio Ziccardi. *The Relationship of Jesus and the Kingdom of God according to Luke-Acts*. Rome: Editrice Pontificia Universita Gregoriana, 2008.

Costas, Orlando E. *Liberating News: A Theology of Contextual Evangelization*. Grand Rapids: Eerdmans, 1989.

Coulter, Dale M., and Amos Yong, eds. *The Spirit, the Affections, and the Christian Tradition*. Notre Dame, IN: University of Notre Dame Press, 2016.

Courey, David J. *What Has Wittenberg to Do with Azusa? Luther's Theology of the Cross and Pentecostal Triumphalism*. New York: Bloomsbury Academic, 2015.

Cox, Harvey G. *Fire from Heaven: The Rise of Pentecostal Spirituality and the Reshaping of Religion in the 21st Century*. Reading, MA: Addison-Wesley, 1995.

Culpepper, R. Alan. "The Gospel of John as a Document of Faith in a Pluralistic Culture." In *What is John?* Vol. 1, *Readers and Readings of the Fourth Gospel*, edited by Fernando F. Segovia, 107–27. Atlanta: Scholars, 1996.

———. "The Gospel of John as a Threat to Jewish-Christian Relations." In *Overcoming Fear between Jews and Christians*, edited by J. H. Charlesworth, with F. X. Blisard and J. L. Gorham, 21–43. New York: Crossroad, 1992.

———. "Inclusivism and Exclusivism in the Fourth Gospel." In *Word, Theology, and Community in John*, edited by John Painter, et al., 85–108. St. Louis: Chalice, 2002.

Cunningham, Mary Kathleen. *What is Theological Exegesis: Interpretation and Use of Scripture in Barth's Doctrine of Election*. Valley Forge, PA: Trinity, 1995.

Curnow, Rohan M. "Which Preferential Option for the Poor? A History of the Doctrine's Bifurcation." *Modern Theology* 31.1 (2015) 27–59.

Dabney, D. Lyle. "Otherwise Engaged in the Spirit: A First Theology for the Twenty-first Century." In *The Future of Theology: Essays in Honor of Jürgen Moltmann*, edited by Miroslav Volf, et al., 154–63. Grand Rapids: Eerdmans, 1996.

———. "Starting with the Spirit: Why the Last Should be First." In *Starting with the Spirit: Task of Theology II*, edited by Stephen Pickard and Gordon Preece, 3–27. Hindmarsh, Australia: Australian Theological Forum, 2001.

Damasio, Antonio R. *Descartes' Error: Emotion, Reason, and the Human Brain*. New York: Putnam, 1994.

Daniels, David D., III. "'Gotta Moan Sometime': A Sonic Exploration of Earwitnesses to Early Pentecostal Sound in North America." *Pneuma: The Journal of the Society for Pentecostal Studies* 30.1 (2008) 5–32.

Davis, Billie. "Perpetuating Pentecost through the Family." In *Nurturing Pentecostal Families: A Covenant to Nurture Our Families*, edited by John Kie Vining, 87–97. Cleveland, TN: Family Ministries/Pathway, 1996.

Davis, Jud. "Acts 2 and the Old Testament: The Pentecost Event in Light of Sinai, Babel, and the Table of Nations." *Criswell Theological Review* 7.1 (2009) 29–48.
Davis, Lennard J., ed. *The Disability Studies Reader*. New York: Routledge, 1997.
Dawkins, Richard. *The Selfish Gene*. New York: Oxford University Press, 1976.
Dawson, Audrey. *Healing, Weakness and Power: Perspectives on Healing in the Writings of Mark, Luke and Paul*. Milton Keynes, UK: Paternoster, 2008.
Dayton, Donald W. *Theological Roots of Pentecostalism*. Peabody, MA: Hendrickson, 1987.
Deddo, Gary W. *Karl Barth's Theology of Relations: Trinitarian, Christological, and Human—Towards an Ethic of the Family*. Issues in Systematic Theology 4. New York: Peter Lang, 1999.
De Klerk, Jilles. "Through Different Eyes: Indonesian Experiences with an Intercultural Reading of John 4." In *Through the Eyes of Another: Intercultural Reading of the Bible*, edited by Hans de Wit et al., 161–75. Elkhart, IN: Institute of Mennonite Studies, and Amsterdam: Vrije Universiteit, 2004.
Del Agua, Agustín. "The Lucan Narrative of the 'Evangelization of the Kingdom of God': A Contribution to the Unity of Luke-Acts." In *The Unity of Luke-Acts*, edited by J. Verheyden, 639–61. Bibliotheca Ephemeridum Theologicarum Lovaniensium 62. Leuven: Leuven University Press and Uitgeverij Peeters, 1999.
Dempster, Murray W. "Paradigm Shifts and Hermeneutics: Confronting Issues Old and New." *Pneuma: The Journal of the Society for Pentecostal Studies* 15.2 (1993) 129–35.
Dempster, Stephen G. "The Canon and Theological Interpretation." In *A Manifesto for Theological Interpretation*, edited by Craig G. Bartholomew and Heath A. Thomas, 131–48. Grand Rapids: Baker Academic, 2016.
DePauw, Karen P., and Susan J. Gavron. *Disability Sport*. 2d ed. Champaign, IL: Human Kinetics, 2005.
Destro, Adriana, and Mauro Pesce. "Fathers and Householders in the Jesus Movement: The Perspective of the Gospel of Luke." *Biblical Interpretation* 11.2 (2003) 211–38.
De Vries, Carl E. "Paul's 'Cutting' Remarks about a Race: Galatians 5:1–12." In *Current Issues in Biblical and Patristic Interpretation: Studies in Honor of Merrill C. Tenney Presented by His Former Students*, edited by G. F. Hawthorne, 115–20. Grand Rapids: Eerdmans, 1975.
Dimant, Devorah. "Dualism at Qumran: New Perspectives." In *Caves of Enlightenment: Proceedings of the American Schools of Oriental Research Dead Sea Scrolls Jubilee Symposium (1947-1997)*, edited by James H. Charlesworth, 55–73. North Richland Hills, TX: Bibal, 1998.
Dinn, Sheila. *Hearts of Gold: A Celebration of Special Olympics and Its Heroes*. Woodbridge, CT: Blackbirch, 1996.
Dokka, Trond Skard. "Irony and Sectarianism in the Gospel of John." In *New Readings in John: Literary and Theological Perspectives*, edited by Johannes Nissen and Sigfeid Pedersen, 84–107. Sheffield: Sheffield Academic Press, 1999.
Doll-Tepper, Gudrun. "Disability Sport." In *The International Politics of Sport in the Twentieth Century*, edited by James Riordan and Arnd Krüger, 177–90. London: E & FN Sponsors, and New York: Routledge, 1999.
Doll-Tepper, Gudrun, Michael Kröner, and Werner Sonnenschein, eds. *New Horizons in Sport for Athletes with a Disability: Proceedings of the International VISTA '99*

Conference, Cologne, Germany, 28 August–1 September 1999. 2 vols. Aachen, Germany: Meyer & Meyer Sport, 2001.

Domning, Daryl P., with Monika K. Hellwig. *Original Selfishness: Original Sin and Evil in the Light of Evolution*. Aldershot, UK: Ashgate, 2006.

Drake, Stillman, trans. *Discoveries and Opinions of Galileo*. Garden City, NY: Doubleday Anchor, 1957.

Dresselhaus, Richard L. "Can Children Receive the Baptism?" In *Questions and Answers about the Holy Spirit*, edited by Hal Donaldson et al., 105–108. Springfield, MO: Gospel, 2001.

Dube, Musa W. "Reading for Decolonization (John 4.1–42)." In *John and Postcolonialism: Travel, Space and Power*, edited by Musa W. Dube and Jeffrey L. Staley, 51–75. The Bible and Postcolonialism 7. New York: Sheffield Academic, 2002.

Dupuis, Jacques. *Toward a Christian Theology of Religious Pluralism*. Maryknoll, NY: Orbis, 1997.

Dutch, Robert S. *The Educated Elite in 1 Corinthians: Education and Community Conflict in Graeco-Roman Context*. New York: T & T Clark International, 2005.

Edwards, Denis. "Original Sin and Saving Grace in Evolutionary Context." In *Evolution and Molecular Biology: Scientific Perspectives on Divine Action*, edited by Robert John Russell et al., 377–92. Vatican City: Vatican Observatory, and Berkeley: Center for Theology and Natural Sciences, 1998.

Eiesland, Nancy. "Avoiding Hospital Chaplains and other Venial Sins." *Candler Connection* (Fall 2008) 8–9.

———. *The Disabled God: Toward a Liberatory Theology of Disability*. Nashville: Abingdon, 1994.

Elbert, Paul. "Genesis 1 and the Spirit: A Narrative-Rhetorical Ancient Near Eastern Reading in Light of Modern Science." *Journal of Pentecostal Theology* 15.1 (2006) 23–72.

Elbert, Paul, and Amos Yong. "Christianity, Pentecostalism: Issues in Science and Religion." In *Encyclopedia of Science and Religion*, edited by J. Wentzel van Huysteen I, 2 vols., 132–35. New York: Macmillan Reference Library, 2003.

Ellingson, Laura L., and Patricia J. Sotirin. *Aunting: Cultural Practices that Sustain Family and Community Life*. Waco, TX: Baylor University Press, 2009.

Ellington, Scott A. "'Can I Get a Witness': The Myth of Pentecostal Orality and the Process of Traditioning in the Psalms." *Journal of Pentecostal Theology* 20 (2011) 54–67.

Elliott, John H. "Temple versus Household in Luke-Acts: A Contrast in Social Institutions." In *The Social World of Luke-Acts: Models for Interpretation*, edited by Jerome H. Neyrey, 211–40. Peabody, MA: Hendrickson, 1991.

Ellis, Stephen, and Gerrie ter Haar. *Worlds of Power: Religious Thought and Political Practice in Africa*. Oxford: Oxford University Press, 2004.

Engelke, Matthew. *A Problem of Presence: Beyond Scripture in an African Church*. Berkeley: University of California Press, 2007.

England, John C., et al., eds. *Asian Christian Theologies: A Research Guide to Authors, Movements, and Sources*. 3 vols. Maryknoll, NY: Orbis, and Delhi: ISPCK/Claretian, 2002.

Epperly, Bruce G. *God's Touch: Faith, Wholeness, and the Healing Miracles of Jesus*. Louisville: Westminster John Knox, 2001.

Ervin, Howard M. *Healing: Sign of the Kingdom*. Grand Rapids: Baker Academic, 2002.

Esler, Philip F. "Paul and the *Agon*: Understanding a Pauline Motif in its Cultural and Visual Context." In *Picturing the New Testament: Studies in Ancient Visual Images*, edited by Annette Weissenrieder et al., 357–84. Wissenschaftliche Untersuchungen Zum Neuen Testament II.193. Tübingen: Mohr Siebeck, 2005.

"Evangelization, Proselytism, and Common Witness—Final Report of the Dialogue between the Roman Catholic Church and Some Classical Pentecostal Churches: 1990-1997." In *Pentecostalism and Christian Unity: Ecumenical Documents and Critical Assessments*, edited by Wolfgang Vondey, 159–98. Eugene, OR: Pickwick, 2010.

Evans, Craig A., and Donald A. Hagner, eds. *Anti-Semitism and Early Christianity: Issues of Polemic and Faith*. Minneapolis: Fortress, 1993.

Everts, Janet M., and Rachel S. Baird. "Phoebe Palmer and Her Pentecostal Protégées: Acts 2.17–18 and Pentecostal Woman Ministers." In *Trajectories in the Book of Acts: Essays in Honor of John Wesley Wyckoff*, edited by Paul Alexander, et al., 146–59. Eugene, OR: Wipf & Stock, 2010.

Falk, Darrell R. *Coming to Peace with Science: Bridging the Worlds between Faith and Biology*. Downers Grove, IL: InterVarsity, 2004.

Farrell, Robin J., et al. "The Driving Force: Motivation in Special Olympics." *Adapted Physical Activity Quarterly* 21.2 (2004) 153–66.

Faupel, David W. *The Everlasting Gospel: The Significance of Eschatology in the Development of Pentecostal Thought*. Journal of Pentecostal Theology Supplement series 10. Sheffield: Sheffield Academic Press, 1996.

Ferm, Deane William. *Third World Liberation Theologies: An Introductory Survey*. Maryknoll, NY: Orbis, 1988.

Fettke, Steven M. "The Spirit of God Hovered Over the Waters: Creation, the Local Church, and the Mentally and Physically Challenged—A Call to Spirit-led Ministry." *Journal of Pentecostal Theology* 17.2 (2008) 170–82.

Fitzgerald, Hayley. *Disability and Youth Sport*. New York: Routledge, 2009.

Fitzmyer, Joseph A. *The Gospel according to Luke (I–IX): Introduction, Translation, and Notes*. The Anchor Bible 28. Garden City, NY: Doubleday, 1983.

Flannery, Edward H. *The Anguish of the Jews: Twenty-three Centuries of Anti-Semitism*. New York: Macmillan, and London: Collier, 1965.

Fleischer, Doris Zames, and Frieda Zames. *The Disability Rights Movement: From Charity to Confrontation*. Philadelphia: Temple University Press, 2001.

Flemming, Dean. *Contextualization in the New Testament: Patterns for Theology and Mission*. Downers Grove, IL: InterVarsity, 2005.

Flynn, Robert J., and Raymond A. Lemay, eds. *A Quarter-Century of Normalization and Social Role Valorization: Evolution and Impact*. Ottawa: University of Ottawa Press, 1999.

Ford, David F. *Christian Reason: Desiring God and Learning in Love*. Cambridge: Cambridge University Press, 2007.

Ford, David F., and Frances Clemson, eds. *Interreligious Reading after Vatican II: Scriptural Reasoning, Comparative Theology, and Receptive Ecumenism*. Malden, MA: Wiley-Blackwell, 2013.

Ford, David F., and Graham Stanton, eds. *Reading Texts, Seeking Wisdom: Scripture and Theology*. Grand Rapids: Eerdmans, 2003.

Forrest, David. "Sport and Gambling." In *Handbook on the Economics of Sport*, edited by Wladimir Andreff and Stefan Szymanski, 40–49. Cheltenham, UK: Edward Elgar, 2006.

Fournier, Marianne. *The Episode at Lystra: A Rhetorical and Semiotic Analysis of Acts 14:7–20a*. American University Studies Series VII, Theology and Religion 197. New York: Peter Lang, 1997.

Fowl, Stephen E. *Engaging Scripture: A Model for Theological Interpretation*. Malden, MA: Blackwell, 1998.

———. *Theological Interpretation of Scripture*. Eugene, OR: Cascade, 2009.

Francoeur, Robert T. *Perspectives in Evolution*. Baltimore: Helicon, 1965.

Freeman, Dena, ed. *Pentecostalism and Development: Churches, NGOs and Social Change in Africa*. New York: Palgrave Macmillan, 2010.

Frei, Hans W. *The Eclipse of Biblical Narrative: A Study in Eighteenth and Nineteenth Century Hermeneutics*. New Haven: Yale University Press, 1974.

Freyne, Sean. "Vilifying the Other and Defining the Self: Matthew's and John's Anti-Jewish Polemic in Focus." In *"To See Ourselves as Others See Us": Christians, Jews, "Others" in Late Antiquity*, edited by Jacob Neusner and Ernest S. Frerichs, 117–43. Chico, CA: Scholars, 1985.

Gabaitse, Rosinah Mmannana. "Pentecostal Hermeneutics and the Marginalisation of Women." *Scriptura* 114 (2015) 1–12.

Gadacz, René R. *Re-thinking Dis-ability: New Structures, New Relationships*. Edmonton, AB: University of Alberta Press, 1994.

Gage, Warren Austin. *The Gospel of Genesis: Studies in Protology and Eschatology*. Winona Lake, IN: Carpenter, 1984.

Gager, John G. *The Origins of Anti-Semitism: Attitudes toward Judaism in Pagan and Christian Antiquity*. Oxford: Oxford University Press, 1983.

Gallegos, John. "African Pentecostal Hermeneutics." In *Pentecostal Theology in Africa*, edited by Clifton R. Clarke, 40–57. Eugene, OR: Wipf & Stock, 2014.

Gard, Michael, and Hayley Fitzgerald. "Tackling *Murderball*: Masculinity, Disability and the Big Screen." *Sport, Ethics and Philosophy* 2.2 (2008) 126–41.

Garrison, Roman. *The Greco-Roman Context of Early Christian Literature*. Sheffield: Sheffield Academic Press, 1997.

Gaventa, Beverly Roberts. *From Darkness to Light: Aspects of Conversion in the New Testament*. Overtures to Biblical Theology 20. Philadelphia: Fortress, 1986.

George, Sherron Kay. *Meeting Your Neighbor: Multiculturalism in Luke and Acts*. NP: Presbyterian Church, U.S.A., 2000.

Gibson, Richard J. "Paul and the Evangelization of the Stoics." In *The Gospel to the Nations: Perspectives on Paul's Mission*, edited by Peter Bolt and Mark Thompson, 309–26. Downers Grove, IL: InterVarsity, and Leicester, UK: Apollos, 2000.

Gifford, Paul. "'Africa Shall Be Saved': An Appraisal of Reinhard Bonnke's Pan-African Crusade." *Journal of Religion in Africa* 17.1 (1987) 63–92.

Gillman, John. *Possessions and the Life of Faith: A Reading of Luke-Acts*. Collegeville, MN: Liturgical, 1991.

Godbey, J. E., and Allen Howard Godbey. *Light in Darkness: or, Missions and Missionary Heroes—An Illustrated History of the Missionary Work Now Carried on By All Protestant Denominations in Heathen Lands*. Boston: Eastern, 1888.

Goff, James R., Jr. *Fields White unto Harvest: Charles F. Parham and the Missionary Origins of Pentecostalism*. Fayetteville, AR: The University of Arkansas Press, 1988.

Goggin, Gerard, and Christopher Newell. *Digital Disability: The Social Construction of Disability in New Media.* Lanham, MD: Rowman & Littlefield, 2003.

Goheen, Michael W., and Christopher J. H. Wright. "Mission and Theological Interpretation." In *A Manifesto for Theological Interpretation*, edited by Craig G. Bartholomew and Heath A. Thomas, 171–96. Grand Rapids: Baker Academic, 2016.

Goldstein, Jeffrey, ed. *Why We Watch: The Attractions of Violent Entertainment.* Oxford: Oxford University Press, 1998.

González, Catherine Gunsalus, and Justo L. González. "Babel and Empire, Pentecost and Empire: Preaching on Genesis 11:1–9 and Acts 2:1–12." *Journal for Preachers* 16.4 (1993) 22–26.

González, Justo L. *Luke.* Belief: A Theological Commentary on the Bible. Louisville: Westminster John Knox, 2010.

Graham, William A. *Beyond the Written Word: Oral Aspects of Scripture in the History of Religion.* Cambridge: Cambridge University Press, 1982.

Grau, Marion. *Rethinking Mission in the Postcolony: Salvation, Society and Subversion.* New York: T & T Clark, 2011.

Greeley, Andrew, and Michael Hout. *The Truth about Conservative Christians: What They Think and What They Believe.* Chicago: The University of Chicago Press, 2006.

Green, Chris E. W. *Sanctifying Interpretation: Vocation, Holiness, and Scripture.* Cleveland, TN: CPT, 2015.

Green, Joel B. "Good News to Whom? Jesus and the 'Poor' in the Gospel of Luke." In *Jesus of Nazareth: Lord and Christ—Essays on the Historical Jesus and New Testament Christology*, edited by Joel B. Green and Max Turner, 59–74. Grand Rapids: Eerdmans, and Carlisle, UK: Paternoster, 1994.

———. *The Gospel of Luke.* Grand Rapids: Eerdmans, 1997.

———. "'In Our Own Languages': Pentecost, Babel, and the Shaping of Christian Community in Acts 2:1–13." In *The Word Leaps the Gap: Essays on Scripture and Theology in Honor of Richard B. Hays*, edited by J. Ross Wagner et al., 198–213. Grand Rapids: Eerdmans, 2008.

———. "Learning Theological Interpretation from Luke." In *Reading Luke: Interpretation, Reflection, Formation*, edited by Craig G. Bartholomew, et al., 55–78. Grand Rapids: Zondervan, 2005.

———. *Practicing Theological Interpretation: Engaging Biblical Texts for Faith and Formation.* Grand Rapids: Baker Academic, 2012.

———. "Scripture and Theology: Uniting the Two So Long Divided." In *Between Two Horizons: Spanning New Testament Studies and Systematic Theology*, edited by Joel B. Green and Max Turner, 23–42. Grand Rapids: Eerdmans, 2000.

———. *Seized by the Truth: Reading the Bible as Scripture.* Nashville: Abingdon, 2007.

———. "'Tell Me a Story': Perspectives on Children from the Acts of the Apostles." In *The Child in the Bible*, edited by Marcia J. Bunge, 215–32. Grand Rapids: Eerdmans, 2008.

———. "'To Turn from Darkness to Light' (Acts 26:18): Conversion in the Narrative of Luke-Acts." In *Conversion in the Wesleyan Tradition*, edited by Kenneth J. Collins and John H. Tyson, 103–18. Nashville: Abingdon, 2001.

Green, Joel B., and Max Turner, eds. *Between Two Horizons: Spanning New Testament Studies and Systematic Theology.* Grand Rapids: Eerdmans, 2000.

Green, Joel B., and David F. Watson, eds., *Wesley, Wesleyans, and Reading Bible as Scripture*. Waco, TX: Baylor University Press, 2012.

Green, Michael. *Evangelism in the Early Church*. Rev. ed. Grand Rapids: Eerdmans, 2003.

Grey, Jacqueline. *Three's a Crowd: Pentecostalism, Hermeneutics, and the Old Testament*. Eugene, OR: Wipf & Stock, 2011.

Griffiths, Paul J. *An Apology for Apologetics: A Study in the Logic of Interreligious Dialogue*. Maryknoll, NY: Orbis, 1991.

Grinnell, Frederick. *Everyday Practice of Science: Where Intuition and Passion Meet Objectivity and Logic*. Oxford: Oxford University Press, 2009.

Groody, Daniel G., ed. *The Option for the Poor in Christian Theology*. Notre Dame, IN: University of Notre Dame Press, 2007.

Groody, Daniel G., and Gustavo Gutiérrez, eds. *The Preferential Option for the Poor beyond Theology*. Notre Dame, IN: University of Notre Dame Press, 2014.

Gundry, Robert H. *Jesus the Word according to John the Sectarian*. Grand Rapids: Eerdmans, 2002.

Gundry-Volf, Judith M. "The Least and the Greatest: Children in the New Testament." In *The Child in Christian Thought*, edited by Marcia J. Bunge, 29–60. Grand Rapids: Eerdmans, 2001.

Haenchen, Ernst. *John: A Commentary on the Gospel of John, Chapters 1–6*. Translated by Robert W. Funk. 2 vols. Philadelphia: Fortress, 1984.

Hagopian, David G., ed. *The G3n3s1s Debate: Three Views on the Days of Creation*. Mission Viejo, CA: Crux, 2001.

Hakola, Raimo. *Identity Matters: John, the Jews and Jewishness*. Supplements to Novum Testamentum 118. Leiden: Brill, 2005.

Hannam, Wilfrid L. *In the Things of My Father: A Study of the Purpose of Luke the Evangelist*. London: Epworth, 1953.

Hardesty, Nancy. *Faith Cure: Divine Healing in the Holiness and Pentecostal Movements*. Peabody, MA: Hendrickson, 2003.

Hardy, Clarence E., III. "Church Mothers and Pentecostals in the Modern Age." In *Afro-Pentecostalism: Black Pentecostal and Charismatic Christianity in History and Culture*, edited by Estrelda Alexander and Amos Yong, 83–93. Religion, Race, and Ethnicity Series. New York: New York University Press, 2011.

Harms, Richard B. *Paradigms from Luke-Acts for Multicultural Communities*. American University Studies Series VII, Theology and Religion 216. New York: Peter Lang, 2001.

Harris, James C. *Intellectual Disability: Understanding Its Development, Causes, Classification, Evaluation, and Treatment*. Oxford: Oxford University Press, 2006.

Harrison, James R. "Paul and the Athletic Ideal in Antiquity: A Case Study in Wrestling with Word and Image." In *Paul's World*, edited by Stanley E. Porter, 81–109. Pauline Studies 4. Leiden: Brill, 2008.

Harrison, Peter. *The Bible, Protestantism and the Rise of Natural Science*. Cambridge: Cambridge University Press, 1998.

———. "Reinterpreting Nature in Early Modern Europe: Natural Philosophy, Biblical Exegesis and the Contemplative Life." In *The Word and the World: Biblical Exegesis and Early Modern Science*, edited by Kevin Killeen and Peter J. Forshaw, 25–44. New York: Palgrave Macmillan, 2007.

Harshaw, Jill R. "Prophetic Voices, Silent Words: The Prophetic Role of Persons with Profound Intellectual Disabilities in Contemporary Christianity." *Practical Theology* 3.3 (2010) 311–29.

Hart, Larry D. *Truth Aflame: Theology for the Church in Renewal*. Rev. ed. Grand Rapids: Zondervan, 2005.

Hart, Trevor. "Tradition, Authority, and a Christian Approach to the Bible as Scripture." In *Between Two Horizons: Spanning New Testament Studies and Systematic Theology*, edited by Joel B. Green and Max Turner, 183–204. Grand Rapids: Eerdmans, 2000.

Hauerwas, Stanley, and William Willimon. *Resident Aliens: Life in the Christian Colony*. Nashville: Abingdon, 1989.

Healey, Joseph, and Donald Sybertz. *Towards an African Narrative Theology*. Maryknoll, NY: Orbis, 1996.

Heaney, Sharon E. *Contextual Theology for Latin America: Liberation Themes in Evangelical Perspective*. Milton Keynes, UK: Paternoster, 2008.

Hedrick, Charles W. "Paul's Conversion/Call: A Comparative Analysis of the Three Reports in Acts." *Journal of Biblical Literature* 100.3 (1981) 415–32.

Hefner, Philip J. *The Human Factor: Evolution, Culture, and Religion*. Minneapolis: Fortress, 1993.

Henderson, Walter E., Jr. "The Athletic Imagery of Paul." *Theological Educator* 56 (1997) 30–37.

Hendricks, William L. *A Theology for Children*. Nashville: Broadman, 1980.

Hengel, Martin. *The Johannine Question*. Translated by John Bowden. London: SCM, and Philadelphia: Trinity Press International, 1989.

Henry, Carl F. H. *Evangelicals at the Brink of Crisis: Significance of the World Congress on Evangelism*. Waco, TX: Word, 1967.

Hess, Richard S., and M. Daniel Carroll R., eds. *Family in the Bible: Exploring Customs, Culture, and Context*. Grand Rapids: Baker Academic, 2003.

Higgs, Robert J., and Michael C. Braswell. *An Unholy Alliance: The Sacred and Modern Sports*. Macon, GA: Mercer University Press, 2004.

Hill, Johnny Bernard. *Prophetic Rage: A Postcolonial Theology of Liberation*. Grand Rapids: Eerdmans, 2013.

Hitching, Roger. *The Church and Deaf People: A Study of Identity, Communication and Relationships with Special Reference to the Ecclesiology of Jürgen Moltmann*. Carlisle, UK: Paternoster, 2003.

Hodges, Zane C. "Coming into the Light—John 3:20–21." *Bibliotheca Sacra* 135 (1978) 314–22.

Hoffman, Shirl James. *Good Game: Christians and the Culture of Sport*. Waco, TX: Baylor University Press, 2010.

Hollenweger, Walter J. *Pentecostalism: Origins and Developments Worldwide*. Peabody, MA: Hendrickson, 1998.

Holmes, Pamela M. S. "Acts 29 and Authority: Towards a Pentecostal Feminist Hermeneutic of Liberation." In *A Liberating Spirit: Pentecostals and Social Action in North America*, edited by Michael Wilkinson and Steven M. Studebaker, 185–209. Eugene, OR: Pickwick, 2010.

Holmes, Urban T. *Turning to Christ: A Theology of Evangelization and Renewal*. Boston: Cowley, 1981.

Holvast, Rene. *Spiritual Mapping in the United States and Argentina, 1989–2005: A Geography of Fear*. Religion in the Americas 8. Leiden: Brill, 2008.
Hordern, William, and Frederick Dale Bruner. *The Holy Spirit: Shy Member of the Trinity*. Minneapolis: Augsburg Fortress, 1984.
Horsfeld, Peter, and J. Kwabena Asamoah-Gyadu. "What Is It about the Book? Semantic and Material Dimensions in the Mediation of the Word of God." *Studies in World Christianity* 17.2 (2011) 175–93.
Howard, Evan B. *Affirming the Touch of God: A Psychological and Philosophical Exploration of Christian Discernment*. Lanham, MD: University Press of America, 2000.
Howell, Kenneth J. *God's Two Books: Copernican Cosmology and Biblical Interpretation in Early Modern Science*. Notre Dame, IN: University of Notre Dame Press, 2002.
Huffey, Rhoda. *The Hallelujah Side*. Orlando, FL: Houghton Mifflin, 2000.
Hughes, Bill, and Kevin Paterson. "The Social Model of Disability and the Disappearing Body: Towards a Sociology of Impairment." *Disability & Society* 12.3 (1997) 325–40.
Hull, John M. *In the Beginning There was Darkness: A Blind Person's Conversations with the Bible*. Harrisburg, PA: Trinity, 2002.
Hull, Judy Brown. *When You Receive a Child: Reflections on Luke 9:46–48*. St. Meinrad, IN: Abbey, 1980.
Hullinger, Jerry M. "The Historical Background of Paul's Athletic Allusions." *Bibliotheca Sacra* 161.643 (2004) 343–59.
Hundley, Raymond C. *Radical Liberation Theology: An Evangelical Response*. Wilmore, KY: Bristol & OMS International, 1987.
Hunt, Stephen, and Nicola Lightly. "Work in Progress: The Religious Beliefs of Young Nigerian Pentecostals." *International Journal of Children's Spirituality* 5.1 (2000) 103.
Hunter, Harold D., and Peter D. Hocken, eds. *All Together in One Place: Theological Papers from the Brighton Conference on World Evangelization*. Journal of Pentecostal Theology Supplement series 4. Sheffield: Sheffield Academic Press, 1993.
Ibita, Ma. Marilou, and Reimund Bieringer. "(Stifled) Voices of the Future: Learning about Children in the Bible." In *Children's Voices: Children's Perspectives in Ethics, Theology and Religious Education*, edited by Annemie Dillon and Didier Pollefeyt, 73–115. Leuven: Uitgeverij Peeters, 2010.
Inch, Morris A. *The Elder Brother: A Christian Alternative to Anti-Semitism*. Lanham, MD: University Press of America, 2005.
Irele, F. Abiola. *The African Imagination: Literature in Africa and the Black Diaspora*. Oxford: Oxford University Press, 2001.
Irvin, Dale T. *Christian Histories, Christian Traditioning: Rendering Accounts*. Maryknoll, NY: Orbis, 1988.
Irvin, Howard M. *Healing: Sign of the Kingdom*. Peabody, MA: Hendrickson, 2002.
Ittmann, Karl. *Work, Gender, and Family in Victorian England*. Washington Square, NY: New York University Press, 1995.
James, Jonathan D. *McDonalisation, Masala McGospel and Om Economics: Televangelism in Contemporary India*. New Delhi: SAGE, 2010.
Jeffrey, David L. "Naming the Father: The Teaching Authority of Jesus and Contemporary Debate." In *After Pentecost: Language and Biblical Interpretation*,

edited by Craig Bartholomew et al., 263–79. Carlisle, UK: Paternoster, and Grand Rapids: Zondervan, 2001.

Jenkins, Philip. *The New Faces of Christianity: Believing the Bible in the Global South.* Oxford: Oxford University Press, 2006.

———. *The Next Christendom: The Coming of Global Christianity.* Oxford: Oxford University Press, 2002.

Jervell, Jacob. "The Future of the Past: Luke's Vision of Salvation History and Its Bearing on His Writing of History." In *History, Literature, and Society in the Book of Acts,* edited by Ben Witherington III, 104–26. Cambridge: Cambridge University Press, 1996.

Jespersen, Ejgil, and Mike McNamee, eds. *Ethics, Dis/Ability and Sports.* New York: Routledge, 2009.

Johns, Cheryl Bridges. *Pentecostal Formation: A Pedagogy among the Oppressed.* Journal of Pentecostal Theology Supplement series 2. Sheffield: Sheffield Academic Press, 1993.

Johnson, Luke Timothy. "The New Testament's Anti-Jewish Slander and the Conventions of Ancient Polemic." *Journal of Biblical Literature* 108.3 (1989) 419–41.

———. *Prophetic Jesus, Prophetic Church: The Challenge of Luke-Acts to Contemporary Christians.* Grand Rapids: Eerdmans, 2011.

———. *Sharing Possessions: Mandate and Symbol of Faith.* Minneapolis: Fortress, 1981.

Jonker, Louis. "Towards a 'Communal' approach for Reading the Bible in Africa." In *Interpreting the Old Testament in Africa: Papers from the International Symposium on Africa and the Old Testament in Nairobi, October 1999,* edited by Mary Getui et al., 77–88. Bible and Theology in Africa 2. New York: Peter Lang, 2001.

Jorgensen, Dan. "Third Wave Evangelism and the Politics of the Global in Papua New Guinea: Spiritual Warfare and the Recreation of Place in Telefolmin." *Oceania* 75 (2005) 444–61.

Juel, Donald H. *Shaping the Scriptural Imagination: Truth, Meaning, and the Theological Interpretation of the Bible,* edited by Shane Berg and Matthew L. Skinner. Waco, TX: Baylor University Press, 2011.

Jung, Lee Hong. "Minjung and Pentecostal movements in Korea." In *Pentecostals after a Century: Global Perspectives on a Movement in Transition,* edited by Allan H. Anderson and Walter J. Hollenweger, 138–60. Journal of Pentecostal Theology Supplement series 15. Sheffield: Sheffield Academic Press, 1999.

Kärkkäinen, Veli-Matti. *A Constructive Christian Theology for the Pluralistic World.* Vol. 3, *Creation and Humanity.* Grand Rapids: Eerdmans, 2015.

———. *An Introduction to Ecclesiology: Ecumenical, Historical, and Global Perspectives.* Grand Rapids: Baker Academic, 2002.

———. *An Introduction to the Theology of Religions: Biblical, Historical and Contemporary Perspectives.* Downers Grove, IL: InterVarsity, 2003.

———. *Toward a Pneumatological Theology: Pentecostal and Ecumenical Perspectives on Ecclesiology, Soteriology and Theology of Mission.* Edited by Amos Yong. Lanham, MD: University Press of America, 2002.

Kee, Howard Clark. *Good News to the Ends of the Earth: The Theology of Acts.* London: SCM, and Philadelphia: Trinity, 1990.

Keener, Craig S. *The Gospel of John: A Commentary.* Vol. 1. Peabody: Hendrickson, 2003.

———. *Paul, Women and Wives: Marriage and Women's Ministry in the Letters of Paul.* Peabody, MA: Hendrickson, 1992.

———. "Power of Pentecost: Luke's Missiology in Acts 1–2." *Asia Journal of Pentecostal Studies* 12.1 (2009) 47–73.

———. *Spirit Hermeneutics: Reading Scripture in Light of Pentecost.* Grand Rapids: Eerdmans, 2016.

Kelber, Werner H. *The Oral and the Written Gospel: The Hermeneutics of Speaking and Writing in the Synoptic Tradition, Mark, Paul, and Q.* Philadelphia: Fortress, 1983.

Kemp, Ian S. "'The Light of Men' in the Prologue of John's Gospel." *Indian Journal of Theology* 15.4 (1966) 154–64.

Kent, Homer A., Jr. *Light in the Darkness: Studies in the Gospel of John.* Grand Rapids: Baker, 1974.

Kerr, John H. *Rethinking Aggression and Violence in Sport.* New York: Routledge, 2005.

Keum, Jooseup, ed. *Together towards Life: Mission and Evangelism in Changing Landscapes.* Geneva: World Council of Churches, 2013.

Kimilike, Lechion Peter. *Poverty in the Book of Proverbs: An African Transformational Hermeneutic of Proverbs on Poverty.* Bible and Theology in Africa 7. New York: Peter Lang, 2008.

Kim, Jean K. *Woman and Nation: An Intercontextual Reading of the Gospel of John from a Postcolonial Feminist Perspective.* Biblical Interpretation Series 69. Boston: Brill, 2004.

Kim, Myung Hyuk. "The Concept of God in Minjung Theology and Its Socio-economic and Historical Characteristics." *Evangelical Review of Theology* 14.2 (1990) 126–49.

Kirk, J. Andrew. *Liberation Theology: An Evangelical View from the Third World.* Atlanta: John Knox, 1979.

Kirsch, Thomas G. *Spirits and Letters: Reading, Writing and Charisma in African Christianity.* Oxford: Berghahn, 2008.

Klein, Ralph W. "A Liberated Lifestyle: Slaves and Servants in Biblical Perspective." *Currents in Theology and Mission* 9.4 (1982) 212–21.

Kliner, David Paul. "Assessing Healing Stories in the Gospels: Analysis of Initiators, Conditions, Touch, and Gender." *Chicago Theological Seminary Register* 86.3 (1996) 33–40.

Knight, Henry H., III, and F. Douglas Powe Jr. *Transforming Evangelism: The Wesleyan Way of Sharing Faith.* Nashville: Discipleship Resources, 2006.

Knitter, Paul F. *Introducing Theologies of Religions.* Maryknoll, NY: Orbis, 2002.

Koenig, John. *Jews and Christians in Dialogue: New Testament Foundations.* Philadelphia: Westminster, 1979.

Kombo, James Henry Owino. *The Doctrine of God in African Christian Thought: The Holy Trinity, Theological Hermeneutics and the African Intellectual Climate.* Studies in Reformed Theology 14. Leiden: Brill, 2007.

Korsmeyer, Jerry D. *Evolution and Eden: Balancing Original Sin and Contemporary Science.* New York: Paulist, 1998.

Koskie, Steven J. "Can We Speak of a Wesleyan Theological Hermeneutic of Scripture Today?" In *Wesley, Wesleyans, and Reading Bible as Scripture*, edited by Joel B. Green and David F. Watson, 195–209. Waco, TX: Baylor University Press, 2012.

Köstenberger, Andreas J. "Sensitivity to Outsiders in John's Gospel and Letters and Its Implications for the Understanding of Early Christian Mission." In *Sensitivity towards Outsiders: Exploring the Dynamic Relationship between Mission and Ethics in the New Testament and Early Christianity*, edited by Jakobus (Kobus) Kok et al., 171–86. Wissenschaftliche Untersuchungen zum Neuen Testament 2.364. Tübingen: Mohr Sieback, 2014.

Krattenmaker, Tom. *Onward Christian Athletes: Turning Ballparks into Pulpits and Players into Preachers*. Lanham, MD: Rowman & Littlefield, 2010.

Krentz, Edgar. "Paul, Games, and the Military." In *Paul in the Greco-Roman World: A Handbook*, edited by J. P. Sampley, 344–83. Harrisburg, PA: Trinity, 2003.

Kuecker, Aaron J. "The Spirit and the 'Other,' Satan and the 'Self': Economic Ethics as a Consequence of Identity Transformation in Luke-Acts." In *Engaging Economics: New Testament Scenarios and Early Christian Reception*, edited by Bruce W. Longenecker and Kelly D. Liebengood, 81–103. Grand Rapids: Eerdmans, 2009.

Kysar, Robert. "Anti-Semitism and the Gospel of John." In *Anti-Semitism and Early Christianity: Issues of Polemic and Faith*, edited by Craig A. Evans and Donald A. Hagner, 113–27. Minneapolis: Fortress, 1993.

———. *Voyages in John: Charting the Fourth Gospel*. Waco, TX: Baylor University Press, 2005.

Ladd, Tony, and James A. Mathisen. *Muscular Christianity: Evangelical Protestants and the Development of American Sport*. Grand Rapids: Baker, 1999.

Lakoff, George, and Mark Johnson. *Philosophy in the Flesh: The Embodied Mind and Its Challenge to Western Thought*. New York: Basic, 1999.

Lalleman, Pieter J. "Healing by a Mere Touch as a Christian Concept." *Tyndale Bulletin* 48.2 (1997) 355–61.

Lambrecht, Jan. "The Relatives of Jesus in Mark." *Novum Testamentum* 16.4 (1974) 241–58.

Lamoureux, Denis O. *Evolutionary Creation: A Christian Approach to Evolution*. Eugene, OR: Wipf & Stock, 2008.

Land, Steven J. *Pentecostal Spirituality: A Passion for the Kingdom*. Journal of Pentecostal Theology Supplement series 1. Sheffield: Sheffield Academic Press, 1996.

Larsen, Timothy, and Daniel J. Treier, eds. *The Cambridge Companion to Evangelical Theology*. Cambridge: Cambridge University Press, 2008.

Lawless, Elaine J. *God's Peculiar People: Women's Voices and Folk Tradition in a Pentecostal Church*. Lexington, KY: University Press of Kentucky, 1988.

Lee, Matthew T., and Amos Yong, eds. *The Science and Theology of Godly Love*. DeKalb, IL: Northern Illinois University Press, 2012.

Levering, Matthew. *Participatory Biblical Exegesis: A Theology of Biblical Interpretation*. Notre Dame, IN: University of Notre Dame Press, 2008.

Levison, John H. *Filled with the Spirit*. Grand Rapids: Eerdmans, 2009.

Lewis, Hannah. *Deaf Liberation Theology*. Aldershot, UK: Ashgate, 2007.

Lieu, Judith M. "Gnosticism and the Gospel of John." *The Expository Times* 90 (1979) 233–37.

Lindbeck, George A. *The Nature of Doctrine: Religion and Theology in a Postliberal Age*. Philadelphia: Westminster, 1984.

Loder, James E., and W. Jim Neidhardt. *The Knight's Move: The Relational Logic of the Spirit in Theology and Science*. Colorado Springs: Helmers & Howard, 1992.

Löfstedt, Torsten. "Gender Roles among Russian and Belarusian Pentecostals." Paper presented to the Sixth International and Multidisciplinary Conference of the European Research Network on Global Pentecostalism (GloPent), Uppsala University, Uppsala, Sweden, 2011.

Lohfink, Gerhard. *The Conversion of St. Paul: Narrative and History in Acts*. Translated by Bruce J. Malina. Chicago: Franciscan Herald, 1976.

Losie, Lynn Allan. "Paul's Speech on the Areopagus: A Model of Cross-cultural Evangelism." In *Mission in Acts: Ancient Narratives in Contemporary Context*, edited by Robert L. Gallagher and Paul Hertig, 221–38. American Society of Missiology 34. Maryknoll, NY: Orbis, 2004.

Lounela, Jaako. *Mission and Development: Finnish Pentecostal, Lutheran and Orthodox Mission Agencies in Development Work in Kenya 1948–1989*. Abo: Abo Akademi University Press, 2007.

Lovett, Leonard. "Liberation: A Dual-Edged Sword." *Pneuma: The Journal of the Society for Pentecostal Studies* 9.2 (1987) 155–71.

Lowther, Roland J. *Spirit and Life: The Practice of Living by the Spirit*. Milton Keynes, UK: Paternoster, 2016.

Macchia, Frank D. "Babel and the Tongues of Pentecost—Reversal or Fulfilment? A Theological Perspective." In *Speaking in Tongues: Multi-Disciplinary Perspectives*, edited by Mark J. Cartledge, 34–51. Eugene, OR: Wipf & Stock, 2012.

———. *Baptized in the Spirit: A Global Pentecostal Theology*. Grand Rapids: Zondervan, 2006.

———. *Justified in the Spirit: Creation, Redemption, and the Triune God*. Pentecostal Manifestos series. Grand Rapids: Eerdmans, 2010.

Maccini, Robert Gordon. "A Reassessment of the Woman at the Well in John 4 in Light of the Samaritan Context." *Journal for the Study of the New Testament* 53 (1994) 35–46.

Machado, Maria das Dores Campos. "Family, Sexuality, and Family Planning: A Comparative Study of Pentecostals and Charismatics in Rio de Janiero." In *More than Opium: An Anthropological Approach to Latin American and Caribbean Pentecostal Praxis*, edited by Barbara Boudewijnse et al., 169–202. Studies in Evangelicalism 14. Lanham, MD: Scarecrow, 1998.

Mackinnon, Edward. "Complementarity." In *Religion and Science: History, Method, Dialogue*, edited by W. Mark Richardson and Wesley J. Wildman, 255–70. London: Routledge, 1996.

Madueme, Hans, and Micheal Reeves, eds. *Adam, the Fall, and Original Sin: Theological, Biblical, and Scientific Perspectives*. Grand Rapids, MI: Baker Academic, 2014.

Malina, Bruce J. *Social-Science Commentary on the Synoptic Gospels*. Minneapolis: Fortress, 2003.

Malina, Bruce J., and Richard L. Rohrbaugh. *Social-Science Commentary on the Gospel of John*. Minneapolis: Fortress, 1998.

Manriquez, Samuel Palma. "Religion of the People and Evangelism: A Pentecostal Perspective." *International Review of Mission* 82.327 (1993) 365–74.

Marino, Bruce R. "The Origin, Nature, and Consequences of Sin." In *Systematic Theology*, edited by Stanley M. Horton, 255–90. Rev. ed. Springfield, MO: Logion, 1995.

Martin, Lee Roy. "'Oh Give Thanks to the Lord for He Is Good': Affective Hermeneutics, Psalm 107, and Pentecostal Spirituality." *Pneuma: The Journal of the Society for Pentecostal Studies* 36 (2014) 1–24.

———. "Psalm 63 and Pentecostal Spirituality: An Exercise in Affective Hermeneutics." In *Pentecostal Hermeneutics: A Reader*, edited by Lee Roy Martin. Leiden: Brill, 2013.

———. "Rhetorical Criticism and the Affective Dimension of the Biblical Text." *Journal for Semitics* 23 (2014) 339–53.

———. *The Unheard Voice of God: A Pentecostal Hearing of the Book of Judges.* Journal of Pentecostal Theology Supplement series 32. Blandford Forum, UK: Deo, 2008.

Martin, Lee Roy, ed. *Pentecostal Hermeneutics: A Reader.* Leiden: Brill, 2013.

Martins, Andrea Damacena, and Lucia Pedrosa de Pádua. "The Option for the Poor and Pentecostalism in Brazil." *Exchange* 31.2 (2002) 136–56.

Masenya, Madipoane (ngwana' Mphahlelej). "The Bible and Prophecy in African-South African Pentecostal Churches." *Missionalia* 33.1 (2005) 35–45.

———. "Foreign on Own Home Front? Ruminations from an African-South African Pentecostal Biblical Scholar." In *Global Renewal Christianity: Spirit-Empowered Movements Past, Present, and Future*, vol. III: *Africa*, edited by Vinson Synan et al., 380–94. Lake Mary, FL: Charisma House, 2016.

Matson, David Lertis. *Household Conversion Narratives in Acts: Pattern and Interpretation.* Journal for the Study of the New Testament Supplement Series 123. Sheffield: Sheffield Academic Press, 1996.

Matthews, Steven. "Reading the Two Books with Francis Bacon: Interpreting God's Will and Power." In *The Word and the World: Biblical Exegesis and Early Modern Science*, edited by Kevin Killeen and Peter J. Forshaw, 61–77. New York: Palgrave Macmillan, 2007.

Maynard-Reid, Pedrito U. *Complete Evangelism: The Luke-Acts Model.* Waterloo, ON: Herald, 1997.

McCall, Bradford. "A Contemporary Reappropriation of Baconian Common Sense Realism in Renewal Hermeneutics." *Pneuma: The Journal of the Society for Pentecostal Studies* 32 (2010) 223–40.

McCarthy, David M. *Sex and Love in the Home: A Theology of the Household.* 2d ed. London: SCM, 2004.

McDonnell, Killian, ed. *Toward a New Pentecost for a New Evangelization: Malines Document I.* 2nd ed. Collegeville, MN: Liturgical, 1993.

McGee, Gary B. *Miracles, Missions, and American Pentecostalism.* American Society of Missiology series 45. Maryknoll, NY: Orbis, 2010.

McGee, Gary B., ed. *Initial Evidence: Historical and Biblical Perspectives on the Pentecostal Doctrine of Spirit Baptism.* Peabody, MA: Hendrickson, 1991.

McGlasson, Paul C. *Another Gospel: A Confrontation with Liberation Theology.* Grand Rapids: Baker, 1994.

McGrath, Alister E. *Science and Religion: An Introduction.* Oxford: Blackwell, 2010.

McNamee, Mike. *The Ethics of Sports: A Reader.* London: Routledge, 2010.

McQueen, Larry R. *Joel and the Spirit: The Cry of a Prophetic Hermeneutic.* Journal of Pentecostal Theology Supplement Series 8. Sheffield: Sheffield Academic Press, 1996.

Medina, Néstor. *Mestizaje: Remapping Race, Culture, and Faith in Latina/o Catholicism.* Maryknoll, NY: Orbis, 2009.

———. "Orality and Context in a Hermeneutical Key: Toward a Latina/o-Canadian Pentecostal Life-Narrative Hermeneutics." *PentecoStudies: An Interdisciplinary Journal for Research on the Pentecostal and Charismatic Movement* 14.1 (2015) 97–123.

Medina, Néstor, and Sammy Alfaro, eds. *Pentecostals and Charismatics in Latin America and Latino Communities*. CHARIS: Christianity and Renewal—Interdisciplinary Studies series. New York: Palgrave Macmillan, 2015.

Meek, James A. *The Gentile Mission in Old Testament Citations in Acts: Text, Hermeneutic, and Purpose*. New York: T & T Clark, 2008.

Meeks, Wayne A. "The Man from Heaven in Johannine Sectarianism." *Journal of Biblical Literature* 91.1 (1972) 44–72.

Melander, Veronica. "'New' Pentecostalism Challenges 'Old' Liberation Theology." *Svensk missionstidskrift* 87.3 (1999) 341–57.

Melcher, Sarah. "'I Will Lead the Blind by the Road They Do Not Know': Disability in Prophetic Eschatology." Paper presented to the Biblical Scholarship and Disabilities Program Unit, Society of Biblical Literature (November 2004) 20–24. http://www.sbl-site.org/assets/pdfs/Melcher_Prophetic_Disability.pdf.

———. "Visualizing the Perfect Cult: The Priestly Rationale for Exclusion." In *Human Disability and the Service of God: Reassessing Religious Practice*, edited by Nancy L. Eiesland and Don E. Saliers, 55–71. Nashville: Abingdon, 1998.

Menuge, Angus J. L. "Interpreting the Book of Nature." *Perspectives on Science and Christian Faith* 55.2 (2003) 88–98.

Menzies, Robert P. "Complete Evangelism: A Review Article." *Journal of Pentecostal Theology* 13 (1998) 133–42.

Mercer, Joyce Ann. *Welcoming Children: A Practical Theology of Childhood*. St. Louis: Chalice, 2005.

Mews, Constant J. "The World as Text: The Bible and the Book of Nature in Twelfth-Century Theology." In *Scripture and Pluralism: Reading the Bible in the Religiously Plural Worlds of the Middle Ages and Renaissance*, edited by Thomas J. Heffernan and Thomas E. Burman, 95–122. Studies in the History of Christian Traditions 123. Leiden: Brill, 2005.

Michalko, Rod. *The Difference that Disability Makes*. Philadelphia: Temple University Press, 2002.

Miller, Donald E., and Tetsunao Yamamori. *Global Pentecostalism: The New Face of Christian Social Engagement*. Berkeley: University of California Press, 2007.

Miller, Ed L. "The True Light Which Illumines Every Person." In *Good News in History: Essays in Honor of Bo Reicke*, edited by Ed L. Miller, 63–82. Atlanta: Scholars, 1993.

Mitchell, B. K. (Bev). "Let There Be Life! Toward a Hermeneutic of Biological and Theological Integration." In *Constructive Pneumatological Hermeneutics in Pentecostal Christianity*, edited by L. William Oliverio Jr. and Kenneth J. Archer, 297-314. CHARIS: Christianity and Renewal—Interdisciplinary Studies series. New York: Palgrave Macmillan, 2016.

Mitchell, David T., and Sharon Snyder. "'Jesus Throws Everything Off Balance': Disability and Redemption in Biblical Literature." In *This Abled Body: Rethinking Disabilities in Biblical Studies*, edited by Hector Avalos et al., 173–83. Atlanta: Society of Biblical Literature, 2007.

Mitchell, David T., and Sharon L. Snyder, eds. *The Body and Physical Difference: Discourses of Disability*. Ann Arbor, MI: The University of Michigan Press, 1997.

Mittelstadt, Martin W. *Reading Luke-Acts in the Pentecostal Tradition*. Cleveland, TN: CPT, 2010.

———. *The Spirit and Suffering in Luke-Acts: Implications for a Pentecostal Pneumatology*. New York: T & T Clark, 2004.
Mittelstadt, Martin W., and Jeff Hittenberger. "Power and Powerlessness in Pentecostal Theology." *Pneuma: The Journal of the Society for Pentecostal Studies* 30.1 (2008) 137-45.
Moberly, R. W. L. *The Theology of the Book of Genesis*. Cambridge: Cambridge University Press, 2009.
Moede, Gerald F. "God's Power and Human Ability." *Ecumenical Review* 36.3 (1984) 290-98.
Moessner, David P. "The 'Script' of the Scriptures in Acts: Suffering as God's 'Plan' for the World for the 'Release' of Sins." In *History, Literature, and Society in the Book of Acts*, edited by Ben Witherington III, 218-50. Cambridge: Cambridge University Press, 1996.
Moon, Cyris H. S. *A Korean Minjung Theology: An Old Testament Perspective*. Maryknoll, NY: Orbis, and Hong Kong: Plough, 1985.
Moore, James F., et al. *Toward a Dialogical Community: A Post-Shoah Christian Theology*. Lanham, MD: University Press of America, 2004.
Moore, Rickie D. "Canon and Charisma in the Book of Deuteronomy." *Journal of Pentecostal Theology* 1 (1992) 75-92.
———. "Deuteronomy and the Fire of God: A Critical Charismatic Interpretation." *Journal of Pentecostal Theology* 7 (1995) 11-33.
———. *The Spirit of the Old Testament*. Journal of Pentecostal Theology Supplement Series 35. Blandford Forum, UK: Deo, 2011.
Moore, Stephen D. *Mark and Luke in Poststructuralist Perspective: Jesus Begins to Write*. New Haven, CT: Yale University Press, 1992.
Morris, Leon. *The Gospel according to John*. Grand Rapids: Eerdmans, 1971.
———. *Jesus is the Christ: Studies in the Theology of John*. Leicester, UK: Inter-Varsity, and Grand Rapids: Eerdmans, 1989.
Motyer, Stephen. *Your Father the Devil? A New Approach to John and "the Jews."* Carlisle, UK: Paternoster, 1997.
Moulaison, Jane Barter. *Lord, Giver of Life: Toward a Pneumatological Complement to George Lindbeck's Theory of Doctrine*. Editions SR 32. Toronto: Wilfred Laurier University Press, 2007.
Mowery, Robert L. "God the Father in Luke-Acts." In *New Views on Luke and Acts*, edited by Earl Richard, 124-32. Collegeville, MN: Liturgical, 1990.
Munyon, Timothy. "The Creation of the Universe and Humankind." In *Systematic Theology*, edited by Stanley M. Horton, 215-53. Rev. ed. Springfield, MO: Logion, 1995.
Murphy, George L. "Reading God's Two Books." *Perspectives on Science and Christian Faith* 58.1 (2006) 64-67.
Myers, William R. "Encouraging Youth to Receive the Baptism in the Holy Spirit." In *Conference on the Holy Spirit Digest: A Condensation of Plenary Sessions and Seminars of the Conference on the Holy Spirit in Springfield, Missouri, August 16-18, 1982*, edited by Gwen Jones, 180-84. Springfield, MO: Gospel, 1983.
Nadar, Sarojini. "'The Bible Says!' Feminism, Hermeneutics and Neo-Pentecostal Challenges." *Journal of Theology for Southern Africa* 134 (2009) 131-46.
Neitz, Mary J. "Family, State, and God: Ideologies of the Right-to-life Movement." *Sociological Analysis* 42.3 (Fall 1981) 265-76.

Nelson, Gertrud Mueller. "Christian Formation of Children: The Role of Ritual and Celebration." In *Liturgy and Spirituality in Context: Perspectives on Prayer and Culture*, edited by Eleanor Bernstein, 114–35. Collegeville, MN: Liturgical, 1990.

Neville, Robert. *Boston Confucianism: Portable Tradition in the Late Modern World*. Albany, NY: State University of New York Press, 2000.

———. *Ritual and Deference: Extending Chinese Philosophy in a Comparative Context*. Albany, NY: State University of New York Press, 2008.

Newbigin, Lesslie. *The Open Secret: An Introduction to the Theology of Mission*. Grand Rapids: Eerdmans, 1995.

Newman, Jay. *Competition in Religious Life*. Editions SR 11. Waterloo, ON: Wilfrid Laurier University Press, 1989.

Neyrey, Jerome H. "Honor and Shame: Loss of Wealth, Loss of Family, Loss of Honor—the Cultural Context of the Original Makarisms in Q." In *The Social World of the New Testament*, edited by Jerome H. Neyrey and Eric C. Stewart, 87–102. Peabody, MA: Hendrickson, 2008.

Ngong, David Tonghou. *The Holy Spirit and Salvation in African Christian Theology: Imagining a More Hopeful Future for Africa*. The Bible and Theology in Africa 8. New York: Peter Lang, 2010.

Nguyen, VanThanh. *Peter and Cornelius: A Story of Conversion and Mission*. Eugene, OR: Pickwick, 2012.

Nickelsburg, George W. E. "Revealed Wisdom as a Criterion for Inclusion and Exclusion: From Jewish Sectarianism to Early Christianity." In *"To See Ourselves as Others See Us": Christians, Jews, 'Others' in Late Antiquity*, edited by Jacob Neusner and Ernest S. Frerichs, 73–91. Chico, CA: Scholars, 1985.

Niditch, Susan. *Chaos to Cosmos: Studies in Biblical Patterns of Creation*. Scholars Press Studies in the Humanities 6. Chico, CA: Scholars, 1985.

Niebuhr, Reinhold. *Man's Nature and His Communities: Essays on the Dynamics and Enigmas of Man's Personal and Social Existence*. New York: Charles Scribner's Sons, 1965.

———. *Moral Man and Immoral Society: A Study in Ethics and Politics*. New York: Charles Scribner's Sons, 1932.

Nielsen, Kim. "Helen Keller and the Politics of Civic Fitness." In *The New Disability History: American Perspectives*, edited by Paul K. Longmore and Lauri Umansky, 268–90. London: New York University Press, 2001.

Noble, Tim. *The Poor in Liberation Theology: Pathway to God or Ideological Construct?* Sheffield, UK: Equinox, 2013.

Noel, Bradley Truman. *Pentecostal and Postmodern Hermeneutics: Comparisons and Contemporary Impact*. Eugene, OR: Wipf & Stock, 2010.

Nolan, Albert, and Richard F. Broderick. *"To Nourish Our Faith": The Theology of Liberation in Southern Africa*. Hilton, S. Africa: Order of Preachers, 1987.

Nolivos, Eloy. "Pentecostalism's Theological Reconstruction of the Identity of the Latin American Family." In *Pentecostal Power: Expressions, Impact and Faith of Latin American Pentecostalism*, edited by Calvin L. Smith, 205–26. Global Pentecostal & Charismatic Studies 6. Leiden: Brill, 2011.

Nolivos, Virginia Trevino. "A Pentecostal Paradigm for the Latin American Family: An Instrument of Transformation." *Cyberjournal for Pentecostal-Charismatic Research* 11 (2002). http://www.pctii.org/cyberj/cyber11.html.

Novak, David. "From Supersessionism to Parallelism in Jewish-Christian Dialogue." In *Jews and Christians: People of God*, edited by Carl E. Braaten and Robert W. Jenson, 95–113. Grand Rapids: Eerdmans, 2003.

Núñez C., Emilio A. *Liberation Theology*. Translated by Paul E. Sywulka. Chicago: Moody, 1985.

O'Brien, Joan, and Wilfred Major. *In the Beginning: Creation Myths from Ancient Mesopotamia, Israel and Greece*. American Academy of Religion Aid for the Study of Religion 11. Chico, CA: Scholars, 1982.

O'Connor, James T. *Liberation: Towards a Theology for the Church in the World, according to the Second General Conference of Latin American Bishops at Medellín, 1968*. Rome: Officium Libri Catholici, 1972.

O'Day, Gail. "Johannine Theology as Sectarian Theology." In *What is John?, Vol. 1, Readers and Readings of the Fourth Gospel*, edited by Fernando F. Segovia, 199–203. Atlanta: Scholars, 1996.

Odegard, Holtan P. *Sin and Science: Reinhold Niebuhr as Political Theologian*. Yellow Springs, OH: Antioch, 1956.

O'Keefe, Cathy. "Leisure at L'Arche: Communities of Faith for Persons with Developmental Disabilities." In *Christianity and Leisure: Issues in a Pluralistic Society*, edited by Paul Heintzman, et al., 109–16. Sioux Center, IA.: Dordt College, 2005.

O'Keefe, Mark. *What Are They Saying about Social Sin?* Mahwah, NJ: Paulist, 1990.

Okpewho, Isidore. *African Oral Literature: Backgrounds, Character, and Continuity*. Bloomington: Indiana University Press, 1992.

Oliverio, L. William, Jr. *Theological Hermeneutics in the Classical Pentecostal Tradition: A Typological Account*. Global Pentecostal and Charismatic Studies 12. Leiden: Brill, 2012.

Oliverio, L. William, Jr., and Kenneth J. Archer, eds. *Constructive Pneumatological Hermeneutics in Pentecostal Christianity*. CHARIS: Christianity and Renewal—Interdisciplinary Studies series. New York: Palgrave Macmillan, 2016.

Olwa, Alfred. "Pentecostalism in Tanzania and Uganda: A Historical and Theological Perspective." In *Global Renewal Christianity: Spirit-Empowered Movements Past, Present, and Future*, vol. III: *Africa*, edited by Vinson Synan, et al., 166–85. Lake Mary, FL: Charisma House, 2016.

Olyan, Saul. *Disability in the Hebrew Bible: Interpreting Mental and Physical Differences*. Cambridge: Cambridge University Press, 2008.

Omenyo, Cephas N. *Pentecost Outside Pentecostalism: A study of the Development of Charismatic Renewal in the Mainline Church in Ghana*. Zoetermeer, The Netherlands: Boekencentrum, 2002.

Omenyo, Cephas N., and Wonderful Adjei Arthur. "The Bible Says! Neo-Prophetic Hermeneutics in Africa." *Studies in World Christianity* 19.1 (2013) 50–70.

O'Neill, Kevin L. *City of God: Christian Citizenship in Postwar Guatemala*. Berkeley: The University of California Press, 2009.

Ong, Walter J. *Orality and Literacy: The Technologizing of the Word*. New York: Routledge, 1982.

———. *The Presence of the Word: Some Prolegomena for Cultural and Religious History*. New Haven, CT: Yale University Press, 1967.

Onyinah, Poku. "New Ways of Doing Evangelism." *International Review of Mission* 103.1 (2014) 121–28.

Ouellet, Marc Cardinal. *Divine Likeness: Toward a Trinitarian Anthropology of the Family.* Translated by Phillip Milligan and Linda M. Cicone. Grand Rapids: Eerdmans, 2006.

Owens, Virginia Stem. "On Praising God with Our Senses." In *The Christian Imagination: Essays on the Literature and the Arts,* edited by Leland Ryken, 375–82. Grand Rapids: Baker, 1981.

Painter, John. "The Quotation of Scripture and Unbelief in John 12.36b–43." In *The Gospels and the Scriptures of Israel,* edited by Craig A. Evans and W. Richard Stegner, 429–58. JSNT Sup 104; Studies in Scripture in Early Judaism and Christianity 3. Sheffield: Sheffield Academic Press, 1994.

Pais, Janet. *Suffer the Children: A Theology of Liberation by a Victim of Child Abuse.* Mahwah, NJ: Paulist, 1991.

Pakenham, Thomas. *The Scramble for Africa: White Man's Conquest of the Dark Continent from 1876 to 1912.* New York: Avon, 1992.

Palmer, Phoebe. *The Promise of the Father.* New York: Garland, 1985.

Parsons, Mikeal C. *Body and Character in Luke and Acts: The Subversion of Physiognomy in Early Christianity.* Grand Rapids: Baker Academic, 2006.

Pecknold, C. C. *Transforming Postliberal Theology: George Lindbeck, Pragmatism and Scripture.* New York: Bloomsbury T & T Clark, 2005.

Penney, John Michael. *The Missionary Emphasis of Lukan Pneumatology.* Journal of Pentecostal Theology Supplement Series 12. Sheffield, UK: Sheffield Academic Press, 1997.

Peters, Ted. *Sin: Radical Evil in Soul and Society.* Grand Rapids: Eerdmans, 1994.

Petersen, Norman R. *The Gospel of John and the Sociology of Light: Language and Characterization in the Fourth Gospel.* Valley Forge, PA: Trinity, 1993.

Petrella, Ivan. *Beyond Liberation Theology: A Polemic.* London: SCM, 2008.

———. *The Future of Liberation Theology.* Aldershot, UK: Ashgate, 2004.

———. "Liberation Theology: A Programmatic Statement." In *Latin American Liberation Theology: The Next Generation,* edited by Ivan Petrella, 147–72. Maryknoll, NY: Orbis, 2005.

Pfitzner, V. C. "Martyr and Hero: The Origin and Development of a Tradition in the Early Christian Martyr—Acts." *Lutheran Theological Journal* 15.1–2 (1981) 9–17.

———. *Paul and the Agon Motif: Traditional Athletic Imagery in the Pauline Literature.* Supplements to Novum Testamentum 16. Leiden: Brill, 1967.

———. "Was St Paul a Sports Enthusiast? Reality and Rhetoric in Pauline Athletic Metaphors." In *Sports and Christianity: Historical and Contemporary Perspectives,* edited by Nick J. Watson and Andrew Parker, 89–111. London: Routledge, 2013.

———. "We are the Champions! Origins and Developments of the Image of God's Athletes." In *Sport and Spirituality: An Exercise in Everyday Theology,* edited by Gordon Preece and Rob Hess, 49–64. Adelaide, Australia: ATF, 2007.

Philip, William J. U. "The Light of Glory: An Exposition of the Prologue of John's Gospel." *Churchman* 116.2 (2002) 113–26.

Phillips, Thomas E. *Reading Issues of Wealth and Poverty in Luke-Acts.* Studies in Bible and Early Christianity 48. Lewiston: Edwin Mellen, 2001.

Pickard, Stephen K. *Liberating Evangelism: Gospel, Theology, and the Dynamics of Communication.* Harrisburg, PA: Trinity, 1998.

Pilgrim, Walter E. *Good News to the Poor: Poverty and Wealth in Luke-Acts.* Minneapolis: Augsburg Fortress, 1981.

Pinnock, Clark H. *Flame of Love: A Theology of the Holy Spirit*. Downers Grove, IL: InterVarsity, 1996.

Plantinga, Richard J. *Christianity and Religious Plurality: Classic and Contemporary Readings*. Oxford: Blackwell, 1999.

Poirier, John C. "Narrative Theology and Pentecostal Commitments." *Journal of Pentecostal Theology* 16.2 (2008) 69–85.

Poirier, John C., and B. Scott Lewis. "Pentecostal and Postmodernist Hermeneutics: A Critique of Three Conceits." *Journal of Pentecostal Theology* 15.1 (2006) 3–21.

Pope-Levison, Priscilla. *Evangelization from a Liberation Perspective*. American University Studies Series VII, Theology and Religion 69. New York: Peter Lang, 1991.

Post, Stephen. G. *More Lasting Unions: Christianity, the Family, and Society*. Grand Rapids, MI: Eerdmans, 2000.

Prior, Michael, CM. *Jesus the Liberator: Nazareth Liberation Theology (Luke 4:16–30)*. New York: Continuum, 1995.

Privett, Peter. "Play." In *Through the Eyes of a Child: New Insights in Theology from a Child's Perspective*, edited by Anne Richards and Peter Privett, 101–24. London: Church, 2009.

Pulikottil, Paulson. "Ramankutty Paul: A Dalit Contribution to Pentecostalism." In *Asian and Pentecostal: The Charismatic Face of Christianity in Asia*, edited by Allan Anderson and Edmond Tang, 245–57. London: Regnum, and Baguio City, Philippines: Asia Pacific Theological Seminary, 2005.

Purves, Alan C. *The Web of Text and the Web of God: An Essay on the Third Information Transformation*. London: Guilford, 1998.

Putney, Clifford. *Muscular Christianity: Manhood and Sports in Protestant America, 1880–1920*. Cambridge, MA: Harvard University Press, 2001.

Quigley, Thomas E., ed. *Freedom and Unfreedom in the Americas: Towards a Theology of Liberation*. New York: Zale S. Koff, and Latin American Bureau USCC, 1971.

Race, Alan. *Christians and Religious Pluralism: Patterns in the Christian Theology of Religions*. Maryknoll, NY: Orbis, 1982.

Rainer, Thom S. "Church Growth and Evangelism in the Book of Acts." *Criswell Theological Review* 5.1 (1990) 57–68.

Ramsey, W. M. *Luke the Physician, and Other Studies in the History of Religion*. Grand Rapids, MI: Baker, 1956.

Rapaka, Yabbaju (Jabez). *Dalit Pentecostalism: A Study of the Indian Pentecostal Church of God*. Lexington, KY: Emeth, 2013.

Reid, Robert G. "Spirit-Empowerment as Resistance Discourse: An Imperial-Critical Reading of Acts 2." In *Trajectories in the Book of Acts: Essays in Honor of John Wesley Wyckoff*, edited by Paul Alexander et al., 21–45. Eugene, OR: Wipf & Stock, 2010.

Reinders, Hans S. *Receiving the Gift of Friendship: Profound Disability, Theological Anthropology, and Ethics*. Grand Rapids, MI: Eerdmans, 2008.

Rensberger, David. "Sectarianism and Theological Interpretation in John." In *What is John?*, vol. 2, *Literary and Social Readings of the Fourth Gospel*, edited by Fernando F. Segovia, 139–56. Atlanta: Scholars, 1998.

Reynolds, Thomas E. *Vulnerable Communion: A Theology of Disability and Hospitality*. Grand Rapids, MI: Brazos, 2008.

Rice, John R. *The Home: Courtship, Marriage and Children*. London: Garland, 1988.

Richie, Tony. "A Discerning Theology of Christian Evangelism Suitable for a Multi-faith World." *Cyberjournal for Pentecostal-Charismatic Research* 23 (2016) http://www.pctii.org/cyberj/cyber23.html.

———. "On 'Christian Witness in a Multi-religious World: Recommendations for Conduct': A Pentecostal Perspective on Evangelism and Religious Pluralism." *One in Christ* 45.2 (2011) 212–22.

Ricoeur, Paul. *The Conflict of Interpretations: Essays in Hermeneutics*, edited by Don Ihde. Evanston , IL: Northwestern University Press, 1974.

Ringe, Sharon H. *Jesus, Liberation, and the Biblical Jubilee: Images for Ethics and Christology*. Overtures in Biblical Theology 19. Philadelphia: Fortress, 1985.

Ringwald, A. "Fight, Prize, Triumph, Victory: ἀγών." In *The New International Dictionary of New Testament Theology*, edited by C. Brown, 644–48. Vol. I. Grand Rapids, MI: Zondervan, 1979.

Roberts, Michael. *Evangelicals and Science*. Westport, CT: Greenwood, 2008.

Robinson, Anthony B., and Robert W. Wall. *Called to Be Church: The Book of Acts for a New Day*. Grand Rapids, MI: Eerdmans, 2006.

Robinson, Thomas A., and Lanette D. Ruff. *Out of the Mouth of Babes: Girl Evangelists in the Flapper Era*. Oxford: Oxford University Press, 2011.

Rodriguez, Darío López. *The Liberating Mission of Jesus: The Message of the Gospel of Luke*. Translated by Stefanie E. Israel and Richard E. Waldrop. Eugene, OR: Pickwick, 2012.

Rodríguez, Rubén Rosario. *Racism and God-Talk: A Latino/a Perspective*. New York: New York University Press, 2008.

Rogers, Eugene F., Jr. *After the Spirit: A Constructive Pneumatology from Resources outside the Modern West*. Grand Rapids: Eerdmans, 2005.

Rogers, Glenn. *Holistic Ministry and Cross-cultural Mission in Luke-Acts*. NP: Mission and Ministry Resources, 2003.

Rogers, Linda J., and Beth Blue Swadener, eds. *Semiotics and Dis/ability: Interrogating Categories of Difference*. Albany, NY: State University of New York Press, 2001.

Rostrup, Barbara J. "Teaching Children about the Baptism in the Holy Spirit." In *Conference on the Holy Spirit Digest: A Condensation of Plenary Sessions and Seminars of the Conference on the Holy Spirit in Springfield, Missouri, August 16–18, 1982*, edited by Gwen Jones, 174–79. Springfield, MO: Gospel, 1983.

Roth, S. John. *The Blind, the Lame, and the Poor: Character Types in Luke-Acts*. Sheffield: Sheffield Academic Press, 1997.

Rouse, Christopher D. "Scripture and the Disabled: Redeeming Mephibosheth's Identity." *Journal of Pentecostal Theology* 17.2 (2008) 183–99.

Rowland, Christopher. "Reading Scripture Eschatologically (2)." In *Reading Texts, Seeking Wisdom: Scripture and Theology*, edited by David F. Ford and Graham Stanton, 257–70. Grand Rapids: Eerdmans, 2003.

Rubio, Julie H. *A Christian Theology of Marriage and Family*. New York: Paulist, 2003.

Ruether, Rosemary Radford. *Faith and Fratricide: The Theological Roots of Anti-Semitism*. New York: Crossroad, 1974.

Russell, Robert John. *Time in Eternity: Pannenberg, Physics, and Eschatology in Creative Mutual Interaction*. Notre Dame, IN: Notre Dame University Press, 2012.

Ryan, Patrick, ed. *The Model of "Church-as-Family": Meeting the African Challenge—Proceedings of the Fourth Interdisciplinary Session of the Faculty of Theology and* the Department of Religious Studies, Catholic University of Eastern Africa, Nairobi. Nairobi: The Catholic University of Eastern Africa, 1999.

Sabourin, Leopold. "Evangelize the Poor (Lk 4:18)." *Religious Studies and Theology* 1 (1981) 101–9.

Salier, Bill. "What's in a World? Κόσμος in the Prologue of John's Gospel." *The Reformed Theological Review* 56.3 (1997) 106–17.

Sanders, Jack T. *Schismatics, Sectarians, Dissidents, Deviants: The First One Hundred Years of Jewish-Christian Relations*. Valley Forge, PA: Trinity, 1993.

Sanders, James A. "Sins, Debts, and Jubilee Release." In *Luke and Scripture: The Function of Sacred Tradition in Luke-Acts*, edited by Craig A. Evans and James A. Sanders, 84–92. Eugene, OR: Wipf & Stock, 2001.

Sanneh, Lamin. *Translating the Message: The Missionary Impact on Culture*. Maryknoll, NY: Orbis, 1989.

Santiago-Vendrell, Angel. "The Gospel in a New Tune! The Appropriation of Ada María Isasi-Díaz's 'Historical Project' by Latina Pentecostals in the Formulation of a Theology of Evangelism." *Feminist Theology* 19.1 (2010) 73–85.

———. "Not by Words Alone! Mujerista and Pentecostal Missiologies of Liberation from the Latina/o Margins." *Journal of Pentecostal Theology* 18.2 (2009) 285–300.

Sawyer, Thomas H., Kimberly H. Bodey, and Lawrence W. Judge. *Sport Governance and Policy Development: An Ethical Approach to Managing Sport in the 21st Century*. Champaign, IL: Sagamore, 2008.

Schaull, Richard, and Waldo Cesar. *Pentecostalism and the Future of the Christian Churches: Promises, Limitations, Challenges*. Grand Rapids: Eerdmans, 2000.

Schipper, Jeremy. *Disability Studies and the Hebrew Bible: Figuring Mephibosheth in the David Story*. New York: T & T Clark, 2006.

Schnackenburg, Rudolf. *The Gospel according to St. John*. Translated by Kevin Smyth. 3 vols. New York: Crossroad, 1982.

Schnelle, Udo. *Antidocetic Christology in the Gospel of John*. Translated by Linda M. Maloney. Minneapolis: Fortress, 1992.

Scroggs, Robin. "The Earliest Christian Communities as Sectarian Movement." In *Christianity, Judaism, and Other Greco-Roman Cultus: Studies for Morton Smith at Sixty*, vol. 2, *Early Christianity*, edited by Jacob Neusner, 1–23. Leiden: E. J. Brill, 1975.

Seal, David. "Sensitivity to Aural Elements of the Text: Some Acoustical Elements in Revelation." *Journal of Biblical and Pneumatological Research* 3 (2011) 38–52.

Seely, Paul H. "The First Four Days of Genesis in Concordist Theory and in Biblical Context." *Perspective on Science and Christian Faith* 49 (1997) 85–95.

Seesengood, Robert P. *Competing Identities: The Athlete and the Gladiator in Early Christian Literature*. Library of New Testament Studies 346. New York: Continuum, 2006.

Segovia, Fernando F. "Inclusion and Exclusion in John 17: An Intercultural Reading." In *What is John?*, vol. 2, *Literary and Social Readings of the Fourth Gospel*, edited by Fernando F. Segovia, 183–210. Atlanta: Scholars, 1998.

———. "The Love and Hatred of Jesus and Johannine Sectarianism." *Catholic Biblical Quarterly* 43.2 (1981) 258–72.

Sepúlveda, Juan. "Pentecostalism and Liberation Theology: Two Manifestations of the Work of the Holy Spirit for the Renewal of the Church." In *All Together in One Place: Theological Papers from the Brighton Conference on World Evangelization*, edited by Harold D. Hunter and Peter D. Hocken, 51–64. Journal of Pentecostal Theology Supplement series 4. Sheffield: Sheffield Academic Press, 1993.

Sevenster, J. N. *The Roots of Pagan Anti-Semitism in the Ancient World.* Supplements to Novum Testamentum 41. Leiden: E. J. Brill, 1975.

Shannahan, Chris. *Voices from the Borderland: Re-imagining Cross-Cultural Urban Theology in the Twenty-First Century.* London: Routledge, 2014.

Shelton, James B. *Mighty in Word and Deed: The Role of the Holy Spirit in Luke-Acts.* Peabody, MA: Hendrickson, 1991.

Sheppard, Gerald T. "Pentecostalism and the Hermeneutics of Dispensationalism: Anatomy of an Uneasy Relationship." *Pneuma: The Journal of the Society for Pentecostal Studies* 6.2 (1984) 5–34.

Shibley, David. *A Force in the Earth: The Move of the Holy Spirit in World Evangelization.* Lake Mary, FL: Creation House, 1997.

Shorter, Aylward, et al. *Theology of the Church as Family of God.* Tangaza Occasional Papers 3. Nairobi: Paulines Africa, 1997.

Sloan, Robert Bryan. *The Favorable Year of the Lord: A Study of Jubilary Theology in the Gospel of Luke.* Austin, TX: Schola, 1977.

Smith, Aaron T. *A Theology of the Third Article: Karl Barth and the Spirit of the Word.* Minneapolis: Fortress, 2014.

Smith, James K. A. *The Fall of Interpretation: Philosophical Foundations for a Creational Hermeneutic.* Downers Grove, IL: InterVarsity, 2000.

———. *Imagining the Kingdom: How Worship Works.* Grand Rapids: Baker Academic, 2013.

———. *Thinking in Tongues: Pentecostal Contributions to Christian Philosophy.* Pentecostal Manifestos series. Grand Rapids: Eerdmans, 2010.

Snyder, Sharon L., Brenda L. Brueggemann, and Rosemarie Garland-Thomson, eds. *Disability Studies: Enabling the Humanities.* New York: Modern Language Association of America, 2002.

Solivan, Samuel. *Spirit, Pathos and Liberation: Toward an Hispanic Pentecostal Theology.* Journal of Pentecostal Theology Supplement Series 14. Sheffield: Sheffield Academic Press, 1998.

Song, C. S. *Tell Us Our Names: Story Theology from an Asian Perspective.* Maryknoll, NY: Orbis, 1984.

Soothill, Jane E. *Gender, Social Change and Spiritual Power: Charismatic Christianity in Ghana.* Leiden: Brill, 2007.

Spawn, Kevin L., and Archie T. Wright, eds. *Spirit and Scripture: Exploring a Pneumatic Hermeneutic.* London: T & T Clark, 2012.

Spinks, D. Christopher. *The Bible and the Crisis of Meaning: Debates on the Theological Interpretation of Scripture.* New York: T & T Clark, 2007.

Spittler, R. S. "Glossolalia." In *The New International Dictionary of Pentecostal and Charismatic Movements*, edited by Stanley M. Burgess and Eduard M. Van Der Maas, 670–76. Grand Rapids: Zondervan, 2002.

Sri, Edward. "Release from the Debt of Sin: Jesus' Jubilee Mission in the Gospel of Luke." *Nova et Vetera* 9.1 (2011) 183–94.

Stackhouse, Max. L. *Covenant and Commitments: Faith, Family, and Economic Life.* Louisville: Westminster John Knox, 1997.

Staley, Jeffrey L. "Stumbling in the Dark, Reaching for the Light: Reading Character in John 5 and 9." *Semeia* 53 (1991) 55–80.

Stanford, Matthew S. *The Biology of Sin: Grace, Hope and Healing for Those Who Feel Trapped*. Downers Grove, IL: Biblical, 2010.
Steinmetz, David C. "The Superiority of Pre-critical Exegesis." In *The Theological Interpretation of Scripture: Classic and Contemporary Readings*, edited by Stephen E. Fowl, 26–38. Cambridge, MA: Blackwell, 1997.
Stephen, M. *A Christian Theology in the Indian Context*. Delhi: ISPCK, 2001.
Stephenson, Christopher A. "The Rule of Spirituality and the Rule of Doctrine: A Necessary Relationship in Theological Method." *Journal of Pentecostal Theology* 15.1 (2006) 83–105.
Stocchino, Gianni. "Full Integration in Italian School during Physical Education and Sports Activities." In *Sport for Persons with a Disability*, edited by Colin Higgs and Yves Vanlandewijck, 105–26. Perspectives: The Multidisciplinary Series of Physical Education and Sport Science 7. Berlin: International Council of Sport Science and Physical Education, 2007.
Stronstad, Roger. *The Charismatic Theology of St. Luke*. Peabody, MA: Hendrickson, 1984.
———. *The Prophethood of All Believers: A Study in Luke's Charismatic Theology*. Sheffield: Sheffield Academic Press, 1999.
———. *Spirit, Scripture, and Theology: A Pentecostal Perspective*. Baguio City, Philippines: Asia Pacific Theological Seminary, 1995.
Studebaker, Steven M. *From Pentecost to the Triune God: A Pentecostal Trinitarian Theology*. Pentecostal Manifestos series. Grand Rapids: Eerdmans, 2012.
———. *A Pentecostal Political Theology for American Renewal: Spirit of the Kingdoms, Citizens of the Cities*. CHARIS: Christianity and Renewal—Interdisciplinary Studies series. New York: Palgrave Macmillan, 2016.
Sung, Bae Hyoen. "Response." In *Pentecostals after a Century: Global Perspectives on a Movement in Transition*, edited by Allan H. Anderson and Walter J. Hollenweger, 161–63. Journal of Pentecostal Theology Supplement series 15. Sheffield: Sheffield Academic Press, 1999.
Synan, Vinson, and Amos Yong, eds. *Global Renewal Christianity: Spirit-Empowered Movements Past, Present, and Future*, vol. I, *Asia and Oceania*. Lake Mary, FL: Charisma House, 2015.
———, eds. *Global Renewal Christianity: Spirit-Empowered Movements Past, Present, and Future*, Vol. IV, *Europe and North America*. Lake Mary, FL: Charisma House, 2016.
———, and J. Kwabena Asamoah-Gyadu, eds. *Global Renewal Christianity: Spirit-Empowered Movements Past, Present, and Future*, vol. III: *Africa*. Lake Mary, FL: Charisma House, 2016.
Tanner, Kathryn. "Workings of the Spirit: Simplicity or Complexity?" In *The Work of the Spirit: Pneumatology and Pentecostalism*, edited by Michael Welker, 87–105. Grand Rapids: Eerdmans, 2006.
Tanzella-Nitti, G. "The Two Books Prior to the Scientific Revolution." *Perspectives on Science and Christian Faith* 57.3 (2005) 235–48.
Tarr, Del. *Double Image: Biblical Insights from African Parables*. Mahwah, NJ: Paulist, 1994.
Teng, Philip. "Evangelism and the Teaching of Acts." In *One Race, One Gospel, One Task: World Congress on Evangelism, Berlin 1966, Official References Volumes*, edited by

Carl F. H. Henry and W. Stanley Mooneyham, 17–19. Vol. II. Minneapolis: World Wide, 1967.

Tennison, D. Allen. "Charismatic Biblical Interpretation." In *Dictionary for Theological Interpretation of the Bible*, edited by Kevin J. Vanhoozer, 106–109. Grand Rapids: Baker Academic, 2005.

Thatcher, Adrian. "Beginning Again with Jesus," in *Children's Voices: Children's Perspectives in Ethics, Theology and Religious Education*, edited by Annemie Dillen and Didier Pollefeyt, 137–61. Bibliotheca Ephemeridum Theologicarum Lovaniensium 230. Leuven: Uitgeverij Peeters, 2010.

———. *Theology and Families*. Malden, MA: Blackwell, 2007.

Thiselton, Anthony C. *The Two Horizons: New Testament Hermeneutics and Philosophical Description*. Grand Rapids, MI: Eerdmans, 1980.

Thomas, John Christopher. *The Spirit of the New Testament*. Blandford Forum, UK: Deo, 2005.

———. "Women, Pentecostals, and the Bible: An Experiment in Pentecostal Hermeneutics." *Journal of Pentecostal Theology* 2.5 (1994) 41–56.

Thomas, John Christopher, and Frank D. Macchia. *Revelation*, The Two Horizons New Testament Commentary. Grand Rapids: Eerdmans, 2016.

Thomas, Nigel, and Andy Smith. *Disability, Sport and Society: An Introduction*. New York: Routledge, 2009.

Thomas, Pradip Ninan. *Strong Religion, Zealous Media: Christian Fundamentalism and Communication in India*. Los Angeles: SAGE, 2008.

Thomas, V. V. *Dalit Pentecostalism: Spirituality of the Empowered Poor*. Bangalore: Asian Trading, 2008.

Thompson, Marianne M. *The Promise of the Father: Jesus and God in the New Testament*. Lousville: Westminster John Knox, 2000.

Thorsen, Jakob Egeris. *Charismatic Practice and Catholic Parish Life: The Incipient Pentecostalization of the Church in Guatemala and Latin America*. Global Pentecostal and Charismatic Studies 17. Leiden: Brill, 2015.

Thorson, Walter R. " Hermeneutics for Reading the Book of Nature: A Response to Angus Menuge." *Perspectives on Science and Christian Faith* 55.2 (2003) 99–101.

Thurston, Bonnie Bowman. "The Gospel of John and Japanese Buddhism." *Japanese Religions* 15.2 (1988) 57–68.

Torres, Sergio, and Virginia Fabella, eds. *The Emergent Gospel: Theology from the Underside of History—Papers from the Ecumenical Dialogue of Third World Theologians, Dar es Salaam, August 5–12, 1976*. Maryknoll, NY: Orbis, 1978.

Toulis, Nicole R. *Believing Identity: Pentecostalism and the Mediation of Jamaican Ethnicity and Gender in England*. Oxford: Berg, 1997.

Treier, Daniel J. *Introducing Theological Interpretation of Scripture*. Grand Rapids: Baker Academic, 2008.

Trevett, Christine. "Asperger's Syndrome and the Holy Fool: The Case of Brother Juniper." *Journal of Religion, Disability & Health* 13.2 (2009) 129–50.

Trulear, Harold D. "Ida B. Robinson: The Mother as Symbolic Presence." In *Portraits of a Generation: Early Pentecostal Leaders*, edited by James R. Goff Jr. and Grant Wacker, 309–24. Fayetteville, AR: University of Arkansas Press, 2002.

Tsakiridis, George. *Evagrius Ponticus and Cognitive Science: A Look at Moral Evil and the Thoughts*. Eugene, OR: Pickwick, 2010.

Turner, Max. *Power from on High: The Spirit in Israel's Restoration and Witness in Luke-Acts*. Journal of Pentecostal Theology Supplement series 9. Sheffield: Sheffield Academic Press, 1996.

Twelftree, Graham H. *People of the Spirit: Exploring Luke's View of the Church*. Grand Rapids: Baker Academic, and London: SPCK, 2009.

Van Buren, Paul M. *A Theology of the Jewish-Christian Reality*. 3 vols. Lanham, MD: University Press of America, 1995.

Van den Toren, Bennie. "Human Evolution and a Cultural Understanding of Original Sin." *Perspectives on Science and Christian Faith* 68.1 (2016) 12–21.

Van der Meer, Jitse M., and Scott Mandelbrote, eds. *Nature and Scripture in the Abrahamic Religions: Up to 1700*. 2 vols. Brill's Series in Church History 36. Leiden: Brill, 2008.

———, eds., *Nature and Scripture in the Abrahamic Religions: 1700–Present*. 2 vols. Brill's Series in Church History 37. Leiden: Brill, 2008.

Van Henten, J. Willem, and Athalya Brenner, eds. *Families and Family Relations as Represented in Early Judaisms and Early Christianities: Texts and Fictions*. Studies in Theology and Religion 2. Leiden: Deo, 2000.

Van Nieuwenhove, Jacques, and Berma Klein Goldewijk, eds. *Popular Religion, Liberation and Contextual Theology: Papers from a Congress (January 3–7, 1990, Nijmegen, the Netherlands) Dedicated to Arnulf Camps OFM*. Kampen: Uitgeversmaatschappij J. H. Kok, 1991.

Vanhoozer, Kevin J. *The Drama of Doctrine: A Canonical-Linguistic Approach to Christian Theology*. Louisville: Westminster John Knox, 2005.

———. *First Theology: God, Scripture and Hermeneutics*. Downers Grove, IL: InterVarsity, 2002.

———. *Is There a Meaning in This Text? The Bible, the Reader, and the Morality of Literary Knowledge*. Grand Rapids, MI: Zondervan, 1998.

Vanhoozer, Kevin J., and Daniel J. Treier. *Theology and the Mirror of Scripture: A Mere Evangelical Account*. Downers Grove, IL: IVP Academic, 2015.

Vanier, Jean. *An Ark for the Poor: The Story of L'Arche*. Toronto: Novalis, 1995.

Villafañe, Eldin. *The Liberating Spirit: Toward an Hispanic American Pentecostal Social Ethic*. Grand Rapids: Eerdmans, 1993.

Volf, Miroslav. *Captive to the Word of God: Engaging the Scriptures for Contemporary Theological Reflection*. Grand Rapids: Eerdmans, 2010.

———. "Materiality of Salvation: An Investigation in the Soteriologies of Liberation and Pentecostal theologies." *Journal of Ecumenical Studies* 26.3 (1989) 447–67.

Vondey, Wolfgang. *Beyond Pentecostalism: The Crisis of Global Christianity and the Renewal of the Theological Agenda*. Pentecostal Manifestos series. Grand Rapids: Eerdmans, 2010.

Von Speyr, Adrienne. *The World of Prayer*. Translated by Graham Harrison. San Francisco: Ignatius, 1985.

Wacker, Grant. *Heaven Below: Early Pentecostals and American Culture*. Cambridge, MA: Harvard University Press, 2001.

———. "Living with Signs and Wonders: Parents and Children in Early Pentecostal Culture." In *Signs, Wonders, Miracles: Representations of Divine Power in the Life of the Church—Papers Read at the 2003 Summer Meeting and the 2004 Winter Meeting of the Ecclesiastical History Society*, edited by Kate Cooper and Jeremy

Gregory, 423–43. Studies in Church History 41. Woodbridge, UK: Ecclesiastical History Society/Boydell, 2005.

Waddell, Robby. *The Spirit in the Book of Revelation*. Journal of Pentecostal Theology Supplement series 30. Blandford Forum, UK: Deo, 2006.

Wainwright, William J. *Reason and the Heart: A Prolegomenon to a Critique of Passional Reason*. Ithaca, NY: Cornell University Press, 1995.

Walaskay, Paul W. *"And so we Came to Rome": The Political Perspective of St Luke*. Society for New Testament Studies Monograph Series 49. Cambridge: Cambridge University Press, 1984.

Walker, Stuart H. *Winning: The Psychology of Competition*. London: W.W. Norton, 1980.

Wall, Robert W. "Canonical Context and Canonical Conversations." In *Between Two Horizons: Spanning New Testament Studies and Systematic Theology*, edited by Joel B. Green and Max Turner, 165–82. Grand Rapids: Eerdmans, 2000.

———. "Reading the Bible from within Our Traditions: The 'Rule of Faith' in Theological Hermeneutics." In *Between Two Horizons: Spanning New Testament Studies and Systematic Theology*, edited by Joel B. Green and Max Turner, 88–122. Grand Rapids: Eerdmans, 2000.

Walls, Andrew. *The Cross-Cultural Process in Christian History: Studies in the Transmission and Appropriation of Faith*. Maryknoll, NY: Orbis, 2002.

Walsh, Adrian J., and Richard Giulianotti. *Ethics, Money and Sport: This Sporting Mammon*. London: Routledge, 2007.

Waltke, Bruce K., with Cathi J. Fredricks. *Genesis: A Commentary*. Grand Rapids: Zondervan, 2001.

Walton, John H. *The Lost World of Genesis One: Ancient Cosmology and the Origins Debate*. Downers Grove, IL: IVP Academic, 2009.

Walton, Steve. "Acts." In *Theological Interpretation of the New Testament: A Book-by-Book Survey*, edited by Kevin J. Vanhoozer et al., 74–83. London: SPCK, and Grand Rapids: Baker Academic, 2008.

Wan-Tatah, Victor. *Emancipation in African Theology: An Inquiry on the Relevance of Latin American Liberation Theology to Africa*. American University Studies VII, Theology & Religion 14. New York: Peter Lang, 1988.

Ware, Frederick L. "On the Compatibility/Incompatibility of Pentecostal Premillenialism with Black Liberation Theology." In *Afro-Pentecostalism: Black Pentecostal and Charismatic Christianity in History and Culture*, edited by Estrelda Alexander and Amos Yong, 191–206. Religion, Race, and Ethnicity Series. New York: New York University Press, 2011.

Wariboko, Nimi. *The Charismatic City and the Public Resurgence of Religion: A Pentecostal Social Ethics of Cosmopolitan Urban Life*. CHARIS: Christianity and Renewal—Interdisciplinary Studies series. New York: Palgrave Macmillan, 2014.

———. *Economics in Spirit and Truth: A Moral Philosophy of Finance*. New York: Palgrave Macmillan, 2014.

———. *Nigerian Pentecostalism*. Rochester, NY: University of Rochester Press, 2014.

———. *The Pentecostal Principle: Ethical Methodology in New Spirit*. Pentecostal Manifestos series. Grand Rapids: Eerdmans, 2012.

———. "Senses and Legal expression in Kalabari Culture." In *The Foundations of Nigeria: Essays in Honor of Toyin Falola*, edited by Adebayo Oyebade, 305–31. Trenton, NJ: African World, 2003.

Warren, E. Janet. *Cleansing the Cosmos: A Biblical Model for Conceptualizing and Counteracting Evil.* Eugene, OR: Pickwick, 2012.

Warrington, Keith. *The Message of the Holy Spirit.* Downers Grove, IL: InterVarsity, 2009.

———. *Pentecostal Theology: A Theology of Encounter.* London: T & T Clark, 2008.

Waters, Brent. *The Family in Christian Social and Political Thought.* Oxford: Oxford University Press, 2007.

Watson, David F. *Honor among Christians: The Cultural Key to the Messianic Secret.* Minneapolis: Fortress, 2010.

Watson, Francis. "Are There Still Four Gospels? A Study in Theological Method." In *Reading Scripture with the Church: Toward a Hermeneutic for Theological Interpretation,* edited by A. K. M. Adam, et al., 95–116. Grand Rapids: Baker Academic, 2006.

———. *Text and Truth: Redefining Biblical Theology.* Grand Rapids: Eerdmans, 1997.

———. *Text, Church and World: Biblical Interpretation in Theological Perspective.* Grand Rapids: Eerdmans, 1994.

Watson, Nick J. "Special Olympians as a "Prophetic Sign" to the Modern Sporting Babel." In *Sports and Christianity: Historical and Contemporary Perspectives,* edited by Nick Watson and Andrew Parker, 167–206. London: Routledge, 2013.

———. "Sport, Disability and the Olympics: An Exploration of the Status and Prophetic Role of the Special Olympic Movement in Light of the London 2012 Olympic and Paralympic Games." *The Bible in Transmission* (Journal of the Bible Society) (Spring 2012) 14–16. Accessed December 4, 2012. http://www.biblesociety.org.uk/uploads/content/bible_in_transmission/files/2012_spring/BiT_Spring_2012_Watson.pdf.

Watson, Nick J., and John White. "'Winning at All Costs' in Modern Sport: Reflections on Pride and Humility in the Writings of C. S. Lewis." In *Sport and Spirituality: An Introduction,* edited by Jim Parry et al., 61–79. New York: Routledge, 2007.

Webb, Stephen H. *The Divine Voice: Christian Proclamation and the Theology of Sound.* Grand Rapids: Brazos, 2004.

Webb-Mitchell, Brent. *Dancing with Disabilities: Opening the Church to All God's Children.* Cleveland: United Church, 1996.

———. *Unexpected Guests at God's Banquet: Welcoming People with Disabilities into the Church.* New York: Crossroad, 1994.

Weber, Hans-Ruedi. *Jesus and the Children: Biblical Resources for Study and Preaching.* Atlanta: John Knox, and Geneva: World Council of Churches, 1979.

Webster, John. *The Domain of the Word: Scripture and Theological Reason.* London: T & T Clark, 2012.

———. *Holy Scripture: A Dogmatic Sketch.* Cambridge: Cambridge University Press, 2003.

———. "Reading Scripture Eschatologically (1)." In *Reading Texts, Seeking Wisdom: Scripture and Theology,* edited by David F. Ford and Graham Stanton, 245–56. Grand Rapids: Eerdmans, 2003.

———. *Word and Church: Essays in Church Dogmatics.* Rev. ed. Edinburgh: T & T Clark, 2016.

Weissenrieder, Annette. *Images of Illness in the Gospel of Luke: Insights of Ancient Medical Texts.* Wissenschaftliche Untersuchungen zum Neuen Testament 2.164. Tübingen: Mohr Siebeck, 2003.

Welchel, Tom, J. Edward Morris, and Cindy McCowan. *Azusa Street: They Told Me Their Stories*. Rev. ed. Mustang, OK: Dare 2 Dream, 2008.

Welker, Michael. *God as Spirit*. Translated by John F. Hoffmeyer. Minneapolis: Fortress, 1995.

———. "What is Creation? Rereading Genesis 1 and 2." *Theology Today* 48 (1991) 56–71.

Wendland, Ernst. "Study Bible Notes for the Gospel of Luke in Chichewa." In *Biblical Texts and African Audiences*, edited by Ernst R. Wendland and Jean-Claude Loba-Mkole, 103–49. Nairobi: Acton, 2004.

Wenk, Matthias. *Community Forming Power: The Socio-Ethical Role of the Spirit in Luke-Acts*. Journal of Pentecostal Theology Supplement Series 19. Sheffield: Sheffield Academic Press, 2000.

Westhelle, Vítor. "Liberation Theology: A Latitudinal Perspective." In *The Oxford Handbook of Eschatology*, edited by Jerry L. Walls, 311–27. Oxford: Oxford University Press, 2008.

White, John. "Idols in the Stadium: Sport as an 'Idol Factory.'" In *The Image of God in the Human Body: Essays on Christianity and Sports*, edited by Donald Deardorff II and John White, 127–72. Lewiston: Edwin Mellen, 2008.

White, Keith J. "Insights into Child Theology through the Life and Work of Pandita Ramabai." *Dharma Deepika: A South Asian Journal of Missiological Research* 12.2 (2008) 77–93.

Wilcox, David L. "A Proposed Model for the Evolutionary Creation of Human Beings: From the Image of God to the Origin of Sin." *Perspectives on Science and Christian Faith* 68.1 (2016) 22–43.

Wilcox, Melissa M. *Coming Out in Christianity: Religion, Identity, and Community*. Bloomington: Indiana University Press, 2003.

Wilkinson, Michael, and Steven M. Studebaker. "A Liberating Spirit: Liberation Theology and the Pentecostal Movement." *The Ecumenist: A Journal of Theology, Culture, and Society* 45.4 (2008) 1–7.

Wilkinson, Michael, and Steven M. Studebaker, eds. *A Liberating Spirit: Pentecostals and Social Action in North America*. Pentecostals, Peacemaking & Social Justice series. Eugene, OR: Pickwick, 2010.

Williams, David M. *Receiving the Bible in Faith: Historical and Theological Exegesis*. Washington, DC: Catholic University of America Press, 2004.

Williams, J. Rodman. *Renewal Theology: Systematic Theology from a Charismatic Perspective*. 3 vols. Grand Rapids: Zondervan, 1988–1992.

Williams, Patricia A. *Doing without Adam and Eve: Sociobiology and Original Sin*. Minneapolis: Fortress, 2001.

Williamson, Clark M. *A Guest in the House of Israel: Post-Holocaust Church Theology*. Louisville: Westminster/John Knox, 1993.

Wimber, John, and Kevin Springer. *Power Evangelism: Signs and Wonders Today*. Ventura, CA: Regal, 1985.

Work, Telford. *Living and Active: Scripture in the Economy of Salvation*. Grand Rapids, MI: Eerdmans, 2001.

World Health Organization and Joint Commission on International Aspects of Mental Retardation. *Mental Retardation: Meeting the Challenge*. Geneva: World Health Organization, 1985.

Worthen, Jeremy. "Babes in Arms: Speechlessness and Selfhood." In *Children of God: Towards a Theology of Childhood*, edited by Angela Shier-Jones, 41–61. Peterborough, UK: Epworth, 2007.

Wyckoff, John W. *Pneuma and Logos: The Role of the Spirit in Biblical Hermeneutics*. Eugene, OR: Wipf & Stock, 2010.

Wyman, David S. *The Abandonment of the Jews: America and the Holocaust 1941–1945*. New York: Pantheon, 1984.

Xie, Ming, ed. *The Agon of Interpretations: Towards a Critical Intercultural Hermeneutics*. Toronto: University of Toronto Press, 2014.

Yamauchi, Edwin M. *Pre-Christian Gnosticism: A Survey of the Proposed Evidences*. Grand Rapids: Eerdmans, 1973.

Yong, Amos. "Academic Glossolalia? Pentecostal Scholarship, Multi-disciplinarity, and the Science-Religion Conversation." *Journal of Pentecostal Theology* 14.1 (2005) 63–82.

———. "Asian American Evangelical Theology." In *Global Theology in Evangelical Perspective: Exploring the Contextual Nature of Theology and Mission*, edited by Jeffrey Greenman and Gene L. Green, 195–209. Downers Grove, IL: InterVarsity, 2012.

———. "Asian American Historicity: The Problem and Promise of Evangelical Theology." *SANACS Journal* [*Society of Asian North American Christian Studies Journal*] 4 (2012–2013) 29–48.

———. "The 'Baptist Vision' of James William McClendon Jr.: A Wesleyan-Pentecostal Response." *Wesleyan Theological Journal* 37.2 (Fall 2002) 32–57.

———. "Between the Local and the Global: Autobiographical Reflections on the Emergence of the Global Theological Mind." In *Shaping a Global Theological Mind*, edited by Darren C. Marks, 187–94. Aldershot, UK: Ashgate, 2008.

———. *Beyond the Impasse: Toward a Pneumatological Theology of Religions*. Grand Rapids: Baker Academic, 2003.

———. *The Bible, Disability, and the Church: A New Vision of the People of God*. Grand Rapids: Eerdmans, 2011.

———. "The Church and Mission Theology in a Post-Constantinian Era: Soundings from the Anglo-American Frontier." In *A New Day: Essays on World Christianity in Honor of Lamin Sanneh*, edited by Akintunde E. Akinade, 49–61. New York: Peter Lang, 2010.

———. "Conclusion: The Missiology of Jamestown: 1607–2007 and Beyond—Toward a Postcolonial Theology of Mission in North America." In *Remembering Jamestown: Hard Questions about Christian Mission*, edited by Amos Yong and Barbara Brown Zikmund, 157–67. Eugene, OR: Pickwick, 2010.

———. *The Cosmic Breath: Spirit and Nature in the Christianity-Buddhism-Science Trialogue*. Philosophical Studies in Science & Religion 4. Leiden: Brill, 2012.

———. "The Demise of Foundationalism and the Retention of Truth: What Evangelicals Can Learn from C. S. Peirce." *Christian Scholar's Review* 29.3 (Spring 2000) 563–88.

———. *The Dialogical Spirit: Christian Reason and Theological Method for the Third Millennium*. Eugene, OR: Cascade, 2014.

———. "Disability and the Gifts of the Spirit: Pentecost and the Renewal of the Church." *Journal of Pentecostal Theology* 19.1 (2010) 76–93.

———. "Disability from the Margins to the Center: Hospitality and Inclusion in the Church." *Journal of Religion, Disability, and Health* 15.4 (2011) 339–50.

———. "Disability, the Human Condition, and the Spirit of the Eschatological Long Run: Toward a Pneumatological Theology of Disability." *Journal of Religion, Disability, and Health* 11.1 (2007) 5–25.

———. *Discerning the Spirit(s): A Pentecostal-Charismatic Contribution to Christian Theology of Religions.* Journal of Pentecostal Theology Supplement series 20. Sheffield: Sheffield Academic Press, 2000.

———. "From Every Tribe, Language, People, and Nation: Diaspora, Hybridity, and the Coming Reign of God." In *Global Diasporas and Mission*, edited by Chandler H. Im and Amos Yong, 253–61. Regnum Edinburgh Centenary Series 23. Oxford, UK: Regnum, 2014.

———. "The Future of Evangelical Theology: Asian and Asian American Interrogations." *The Asia Journal of Theology* 21.2 (October 2007) 371–97.

———. *The Future of Evangelical Theology: Soundings from the Asian American Diaspora.* Downers Grove, IL: IVP Academic, 2014.

———. "Global Renewal Christianity and World Christianity: Treks, Trends, and Trajectories." In *World Christianity: Perspectives and Insight—Essays in Honor of Peter C. Phan*, edited by Jonathan Y. Tan and Anh Q. Tran, 48–65. Maryknoll, NY: Orbis, 2016.

———. "Glocalization and the Gift-Giving Spirit: Informality and Shalom beyond the Political Economy of Exchange." *Journal of Youngsan Theology* 25 (2012) 7–29.

———. "God and the Evangelical Laboratory: Recent Conservative Protestant Thinking about Theology and Science." *Theology & Science* 5.2 (2007) 203–21.

———. "Guests, Hosts, and the Holy Ghost: Pneumatological Theology and Christian Practices in a World of Many Faiths." In *Lord and Giver of Life: Perspectives on Constructive Pneumatology*, edited by David H. Jensen, 71–86. Louisville: Westminster John Knox, 2008.

———. "The Hermeneutical Trialectic: Notes toward Consensual Hermeneutic and Theological Method." *Heythrop Journal* 45.1 (2004) 22–39.

———. *Hospitality and the Other: Pentecost, Christian Practices, and the Neighbor.* Faith Meets Faith series. Maryknoll, NY: Orbis, 2008.

———. "The Im/Migrant Spirit: De/Constructing a Pentecostal Theology of Migration." In *Theology of Migration in the Abrahamic Religions*, edited by Peter C. Phan and Elaine Padilla, 133–53. New York: Palgrave Macmillan, 2014.

———. "Improvisation, Indigenization, and Inspiration: Theological Reflections on the Sound and Spirit of Global Renewal." In *The Spirit of Praise: Music and Worship in Global Pentecostal-Charismatic Christianity*, edited by Monique Ingalls and Amos Yong, 279–88. University Park, PA: Penn State University Press, 2015.

———. "Informality, Illegality, and Improvisation: Theological Reflections on Money, Migration, and Ministry in Chinatown, NYC, and Beyond." In *New Overtures: Asian North American Theology in the 21st Century—Essays in Honor of Fumitaka Matsuoka*, edited by Eleazar S. Fernandez, 248–68. Upland, CA: Sopher, 2012.

———. *In the Days of Caesar: Pentecostalism and Political Theology.* Grand Rapids, MI: Eerdmans, 2010.

———. "Justice Deprived, Justice Demanded: Afropentecostalisms and the Task of World Pentecostal Theology Today." *Journal of Pentecostal Theology* 15.1 (2006) 127–47.

———. *The Missiological Spirit: Christian Mission Theology for the Third Millennium Global Context*. Eugene, OR: Cascade, 2014.

———. "Pentecostalism and Science: Challenges and Opportunities." In *Proceedings of the Inaugural Faith and Science Conference, Springfield, Missouri, June 27–28, 2011*, edited by David R. Bundrick and Steve Badger, 133–47. Springfield, MO: Gospel, 2012.

———. "Pentecostalism and the Theological Academy." *Theology Today* 64.2 (2007) 244–50.

———. "Pentecostalism, Science, and Creation: New Voices in the Theology-Science Conversation." *Zygon: Journal of Science and Religion* 43.4 (2008) 875–989.

———. "Pentecostal and Charismatic Theology." In *The Routledge Companion to Modern Christian Thought*, edited by Chad Meister and James Beilby, 636–46. London: Routledge, 2013.

———. "Pentecostal Theology." In *Brill's Encyclopedia of Global Pentecostalism*, edited by Todd Johnson, et al. Leiden: Brill, forthcoming.

———. *Pneumatology and the Christian-Buddhist Dialogue: Does the Spirit Blow through the Middle Way?* Studies in Systematic Theology 11. Boston: Brill, 2012.

———. "Poured Out on All Flesh: The Spirit, World Pentecostalism, and the Performance of Renewal Theology." *PentecoStudies: An Interdisciplinary Journal for Research on the Pentecostal and Charismatic Movement* 6.1 (2007) 16–46.

———. "The Power of Language: The Implications of Pentecost for Global Worship." *Reformed Worship* 119 (March 2016) 28–33.

———. "Proclamation and the Third Article: Toward a Pneumatology of Preaching." In *Third Article Theology: A Pneumatological Dogmatics*, edited by Myk Habets, 367–95. Minneapolis: Fortress, 2016.

———. "Renewed and Always Renewing: Pentecostal Ecclesiologies." In *The Oxford Handbook of Ecclesiology*, edited by Paul Avis. Oxford: Oxford University Press, forthcoming.

———. "Restoring, Reforming, Renewing: Accompaniments to *The Cambridge Companion to Evangelical Theology*." *Evangelical Review of Theology* 33.2 (2009) 179–83.

———. Review of *Asian Christian Theologies*, edited by John C. England, et al. *Evangelical Review of Theology* 29.4 (2005) 372–74.

———. "Salvation, Society, and the Spirit: Pentecostal Contextualization and Political Theology from Cleveland to Birmingham, from Springfield to Seoul." *Pax Pneuma: The Journal of Pentecostals & Charismatics for Peace & Justice* 5.2 (2009) 22–34.

———. "Sanctification, Science, and the Spirit: Salvaging Holiness in the Late Modern World." *Wesleyan Theological Journal* 47.2 (2012) 36–52.

———. "Science and Religion: Introducing the Issues, Resolving the Debates—A Review Essay." *Christian Scholar's Review* 40.2 (2011) 189–203.

———. "Sons and Daughters, Young and Old: Toward a Pentecostal Theology of the Family." *PentecoStudies: An Interdisciplinary Journal for Research on the Pentecostal and Charismatic Movement* 10.2 (2011) 147–73.

———. *The Spirit and the Missio Dei: Trinitarian Mission in Canonical Perspective*. Work in progress.

———. "The Spirit, Christian Practices, and the Religions: Theology of Religions in Pentecostal and Pneumatological Perspective." *Asbury Journal* 62.2 (2007) 5–31.

———. *The Spirit of Creation: Modern Science and Divine Action in the Pentecostal-Charismatic Imagination.* Pentecostal Manifestos series. Grand Rapids, MI: Eerdmans, 2011.

———. "The Spirit of an Evolving Creation: Surmisings of a Pentecostal Theologian." In *How I Changed My Mind about Evolution: Evangelicals Reflect on Faith and Science*, edited by Kathryn Applegate and J. B. Stump, 167–72. Downers Grove, IL: InterVarsity, 2016.

———. "The Spirit of Hospitality: Pentecostal Perspectives toward a Performative Theology of the Interreligious Encounter." *Missiology: An International Review* 35.1 (2007) 55–73.

———. *Spirit of Love: A Trinitarian Theology of Grace.* Waco, TX: Baylor University Press, 2012.

———. *The Spirit Poured Out on All Flesh: Pentecostalism and the Possibility of Global Theology.* Grand Rapids: Baker Academic, 2005.

———. "The Spirit Says Come: Gifts, Kings, Nations, and Cultures on the Way to the New Jerusalem." Plenary address, Society for Pentecostal Studies Annual Meeting, Urshan Theological Seminary, St. Louis, Missouri, March 9–11, 2017.

———. "The Spirit, Vocation, and the Life of the Mind: A Pentecostal Testimony." In *Pentecostals in the Academy: Testimonies of Call*, edited by Steven M. Fettke and Robby Waddell, 203–20. Cleveland, TN: CPT, 2012.

———. *Spirit-Word-Community: Theological Hermeneutics in Trinitarian Perspective.* Aldershot, UK: Ashgate, and Eugene, OR: Wipf & Stock, 2002.

———. *Theology and Down Syndrome: Reimagining Disability in Late Modernity.* Waco, TX: Baylor University Press, 2007.

———. "Whither Asian American Evangelical Theology? What Asian? Which American? Whose *Evangelion*?" *Evangelical Review of Theology* 32.1 (2008) 22–37.

———. *Who is the Holy Spirit? A Walk with the Apostles.* Brewster, MA: Paraclete, 2011.

———. "Worship in Many Tongues: The Power of Praise in the Vernacular." *Worship Leader* 122 (May–June 2015) 14–17.

Yong, Amos, ed. *The Spirit Renews the Face of the Earth: Pentecostal Forays in Science and Theology of Creation.* Eugene, OR: Pickwick, 2009.

Yong, Amos, and Jonathan A. Anderson. *Renewing Christian Theology: Systematics for a Global Christianity.* Waco, TX: Baylor University Press, 2014.

Yong, Amos, and James K. A. Smith, eds. *Science and the Spirit: A Pentecostal Engagement with the Sciences.* Bloomington, IN: Indiana University Press, 2010.

Yoo, Tae Wha. *The Spirit of Liberation: Jürgen Moltmann's Trinitarian Pneumatology.* Studies in Reformed Theology 2. Zoetermeer, The Netherlands: Uitgeverij Meinema, 2003.

York, John O. *The Last Shall Be First: The Rhetoric of Reversal in Luke.* Journal of the Study of the New Testament Supplement Series 46. Sheffield: JSOT, 1991.

Young, Frances M., ed. *Encounter with Mystery: Reflections on L'Arche and Living with Disability.* London: Darton, Longman and Todd, 1997.

Young, Kevin. *Sport, Violence and Society.* London: Routledge, 2012.

Yun, Koo Dong. *Baptism in the Holy Spirit: An Ecumenical Theology of Spirit Baptism.* Lanham, MD: University Press of America, 2003.

———. *The Holy Spirit and Ch'i (Qi): A Chiological Approach to Pneumatology.* Eugene, OR: Pickwick, 2012.

———. "Pentecostalism from Below: Minjung Liberation and Asian Pentecostal Theology." In *The Spirit in the World: Emerging Pentecostal Theologies in Global Contexts*, edited by Veli-Matti Kärkkäinen, 89–114. Grand Rapids: Eerdmans, 2009.

Zalanga, Samuel, and Amos Yong. "What Empire? Which Multitude? Pentecostalism and Social Liberation in North America and Sub-Saharan Africa." In *Evangelicals and Empire: Christian Alternatives to the Political Status Quo*, edited by Bruce Ellis Benson and Peter Goodwin Heltzel, 237–51. Grand Rapids: Brazos, 2008.

Zimmerman, Jens. *Recovering Theological Hermeneutics: An Incarnational-Trinitarian Theory of Interpretation*. Grand Rapids: Baker Academic, 2004.

Zoerink, Dean A., and Joseph Wilson. "The Competitive Disposition: Views of Athletes with Mental Retardation." *Adapted Physical Activity Quarterly* 12.1 (1995) 34–42.

Subject Index

ableism, 90n35, 231
abortion, 99
Abraham, Shaibu, 170
absolutism, 212
academic disciplines, 97
Acheampong, Joseph Williams, 55n40
Adam and Eve, 147, 148
addictions, 145
affections, 38, 58, 66, 91, 93, 94n48
affluence, 156
Afrikaner, 166
agonism, 233
Albl, Martin, 232
Alfaro, Sammy, 170
altruism, 144, 160n62
Ambrose (of Milan), 46n7
analogy, 253
anonymous Christian, 206
anthropology, theological, 17-19, 150, 257
anti-Judaism, 204, 213
anti-Semitism, 204, 205
Apartheid, 166
apologetics
    classical, 256
    interreligious, 219
    scientific, 247
Apostolic Faith, 57-62
apostolic, post- , 36
apostolic, theology of, 71-75
apostolicity, 14
Archer, Kenneth J., 9, 10, 241n10
Aristotle, 30

Asian American, 15, 32-34
    epistemologies, 39
    hermeneutics, 37
    hybridity, 37-38n29
Asumang, Annang, 55n39
atheism, 148
athleticism, 233
atonement, 211
Augustine, 46n7, 144, 250
Aune, David E., 209n44
Azusa Street, 28, 33n18, 53, 75, 110, 122, 149

Bacon, Francis, 251
baptism, 129, 244
    and the Holy Spirit, 122, 241
Barth, Karl, 4, 5, 113n44, 113-14n44, 165, 260
beauty, 260
Beckford, Robert, 172, 173
Bernard, David K., 34n21
biblicism, 55, 63, 164
Billings, J. Todd, 259n4
birth control, 99
Black Pentecostalism, 172
blindness, 91
Blumhofer, Edith, 114n45
Boesak, Allan, 166
Brown, Raymond E., 218n71
Bruce, F. F., 112-13n41, 131n39
Brusco, Elizabeth, 101
Buddha, 30
Bultmann, Rudolf, 209n40

SUBJECT INDEX

Calvinism, 166
canon within the canon, 124, 262, 263n14
capitalism, 167
Cartledge, Mark J., 117
causality, 53 251
cessationism, 187n26
Chan, Simon, 171n39
charism, 10, 178
Charlesworth, James H., 209n44
Chaves, João B., 165
child or children, 56, 91, 117
    abuse of, 123, 137
    blessing of, 115
    evangelists, 122
christology, 61, 64, 135, 150, 177n63, 192, 219, 261
church mothers, 116n52
civil rights movement, 224
clash of civilizations, 182n11
Clayton, Philip, 254n46
Cleveland School, 8, 9, 28n4, 36n24
cognition, 66, 94n48
commercialism, 225, 227, 233
common descent, 148
common good, 233, 236
commonsense realism, 240
community, 154
    apostolic, 175, 176
competition, 225, 227, 235, 236
complementarity, 249n32, 250, 254
concordism, 238, 239, 246, 250, 252, 253
concupiscence, 145
Cone, James H., 165, 166
confession, Christian, 57-62, 71-75
confessionalism, 3
Confucius, 30
conservativism, 113, 123
consumerism, 137
contextualization, 15, 164
Conzelmann, Hans, 155n45
Costantino, Antonio Ziccardi, 68n18
Costas, Orlando E., 188n29
Cox, Harvey G., 168
creation, 24, 149, 150, 159, 173, 239, 252

narratives, 244-49
creationism, 238, 239, 245
    ancient earth, 146
    old earth, 148
    progressive, 150n30, 254n47
    young earth, 148, 254n47
creativity, 136, 172, 225
creator, 261
criminality, 145
criticism, biblical, 61, 62, 239
Culpepper, R. Alan, 220
culture, 223-28
Cunningham, Mary Kathleen, 5

Dalit, 170
Daniels, David D. III, 90
Dead Sea Scrolls, 209
deafness, 91
death, 149
debt, cancellation of, 156n48
deculturation, 31n14
demonic, 212
development, 31, 147
dialogue, 219
dichotomies, 215
disability, 17, 79, 80-83, 95-98, 232
    theology of, 12, 23, 95-98
discernment, 253
dispensationalism, 126
dissonance, cognitive, 66
doctrine, cultural-linguistic theory of, 29-31
Dread theology, 172
dreams and visions, 89, 125, 126
dualism, 218, 220, 230

ecclesiology, 61, 66, 107, 117, 230, 231, 232, 259, 264
ecology, 173
economics, 172
ecumenism, 261
egalitarianism, 106, 154, 156
egocentrism, 225, 233
Eiesland, Nancy, 81, 83
eisegesis, 50, 242
Elbert, Paul, 246-47
embodiment, 93, 153
emotions, 39, 66

emperor worship, 223
empiricism, 143
Engelke, Matthew, 50n21, 51n23
environment, 160n63
epistemology, 46, 89, 93, 94, 146, 153, 252
eschatology, 13, 18, 41n39, 100, 104-108, 121, 126, 128, 127-34, 136, 159
ethics, 212, 218, 220, 225, 234
ethnicity, 173, 214
ethnocentrism, 153, 158
eunuchs, 85
Eurocentrism, 179
evangelicals, 148, 150, 237, 238, 245, 247n27, 249, 255
evangelism, 21, 180-86, 219, 224
evolution, 144, 146-48, 150 159, 245, 254n47
exclusivism, 197, 200, 210, 211, 212
exegesis, 5, 50, 242
exorcisms, 68, 92, 243n16, 182, 191
extra Ecclesiam nulla salus, 197

faith-seeking-understanding, 143
fall, 150, 159, 246
falsifiability, 247n27
family
    extended, 111n37, 117
    values, 116
fathers, 116
Fatherhood of God, 110, 111, 112
Fee, Gordon D., 10n42
feelings, 39
feminism, 106n22, 111n38
fideism, 247n27
filial love, 117
Fivefold gospel, 103n15, 103
flesh, 153
forgiveness, 152n34, 155n44
Fourfold Gospel, 81
Fowl, Stephen E., 7n31
Friday Apostolics, 50
Friday Masowe, 52
fundamentalism, 52, 56n45, 63, 113, 123, 132, 237n2, 240

Gabaitse, Rosinah Mmannana, 56n45
Gadamer, Hans George, 260
Galileo, 251n38
globalization, 123, 173
glossolalia, 38n31, 87n28, 97n60, 124, 126, 253n45
Gnosticism, 209
Godly Love, 160n62
goodness, 260
grace, 154
Graham, William, 49n19
Grau, Marion, 180
Great Commission, 126
Greco-Roman games, 229
greed, 155
Green, Chris E. W., 8n34, 264n16
Green, Joel B., 4, 7n31, 112n39, 128n31, 258n1
guilt, 144, 150
Gundry, Robert H., 215n61

Hakola, Raimo, 202n16, 211
hamartiology, 20, 141, 142, 143, 149, 151, 157, 257
Hannam, Wilfrid L., 131n37
hard sayings, 109, 113, 131, 220
Harms, Richard B., 177n61
Hart, Larry D., 150n30
Hauerwas, Stanley, 180
healing, 49, 54, 65, 70, 81-83, 82n8, 85, 86, 88, 90, 92, 93, 103, 122, 175, 176, 182, 191
healthism, 227
hearing, 88, 89, 90
heart, 40, 241
Hellenism, 209
hermeneutical circle, 109, 137, 260
hermeneutics, 48, 55, 67, 124, 238-44
    African, 53
    apostolic, 21-24, 36n24
    Asian American, 37
    canonical, 212
    charismatic, 70
    christological, 262n12
    communal, 56
    conflationist, 55

hermeneutics (continued)
  disability, 17, 232
  feminist, 106n22
  global, 27
  improvisional, 258
  intercultural, 259
  interreligious, 259
  ordinary language, 48
  Pentecost, 8-11, 14-17, 35-42, 53, 151-61, 239-44
  pentecostal, 8-11, 35-42
  pneumatological, 10, 12, 72, 255
  postcolonial, 63n1
  postmodern, 46
  reader-response, 37, 53, 54, 58n48, 124
  scriptural, 1-14
  this-is-that, 37, 59n52, 66, 68n12, 70, 242-44, 246, 247, 255
  transcultural, 28-31
  triadic, 34
hierarchies, 154
historians, 253
historical criticism, 2, 61, 124, 126, 240, 243, 248, 249, 256
historical-grammatical method, 243n17
historicity, 241, 243
Holiness movement, 110
Hollenweger, Walter J., 53
Holy Spirit, 65, 209
  baptism of/in, 122, 241
homosexuality, 99, 117
Hoskyns, E. C., 215n62
hospitality, 12, 220
household, 108, 129
Hugh of St. Victor, 250
Hull, John M., 90n31
humility, 194
husbands and wives, 116
hybridity, 15, 37-38n30

idolatry, 226
image of God, 248
imagination, 16, 35, 72, 76, 83, 136, 252

  scriptural, 50-57
incarnation, 156, 173, 174, 208, 258, 262
inclusion, 235
inclusivism, 218
inerrancy, 212, 240
infallibility, 212, 240
infant baptism, 108n28
infants, 132, 133, 134
initiation, Christian, 122
intellectual disability, 223, 227, 231, 235
intelligent design, 148, 253n43, 254n47
interculturalism, 41, 261
interdisciplinarity, 143-51, 167, 173, 252, 253, 260, 261
interfaith encounter, 12, 260n6, 26, 184
interpretation, 1-14, 36
  allegorical, 36, 245, 251
  criteria of, 61, 261
  literal, 251
  moral, 36, 245, 251
  pentecostal, 151-61
  pneumatological, 258, 262
  science of, 35-38
  sighs of, 38-40
  signs of, 40-42
  sociological, 211n51
  spiritual, 5, 36, 245, 251
  teleological, 67-71, 263-66
  theological, 1-14
  trinitarian, 4-8
interrelationality, 60
intersubjectivity, 60
Israel, 189

Jenkins, Philip, 168
Jesus Christ
  as child, 137
  as evangelist, 187-89
  as Messiah, 189
Jews, 201-207
Johnson, Luke Timothy, 204
Jones, Major, 165
Jubilee, 156, 175
Judaism, 204, 205

SUBJECT INDEX 313

Juel, Donald H., 16
justification, 125

Kärkkäinen, Veli-Matti, 141n2
katelaben, 207
Kee, Howard Clark, 70n22
Keener, Craig S., 10n42, 116n51, 218
Kelber, Werner H., 46n8
Keller, Helen, 94n47
kerusso, 186
kingdom of God, 84-85; *see* reign of God
Kirk, J. Andrew, 164, 165
Kirsch, Thomas, 51
Koenig, John, 204n24
kyrios, 189-90

Lambrecht, Jan, 113n42
L'Arche, 228
last days, 126
leisure, 225
Levering, Matthew, 265n19
Levison, John H., 92n40, 262n11
lex orandi lex credenda, 60
liberation theology, 20, 55, 58, 83, 133n41, 156n50, 162, 163, 167, 172-78
light and darkness, 199-201
liminality, 265
literalism, 124, 252
literary method, 243, 243n17
literature, 46
Logos, 208, 213, 219
Lohfink, Gerhard, 74n31, 74n33
Lowther, Roland J., 260n7
Luke, Saint
    ethics of, 155
    and evangelism, 185
    historian, 128n29
    priority of, 263n14
    and sin, 155-58
    theologian, 128

Macchia, Frank D., 8n34, 90n32, 152n36
Maccini, Robert Gordon, 216n67

Machado, Maria das Dores Campos, 102
market economy, 172
Masenya, Madipoane, 54n34
Masowe Apostolics, 50
master-slave relations, 106
materialism, 227
Maynard-Reid, Pedrito, 185
Meek, James A., 73n30
Mercer, Joyce Ann, 137
method, 159, 174
    apostolic, 71-75, 258n1, 262n12
    empirical, 154
    theological, 63-76
migration, 41, 123
militarism, 230
ministry, 121
Minjung theology, 166, 170
miraculous, 242
missiology, 61, 167, 185, 193, 213, 264, 265
mission, theology of 16
missionaries, 113n44
Mittelstadt, Martin W. (Marty), 112n40, 116n51
Moberly, R. W. L., 245n23
modernism, 240, 242
Moore, Rickie D., 8, 9, 240
Moore, Stephen D., 91n37
moral responsibility, 137
mothers, 116
Motyer, Stephen, 204
Moulaison, Jane Barter, 3n6
multiculturalism, 29, 30, 259
multidisciplinarity, 252
multivocality, 166, 174, 177
Munyon, Timothy, 150n30
Murphy, George L., 253n43

nationalism, 223
narrative method, 243, 243n17
natural selection, 144
nature, books of, 239, 249, 251, 253n43
Neitz, Mary Jo, 102
neo-orthodoxy, 166
neuroscience, 144
new creation, 248

SUBJECT INDEX

Ngong, David Tonghou, 171
Niebuhr, Reinhold, 19, 143, 146
Nolivos, Virginia Trevino, 103
normalization, 90

Odegard, Holtan P., 143n5
Oliverio, L. William, Jr., 10
Olwa, Alfred, 54n34
Olympics, 226, 229, 234
Omenyo, Cephas N., 54n33
Ong, Walter J., 45, 47n9
ontology
    incarnational, 260
    interrelational, 53
    intersubjective, 53
oppressed, 156
oral communication, 47
orality, 16, 45-57, 60-61
original sin, 144, 146, 147, 149, 150
origins, 159
orphanages, 122
orthodoxy, 42, 57, 59, 60, 61
orthopathy, 39, 40, 42, 57, 59, 61, 169
orthopraxy, 40, 42, 57, 58, 59, 61

Palmer, Phoebe, 110n31
palpability, 93
Paralympics, 224, 234
Parsons, Mikeal C., 84
participation, 240, 241
passions, 39, 169
Peirce, Charles Sanders, 7n31, 40
Pentecost, Day of, 6n23, 120
    hermeneutics of, 8-11, 14-17, 35-42, 53, 151-61, 239-44
    principle, 172
    spirituality, 172
    worship, 93
Pentecostal Studies, 80-83
Pentecostalism
    American, 33-34
    Asian, 33-34
    Black church, 172
    global, 168
perceptivity, 91, 153
perfectionism, 227

performance-enhancement, 225, 226
personality disorders, 145
phenomenology, 50-57, 61
Philemon, 106
Philip, Saint, 129
physiognomy, 84
pietism, 244
Pinnock, Clark H., 13n48
Plato, 30
play, 136
pluralism, 7, 173, 177, 218
pneumaticism, 55
pneumatology, 13, 120, 122-27, 135, 142, 262n11
    and epistemology, 89
    and creation, 24
    and environment, 160n63
    and imagination, 16, 35, 72, 76, 83, 252
    and postcoloniality, 192, 193
    and religions, 12, 22
    and soteriology, 19-21, 257
    and thinking, 74
Poirier, John C., 242-43n15
political correctness, 259
political theology, 165, 172
polyvocality, 259
poor, 156
postcolonialism, 63n1, 164, 180, 192, 193
postconservativism, 165
postliberalism, 2, 3
postmodernism, 46
poverty, 156n47, 164, 167
power encounters, 182
power evangelism, 182
powers, 57
practices, 61, 138, 253
praeparatio, 207
praxis, 57-62, 69
preferential option for the poor, 163-68, 177
premodernism, 5
pride, 145
primitivism, 124
principalities and powers, 55, 177
profits, 56n43

prophets, 56n43
proselytism, 181n10
punishment, 150

Qumran, 207-13

race, 172, 173
racism, 146
rage, 145
Rahner, Karl, 206
rationalism, 136
reader-response hermeneutics, 37, 53, 54, 124
reading, transformative, 264
reason, 94
reconciliation, 159
redemption, 142
Reformation, 251
regeneration, 125
reign of God, 17n57, 18, 19, 41, 56, 68-69, 100, 107, 112-13, 115, 117, 121, 129-38, 142, 157, 159, 160, 164, 176, 189-94, 236, 259, 263, 265
religions, 12, 22
religious pluralism, 199
Renaissance, 251
Rensberger, David, 213n56
restoration of Israel, 130
restorationism, 124, 243
resurrection, 154
revelation, 208n36
Richie, Tony, 182
Ricoeur, Paul, 255
Roberts, J. Deotis, 165
Rodgers, Darrin, 114n45
Rodríguez, Dario Lopez, 133n41, 156n50, 170
Rodríguez, Rubén Rosario, 31n14
ruah, 252
Rule of Faith, 2-4
Russian Church, 102

salvation, 198
salvation history, 241, 248
Samaria, 158
Samaritan, 214, 216
sanctification, 125, 151, 241

Sanneh, Lamin, 192n42
Schnackenburg, Rudolf, 203n18, 207, 216n63
Schnelle, Udo, 202n16
science and theology, 20, 23, 24, 142, 144, 146, 150, 160, 254
science and sciences, 148
  biological, 160
  evolutionary, 144
  modern, 239, 247n27
  natural, 160, 249
  of interpretation, 35-38
  social, 160
  theories of, 256
scientific method, 251, 252
scientific theology, 161
scientism, 148
scientists, 253
Scriptural Reasoning, 3, 52
sectarianism, 207-13
seeing, 88, 89
Segovia, Fernando F., 214, 215
self-control, 224
self-discipline, 225
selfish gene, 144
semper reformanda, 264
sensorium, 18, 93, 94, 153
sexual mores, 99
Seymour, William, 53, 114n45
Shankara, 30
Shaul, Richard, 170
signs and wonders, 73, 122n15, 144n45, 154, 181, 182, 190, 191, 242
sin, 82, 146-49, 159-61
  effects of, 160
  inherited, 150
  original, 147, 149, 150
  pentecostal views of, 149
  sociality of, 146
  universality of, 147, 149, 150
skepticism, 239
Smith, Aaron T., 5n14
social justice, 169
socialism, 167
sociality, 134
Society for Pentecostal Studies, 83n15

sociobiology, 144
solidarity, 163
Solivan, Samuel, 169, 259n3
soteriology, 19-21, 107, 125, 197, 230, 257
Spawn, Kevin L., 10
Special Olympics, 224, 227, 228, 234, 235
speech-acts, 21, 59, 60, 87
Spinks, D. Christopher, 7n31
Spirit Apostolic Church, 51
Spirit Christology, 128, 130-31, 170, 261
spirits, territorial, 182
Spiritual Apostolics, 52
spiritual gifts, 75, 119, 124
spiritual warfare, 182, 187n26, 230
spirituality, 93, 94, 124, 172
    evangelical, 102, 168
sports, 225, 226
Stanford, Matthew S., 20, 145
Stephen, M, 170-71n38
subjectivity, 242
suffering, 169
symbolism, 250
synagogue, 202-203
syncretism, 15
systematic theology, 13

tactility, 66, 93
Tanner, Kathryn, 161n64
Tarr, Del, 53n31
technology, 183
teleology, 67-71, 145, 263-66
Teng, Philip, 188n27
territorial spirits, 182
Thatcher, Adrian, 137
theological method, 63-76
theology, 12, 165
    apostolic, 71-75
    charismatic, 23
    disability, 12, 19n61, 162n3, 222
    Dread, 172
    eschatological, 121, 128, 159
    evangelical, 163-68
    global, 165
    holistic, 164
    natural, 253n43

performative, 213, 218-21
pneumatological, 13, 120
political, 165, 172
reversal of, 157
systematic, 13
trinitarian, 120
urban, 167
Theosis, 264n16
Third Article theology, 133-38, 152
this-is-that, 24, 36, 39, 40, 41, 59, 66, 70, 184, 240, 242, 243, 244-49, 255, 256
Thomas, John Christopher, 8-9, 8n34
Thurston, Bonnie Bowman, 219n74
touch, 92
Tower of Babel, 153
transculturalism, 41
transdisciplinarity, 141
transnationalism, 41, 173
Treier, Daniel J., 15
Trinitarianism, 64, 66, 67, 120, 174, 257, 261, 263
    fellowship, 265
    interpretation, 4-8, 263-66
triumphalism, 194, 215
truth, 209, 260
Twelftree, Graham H., 157n53, 185n25, 243n16

unbelief, 200
unevangelized, 217
union with God, 241
universality, 149, 158

Vanhoozer, Kevin J., 4, 7, 263-64
Vatican II, 212
verbalization, 53
vernacularization, 192n42
Villafañe, Eldin, 169
violence, 233
virtues, 235
Volf, Miroslav, 169
Vondey, Wolfgang, 136, 239n5
Von Speyr, Adrienne, 131n38
vulnerability, 136, 137

Wall, Robert W., 4, 13n49

Walls, Andrew, 189n33
Walton, John H., 245n23
Walton, Steve, 17n57
Wariboko, Nimi, 49n16, 171, 172
Warren, E. Janet, 161n65
Waters, Brent, 107n26
Watson, Francis, 113n42
Watson, Nick J., 227
weakness, 232, 233, 236
wealth, 156
Webb, Stephen H., 50n20
Welker, Michael, 152n36, 262n11
Wesleyan theology, 4, 151, 244
Williams, J. Rodman, 150n30
Willimon, William, 180

Wimber, John, 182
witness, 40, 88-95
woman, 56, 111n38
Worthen, Jeremy, 133n42
Wright, Archie T., 10
Wyckoff, John W., 10n42
Wyman, David S., 205n28

xenophobia, 159

Yun, Koo Dong, 170

Zalanga, Samuel, 55n39
Zimmerman, Hans, 5n15

Scripture Index

OLD TESTAMENT

Genesis
1	246
1–2	244, 245, 247, 255, 257–258
1:1–2:4	245
1:11–12	247
1:2	245
1:24	247
1:25	247
1:28	248
2	245
2:7	248
8:20–22	91n37

Exodus
4:10–12	87

Leviticus
21:17–23	85

Deuteronomy
23:1	85

1 Samuel
17:35	52

Psalms
2:2	190
19:1	250

Proverbs
3:12	123
13:24	123

Isaiah
34:4	250
42:6	158
49:6	158
53:7–8	117
56:3–5	85
61:1–2	65, 156, 176, 187
66:1–2	72

Jeremiah
31:8–9	86

Joel
2:28	67

Amos
9:11–12	73

Micah
4:6–7	86

Zephaniah

3:19	86

Zechariah

1:67	130

NEW TESTAMENT

Matthew

4:16	198n4
5:47	220
6:7	204n22
6:32	204n22
22:29	251

Mark

3:20–21	112n40

Luke

1:1–4	239
1:17	130
1:19	186
1:22	87
1:35	130, 187
1:39–41	111
1:41	130
1:44	130
1:46–55	131
1:52–53	86n24, 157n51
1:55	109
1:59–60	111
1:62–63	87
1:72	109
1:77	155n44
1:79	198n4
1:80	130
2:1	12, 188
2:20	89
2:25–32	130
2:25–35	92
2:30	89
2:30–32	158
2:40	130
2:44	111n37
2:46–49	131
2:51	130, 131
2:52	131
3:1	188
3:3	155n44, 186
3:6	89
3:18	186
3:33	187
3:38	158
4:1	133, 187
4:1–13	157
4:14	133, 187
4:14–21	175–176
4:16–18	156n47
4:18	81, 133, 188
4:18–19	65, 128, 156
4:18–21	188
4:19	68
4:43	68
4:44	186
5:8	155n44
5:13	92
5:20–24	155n44
5:30–32	155n44
6:19	92
6:32–34	155n44
6:36	131
7:11–17	133
7:14	92
7:22	81, 176
7:34	155n44
7:36–50	92, 155n44
8:1	68, 186
8:19–21	112n40
8:41–56	133
8:44	92
9:2	68
9:11	68
9:37–45	133
9:47–48	132
9:52	158
9:60	68, 112
10:9	68
10:21	132
10:24	89
10:25–37	158n55

Luke (continued)

11:2	68
11:4	155n44
11:11–13	133
11:13	109, 110, 135
11:20	68
12:30–32	131
12:32	68, 110
12:53	112
13:2	155n44
13:12–13	92
13:30	86n24, 157
14:7–24	85
14:11	157
14:13	85
14:21	85
14:23	85
14:26	112, 131
15:2	155n44
15:7	155n44
15:10	155n44
15:18	155n44
15:21	155n44
16:1–15	156n47
17:3–4	155n44
17:11	158n55
17:21	68, 176
18:9–11	156n47
18:13	155n44
18:14	157
18:15	91
18:15–17	115, 132
18:18–20	115
18:20	132
18:27	98
18:29	113, 131
18:35–43	89
19:1–10	156n47
19:7	155n44
19:9	85
19:11	68
19:11–27	156n47
20:9–26	156n47
21:1–4	156n47
21:16	113, 132
21:31	68
22:16	68
22:51	92
24:7	155n44
24:32	91
24:37	65
24:39	91
24:47	155n44, 158
24:49	65, 109, 133, 135

John

1:3	207
1:4–5	207
1:5	199
1:7	199
1:9	208
1:10	208
1:11	208
1:12	208, 220
1:33	218
1:47	206
1:49	206
3:8	256
3:16	31, 213, 217
3:17	217
3:17–21	217
3:18–21	218
3:19–21	200
3:20	215
3:20–21	200n10
3:36	218
4	216
4:9	216
4:21	216
4:39–40	216
4:42	214
5:18	202
5:24	218
5:28–29	218
6:40	218
6:51	214
6:70	215
6:71	215
7–8	203
7:1–9	202
7:7	200
7:10–11	201
7:12–13	202
7:14	201

7:37	201
7:37–38	201
7:44	202
7:49	203
7:53–8:11	201
8:12	199, 200n12, 201
8:13	201
8:13–20	202
8:20	201
8:21–26	202
8:22	201
8:23	200n12
8:31	206
8:31–42	202
8:44	202, 204
8:48	202
8:59	202
9	203, 215
9:2–3	82
9:3	216
9:4	203, 216n63
9:22	202
9:34	203
9:38	203n21
9:39	200n12
10:16	214
10:17–18	211
10:19	202
10:31	202
10:39	202
11:9–10	203
11:10	216n63
11:35–36	199
11:51–52	214
11:53–57	202
12:23–36	211
12:24	154
12:31	200n12, 209
12:35–36	203
12:36–43	203n21
12:37–46	203
12:42	202
12:46	199
13:1	200n12
13:27	216n63
13:30	203, 215
14:30	209
15:4	218
15:7	218
15:18–24	200
16:2	202
16:11	209
16:13	6n26
17:9	214
17:14	200
17:14–16	214
17:18	214
17:21	214
19:15	203
19:38	215
19:39	215
20:31	242

Acts

1	59
1:1	239
1:2	65
1:3	190
1:4	109, 135
1:6	68, 190
1:7–8	68
1:8	40, 59, 65, 67, 152, 155, 158n55, 175, 183, 189, 258, 264
1:22	193
2	11, 18, 29, 34, 35, 44, 59, 64, 86n26, 87, 104, 105, 111, 119, 124, 125, 152n34, 154, 155, 173n50, 174, 187, 257
2:1–21	175
2:2–3	38, 87
2:2–4	58, 153
2:3	38
2:4	38
2:5	69, 153
2:6	60, 87, 153, 174
2:6–8	30
2:7	60, 153
2:7–11	88, 153
2:8	38, 174
2:9–11	37–38n29
2:10	152

Acts (continued)

2:11	69, 86, 87, 153, 174, 253
2:12	60, 153, 265
2:12–13	104
2:14–40	65
2:16–21	60, 125
2:17	38, 58, 64, 67, 86, 89, 125, 126, 153, 174, 187, 265
2:17–18	105, 154
2:18	187
2:19–20	154
2:20	40, 107, 126
2:21	59, 105, 107, 126
2:22–36	60, 65
2:22–40	175
2:24	154
2:25–28	154
2:29–30	154
2:31	154
2:32–33	65, 128
2:33	67, 87, 112, 135, 177, 184, 187
2:33–36	154
2:36	65, 127
2:37–39	127
2:38	69, 152n34, 258
2:39	59, 108, 135, 184
2:41	174
2:41–47	175
2:42–47	117, 154
2:44–45	175
2:44–46	193
3:17	89
3:19	152n34
3:25	107
4:17–20	190
4:20	89
4:26	190
4:32–37	117, 193
4:33	193
5:15–16	92
5:16	81, 176–177
5:31	152n34
5:42	189
6:1–7	117
6:3	71
6:5	71
6:7	71
6:8	71
6:9	72
6:10	71
6:13	72
7:2–19	72
7:22	72
7:29	128
7:29–30	72
7:48	72
7:49–50	72
7:55	72
7:60	152n34
8:1–4	69
8:2–25	158n55
8:4	186
8:5	189, 190
8:6	89
8:7	81
8:12	68, 190
8:32–33	117
8:38	85
8:39	186
9:1–19	74
9:2	186
9:3	74
9:20	186
9:22	189
10–15	6
10:2	129
10:34	181
10:34–35	69
10:35	190
10:38	65, 81, 128, 175, 187
10:42	186
10:43	152n34
10:44–48	69
11:14	129
11:20	186, 190
13:5	186
13:16–41	191n38
13:24	186
13:32	186
13:33	129
13:38	186

13:38–39	152n34
13:47	158
14:7	186
14:8–10	191
14:15	186
14:15–17	69
14:15–18	191
14:21	186
14:21–22	190, 191
14:22	68
15	60nn56–57
15:2	73
15:3	73
15:5	73
15:6–11	73
15:8	73
15:12	73
15:12–29	60
15:15–17	60n56
15:16–18	36n24
15:17–18	73
15:21	186
15:28	36n24, 60n56, 73, 265
15:35–36	186
16:10	186
16:15	129
16:16–17	186
16:31–34	129
16:33	108
17:3	189
17:6	134, 157
17:13	186
17:18	193
17:22–34	191
17:24	190
17:28	69
17:32	193
18:5	189
18:8	129
18:28	189
19:8	68
19:10	188
19:12	92
19:14	129
20:25	68, 186, 190
21:5	129
21:9	129, 186
22:2–21	74
22:3–5	74
22:4–16	74
22:6	74
22:9	74
22:11	74
22:12	74
22:15	89, 188
26:2–23	74
26:6–8	74
26:12–18	74
26:15–18	74
26:18	74, 152n34, 198n4
26:23	74, 188, 189
28	81
28:2	69
28:7	69
28:8–10	70
28:9	81
28:23	68
28:31	68, 70, 186, 190

Romans

1:4	64, 154
1:18–32	204n22
1:20	250
5	147
8:15–16	261
8:23	38, 248
8:26	38, 57–58
9:2–3	234
10:9–13	197
14:17	265

1 Corinthians

1	230
1:20	231
1:21	231
1:23	231
1:25	231, 233
1:27	231
1:27–28	231
1:28	231
2:2	231, 232
6:9–10	204n22
9	230

1 Corinthians (*continued*)

9:7	229
9:22	69
9:24–27	228, 257
12	193, 230, 231, 258
12:3	64
12:4	178
12:11	135
12:13	261
12:15–16	233
12:18	233
12:22	96, 232
12:24	232
12:24–26	96
12:25	233
12:26	232, 233
13:12	41, 194, 254, 261
14:8	229
15:57–58	229
16:13	230

2 Corinthians

2:14	230
2:14–16	91n37
3:6	51n23
6:14	198n4
7:7	230
10:3–6	230
13:13	259

Galatians

2:19–20	232
5:15	233

Ephesians

1:4	5
2:11–12	204n22
5:2	91n37
5:8	198n4
5:22–23	116
6:1–3	117
6:4	116, 123

Philippians

4:18	91n37

Colossians

1:13	198n4
4:14	84

1 Thessalonians

4:5	204n22
4:13	204n22
5:4–5	198n4

2 Timothy

1:5	116
3:16	264
3:16–17	241

Titus

1:12	204n22

Hebrews

4:12	51n23
12:6	123

1 Peter

1:14	204n22
1:18	204n22
2:9	198n4
4:3–4	204n22

1 John

3:2	261

2 John

11	220

3 John

8	220

Revelation

6:14	250
19:20	52
21:4	82

www.ingramcontent.com/pod-product-compliance
Lightning Source LLC
Chambersburg PA
CBHW030433300426
44112CB00009B/976